1   BEE-EATER
2   HOUSE SPARROW
3   STARLING
4   CHAFFINCH
5   HOUSE MARTIN
6   SWALLOW
7   WOOD PIGEON
8   JACKDAW
9   LITTLE OWL
10   WHINCHAT
11   KESTREL
12   RED-BACKED SHRIKE
13   MAGPIE
14   WAGTAIL
15   SKY LARK
16   LAPWING
17   PHEASANT
18   BLACKBIRD
19   PARTRIDGE
20   ROOK

Capt Cook.
Happy bird watching,
 Feb '72

A Field Guide
to the Birds of Britain
and Europe

A Field Guide

To the Birds of Britain

and Europe

A FIELD GUIDE
TO THE
BIRDS OF BRITAIN
AND EUROPE

by

ROGER PETERSON

GUY MOUNTFORT

P. A. D. HOLLOM

*Revised and Enlarged Edition
in collaboration with
I. J. Ferguson-Lees
and D. I. M. Wallace*

Introduction by
SIR JULIAN HUXLEY

COLLINS
14 ST JAMES'S PLACE
LONDON

1st impression 1954
2nd impression 1954
3rd impression 1954
4th impression 1956
5th impression 1958
6th impression 1959
7th impression 1961
8th impression 1963
9th impression 1964
Revised and Enlarged Edition 1965
11th impression 1965
12th impression 1967
13th impression 1971

TO OUR
LONG-SUFFERING WIVES

She laments, sir, . . . her husband
goes this morning a-birding.
SHAKESPEARE—*Merry Wives of Windsor*

ISBN 0 00 212020 8

*Printed in Great Britain
Collins Clear-Type Press
London and Glasgow*

Introduction to the first Edition
by Sir Julian Huxley

In common with every British ornithologist who has ever travelled (or ever intends to travel) on the Continent, I have often longed for a good handy book on the birds of Europe. Without such a guide, how could I be sure that the woodpecker I saw near Paris was a Middle Spotted Woodpecker? How could I find out the name of the strange warbler I heard in the woods of North Italy? How could I distinguish the two species of tree creepers on the Continent? How should I learn all the exciting new species of birds to be seen, or expected, in Switzerland or in Portugal? And I am sure that Continental ornithologists must share that longing, for the boundaries between their countries are, biologically speaking, even more artificial than that between our islands and the rest of Europe. The only handy works on the subject are half a century old, and have no pictures. One cannot carry around large systematic works like Dresser's *Birds of Europe*, and anyhow they are not designed to help the observer in the field.

What are the criteria for a good book on European birds, which will meet the needs of the field naturalist? In the first place it must be in one volume, and not too bulky to travel with, or for actual use in the field. Secondly, it must be fully illustrated, and must concentrate first and foremost on helping the naturalist to identify the new species with which he is confronted on his travels. Thirdly, it should help the naturalist to understand something of the distribution of the birds he sees. Finally, it should be scientific, based on the latest facts and the best theoretical interpretations.

This new Field Guide to the Birds of Britain and Europe seems to me to meet these requirements admirably. All three of its authors have special qualifications for the task. Guy Mountfort had for long planned to write a handbook of Continental birds. He was Secretary of the British Ornithologists' Union, and has travelled and observed birds in more than a hundred different countries. For ten years he lived on the Continent, where he made an intensive study of West European birds.

Roger Peterson is a passionate lover and student of birds. He has the distinction of having produced a bird book whose sales far exceed those of any other ever written. His success has been due to the combination of high artistic skill with personal knowledge of birds in the field. This led to the designing of his particular method of illustration for identification, in which the bird is portrayed with pointers indicating the special features by which it can be distinguished. His systematic working out of this method, first for birds, then for mammals, then for other organisms, has met with an overwhelming response from amateur naturalists in America. Though an American, he has a wide knowledge of Europe, and has spent much of the last three years travelling there to familiarise himself with European birds.

Finally, P. A. D. Hollom, widely travelled and known to British ornithologists as the editor of *The Popular Handbook of British Birds* and an editor of the magazine *British Birds*, has made a specialist study of the geographical distribution of the birds of the Old World.

Guy Mountfort met Roger Peterson in 1949 on Hawk Mountain in Pennsylvania, where ornithologists gather annually to watch the spectacular migration of birds of prey—buzzards, eagles, hawks and falcons—riding the thermal currents above the range of the Kittatinny Mountains. Within a few minutes of their meeting, they had enthusiastically decided to go into partnership in the publication of a Field Guide to European birds, on the same general pattern as that of Peterson's Field Guides to American birds, which had been so successful in the New World, and which had already made their influence felt in the bird literature of Europe. And when it was later discovered that Hollom too had been planning a book on European birds, they decided to collaborate.

During the next three years, the authors travelled all over Europe, from Arctic Lapland to Southern Spain, from Britain to Turkey, putting the final touches to their field notes and contacts with foreign ornithologists, and combing through all the relevant literature. Between the three of them they have seen and watched in their natural habitats all but an insignificant fraction of the 583 species described in this book. Peterson has been primarily responsible for the illustrations and the accompanying caption pages, Mountfort for the main descriptive text, and Hollom for the maps and notes on distribution; however, the book is not just the sum of three separate contributors, but in all respects a product of close and critical teamwork.

The result seems to me extremely satisfactory. In spite of dealing with 583 distinct species, the book is of manageable size, a field guide to be consulted on the spot. Of these 583 species it has more than 1200 illustrations, the majority in colour, and all drawn on Peterson's system, so as to facilitate quick and accurate identification of birds of either sex and every age. Hollom has provided maps of the breeding and winter distributions of all the species in Europe. It is remarkable that we have had to wait so long for this visual aid to the study of ornithology, and I am sure that this feature will be of the greatest value to all serious students. Finally, Mountfort's text conveys the maximum of necessary information in the minimum of space. The common names of the birds are given for the most ornithologically important European languages, and facts are included on voice, behaviour, habitats and nest-sites, which may help identification and pave the way for further study, though obviously a pocket-size field guide cannot be expected to cover all aspects of ornithology.

The birds are arranged according to the latest scientific classification, thus indicating their true relationships. And, while due recognition has been given to the facts of subspecific differentiation, emphasis is laid throughout on the species as the primary unit of study; subspecies which are recognisable in the field are briefly listed and described at the end of the account of each species.

The publication of this Field Guide seems to me an event of considerable importance to science as well as to natural history. It will certainly extend the range of interest of ornithologists in this country; it will promote international liaison between the naturalists of Western Europe; it will help to convince them that the study of the natural history of single countries is insufficient and that European ornithology deserves to be pursued in its entirety. It will, I hope, pave the way for a comprehensive handbook of the European birds, which will perform the same sort of service to European ornithology as *The Handbook of British Birds* has done for ornithology in these islands. I congratulate authors and publisher alike on their enterprise.

JULIAN HUXLEY

Preface to the First Edition

> " *Though it must not be said that every species of birds has a manner peculiar to itself, yet there is somewhat in most genera at least that at first sight discriminates them, and enables a judicious observer to pronounce upon them with some certainty.*"
>
> GILBERT WHITE, 1778

No branch of natural history has been endowed with a richer literature than ornithology. New books about birds, good, bad, and indifferent, pour forth upon a seemingly insatiable public at an average of one for every two weeks of the year, in Great Britain alone. To produce yet another, requires a word of explanation.

People whose vocation in life it is to sell books, affirm that a major part of to-day's demand for those about birds takes two forms and stems from two sources. Knowledgeable ornithologists who already possess one or several of the encyclopædic works, such as Witherby's five volume *Handbook of British Birds*, ask for a similarly authoritative and complete reference book "small enough to carry in the pocket." A far more clamorous demand is for a "really simple" book, which will enable the general public to identify birds "at a glance" and without expert knowledge. Both demands, for quite different reasons, are *cris du coeur*. The experienced ornithologist is understandably loath to carry several heavy and costly volumes with him on his expeditions, and the existing single volume works omit, for reasons of space, the very rarities which he is ever seeking. Beginners, and the vast numbers of people whose interest is often more sentimental than scientific, long for a book which will enable them to identify the birds they see around the garden, without having to disentangle the wealth of detail and technicalities which confuses them in much of the existing literature.

There is, we are told, also a third demand, from the growing numbers of bird watchers who travel each year to new ornithological territories, where unfamiliar birds occur. Because of currency or linguistic difficulties, the local handbooks, which are available in some countries, are often debarred to them. Hence the call for a book which includes illustrations of *all* European species. In this category nothing has been produced since Dresser's monumental nine-volume masterpiece of 1871-80, which to-day costs around £100.

A Field Guide to the Birds of Britain and Europe attempts to fulfil all three of these seemingly conflicting requirements. Absolute simplicity is its keynote. It is non-technical. It embraces all the birds of Europe, including rare vagrants, from the tundra of northern Finland to the Mediterranean islands, westwards to Iceland, and eastwards to the Black Sea.

The birds are arranged in the latest order of classification, which is now internationally accepted. The scientific names used in the latest British check-list have been incorporated. Vernacular names are given in English, Dutch, French, German and Swedish, and, because many European species are conspecific with those in the United States and Canada, the North American equivalents are also shown, where they differ from the British. The English vernacular names are those in popular usage, for this, as David Lack has pointed out, must always be the ultimate criterion.

The illustrations are primarily patternistic and functional, rather than "portraits." All are drawn strictly to scale. Similar species are shown adjacent to each other and in identical positions, occasionally regardless of systematic relationship, in order to assist comparison. Arrows indicate clearly the significant "field marks" not shared by related species. Further comparisons are given in the accompanying text. Descriptive detail of only general (i.e. non-specific) interest has been ruthlessly expunged; notes on behaviour are included only where they aid identification. Maps show the summer and winter ranges of the species, excepting those of only accidental occurrence, or where a written description can give the information more clearly. Finally, the dimensions of the Field Guide fulfil the requirement that it should literally "fit in the pocket." Those who prefer their bird books to be specialised, narrative, or even anthropomorphic in form, will find a wide choice in every bookshop: in this respect the Field Guide is non-competitive and supplementary to existing literature on the subject.

The information on which this book is based has been compiled from various sources. First, the authors' own field notes, made during many years of travel and study. Second, from intimate collaboration with leading ornithologists throughout Europe, who have generously made available their own records on such subjects as local distribution of species. Third, from a continuing study of all available ornithological literature and periodicals—not excepting the Russian. Fourth, from critical examination of skins and living birds in various museums and private collections, notably those of the British Museum of Natural History, the Zoological Society of London, the Wildfowl Trust, the Smithsonian Institution of Washington, D.C., and the American Museum of New York.

To the painstaking staffs of these institutions is due the warmest gratitude of the authors. Special mention must also be made of the invaluable advice and facilities provided by Peter Scott in the final preparation of the texts and illustrations concerning ducks, geese, and swans, all of which have had the benefit of his expert scrutiny.

To Sir Landsborough Thomson and Dr. David Lack thanks are due for guidance on the complex subject of vernacular nomenclature. Acknowledgment is also made to Dr. François Bourlière, for assistance in compiling the critical list of Continental literature shown in the appendix.

Space unfortunately does not permit the authors to acknowledge individually in print all the help so freely given by ornithologists in many countries. If the Field Guide has merit, it must stem from the fact that it reflects the collaboration of so wide, so distinguished, and so truly international a board of advisers. The authors' thanks must, however, be recorded for particular assistance received from the following:

Austria—Dr. G. Rokitansky.

Belgium—C. Dupont, J. Spaepen.

Bulgaria—Dr. J. M. Harrison.

Czechoslovakia—Dr. W. Cerny, F. J. Turcek.

Denmark—Miss H. I. Jørgensen, Dr. P. Jespersen, Dr. Finn Salomonsen.

Estonia—J. Lepiksaar.

Finland—Dr. O. Kalela.

France—P. Barruel, G. Berthet, R. D. Etchécopar, Dr. C. Ferry, F. Hüe, H. Lomont, N. Mayaud, G. Olivier, A. Rivoire, G. Tallon.

Germany—G. Niethammer, Prof. E. Stresemann.

Great Britain—W. B. Alexander, D. G. Andrew, Mrs. Mary Bannerman, Miss P. Barclay-Smith, C. I. Blackburne, A. R. M. Blake, H. H. Davis, A. E. Doerr, James Fisher, D. Goodwin, Dr. J. M. Harrison, Capt. Collingwood Ingram, J. D. Macdonald, Col. R. Meinertzhagen, E. M. Nicholson, G. Pollard, W. R. Trevelyan. N. J. P. Wadley, K. Williamson.

Greece—Dr. W. Makatsch, P. Zervas.

Holland—Dr. G. C. A. Junge, J. Kist, J. E. Sluiters, M. J. Tekke.

Hungary—Dr. A. Keve, Dr. Z. Tildy.

Italy—Prof. F. Caterini, Prof. A. Ghigi, Prof. E. Moltoni.

Ireland—G. R. Humphreys.

Iceland—Dr. Finnur Gudmundsson.

Latvia and Lithuania—B. Berzins.

Norway—Dr. H. M. S. Blair, Dr. Y. Hagen, Prof. H. L. Løvenskiold.
Poland—Z. Godyn.
Portugal—H. W. Coverley.
Roumania—Prof. D. Lintia.
Switzerland—P. Géroudet.
Sweden—C. F. Lundevall, Dr. G. Svärdson.
Spain—Don Mauricio Gonzalez Diez, Capt. P. W. Munn.
Turkey—Dr. S. Ergene.
United States of America—H. Diegnan, L. S. Pearl, R. H. Pough.
Yugoslavia—R. Csornai, Prof. R. Kroneisl.

R. T. P., G. R. M., P. A. D. H. 1953

Preface to the Revised Edition

Since its first appearance in 1954 the English edition of the Field
Guide has been reprinted with minor revisions nine times. The
book has now appeared in eleven foreign-language editions, many
of which have also been reprinted several times. Other foreign
editions are in preparation. With the single exception of its earlier
companion volume, *A Field Guide to the Birds* (of North America)
it has now sold more copies than any book on birds yet produced
in any country. This gratifying response encourages the authors
to believe that the time has come to produce an enlarged and
completely revised edition.

A number of new species of birds have been added to the European
list in the past decade. Twenty-one of those previously treated
only as rare vagrants from North America, Africa or Asia have now
been recorded in Europe more than twenty times and have therefore
now been given full descriptive treatment and are illustrated on
new colour plates. Many other vagrant species which have only
recently been recorded in Europe have been added to the Accidentals
Section. The scientific nomenclature and order of species have been
fully revised. Down to familial level the sequence follows that of
the *Check-List of Birds of the World* by J. L. Peters and successors
(as completed by Ernst Mayr and J. C. Greenway, Jr. in *Breviora*);
it therefore agrees with the order of families used in *A New
Dictionary of Birds* edited by Sir A. Landsborough Thomson.
Within the families it follows the sequence of species adopted by
Charles Vaurie in *The Birds of the Palearctic Fauna*, with one or
two very minor modifications. The scientific nomenclature also

largely follows Vaurie, to whom the authors are particularly indebted for his generous co-operation.

A number of plates in colour and black and white have been altered in the light of further experience gained in the countries where the species concerned breed. In one or two instances, where minor corrections did not warrant the high cost of new colour plates, attention has been drawn to them in the text. Several new line drawings have been added. All the distribution maps have been revised on the basis of the recent information from all Europe, for the geographical range of birds is, of course, constantly changing. The text matter has been rewritten to embody improvements in methods of identification; this applies particularly to the more difficult groups, such as the immature eagles and terns, the small waders and the warblers, where even the experts have trouble in separating closely similar species. Certain previously admitted British records (the now discredited "Hastings Rarities") have been corrected. It is hoped that beginners will find the introductions to each family group more helpful in their revised form.

Ornithologists throughout Europe have collaborated in these revisions, but our chief indebtedness is to I. J. Ferguson-Lees and D. I. M. Wallace, two of Britain's leading experts, who have worked tirelessly with us for eighteen months perfecting the texts.

R.T.P., G.R.M., P.A.D.H. 1965

Contents

Illustrations

A Note to British Readers

This Field Guide covers all the birds of Britain. It also includes all European birds found this side of Russia, the majority of which are on the British list. For the convenience of users in Britain who will turn to the colour plates first when they see a new bird, the following symbols are employed on the caption pages, opposite the illustrations:

● **RESIDENT, REGULAR, OR FREQUENT ANNUAL** occurrence in the British Isles. ("British Isles" is here used to include Eire.)

○ **OCCASIONAL, OR VERY RARE** in the British Isles. Twenty occurrences or more; may occur in numbers during occasional "invasions."

△ **ACCIDENTAL** in the British Isles. Fewer than twenty occurrences in total, or very rare in recent years. No symbol means that the bird is not on the British list.

The following sex symbols are used on the illustrations:

♂ means **male**   ♀ means **female**

ABOUT THE MAPS

Black area—Summer
Dotted line—Winter

The solid black areas represent the bird's breeding range. The area below the heavy dotted line, or enclosed by it, is the bird's winter range. This does not mean that the bird occurs everywhere within these limits, but locally where its proper habitat is available. Additional information is given in abbreviated form in the space between the two maps. For example, if the bird's winter range is identical with its breeding range, or if the bird entirely leaves the map area, it is so stated, and the dotted line is not used. Thus: "Resident" (if all the year); "Partial migrant" (if many but not all individuals leave northern part of range in winter); "Summer visitor" (if the species winters entirely outside Europe). In the few cases where maps are inappropriate, brief information on range is given in the main text. This is the first time range has been mapped for many species; further information will be welcomed by the authors, who may be contacted c/o the publishers.

THE GEOGRAPHICAL AREA
EMBRACED BY THE
FIELD GUIDE.

The birds described are those resident or occurring
within the unshaded portion of the map, that is to say
in the British Isles and Eire, Iceland and continental
Europe, eastwards to the 30° line of longitude. The
islands of the Mediterranean basin are included, but
Turkey and North Africa are excluded.

How to Identify Birds

MANY PEOPLE who are already mildly interested in birds are afraid to pursue the subject because, as they sometimes express it, they "cannot tell a robin from a sparrow." Others, perhaps have shied away from an unfamiliar terminology. Such people do themselves needless injustice. The enjoyment of birds, whether casual or absorbing, which man has developed during centuries of sentimental attachment, depends neither upon intensive study nor academic qualifications. Those who claim to be unable to distinguish a robin from a sparrow certainly recognise an eagle, a gull, a duck, an owl, and many others of the various families. They are, in fact, already quite a long way on the road to "knowing the birds."

But the terms "eagle," "gull," or "duck," are very broad. There are about fifty different species of eagles in various parts of the world, and many more species of gulls and ducks. The purpose of this book is to show, without recourse to complicated symbols, how to distinguish, at reasonable distance, all the species of birds inhabiting or visiting Great Britain and the European continent.

We are concerned in Europe with only 469 basic species. All these are given full treatment in this book. An additional 114 species have occurred in Europe fewer than twenty times: these are described briefly in the appendix of "Accidentals" (page 312). The more complex subject of subspecies is discussed on page xxvii. Those subspecies which are recognisable in the field are also briefly described in the main text, and bring the total to over 600.

What to Look For

The identification of birds is largely a matter of knowing what to look for—the "field marks." Exact diagnosis then depends upon a process of elimination, by comparison with other species which the bird may resemble. The arrows on the illustrations facilitate this process. But appearance is only one factor. Call-notes, song, attitudes, behaviour, habitat and range are also important.

What is its Size?

First acquire the habit of comparing strange birds with some familiar "yard stick"—a House Sparrow, a Blackbird, a Pigeon, etc., so that you can say to yourself "smaller than a Blackbird, a little larger than a Sparrow," etc. The measurements quoted in this book indicate the *average* length of the bird from bill-tip to tail-tip.

What is its Shape?

Is it plump, like a Robin (left); or slender, like a Wagtail (right)?

What shape are its wings? Are they sharply pointed, like a Swallow's (left); or short and rounded, like a Warbler's (right)?

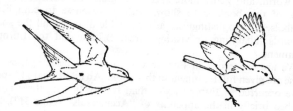

What shape is its bill? Is it small and fine, like a Warbler's (1); stout and short, like a seed-cracking Sparrow's (2); dagger-shaped, like a Tern's (3); or hook-tipped, like a Kestrel's (4)?

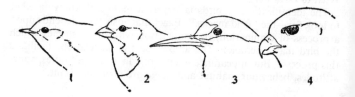

Is its tail deeply forked, like a Swallow's (*a*); short and square-ended, like a Starling's (*b*); deeply notched, like a Linnet's (*c*); rounded, like a Cuckoo's (*d*); or wedge-shaped, like a Raven's (*e*)?

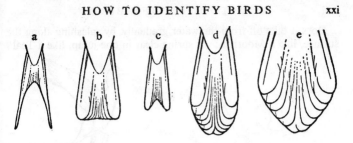

How does it Behave?

Some birds have very characteristic habits. Does it constantly wag its tail, like a Wagtail; quiver its tail, like a Redstart; cock its tail vertically, like a Wren; or sit bolt upright, with its tail downwards, like a Spotted Flycatcher?

Does it climb trees? If so, does it climb upwards in spirals, like a Tree Creeper (1); in short jerks, braced on its stiff tail, like a Woodpecker (2); or does it climb, without using its tail as a prop, as readily downwards as upwards, like a Nuthatch (3)?

If it feeds on the ground, does it walk, like a Jackdaw; hop, like a House Sparrow; run spasmodically, like a Wagtail; or shuffle along, close to the ground, like a Dunnock?

If it swims, does it sit high in the water, like a Moorhen (a); or low, with its back almost awash, like a Diver (b)? Does it dive, like a Coot (c); or merely "up-end," like a Mallard (d)?

Does it take off from the water gradually, by splashing along the surface, like a Moorhen; or spring clear in one jump, like a Teal?

Does it hover over the water and dive headlong, like a Tern, or a Kingfisher; or plunge after fish feet-first, like an Osprey; or walk deliberately beneath the water, like a Dipper?

Does it wade? If so, does it stand motionless in the shallows for long periods, like a Heron; or run quickly along the margins, like a Sandpiper; or chase the receding waves, like a Sanderling?

How does it Fly?

Is its flight deeply undulating, like a Woodpecker's (1); or straight and fast, like a Starling's (2)?

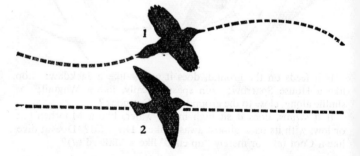

Does it beat its wings slowly, like a Heron; or rapidly, like a Mallard; or with alternate periods of wing-beats and "shooting," like a Fieldfare; or does it soar on motionless wings, like a Buzzard?

What are its Field Marks?

A few birds can be instantly identified by colour alone. There is no mistaking the brilliant yellow and black of a male Golden Oriole, for example. But we need also to look for certain field marks to distinguish most species. These take various forms. They are indicated by pointers on the illustrations in the Field Guide, and correspond to the italicised portions of the accompanying descriptive texts. Obscure field marks are included only when the problem of identification demands completeness.

Many birds are more or less spotted or streaked below. Are these marks nearly all over the under-parts, as in the Song Thrush (*a*); only on the upper-breast, as in the Sky Lark (*b*); or only on the flanks, as in the Redpoll (*c*)?

Does the tail have a distinctive pattern? Has it a white tip, as in the Hawfinch (1); white outer feathers, as in the Chaffinch (2); or white side patches, as in the Whinchat (3)?

Some birds show a conspicuous white rump in flight—Jay, House Martin, Bullfinch, the Wheatears, many waders, and the Hen Harrier, to mention a selection. Where so many species share such a prominent feature, it is necessary to look for additional field marks.

WHEATEAR   HOUSE MARTIN

Wing-bars are very important in such families as the warblers; some are conspicuous, some obscure, some single, some double.

Eye-stripes are equally important in many small passerines (perching birds). Does the bird have a stripe above, through, or below the eye—or a combination of two, or three, of these stripes? Some warblers have distinctively coloured eyes, or eye-rims, or "moustachial" stripes. These details are useful only when the bird permits close examination, of course.

Wing patterns should always be noted, particularly with ducks and waders. Wings may be all-dark, or all-white, or half-and-half, or show conspicuous patches of white, or colour. The exact location of such marks on the wings, above or below, is important.

Unpatterned wing   Wing stripe   Wing patch

Call Notes and Song

Expert ornithologists often rely on their ears as much as on their eyes, to identify birds. It is difficult to portray bird voices in writing, because birds rarely make "human" sounds, and our interpretations vary: one person hears a call-note as "*teu*," another as "*chew*" or "*sioo*." It must be remembered, also, that birds, like humans, often develop dialectic variations in their "speech." In the Field Guide an attempt has been made to portray the chief call-notes and song phrases by simplified phonetics and similes; but the best way to learn voice identification is to go out with someone who knows the birds, and to obtain first-hand teaching. There are several sets of published gramophone records of bird songs, which are also an invaluable aid, even to the expert.

Where is it Found?

Birds which beginners may have difficulty in identifying by appearance alone, can often be placed by knowledge of the typical habitats. The Long-tailed Duck is likely to be seen only on salt water, but the Pintail, a duck which also has a longish, pointed tail, frequents fresh water. Wood Warblers are birds of the upper leaf canopy of the beech and oak woods, and do not occur out on the low, bushy scrub where one would seek the Grasshopper Warbler. Birds have quite strict limits of geography, habitat, and vegetation. Outside these they are seldom found, except during migration, when they may occur in very unlikely places. The range maps and notes on habitat and distribution, which are included in the Field Guide, should always be consulted in cases of doubtful identification.

When is it Found?

It is always interesting to learn the seasons during which different migratory species may occur in one's area. Most good field workers keep a diary of arrival and departure dates. In a few years it becomes possible to forecast with some accuracy when the first Chiffchaff, or Swift, or Redwing, should appear. These dates may be pencilled in the margins of the Field Guide—for it is intended, not as an ornament to the bookshelf, but as a working companion.

Caution!

Where rarities are concerned, great caution should always be exercised. Rare, wind-drifted vagrants may occur in almost any locality, particularly in coastal areas, and on isolated islands. Detailed written notes and sketches should be made of any suspected rarity *on the spot*. If possible, an experienced member of the local ornithological society should be invited by telephone to corroborate the discovery. Before unusual "sight records" can be accepted, at least two independent sets of field notes are usually required for critical examination by the ornithological authorities.

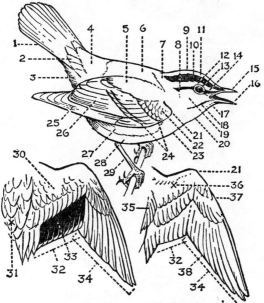

Upper wing (*Duck*)   *Under wing*

TOPOGRAPHY OF A BIRD

Key showing terms used in this volume

1 Outer tail-feathers
2 Upper tail-coverts
3 Under tail-coverts
4 Rump
5 Scapulars
6 Back
7 Nape
8 Eye-stripe
9 Crown
10 Head-stripe
11 Crown-stripe
12 Supercilium (eye-brow)
13 Eye-ring
14 Lores
15 Upper mandible
16 Lower mandible
17 Chin
18 Moustachial stripe
19 Ear-coverts (cheek)
20 Throat
21 Bend of wing
22 Carpal (wrist)
23 Breast
24 Wing-bars
25 Primaries
26 Secondaries
27 Flanks
28 Belly
29 Tarsus
30 Wing-coverts
31 Scapulars
32 Secondaries
33 Speculum (duck)
34 Primaries
35 Axillaries
36 Wing-linings
37 Fore-edge of wing
38 Rear-edge of wing

Check-List

This list of European birds may be used to record the species you have seen. Accidentals can be entered at the end.

.... Red-throated Diver
.... Black-throated Diver
.... Great Northern Diver
.... White-billed Diver
.... Little Grebe
.... Black-necked Grebe
.... Slavonian Grebe
.... Red-necked Grebe
.... Great Crested Grebe
.... Fulmar
.... Cory's Shearwater
.... Great Shearwater
.... Sooty Shearwater
.... Manx Shearwater
.... Storm Petrel
.... Wilson's Petrel
.... Leach's Petrel
.... White Pelican
.... Dalmatian Pelican
.... Gannet
.... Cormorant
.... Shag
.... Pygmy Cormorant
.... Bittern
.... American Bittern
.... Little Bittern
.... Night Heron
.... Squacco Heron
.... Cattle Egret
.... Great White Egret
.... Little Egret
.... Grey Heron
.... Purple Heron
.... White Stork
.... Black Stork
.... Spoonbill
.... Glossy Ibis
.... Greater Flamingo
.... Canada Goose
.... Barnacle Goose
.... Brent Goose
.... Red-breasted Goose
.... Grey Lag Goose
.... White-fronted Goose
... Lesser White-fronted Goose

.... Bean Goose
.... Pink-footed Goose
.... Snow Goose
.... Mute Swan
.... Whooper Swan
.... Bewick's Swan
.... Ruddy Shelduck
.... Shelduck
.... Mallard
.... Teal
.... Blue-winged Teal
.... Baikal Teal
.... Gadwall
.... Wigeon
.... American Wigeon
.... Pintail
.... Garganey
.... Shoveler
.... Marbled Teal
.... Red-crested Pochard
.... Pochard
.... Ferruginous Duck
.... Tufted Duck
.... Scaup
.... Mandarin Duck
.... Eider
.... King Eider
.... Steller's Eider
.... Common Scoter
.... Velvet Scoter
.... Surf Scoter
.... Harlequin Duck
.... Long-tailed Duck
.... Goldeneye
.... Barrow's Goldeneye
.... Smew
.... Red-breasted Merganser
.... Goosander
.... White-headed Duck
.... Osprey
.... Black-winged Kite
.... Honey Buzzard
.... Red Kite
.... Black Kite
.... Goshawk

....Levant Sparrow Hawk
....Sparrow Hawk
....Rough-legged Buzzard
....Long-legged Buzzard
....Buzzard
....Booted Eagle
....Bonelli's Eagle
....Tawny Eagle
....Spotted Eagle
....Lesser Spotted Ealge
....Imperial Eagle
....Golden Eagle
....White-tailed Eagle
....Short-toed Eagle
....Hen Harrier
....Pallid Harrier
....Montagu's Harrier
....Marsh Harrier
....Egyptian Vulture
....Bearded Vulture
....Black Vulture
....Griffon Vulture
....Gyr Falcon
....Saker
....Lanner
....Peregrine
....Hobby
....Eleonora's Falcon
....Merlin
....Red-footed Falcon
....Lesser Kestrel
....Kestrel
....Willow Grouse
....Red Grouse
....Ptarmigan
....Hazel Grouse
....Black Grouse
....Capercaillie
....Rock Partridge
....Chukar
....Barbary Partridge
....Red-legged Partridge
....Partridge
....Quail
....Pheasant
....Andalusian Hemipode
....Crane
....Demoiselle Crane
....Water Rail
....Spotted Crake
....Little Crake
....Baillon's Crake
....Corncrake

....Moorhen
....Purple Gallinule
....Coot
....Crested Coot
....Great Bustard
....Little Bustard
....Houbara Bustard
....Oystercatcher
....Ringed Plover
....Little Ringed Plover
....Kentish Plover
....Greater Sand Plover
....Dotterel
....Golden Plover
....Lesser Golden Plover
....Grey Plover
....Killdeer
....Sociable Plover
....Lapwing
....Spur-winged Plover
....Turnstone
....Little Stint
....Temminck's Stint
....White-rumped Sandpiper
....Pectoral Sandpiper
....Purple Sandpiper
....Dunlin
....Curlew Sandpiper
....Knot
....Sanderling
....Ruff
....Buff-breasted Sandpiper
....Broad-billed Sandpiper
....Long-billed Dowitcher
....Spotted Redshank
....Redshank
....Marsh Sandpiper
....Greenshank
....Greater Yellowlegs
....Lesser Yellowlegs
....Green Sandpiper
....Wood Sandpiper
....Common Sandpiper
....Terek Sandpiper
....Black-tailed Godwit
....Bar-tailed Godwit
....Curlew
....Slender-billed Curlew
....Whimbrel
....Upland Sandpiper
....Woodcock
....Snipe
....Great Snipe

.... Red-rumped Swallow
.... House Martin
.... Richard's Pipit
.... Tawny Pipit
.... Tree Pipit
.... Petchora Pipit
.... Meadow Pipit
.... Red-throated Pipit
.... Water/Rock Pipit
.... Yellow Wagtail
.... Grey Wagtail
.... Pied/White Wagtail
.... Red-backed Shrike
.... Masked Shrike
.... Woodchat Shrike
.... Lesser Grey Shrike
.... Great Grey Shrike
.... Waxwing
.... Dipper
.... Wren
.... Alpine Accentor
.... Dunnock
.... Cetti's Warbler
.... Savi's Warbler
.... River Warbler
.... Pallas's Grasshopper Warbler
.... Grasshopper Warbler
.... Lanceolated Warbler
.... Moustached Warbler
.... Aquatic Warbler
.... Sedge Warbler
.... Blyth's Reed Warbler
.... Marsh Warbler
.... Reed Warbler
.... Great Reed Warbler
.... Icterine Warbler
.... Melodious Warbler
.... Olive-tree Warbler
.... Olivaceous Warbler
.... Barred Warbler
.... Orphean Warbler
.... Garden Warbler
.... Blackcap
.... Whitethroat
.... Lesser Whitethroat
.... Rüppell's Warbler
.... Sardinian Warbler
.... Subalpine Warbler
.... Spectacled Warbler
.... Dartford Warbler
.... Marmora's Warbler
.... Willow Warbler
.... Chiffchaff

.... Bonelli's Warbler
.... Wood Warbler
.... Yellow-browed Warbler
.... Pallas's Leaf Warbler
.... Arctic Warbler
.... Greenish Warbler
.... Goldcrest
.... Firecrest
.... Fan-tailed Warbler
.... Pied Flycatcher
.... Collared Flycatcher
.... Red-breasted Flycatcher
.... Spotted Flycatcher
.... Whinchat
.... Stonechat
.... Wheatear
.... Pied Wheatear
.... Black-eared Wheatear
.... Desert Wheatear
.... Isabelline Wheatear
.... Black Wheatear
.... Rufous Bush Chat
.... Rock Thrush
.... Blue Rock Thrush
.... Black Redstart
.... Redstart
.... Robin
.... Nightingale
.... Thrush Nightingale
.... Bluethroat
.... Red-flanked Bluetail
.... Olive-backed Thrush
.... Eye-browed Thrush
.... Black-throated Thrush
.... Dusky/Naumann's Thrush
.... Fieldfare
.... Ring Ouzel
.... American Robin
.... Blackbird
.... Siberian Thrush
.... Redwing
.... Song Thrush
.... Mistle Thrush
.... White's Thrush
.... Bearded Reedling
.... Long-tailed Tit
.... Marsh Tit
.... Willow Tit
.... Sombre Tit
.... Siberian Tit
.... Crested Tit
.... Coal Tit
.... Blue Tit

....Azure Tit
....Great Tit
....Penduline Tit
....Nuthatch
....Corsican Nuthatch
....Rock Nuthatch
....Wall Creeper
....Tree Creeper
....Short-toed Tree Creeper
....Corn Bunting
....Yellowhammer
....Rock Bunting
....Cinereous Bunting
....Ortolan Bunting
....Cretzschmar's Bunting
....Cirl Bunting
....Little Bunting
....Rustic Bunting
....Yellow-breasted Bunting
....Black-headed Bunting
....Reed Bunting
....Lapland Bunting
....Snow Bunting
....Chaffinch
....Brambling
....Citril Finch
....Serin
....Greenfinch
....Siskin
....Goldfinch
....Twite

....Linnet
....Redpoll
....Arctic Redpoll
....Trumpeter Bullfinch
....Scarlet Rosefinch
....Pine Grosbeak
....Parrot Crossbill
....Crossbill
....Two-barred Crossbill
....Bullfinch
....Hawfinch
....House Sparrow
....Spanish Sparrow
....Tree Sparrow
....Rock Sparrow
....Snow Finch
....Rose-coloured Starling
....Starling
....Spotless Starling
....Golden Oriole
....Siberian Jay
....Jay
....Azure-winged Magpie
....Magpie
....Nutcracker
....Chough
....Alpine Chough
....Jackdaw
....Rook
....Carrion/Hooded Crow
....Raven

Accidentals

....
....

....
....

....
....

....
....

....
....

....
....

The British
Ornithological Societies

The principal British societies are listed below. They do not compete but, between them, cater for every ornithological interest.

The senior society is the BRITISH ORNITHOLOGISTS' UNION, founded in 1859, for the advancement of the science of ornithology. Its interests are not restricted to Britain, but are world-wide. The B.O.U. issues an important quarterly journal, *The Ibis*, in which authoritative papers are published on such subjects as ecology, behaviour, taxonomy and reviews of British and foreign ornithological literature. Scientific meetings are arranged and in all international ornithological affairs the B.O.U. takes a leading part. Address: *c/o The Bird Room, British Museum (Natural History), London, S.W.7.*

The BRITISH ORNITHOLOGISTS' CLUB recruits its members from the B.O.U. The club meets in London nearly every month at a dinner, which is followed by short communications, films and lectures. The Club *Bulletin*, published monthly except July-September, contains articles relating to the subjects discussed, and descriptions of new species and races. Address: *c/o The Bird Room, British Museum (Natural History), London, S.W.7.*

The BRITISH TRUST FOR ORNITHOLOGY is the focal point for organised field work. Its aim is the encouragement of individual and group research. Members take part in bird ringing and nest recording schemes and population studies. Courses are organised at Field Centres, and many meetings are held with local societies. Bulletins, reports, the quarterly *Bird Study* and field guides are published, and a fine collection of ornithological books is maintained, in conjunction with Oxford University, at the Alexander Library. Address: *Beech Grove, Tring, Herts.*

THE ROYAL SOCIETY FOR THE PROTECTION OF BIRDS is concerned with the scientific application of conservation and strives constantly to improve the Wild Birds Protection Acts. It educates the public by means of films, exhibitions and meetings, and finances and manages a network of bird sanctuaries. The Society produces an illustrated magazine, *Birds*, and many other publications. Address: *The Lodge, Sandy, Beds.*

The WILDFOWL TRUST has a unique collection of ducks, geese and swans from all parts of the world. It offers ideal conditions for studying every species occurring in Britain. A large decoy is maintained for catching and ringing ducks, and it is possible to watch flocks of wild geese feeding in the adjoining fields at appropriate seasons. The Trust publishes a lavishly illustrated *Annual Report* and periodical bulletins. Address: *Slimbridge, Glos.*

DIVERS: Gaviidae

Large swimming birds of open waters, with sharp-pointed bills. Longer-bodied and thicker-necked than grebes. Dive and swim expertly under water. Submerge quickly when alarmed, or swim with only head above water. Outline in flight is hunchbacked, with slight downward sweep to extended neck. Wings rather small and pointed. In flight, feet project behind rudimentary tail. Voices wailing. Sexes similar. Ground nesting.

RED-THROATED DIVER *Gavia stellata* page 4
 Du – Roodkeelduiker   Fr – Plongeon catmarin
 Ge – Sterntaucher   Sw – Smålom
     N.Am – Red-throated Loon

Identification: 21-23″. Smaller than Great Northern; about size of Black-throated, but with smaller head. Slender *up-tilted* bill affords quick identification even at distance. In breeding plumage has grey head, *red throat-patch* (looks black at distance) and grey-brown *unpatterned* upper-parts. Winter plumage paler than Black-throated, being finely speckled with white; under-parts white; extensive white from sides of head to forehead gives white-faced appearance. Bills of Black-throated and Great Northern are straight, not up-tilted; latter's is also much stouter. (But see also rare White-billed Diver.) Occasionally seen in flocks along coast in winter.

Voice: A repeated, guttural, quacking "*kwuck,*" less deep than similar note of Black-throated; also a high wailing and a goose-like clamour.
Habitat: Mainly coastal waters in winter. Nests on margins of quite small but deep lochs and northern coastal lagoons. Map p. 2.

BLACK-THROATED DIVER *Gavia arctica* page 4
 Du – Parelduiker   Fr – Plongeon arctique
 Ge – Prachttaucher   Sw – Storlom
     N.Am – Pacific Loon

Identification: 23-27″. Smaller than Great Northern; near size of Red-throated. Distinguished in breeding plumage by grey crown and hind neck and *straight,* slender, black bill; throat *black,* narrowly striped with white on sides of neck and breast; squarish white spots on upper-parts are arranged in *two distinct patches either side.* In winter looks like small Great Northern, but forehead is blacker than crown and hind neck, both of which are often greyer than back; Great Northern looks obscurely barred above, whereas Black-throated looks uniform blackish and immature is "scaly"; smaller size, *less heavy bill* and less angular contours of head are best distinctions; immature otherwise indistinguishable from young Great Northern. Distinguished from winter Red-throated by darker appearance and black forehead

1

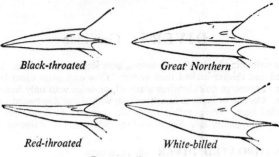

Black-throated   *Great Northern*

Red-throated   *White-billed*

BILLS OF DIVERS

instead of white face; bill is often as slender, but is *straight*, not up-tilted and is bluish with black tip.

Voice: A deep, barking "*kwow*"; a shrill, rising wail.

Habitat: Winters mainly along sea-coasts. In breeding season frequents lakes with or without trees, among inland hills or coastal lowlands. Nests on islets or verges of deeper and usually larger lakes than Red-throated. Map below.

GREAT NORTHERN DIVER *Gavia immer*   page 4
   Du – IJsduiker   Fr – Plongeon imbrin
   Ge – Eistaucher   Sw – Islom
       N.Am – Common Loon

Identification: 27-32″. Size of goose. Distinguished in breeding plumage by *chequered black and white upper-parts*, glossy black head and neck, *striped black and white collar and massive dagger-shaped bill*. In winter, upper-parts are dark grey-brown; crown blacker; cheeks, throat and under-parts white, with suggestion of dark collar at base of neck; pattern of breeding plumage often retained into early

← RED-THROATED
 DIVER
*Partial migrant.
Vagrant south to
Medit. islands*

BLACK-THROATED →
 DIVER
*Mainly migrant.
Vagrant Faeroes,
Ireland, W. Med.*

winter. Flight with slightly drooping neck, and feet projecting behind. Thrashes along surface before taking off; alights breast-first with great splash. Seldom on land. Distinguished from Cormorant when swimming by *horizontal* (not up-tilted) bill; in flight by much shorter neck and tail, and more white on under-parts. See other divers.

Voice: Flight-call a short, barking "*kwuk*"; on breeding grounds has long wailing cries and weird quavering "laughter."

Habitat: Frequents northern lakes, nesting on islets and on grassy promontories. Winters along sea-coasts, occasionally inland. Map below.

WHITE-BILLED DIVER *Gavia adamsii* page 4
　　　Du – Geelsnavelduiker　　　　　　Fr – Plongeon à bec blanc
　　　Ge – Gelbschnäbliger Eistaucher　Sw – Vitnäbbad islom
　　　N.Am–Yellow-billed Loon

Identification: Similar in size and appearance to Great Northern, but bill is *yellowish or ivory white*, not black. However, winter bills of many Great Northerns are bluish-white, especially towards the base. Bill of Great Northern appears quite straight, while that of the rare White-billed is straight above, angled below, giving a distinctly *up-turned* effect (see diagram). Behaviour, voice, habitat and breeding details are similar. Reaches Norwegian coasts in winter from east Arctic. Vagrant southwards to Britain, Austria, Italy.

GREBES: Podicipitidae

Exclusively aquatic; infrequent fliers but expert divers. Distinguished from ducks by pointed bills and "tailless" appearance. Their feet, instead of being webbed, are lobed (flaps along toes). The larger grebes often

← GREAT
NORTHERN
DIVER
Mainly mig. Winter limits dotted.
Vagrant s. to Italy.
Non-breeders s. to Hebrides

LITTLE GREBE →
Partial migrant.
Vagrant Finland (has bred), Norway, Faeroes

GREBES AND DIVERS

● **SLAVONIAN GREBE** page 7
   Summer: Golden "horns"; chestnut neck.
   Winter: Black and white pattern; straight bill; black cap above eye.

● **BLACK-NECKED GREBE** 6
   Summer: Golden ear "fans"; black neck.
   Winter: Like Slavonian Grebe, but greyer neck; up-turned bill; black cap to below eye.

● **RED-NECKED GREBE** 7
   Summer: Reddish neck, white chin and cheek.
   Winter: Grey neck; no white above eye; yellow-based bill.

● **LITTLE GREBE** 6
   Summer: Puffy, dark; light patch on bill,
   Winter: Pale below. Identify by shape and bill.

● **GREAT CRESTED GREBE** 7
   Summer: White neck; black "horns"; rusty frill.
   Winter: Looks white; pinkish bill; white above eye.

● **RED-THROATED DIVER** 1
   Summer: Grey head; dark red throat; plain back.
   Winter: Pale face; speckled back; thin up-turned bill.

● **BLACK-THROATED DIVER** 1
   Summer: Grey crown; back spots in patches.
   Winter: Dark as Great Northern, but paler crown; bill slender, but not upturned.

● **GREAT NORTHERN DIVER** 2
   Summer: Black head, all-checkered back, stout bill.
   Winter: Dark back; stout straight bill.

△ **WHITE-BILLED DIVER**
   Plumages like those of Great Northern Diver.
   Recognised by stout, whitish, upturned bill.

 DIVERS IN FLIGHT are hunch-backed, with a slight downward sweep to the neck and the feet projecting behind.

Summer

Winter

SLAVONIAN GREBE

Summer

Winter

BLACK-NECKED GREBE

Summer

Winter

RED-NECKED GREBE

Summer

Winter

LITTLE GREBE

Summer

Winter

GREAT CRESTED GREBE

Summer

Winter

RED-THROATED DIVER

Summer

Winter

BLACK-THROATED DIVER

Winter

Summer

WHITE-BILLED DIVER

Winter

GREAT NORTHERN DIVER

LEACH'S
PETREL

STORM
PETREL

WILSON'S
PETREL

Western
Mediterranean
form

FULMAR

FULMAR
Dark phase

Light phase

Atlantic
form

MANX
SHEARWATER

SOOTY
SHEARWATER

GREAT
SHEARWATER

CORY'S
SHEARWATER

Immature

Adult

Changing
immature

GANNET

Plate 2 5

SEA BIRDS

PETRELS (little dark sea birds with white rump patches) are usually seen skimming or flitting low over the waves.
FULMARS and SHEARWATERS fly with several flaps and a glide, banking on stiff sabre-like wings in the wave-troughs.

● **LEACH'S PETREL** page 14
    Tail fork seldom visible; bounding flight.

● **STORM PETREL** 13
    Square-ended tail; flitting flight.

△ **WILSON'S PETREL** 13
    Long legs, yellowish feet; bat-like wing-beats.

● **FULMAR** 10
    Bull-necked; stubby bill; stiff-winged, gliding flight.
    Light phase: White head; light patch at base of primaries. *Dark phase:* Smoky grey.

● **MANX SHEARWATER** 12
    Black above, white below; no patch at base of tail.
    W. Med. form; browner above and below.

● **GREAT SHEARWATER** 11
    Black cap; white cheek and patch at base of tail; flight like Manx.

○ **CORY'S SHEARWATER** 11
    No head pattern; yellow bill; flight like Fulmar.

● **SOOTY SHEARWATER** 12
    Dark all over; looks narrower-winged than Manx.

● **GANNET** 18
    Adult: White; pointed tail; large black wing-tips.
    Immature: Brown, pointed tail.
    Changing immature: White patched with dark.

Other sea birds which spend most of their time flying: skuas (Plate 35), gulls (Plates 37, 38), terns (Plates 39, 40, 41).

hold their thin necks quite erect; divers and ducks do so usually only when alarmed. Sexes similar. Floating nests.

LITTLE GREBE *Podiceps ruficollis*　　　　　　　　page 4
　　　　Du – Dodaars　　　　　　　Fr – Grèbe castagneux
　　　　Ge – Zwergtaucher　　　　　Sw – Smådopping

Identification: 10½″. Smallest grebe. Blunt-ended and short-necked, with short, relatively stouter bill than other grebes. In summer, is dark brown above, paler below, with *chestnut cheeks and throat.* Yellowish-green at base of bill makes *distinctive light spot* on dark head. Much paler in winter, with white throat and buffish neck. Juvenile has bold white streaks on side of head. Flight low and rapid, showing very little white on secondaries. Behaviour more skulking than other grebes, but flies more readily.

Voice: Call-note a loud, high whinneying trill, often prolonged, sometimes rising and falling; also a short "*whit, whit.*"

Habitat: Frequents and breeds on ponds, lakes, reservoirs, backwaters, etc. Winters in estuaries, also inland. Map p. 3.

BLACK-NECKED GREBE *Podiceps nigricollis*　　　　page 4
　　　　Du – Geoorde fuut　　　　　Fr – Grèbe à cou noir
　　　　Ge – Schwarzhalstaucher　　Sw – Svårthalsad dopping
　　　　　　　　N.Am – Eared Grebe

Identification: 12″. Distinguished from Slavonian Grebe in breeding season by black neck, *high black forehead and crown* and less conspicuous tuft of *fan-shaped golden feathers from behind eye.* In winter looks chiefly dark above and white below, but is duskier than Slavonian (which see for other differences) and has more slender, slightly up-tilted bill. Juvenile often has less tip-tilted bill and is doubtfully distinguishable from young Slavonian.

Voice: Call-note a quiet "*poo-eep*," also a variety of chattering and crooning notes.

← Black-necked Grebe
Partial migrant. Sporadic Britain, formerly bred Ireland. Vagrant Norway, Finland

Slavonian Grebe →
Partial migrant. Vagrant s. to Med. islands

Habitat: As Slavonian Grebe. Breeds in small scattered groups in reedy shallows of ponds, lakes, lagoons. Winters on open lakes and along coasts. Map p. 6.

SLAVONIAN GREBE *Podiceps auritus* page 4

Du – Kuifduiker   Fr – Grèbe esclavon
Ge – Ohrentaucher   Sw – Svarthakedopping
N.Am – Horned Grebe

Identification: 13″. Larger than Little Grebe; smaller than Great Crested. In breeding plumage has large, glossy black head, with a *broad golden stripe through eye*, forming short "horns," *dark chestnut* neck and flanks. Upper-parts dark, under-parts silky-white. Broad white wing-bar conspicuous in flight. In winter, looks dark above and white below, like Black-necked, but distinguished by flat black crown ending sharply *at eye-level*, more extensive white on head and neck tending to meet on nape, *straight, stubbier,* (not up-tilted), bill and *snake-like head and neck.*
Voice: Has wide vocabulary when breeding; chief note a long, low trill.
Habitat: Ponds and lakes. Nests in inland shallows. Winters chiefly in sheltered bays and estuaries, but also on fresh water. Map p. 6.

RED-NECKED GREBE *Podiceps grisegena* page 4

Du – Roodhalsfuut   Fr – Grèbe jougris
Ge – Rothalstaucher   Sw – Gråhakedopping

Identification: 17″. A thick-set grebe with a large, bulbous head. Identified in summer by *pale grey cheeks* contrasting with black crown (with small black ear-tufts), *rich chestnut neck* and bright yellow base to dark-tipped bill. Upper-parts grey-brown, under-parts silky-white. In winter looks grey and white, somewhat resembling dusky winter Great Crested, but distinguished by smaller size, thicker, greyer neck and cheeks, *lack of white supercilium,* black crown *extending to eye-level* and *yellow* (not pink) on dark-tipped bill. See also winter Red-throated Diver.
Voice: A high "*keck*"; also a long, wailing, neighing "song."
Habitat: Winters mainly along coasts; breeds in reeds and overgrown pools and quiet waters. Map p. 10.

GREAT CRESTED GREBE *Podiceps cristatus* page 4

Du – Fuut   Fr – Grèbe huppé
Ge – Haubentaucher   Sw – Skäggdopping

Identification: 19″. Largest grebe. Easily identified by *blackish ear-tufts,* and, in breeding season, by *prominent chestnut and black frills* on sides of head. Appearance "tailless," with slender neck, grey-brown upper-parts and gleaming satiny-white under-parts. In winter, lacks frills and looks white-headed, with dark crown and white stripe over eye; dis-

LONG-LEGGED MARSH BIRDS
(Bitterns, Herons, Cranes)

● **BITTERN**   page 23
   Tawny-brown; barred and mottled. Bill often pointed
   upwards.

○ **AMERICAN BITTERN**   23
   Smaller than Bittern; more streaked, less barred.
   Conspicuous black neck patch.

○ **LITTLE BITTERN**   24
   Very small; large creamy wing-patch.
   Male: Black back. *Female:* Brown back.
   Juvenile: Brownish; streaked wings.

○ **NIGHT HERON**   24
   Adult: White breast, black back, black crown.
   Immature: Brown; whitish spots on back and wings.

● **GREY HERON**   27
   Large, pale grey; dark flight-feathers.

○ **PURPLE HERON**   30
   Darker, more slender than Grey Heron; kinked chestnut neck. Immature sandier.

○ **CRANE**   109
   Long white cheek stripes; drooping feathers over tail.

  DEMOISELLE CRANE   109
   Smaller than Crane; black breast; white head tufts.

HERONS (including bitterns and egrets) fly with their necks tucked back to their shoulders; Cranes and all other large long-legged marsh birds fly with their necks extended.

NIGHT HERON

BITTERN

AMERICAN BITTERN

LITTLE BITTERN

Juv

Adult

Juv

NIGHT HERON

Adult

Juv

GREY HERON

PURPLE HERON

Adult

CRANE

DEMOISELLE CRANE

Breeding

LITTLE EGRET

Breeding

GREAT WHIT EGRET

Breeding

Non-breeding

Breeding

Non-breeding

Juvenile

CATTLE EGRET

Adults

SQUACCO HERON

SQUACC HERON

SPOONBILL

Juvenile

Adult

GLOSS IBIS

GREATER FLAMINGO

WHITE STORK

BLACK STORK

Plate 4 9

LONG-LEGGED MARSH BIRDS
(Herons, Spoonbill, Glossy Ibis, Flamingo, Storks)

○ **LITTLE EGRET**   page 27
   Small, white; yellow feet, slender black bill.

△ **GREAT WHITE EGRET**   26
   Large, white; blackish feet.

△ **CATTLE EGRET**   25
   Looks white; heavy "jowl," reddish legs and bill.
   Buffish plumes lost after breeding; bill and legs may
   then be yellowish or dusky.

△ **SQUACCO HERON**   25
   Adult: Looks sandy-brown; almost white in flight;
   greenish legs.
   Juvenile: Striped breast.

● **SPOONBILL**   31
   Adult: White; long, black, spatulate bill.
   Juvenile: Pinkish spatulate bill; black wing-tips.

○ **GLOSSY IBIS**   31
   Dark glossy body; decurved bill.

△ **GREATER FLAMINGO**   32
   Bright crimson on wings; very long neck and legs.

○ **WHITE STORK**   31
   White, with black on wings; red bill.

△ **BLACK STORK**   31
   Black, with white belly; red bill.

WHITE STORK   FLAMINGO   BLACK STORK

tinguished from Red-necked by larger size, thinner neck, white super-cilium, *pink* (not yellow and black) bill. Juvenile has black and white striped head and neck, without tufts or frills. Flight low, showing conspicuous white on secondaries, with head and neck low-hung. Has elaborate display ceremonials.

Voice: A barking *"kar-arr,"* a shrill *"er-wick"* and various trumpeting, moaning and whirring noises.

Habitat: Lakes, gravel pits, reservoirs; winters also on coast. Breeds where vegetation provides anchorage, usually near water's edge. Map below.

PETRELS AND SHEARWATERS:
Procellariidae

Oceanic, visiting land only when breeding; tube-like external nostrils. Shearwaters have slender bills, and are longer-bodied than the smaller petrels; they bank and glide on long, narrow, stiff wings. Fulmars are stouter and more gull-like, but also fly on stiff wings. Sexes similar. Hole or cliff nesting.

FULMAR *Fulmarus glacialis*

Du – Noordse stormvogel	Fr – Pétrel fulmar	page 5
Ge – Eissturmvogel	Sw – Stormfågel	

Identification: 18½″. Gull-like in appearance, but is stubbier, with distinctive flight, gliding and banking on stiff wings, close to waves. Distinguished from gulls by *thick bull-neck, and lack of black tips to narrow wings.* Bill yellow, thick and short, with "tubed" nostrils. Legs bluish. In light phase head and under-parts are white; back, wings *and tail* grey; wings have pale patch at base of primaries. In dark northern phase (so-called "Blue Fulmar") plumage is smoky grey, with darker wing-tips; much too pale and too stubby-billed to be

← Red-necked
Grebe
Partial migr. Has bred France, Holland, Italy. Vagrant w. to Spain, Ireland, Faeroes

Great Crested
Grebe →
Partial migrant

mistaken for slender-billed Sooty Shearwater. Follows ships. Swims buoyantly, rising from water with some difficulty. On land shuffles on tarsi, sometimes aided by wings; may rise on feet briefly. Common in all northern waters, often in vast numbers.

Voice: Usual note a hoarse chuckling or grunting "*ag-ag-ag-arr*."

Habitat: Strictly pelagic. Breeds colonially on oceanic cliffs and islands; locally on inland cliffs and grassy hill-sides. Map below.

CORY'S SHEARWATER *Procellaria diomedea* page 5

Du – Cory's pijlstormvogel   Fr – Puffin cendré
Ge – Gelbschnabel-Sturmtaucher   Sw – Gulnäbbad lira

Identification: 18″. A large grey-brown shearwater, heavier built and looking broader-winged than Great. Further distinguished by *grey-brown hood* (not black cap) *merging gradually* into white throat. Thick bill is *yellow*. Sometimes has narrow white patch at base of tail, as in Great, but more often this is indistinct or lacking. *Never has white collar*. Under-parts pure white, without dark smudges on flanks and belly which occur in Great, but has greyish mottling on sides of breast. Flight action recalls Fulmar rather than Great Shearwater, typically 5-8 flaps followed by a long glide with slightly depressed wings. Nocturnal at breeding grounds. See also Manx Shearwater.

Voice: On breeding grounds, a long wailing note and a gull-like "*ia-gowa-gow*."

Habitat: Pelagic, occasionally off-shore. Breeds socially in crevices among rocks on islands. Mainly resident in Mediterranean. In autumn occurs off S.W. England, Ireland. Vagrant in North Sea, Faeroes and inland to Switzerland, Czechoslovakia, Austria. Map below.

GREAT SHEARWATER *Puffinus gravis* page 5

Du – Grote pijlstormvogel   Fr – Puffin majeur
Ge – Grosser Sturmtaucher   Sw – Större lira

Identification: 18″. Distinguished by *dark cap*, sharply contrasting with pure white throat (head looks narrow), almost complete *white collar*,

← FULMAR
*Winter at sea from
Arctic to dotted
line. Vag. Finland,
Czechoslo., Yugo.,
Switz., Portugal*

CORY'S SHEAR-
WATER →
*Black line marks
n. limit of nesting*

and *dark, slender bill. Narrow white patch at base of tail.* Upper-parts
dark brown, under-parts white, with indistinctly spotted flanks and
dark patch on belly. Whitish under-surfaces of wings have darker
margins than Cory's. During moult shows irregular white line along
centre of upper surface of wing. Flight as Manx; latter is much smaller,
blacker above and lacks white tail-patch. See also Cory's.
Voice: Feeding notes raucous and gull-like.
Habitat and Range: Pelagic, occasionally off-shore. Breeds in burrows
on Tristan da Cunha islands, in S. Atlantic, visiting eastern N. Atlantic
(Iceland to Portugal) in summer and autumn. Vagrant in North Sea,
also in Mediterranean east to Sardinia.

SOOTY SHEARWATER *Puffinus griseus* page 5
Du – Grauwe pijlstormvogel   Fr – Puffin fuligineux
Ge – Dunkler Sturmtaucher   Sw – Grå lira
Identification: 16″. Heavy-bodied and narrow-winged. Looks all
black at a distance, gliding close to waves in typical shearwater fashion.
Often associates with Great Shearwater and has similar behaviour.
Distinguished from all other shearwaters in European and N. African
waters (except dark example of W. Mediterranean race of Manx *P.p.
mauretanicus*) by *uniform sooty plumage.* Under-surfaces of wings have
pale areas, usually in form of indistinct whitish stripe along centre of
wing. See also dark form of Fulmar and of W. Mediterranean race of
Manx; also immature Gannet and dark skuas. Silent at sea.
Habitat and Range: Pelagic and off-shore in summer. Breeds in burrows
on islands in southern hemisphere. In summer and autumn visits
Atlantic, N. to Iceland and Norway. Vagrant to southern North Sea
and English Channel, rarely Mediterranean.

MANX SHEARWATER *Puffinus puffinus* page 5
Du – Noordse pijlstormvogel   Fr – Puffin des Anglais
Ge – Schwarzschnabel-Sturmtaucher   Sw – Mindre lira
Identification: 14″. Distinguished from other shearwaters by *sharply
contrasting black upper-parts and pure white under-parts.* Bill slender.
Usually seen in scattered groups, gliding on stiff wings with occasional
wing-beats. Veers from side to side to follow wave contours, showing
alternate black and white. Does not follow ships. Swims frequently,
flocks congregating on water at evening near breeding grounds.
Nocturnal at breeding grounds. Above description refers to Atlantic
P.p. puffinus; E. Mediterranean race *P.p. yelkouan* is less sharply contrasted; W. Mediterranean (Balearic) race *P.p. mauretanicus* is browner
and even less contrasted; individuals with dark under-parts may be
mistaken for Sooty Shearwater, paler individuals for Cory's, but Manx
is much smaller and slimmer than both.
Voice: Various wild crowing and crooning notes at breeding grounds.
Habitat: Off-shore waters rather than pelagic. Breeds locally in dense
colonies in burrows, on islands and cliff-tops. Map p. 13.

STORM PETRELS: Hydrobatidae

Small, blackish oceanic birds with white rumps, flitting erratically over the waves. Sexes similar. Hole nesting.

STORM PETREL *Hydrobates pelagicus*   page 5
    Du – Stormvogeltje   Fr – Pétrel tempête
    Ge – Sturmschwalbe   Sw – Stormsvala
Identification: 6″. Smallest European sea-bird. A long-winged blackish bird with a *conspicuous white rump* and a squared black tail. Has short, faint wing-bar. *Usually seen following ships* well out from land, with weak flitting flight just above waves, at times "pattering" briefly on surface with dangling black feet. Nocturnal on land. Distinguished from Leach's Petrel by blacker coloration, smaller size, squared tail and weak flight. Rare Wilson's Petrel (which also follows ships habitually) has longer legs and yellow feet, which extend beyond tail.
Voice: Makes sustained, rising and falling purring noise in nest burrow, terminating with characteristic "hiccough"; also has several squeaking and crooning notes.
Habitat: Strictly pelagic, except in breeding season. Nests colonially under rocks, in stone walls, etc., on islands. Map below.

WILSON'S PETREL *Oceanites oceanicus*   page 5
    Du – Wilson's stormvogeltje   Fr – Pétrel océanite
    Ge – Buntfüssige Sturmschwalbe   Sw – Havslöpare
Identification: 7″. Very similar to Storm Petrel, but feet have *yellow webs* and extend *beyond* the short squarish tail. Has less obvious area of grey on wing-coverts than Leach's, but more than Storm Petrel. Follows ships. Distinctive flight, alternately gliding and fluttering with

← MANX SHEAR-
WATER
Partial migrant. Occurs North Sea, Portugal; vag. Bulgaria, Switzerland, Austria, Sweden

STORM PETREL →
Black line encloses nesting areas. Prob. breeds Aegean. Partial migrant. Vagrant inland

bat-like wing-beats; often "walks" along surface of water with out-spread wings. A wanderer from Antarctic and sub-Antarctic breeding grounds, which in summer reaches the seas south-west of Ireland and the Bay of Biscay. Stragglers reach the British Isles. Vagrant to the Mediterranean.

LEACH'S PETREL *Oceanodroma leucorrhoa*   page 5

Du – Vaal stormvogeltje   Fr – Pétrel culblanc
Ge – Wellenläufer   Sw – Klykstjärtad stormsvala

Identification: 8″. Distinguished from Storm Petrel by longer wings and body, distinctive *bounding* flight, constantly changing speed and direction; at short range also by browner plumage, grey centre to white rump, *pale grey wing-coverts* and, though difficult to see, by forked tail. Unlike Storm Petrel, *does not follow ships*. Nocturnal at breeding grounds. See also Wilson's Petrel.
Voice: Normally silent, but at night on breeding grounds a rhythmic series of purring *"wirra-wirra"* notes, punctuated by an emphatic *"wicka, wicka,"* which is also heard in flight. Long crooning notes heard from nest burrows.
Habitat: As Storm Petrel, but usually excavates nest burrows in peaty ground. Map p. 15.

WHITE PELICAN   DALMATIAN PELICAN

PELICANS: Pelecanidae

WHITE PELICAN *Pelecanus onocrotalus*

Du – Gewone pelikaan   Fr – Pélican blanc
Ge – Rosapelikan   Sw – Pelikan

Identification: 55-70″. Huge wing-span. *White, with blackish primaries*, long yellowish bill and throat-pouch and flesh-coloured feet. In breeding plumage both sexes have short, shaggy crest on back of head and rosy tint on plumage. At short range, yellowish tuft of feathers at base of neck, and red eye are visible. Juvenile brown, becoming dingy white irregularly speckled with brown. Flight leisurely, with short periods of gliding, head carried well back on shoulders. Flies in regular lines, often at great height. Shows black wing-tips above, *whole rear-edges of wings dark below*. White Stork and Gannet are also white with black wing-tips, but both fly with extended necks and have different bill shapes; Gannet has narrower, angular, pointed wings and longer, pointed tail; Dalmatian Pelican seen from below shows no black on wings (see diagram).

Habitat and Range: Large inland waters, marshes and shallow coastal lagoons. Nests colonially among reeds. Breeds Roumania. Greece in winter. Accidental W. to Sweden, Germany, Spain.

DALMATIAN PELICAN *Pelecanus crispus*   page 14

    Du – Kroeskoppelikaan   Fr – Pélican frisé
    Ge – Krauskopfpelikan   Sw – Krushuvad pelikan

Identification: Difficult to distinguish from White Pelican except in flight; ranges overlap. In flight shows dusky secondaries and black wing-tips above, *all dirty white below*. Size usually slightly larger. At short range upper-parts look dirty white (instead of faintly rose-white); under-parts *dull greyish-white* with large yellowish patch (not tufted) on lower throat; primaries dark brown; legs lead grey (not flesh); feathers on back of head only slightly elongated and curly (not shaggy or crested); eye pale yellowish (not red). Juvenile resembles young White Pelican, distinguishable only at short range by feathers on forehead ending in nearly straight line, instead of in a point above upper mandible (adults have similar distinction). Behaviour, flight and habitat as White Pelican. Map below.

← LEACH'S PETREL
Summer vis. within black line. Vag. e. to Finland, Austria, Sicily. Has bred Ireland

DALMATIAN
PELICAN →
Partial migrant. Vag. cent. Europe, n. to E. Prussia, w. to Spain

SWANS AND GEESE

● **BEWICK'S SWAN** page 43
    Adult: Rounded head; base of bill yellow.
    Immature: Dingy; bill dull flesh to base.

● **WHOOPER SWAN** 43
    Adult: Flat profile; yellow on bill more extensive,
    forming point.
    Immature: Larger than Bewick's; longer neck.

● **MUTE SWAN** 42
    Adult: Bill orange, with black knob.
    Immature: Bill flesh, black at base.

○ **SNOW GOOSE** 42
    Adult: White, with black wing tips.
    Immature: Dingier; bill dark.

● **BARNACLE GOOSE** 33
    Black chest and neck; white face.

● **CANADA GOOSE** 33
    Black neck, light chest; white throat-patch.

● **BRENT GOOSE** 34
    Black chest and neck; small white neck-spot.
    Immature birds lack the neck-spot.
    Dark-bellied form: East and South coasts.
    Pale-bellied form: In Britain, mainly West, especially
    Ireland.

△ **RED-BREASTED GOOSE** 35
    Chestnut breast; broad white flank-stripe; head
    pattern.

Juv   Juv   Juv

Adult   Adult   Adult

BEWICK'S   WHOOPER   MUTE

MUTE SWAN

WHOOPER SWAN
BEWICK'S SWAN

Adult

SNOW
GOOSE

BARNACLE   GOOSE

CANADA   GOOSE

Light-bellied
form

Dark-bellied
form

BRENT GOOSE

RED-BREASTED
GOOSE

Juv

Adult
WHITE-FRONTED

Greenland form

LESSER
WHITE-
FRONTED

BEAN

Adult

Juv

WHITE-FRONTED
GOOSE

GREENLAND
WHITE-FRONTED
GOOSE

BEAN GOOSE

LESSER
WHITE-FRONTED
GOOSE

Eastern form

Western

PINK-FOOTED
GOOSE

GREY LAG
GOOSE

PINK-FOOTED

Western

Eastern

GREY LAG

Plate 6   **17**

GREY GEESE

THE BEST PLACE in Europe to study geese is the New Grounds of the Wildfowl Trust, at Slimbridge. Captive examples of all birds shown on this plate can be studied there and during winter many can be seen in a wild state. The Director of the Trust, Peter Scott, has guided the preparation of the goose plates.

Grey Geese with ORANGE Legs

● **WHITE-FRONTED GOOSE**   page 35
> Pink bill; white patch above base of bill and black blotches on belly are lacking in juvenile.

  ● **GREENLAND WHITE-FRONTED GOOSE**   35
> A subspecies; winters mostly in Ireland and western Scotland.
> Darker; bill yellow (nail horn-colour, not white).

○ **LESSER WHITE-FRONTED GOOSE**   38
> Smaller; stubby bill; *yellow ring* around eye; white more extensive on forehead. A distinct species.

● **BEAN GOOSE**   39
> Dark head and neck; bill yellow with black markings, but variable.

Grey Geese with PINK Legs

● **PINK-FOOTED GOOSE**
> Small dark head; dark neck; bill black and pink.   39

● **GREY LAG GOOSE**   35
> Large and pale; orange-yellow bill has no black.

EASTERN GREY LAG   35
> Paler, with broad, light feather edges; pink bill.

GANNETS: Sulidae

GANNET *Sula bassana*   page 5
  Du – Jan van Gent   Fr – Fou de Bassan
  Ge – Basstölpel   Sw – Havssula

Identification: 36″. A goose-size white sea-bird, identified by *extensive black tips to long, narrow wings*. Twice the size of Herring Gull, *with much longer neck* and *larger, pointed bill* often pointing downward, and *pointed tail* (not fan-shaped). Immature is dusky, closely speckled with white, or boldly pied blackish-brown and white, according to age, but easily identified by characteristic actions and by "cigar-shaped" body. Direct flight usually low, with brief periods of gliding, but wheels majestically when feeding. Plunges headlong after fish, sometimes from 100 ft. or more. (Gulls sometimes drop into sea for food, but Gannet's submerging plunge is spectacular.)

Voice: Usual note a barking "*arrah*."

Habitat: Strictly maritime, often seen far out to sea. Breeds in dense colonies on ledges of steep rocky island cliffs. Map below.

CORMORANTS: Phalacrocoracidae

Large, long-billed dark water-birds, larger (except Pygmy Cormorant) than any duck. Sometimes confused with divers, but tail and wings longer and bill hook-tipped. In flight, neck held slightly above horizontal (divers' necks droop slightly). Fly in line or "V" formation, like geese. Often perch with wings half open. When swimming, resemble divers, but with necks more erect, bills tilted slightly upward. Rock or tree nesting.

← GANNET
Partial mig. Black line encloses nest colonies. Vag. E. Med., Baltic to Finland, Austria

CORMORANT →
Mainly res. Winter all coasts except E. Baltic. Passage central Europe.

CORMORANT
Breeding adult

CORMORANT
Atlantic form

Adult

CORMORANT
Continental form

Adult

CORMORANT
Immature

SHAG
Adult

SHAG
Adult   Immature

Adult

PYGMY
CORMORANT

Cormorant

Shag

Cormorants and Shags (above) stand upright, often hold a 'spread-eagle' pose. Cormorants swim with the bill tilted slightly upward.

THE CORMORANTS

GEESE AND SWANS IN FLIGHT

Most geese and swans fly in line or "V" formation.

● **BRENT GOOSE**   page 34
    Small: black chest, neck and head.
    Pale-bellied form: Light under-parts.
    Dark-bellied form: Dark under-parts.

● **BARNACLE GOOSE**   33
    Black chest and neck; white face.

● **CANADA GOOSE**   33
    Black neck "stocking"; light chest; white throat-
    patch.

● **WHOOPER SWAN**   43
    All white; very long neck.
    Bewick's Swan is smaller, shorter-necked.

● **MUTE SWAN**   42
    Knob on forehead.
    Wings make "singing" sound in flight.

○ **SNOW GOOSE**   42
    White; black primaries.

BRENT GOOSE

Light-bellied form

Dark-bellied form

below

BARNACLE
GOOSE

above

above

CANADA GOOSE

WHOOPER SWAN

MUTE SWAN

SNOW GOOSE

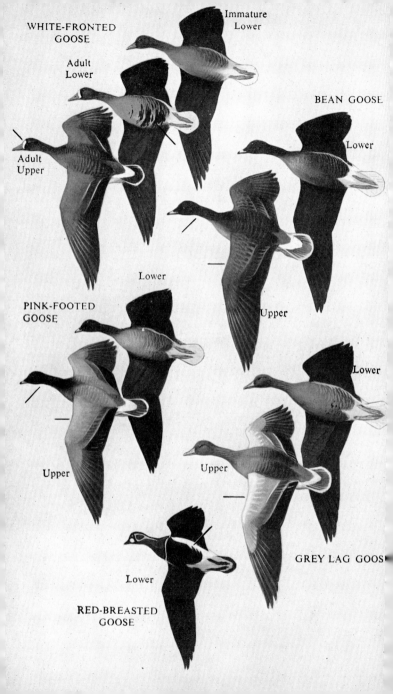

WHITE-FRONTED
GOOSE

Immature
Lower

Adult
Lower

Adult
Upper

BEAN GOOSE

Lower

Lower

PINK-FOOTED
GOOSE

Upper

Upper

Lower

GREY LAG GOOSE

Upper

Lower

RED-BREASTED
GOOSE

Plate 8   21

CHIEFLY GREY GEESE, IN FLIGHT

FOR THE MOST PART, the grey geese on the wing all look very similar and it requires much experience to separate them at a distance. Their voices (below) are useful clues. At close range the bill and leg colours as shown on Plate 6 are distinctive.

● **WHITE-FRONTED GOOSE** page 35

Fore-wing brownish; adult shows black blotches on breast. At close range, orange legs, pink bill, white forehead.
Greenland Whitefront has yellow bill.
Voice: Musical, high-pitched, usually disyllabic, sometimes trisyllabic. "*Kow-lyow*" or "*lyo-lyok*," etc.

● **BEAN GOOSE** 39

Dark; no fore-wing contrast; orange feet; black and yellow bill.
Voice: Reedy and bassoon-like "*ung-unk*," not unlike lower notes of Pink-foot. Relatively silent.

● **PINK-FOOTED GOOSE** 39

Fore-wing blue-grey; pale body; very dark head; pink feet.
Voice: Musical "*ung-unk*," higher than Bean. Sometimes "*king-wink*," or often repeated "*wink-wink-wink*."

● **GREY LAG GEESE** 35

Fore-wing strikingly pale grey; rather large; pale head.
Voice: "*aahng-ung-ung*," or "*gaahnk*," very like farmyard goose.

△ **RED-BREASTED GOOSE** 35

Black belly; rufous chest; white stripes.

CORMORANT   *Phalacrocorax carbo*   page 19
     Du – Aalscholver   Fr – Grand Cormoran
     Ge – Kormoran   Sw – Storskarv

Identification: 36″. A large blackish water bird, easily confused with Shag, but distinguished by larger size, *white chin and cheeks* and, in breeding birds, by *white patch on thighs*, and lack of crest. Juvenile brownish above, distinguished from young Shag by *whitish under-parts* and heavier bill. Perches *upright* on rocks, often with wings hanging half open. Swims low in water like diver, but with neck more erect, bill slightly raised. Flight fairly rapid and direct, neck extended and slightly above horizontal; parties usually fly in line or "V" formation. Sociable. In breeding season most Continental and some British birds have almost completely white head and neck.

Voice: Usual note a low, guttural "*r-rah.*"

Habitat: Coasts, estuaries, coastal lakes, also inland waters. Breeds colonially, sometimes near Shags, on rocky ledges, also on inland lake islands and trees. Map p. 18.

SHAG   *Phalacrocorax aristotelis*   page 19
     Du – Kuifaalscholver   Fr – Cormoran huppé
     Ge – Krähenscharbe   Sw – Toppskarv

Identification: 30″. Smaller than Cormorant, with slightly thinner, shorter neck, slighter head and *smaller bill.* Distinguished by *lack of white on face*; also lacks white thigh-patch of breeding Cormorant; at short range by *green-black* instead of bronze-black plumage; in breeding season has short, upstanding crest. Eyes pale blue-green. Immature distinguished from young Cormorant by dark brown plumage with *little, if any,* white on breast (except young of Med. race, which show some white below); bill is more slender than adult's and much finer than young Cormorant's.

Voice: Usual note a loud, rasping croak. At nest, a deep grunt and loud hissing.

Habitat: Maritime, frequenting rocky coasts and islands with steep cliffs and sea caves; in winter occasionally inland. Breeds colonially

← Shag
Mainly resident.
Vagrant inland,
Sweden, Denmark,
Holland, Belgium

Pygmy
Cormorant →
Partial migrant.
Vagrant n. and w.
to Sweden, France,
Italy

(sometimes singly) on rocky ledges and among boulders. Map p. 22.

PYGMY CORMORANT *Phalacrocorax pygmaeus*   page 19
    Du – Dwergaalscholver   Fr – Cormoran pygmée
    Ge – Zwergscharbe   Sw – Dvärgskarv
Identification: 19". Very much smaller and more active than Cormorant, recalls Coot in flight, but with long tail and *rather small, round head*. In summer, both sexes have dark red-brown head, glossy greenish-black plumage, spotted with white, except for dark grey "saddle" across centre of back and wing-coverts. Outside breeding season white spots are absent, throat is white, breast red-brown. Juvenile has white chin, brown throat and breast, brownish-white under-parts and yellowish bill. See also Shag.
Habitat: Prefers inland waters, including rivers and marshes, to seacoast. Breeds colonially, building untidy nest on bushes in marsh. Map p. 22.

HERONS AND BITTERNS: Ardeidae

Wading birds with long necks, long legs and longish pointed bills. In sustained flight, heads are tucked back on shoulders. Specialized plumes on head, scapulars and neck. Soft parts change colour when breeding. Sexes similar except Little Bittern. Tree or reed nesting.

BITTERN *Botaurus stellaris*   page 8
    Du – Roerdomp   Fr – Butor étoilé
    Ge – Grosse Rohrdommel   Sw – Rördrom
Identification: 30". A large, brown, heron-like marsh bird, *richly mottled and barred*, with large green legs and feet and *distinctive voice*. When hiding, bill is pointed vertically in characteristic elongated pose; walks with shoulders hunched, head lowered. Flight slow and reluctant, neck retracted when well under way: broad rounded wings *distinctively barred black and brown*. Skulking, solitary and usually crepuscular, hiding in reeds by day. Can be confused with immature Night Heron, which is much smaller and spotted. See also American Bittern.
Voice: A harsh "*aark*." Song, 2-3 quiet grunting notes, an audible intake of breath followed by a deep, booming "*woomp*," like distant fog-horn, sometimes audible for a mile.
Habitat: Dense reed-beds in fens, marshes, backwaters, lake shores. Nests among reeds. On Continent sometimes nests around small ponds in cultivated regions. Map p. 24.

AMERICAN BITTERN *Botaurus lentiginosus*   page 8
    Du – Amerikaanse Roerdomp   Fr Butor d'Amérique
    Ge – Amerikanische Rohrdommel Sw – Amerikansk rördrom
Identification: 26". Distinguished from European Bittern by *smaller*

size, finely freckled upper-parts (not boldly mottled and streaked), slightly narrower, *black-tipped* wings (not barred black and brown), *chestnut* crown and *long black streak down side of neck*. Behaviour and flight are similar to European. Immature Night Heron is about same size, but is greyer, without the black wing-tips.

Voice: When flushed, a rapid, throaty "*kok-kok-kok*."

Habitat and Range: More likely to be seen in open meadows than European species. Vagrant to Britain, Channel Isles, Ireland, Faeroes, Iceland.

LITTLE BITTERN *Ixobrychus minutus*   page 8
    Du – Wouwaapje   Fr – Butor blongios
    Ge – Zwergrohrdommel   Sw – Dvärgrördrom

Identification: 14″. Distinguished from other small herons by *very small size*, dark crown and upper-parts, very conspicuous *buffish-white wing-coverts* and under-parts. Male's crown and back are greenish-black. Female is streaky dark brown above, streaky buff below, with less conspicuous buff wing-coverts. Bill yellowish (red at base when breeding). Legs green. Juvenile heavily streaked above and below. Flight usually very low, with rapid wing-beats and long glides. In flight *pale coverts contrast strongly with dark wings and back*. Skulking and chiefly crepuscular except in breeding season.

Voice: A variety of short croaking notes. Song (day or night) a deep thump, repeated at about 2 seconds' interval, sometimes for hours.

Habitat: Overgrown river banks, backwaters, ponds, wooded swamps, reed-beds. Nests near water, occasionally in small scattered groups. Maps below.

NIGHT HERON *Nycticorax nycticorax*   page 8
    Du – Kwak   Fr – Héron bihoreau
    Ge – Nachtreiher   Sw – Natthäger

Identification: 24″. A stocky, rather short-legged heron. Adult is *black-backed* and pale below, with a *black cap*, long drooping white crest, red eyes, and stout bill. Legs yellowish (dull red in breeding

← BITTERN
*Partial migrant.
Has bred Finland.
Vagrant Ireland,
Iceland, Norway*

LITTLE BITTERN →
*Summer visitor,
occas. winter. Vag-
rant n. to Brit. Is.,
Iceland, Finland*

season). Immature dark brown above, boldly spotted with buff; no crest; in bad light may be confused with much larger Bittern, but latter has mottled golden-brown plumage. Has stumpy silhouette in flight. Crepuscular, except in breeding season. Usually spends day hidden and inactive, often in trees, flying to feed at dusk.

Voice: A hoarse *"guark,"* or *"guok,"* usually at dusk.

Habitat: Dense tangled swamps, overgrown river banks, marshes with trees; feeds at dusk in drains, at edges of pools, or in open marshes. Nests colonially, often with allied species, in thickets, trees, locally also in reed beds. Map below.

SQUACCO HERON *Ardeola ralloides* page 9

Du – Ralreiger	Fr – Héron crabier
Ge – Rallenreiher	Sw – Rallhäger

Identification: 18″. Stocky and thick-necked, with *pale buff plumage, white wings*; long drooping crest. Bill black and blue when breeding, dark-tipped greenish in winter. Legs greenish (pink at height of breeding season). On ground looks stocky, thick-necked, dingy yellowish-brown; in flight suddenly reveals conspicuous white wings, rump and tail; can then be confused with Little and Cattle Egrets, but darker back and head are distinctive.

Voice: In breeding season a harsh, crow-like *"karr,"* usually at dusk.

Habitat: As Little Egret, though less often in open. Nests singly, or in scattered groups, among allied species, in reed-beds, bushes, trees. Map below.

CATTLE EGRET *Bubulcus ibis* page 9

Du – Koereiger	Fr – Héron garde-boeufs
Ge – Kuhreiher	Sw – Kohäger

Identification: 20″. Looks white in distance. Slightly smaller, much *stockier and thicker-necked* than Little Egret, with which it often nests.

← Night Heron
*Summer visitor.
Has bred Germany.
Annual Switzer-
land. Vag. n. to
Brit. Is., Faeroes,
Scand., Finland*

Squacco Heron →
*Summer visitor.
Annual Switzer-
land. Vagrant n.
to Brit. Is., Den-
mark, Sweden*

Heavy jowl is distinctive. Distinguished at short range by long buff tufts on crown, chest and mantle; in winter, buff is very pale, When breeding the bill is yellow with a red base, legs reddish; in winter the bill is yellowish, legs dusky. Eye reddish. Juvenile lacks buff tufts, has yellow bill, greenish-brown legs. Flight and actions like Little Egret. Sociable. Unlike Little Egret, *usually feeds among grazing cattle.* Can be confused with Squacco Heron in flight (see above).

Voice: A variety of croaking notes in breeding season.

Habitat and Range: Less aquatic than most herons. Usually among feeding cattle in meadows, marshes, or in dry open country. Nests colonially, often with allied species, in reed-beds, bushes, or trees, over water or on dry land. Resident S. Spain, Portugal. Vagrant to rest of Mediterranean (has bred France), Britain, Denmark, Hungary, Balkans.

GREAT WHITE EGRET *Egretta alba* page 9
Du – Grote zilverreiger   Fr – Grande aigrette
Ge – Silberreiher   Sw – Ägretthäger
N.Am – American Egret

Identification: 35″. Much larger than Little Egret (which also has dazzling white plumage) and has slimmer shape and no real crest. Neck is *very long, thin and angular.* Bill can be all yellow, or partly black from tip. Legs *and feet* greenish-black (Little Egret's feet are yellow); when breeding, upper parts of legs are pinkish-orange. Scapulars greatly elongated in breeding season to form hazy, drooping "cloak" extending below tail. Squacco and Cattle Egret, which look white in distant flight, are much smaller and stockier.

Voice: Has occasional croaking note "*kraak*".

Habitat: Lake and river banks, open swamps, lagoons. Nests in dense reed-beds, usually in scattered groups, rarely in bushes or trees. Map below.

← GREAT WHITE EGRET
*Partial migrant
Has bred Czecho.
Vagrant to Sweden,
Britain, Balearics*

LITTLE EGRET →
*Partial migrant.
Regular spring
Switzerland. Vagrant n. to Brit. Is.,
Denmark, Baltic
Provinces*

LITTLE EGRET *Egretta garzetta* page 9
    Du – Kleine zilverreiger   Fr – Aigrette garzette
    Ge – Seidenreiher   Sw – Silkeshäger

Identification: 22". A small snow-white heron with long, slender, black bill, black legs and *yellow feet*, latter conspicuous in flight. Feet become reddish in spring. (Great White Egret is much larger, and has black feet; Cattle Egret and Squacco Heron in flight both look white in distance, but they are much stockier, thicker-necked birds, with shorter bills). In summer, adults have *very long, drooping crest* and greatly elongated scapulars, forming hazy drooping "cloak." Feeds in open in shallow water, *not among grazing cattle* like Cattle Egret.
Voice: In breeding season, a croaking "*kark*" and a bubbling "*wulla-wulla-wulla.*"
Habitat: Marshes, lagoons, swamps. Nests in colonies, often with other herons, in bushes or trees, in wet marsh, swamps, dry open country, sea cliffs and woods. Map p. 26.

GREY HERON *Ardea cinerea* page 8
    Du – Blauwe reiger   Fr – Héron cendré
    Ge – Fischreiher   Sw – Grå häger

Identification: 36". Distinguished from other herons by *large size, grey upper-parts, white head and neck with broad streak from eye to tip of long, graceful crest.* Long, dagger-shaped bill is yellowish, legs brownish, both becoming reddish in early spring. Stands motionless for long periods in or near water, with long neck erect, or head sunk between shoulders; also perches in trees. Flight powerful, with slow, deep wing-beats; flight silhouette is distinctive, with *head back between shoulders* and legs extended.
Voice: A deep, harsh "*frarnk.*" Numerous croaking and retching notes and bill-snapping in breeding season.
Habitat: Water meadows, rivers, lakes, sea-shores. Nests in colonies, usually in tall trees. Map below.

← GREY HERON
*Partial migrant.
Summers S. Italy,
N. E. Spain*

PURPLE HERON →
*Summer visitor.
Has bred Ger-
many. Vag. n. to
British Isles, Fae-
roes, Scandinavia*

SURFACE-FEEDING DUCKS
(Marshes and Ponds)

● **MALLARD** page 45
Male: Green head; white
neck ring; purplish-brown
breast.
Female: Some orange on bill;
whitish tail.

● **PINTAIL** 50
Male: Needle tail; neck stripe.
Female: Grey bill; slender
pointed tail.

● **GADWALL** page 47
Male: Grey body; black rear.
Female: Orange-sided bill; white speculum (in flight).

● **WIGEON** 47
Male: Chestnut head; buff crown.
Female: Short blue-grey bill; light shoulders (not
often visible when swimming).

● **SHOVELER** 51
Male: Spoon-like bill; dark chestnut sides.
Female: Spoon-like bill; blue shoulders (in flight).

● **MANDARIN** 57
Male: Orange "side-whiskers"; orange "sails."
Female: White mark around eye; white chin.

● **TEAL** 46
Male: Small; grey with dark head; horizontal white
stripe above wing.
Female: Small size; green speculum.

● **GARGANEY** 51
Male: White stripe on head; bluish shoulder patch.
Female: From Teal by greyer wings; obscure
speculum.

MARBLED TEAL 54
Mediterranean. Dappled plumage.
Shaggy head; dark smudge through eye; white tail.

MALLARD ♂ ♀

PINTAIL ♂ ♀

GADWALL ♂ ♀

WIGEON ♂ ♀

SHOVELER ♂ ♀

MANDARIN ♂ ♀

TEAL ♂ ♀

GARGANEY ♂ ♀

MARBLED TEAL ♂

GOLDENEYE

BARROW'S GOLDENEYE

FERRUGINOUS DUCK

SCAUP

TUFTED DUCK

POCHARD

RED-CRESTED POCHARD

Plate 10   29

DIVING DUCKS
(Goldeneyes and Pochards, etc)

DIVING DUCKS (ducks of open waters and sea) patter along the surface when taking flight. Surface-feeding ducks (marsh ducks, Plate 9) spring directly up from the water.

● **GOLDENEYE**   page 63
Male: Round white spot before eye.
Female: Grey body; brown head; white collar; white on wing visible when swimming.

BARROW'S GOLDENEYE   64
Iceland.
Male: White crescent on face; blacker above than Goldeneye.
Female: Very similar to Goldeneye (see text).

○ **FERRUGINOUS DUCK**   55
Male: Deep mahogany; white under tail-coverts.
Female: Similar, but duller.

● **SCAUP**   56
Male: Black fore-parts; pale back; blue bill. "Black at both ends, white in the middle."
Female: Sharply defined white patch at base of bill.

● **TUFTED DUCK**   56
Male: Black fore-parts; black back; drooping crest.
Female: From female Scaup by suggestion of crest. White at base of bill restricted or absent.

◉ **POCHARD**   55
Male: Grey; black chest; chestnut head.
Female: Buff mark around eye and base of bill; blue band on bill.

● **RED-CRESTED POCHARD**   54
Male: From Pochard by red bill and white sides.
Female: Pale cheek; from female Common Scoter by paler plumage; white wing-patch; red on bill.

PURPLE HERON *Ardea purpurea*   page 8
    Du – Purperreiger   Fr – Héron pourpré
    Ge – Purpurreiher   Sw – Purpurhäger
Identification: 31″. Distinguished from Grey Heron by smaller size, much darker coloration, and, when perched, by much more serpentine appearance. Upper-parts and wings dark grey, with elongated chestnut feathers drooping from mantle; crown and crest black; *very long thin chestnut neck boldly striped black*; centre of breast chestnut, rest of under-parts black. Immature is sandier, with chestnut crown, no black on head or neck, and buffish under-parts. In flight, neck bulge *hangs lower and is more angular* and feet look larger than in Grey Heron; latter shows more contrasted wing-pattern. Seldom in trees.
Voice: Higher pitched than Grey Heron, "*rrank*."
Habitat: Swamps, overgrown ditches, dense reed-beds, etc. Breeds in colonies, sometimes with other species, in reed-beds, occasionally in bushes. Map p. 27

STORKS: Ciconiidae

Large, with long legs, long necks and long, straight bills. Flight slow and deliberate, with neck extended but slightly drooped. Gait a sedate walk. Sexes similar. Tree or roof nesting.

WHITE STORK *Ciconia ciconia*   page 9
    Du – Ooievaar   Fr – Cigogne blanche
    G – Weissstorch   Sw – Vit stork
Identification: 40″. Easily identified by large size, white plumage with *jet-black flight feathers* and long, *bright red bill and legs*. Perches on trees and buildings, often on one leg. Walks deliberately. Often soars or flies at great height. Wing-beats are slow. Flight silhouette distinguished from heron's, pelican's and Egyptian Vulture's by long,

← WHITE STORK
*Summer vis; some
winter Spain, Port.
Has bred France,
Italy. Vag. Brit.
Is., Norway, Fin-
land*

BLACK STORK →
*Summer vis.
Bred Denmark,
Sweden, Austria.
Vag. to England,
Norway, Finland*

extended neck. Migrates in irregular flocks, *not* in regular formations. Sociable. See also immature Spoonbill.

Voice: Occasional hissing and coughing notes during breeding season; loud, rhythmic bill-clattering frequent during display.

Habitat: Marshes, water-meadows and grassy plains; in breeding season usually near houses. Nests on buildings, haystacks, or stork-poles, also in trees. Map p. 30.

BLACK STORK *Ciconia nigra*   page 9

    Du – Zwarte ooievaar   Fr – Cigogne noire
    Ge – Schwarzstorch   Sw – Svart stork

Identification: 38″. Distinguished from White Stork by glossy *black plumage*, with *white under-parts*. Shy and solitary.

Voice: Has considerable range, varying from a hoarse gasping, to a noise like sharpening a saw, and several quite musical notes. Bill-clattering less frequent than with White Stork.

Habitat: Wild marshy tracts or meadows among coniferous or mixed forests. Nests at considerable height in forest trees. Map p. 30.

SPOONBILLS AND IBISES:
Threskiornithidae

Resemble small herons or storks in general form, but with long and decurved or flattened and spatulate bills. Necks extended in flight. Sexes similar. Reed, bush or tree nesting.

SPOONBILL *Platalea leucorodia*   page 9

    Du – Lepelaar   Fr – Spatule blanche
    Ge – Löffler   Sw – Skedstork

Identification: 34″. Easily identified by *snow-white plumage* and *long, spatulate bill*. Adults have ochre tinge at base of neck and, in summer, a *pendant "horse-tail" crest*. Legs and bill black, latter with yellow tip. Immature has black tips to wings, no ochre on neck, greyish-pink bill and yellowish to greyish legs. Flight regular and slow, gliding and soaring on extended wings; parties usually in file. Distinguished in flight from all "white" heron-like birds by *extended*, slightly sagging neck and spatulate bill.

Voice: Occasional grunting noise in breeding season. Bill-clattering occurs when excited.

Habitat: Shallow, open water, reedy marshes, estuaries. Breeds in colonies in large reed-beds, on small bare islands, locally in trees or bushes. Map p. 32.

GLOSSY IBIS *Plegadis falcinellus*   page 9

    Du – Ibis   Fr – Ibis falcinelle
    Ge – Brauner Sichler   Sw – Svart ibis

Identification: 22". Bill curlew-shaped, but plumage is *uniform, almost black*. At close range plumage is glossed with purple, bronze and green. Immature is *dull* dark brown. Flight silhouette is distinctive, with narrow body, long round-tipped wings, extended neck and trailing legs; shallow, rapid wing-beats with occasional gliding can cause confusion with Pygmy Cormorant. Perches freely on trees. Has infrequent, long croak.

Habitat: Marshes, mud-flats. Breeds in colonies, frequently with herons or egrets, in large reed-beds among shallow water, occasionally in bushes or trees. Map below.

FLAMINGOS: Phoenicopteridae

GREATER FLAMINGO *Phoenicopterus ruber*   page 9
Du – Ge – Sw – Flamingo   Fr – Flamant rose

Identification: 50". Unmistakable. An extremely slender, white and rose-pink wading bird, with *abnormally long legs and neck and grotesque down-curved bill*. In flight, *neck and legs are extended* and slightly drooped, wings show magnificent combination of *crimson and black*. Immature is dingy grey-brown. Walks sedately, dipping bill or head in shallow water to feed. Strictly gregarious. Beware "escaped" Chilean race (immature has grey legs, pink "knees"; adult has all-pink plumage).

Voice: A goose-like gabble and many trumpeting cries, *"ar-honk,"* etc., particularly in flight.

Habitat and Range: Shallow coastal lagoons, or flood waters, lakes, mudflats, etc. Breeds colonially on mud banks, or in shallow water, building mud-heap nest, a few inches above water. Breeds S. France, resident but rarely breeding S. Spain. Vagrant to British Isles and most European countries. N. to Finland, but chiefly Mediterranean.

← SPOONBILL
Mainly summer vis. Bred Denmark, Czecho. Vag. n. to Iceland, Finland, Ireland

GLOSSY IBIS →
Summer vis. Has bred Spain, Portugal. Vag. n. to Brit. Is., Iceland, Scandinavia

GEESE, SWANS AND DUCKS:
Anatidae

Geese are large, noisy waterfowl: heavier and longer-necked than ducks. Chiefly terrestrial feeders. Sexes similar. Ground and cliff nesting.

Swans are larger, with much longer, more slender necks; like some geese they migrate in lines or V-shaped flocks. Sexes similar. Ground nesting.

Shelducks are goose-like ducks. Sexes similar. Hole nesting.

Surface-feeding Ducks feed by dabbling or "up-ending"; taking flight they spring off the water; usually have brightly coloured speculum (rectangular patch) on secondaries; in eclipse (late summer) plumage, males tend to resemble females. Ground or hole nesting.

Diving Ducks dive for food and patter along surface before flying. Wingbars and patches are important. Hole or ground nesting.

Saw-bills have slender, toothed bills; most have crests and are slender-bodied, more like divers than ducks; in flight appear long-drawn, with bill, head, neck and body horizontal. Ground or hole nesting.

CANADA GOOSE *Branta canadensis*   pages 16, 20
>   Du – Canadese gans   Fr – Bernache du Canada
>   Ge – Kanadagans   Sw – Kanadagås

Identification: 36-40″. Largest goose occurring in Europe. Black head and *long black neck contrast strongly with whitish breast and brown body*. Distinguished from other "black geese" by large size and *broad white patch from throat on to cheek*. Bill and legs black. Distinguished from much smaller Barnacle by *brown body* (not grey), white patch on cheeks (not including face), black extending only to base of neck (not to breast). Brent is even smaller, without white on head. Gregarious outside breeding season. Normally diurnal, grazing in fields like "grey geese," but sometimes also "up-ending" in water. Chiefly a fresh-water species. Flies in regular chevron or line formations.

Voice: Flight-note a resonant "*aa-honk*," second syllable rising.

Habitat and Range: Fields and open marshes near fresh water; sometimes among trees and along seashores. Introduced into Europe and occurs frequently in parks. Breeds singly or in small groups on bushy islets in lakes. Feral breeder in Britain, Sweden; has occurred in Ireland, Faeroes, Norway, Denmark, Holland, Belgium and France.

BARNACLE GOOSE *Branta leucopsis*   pages 16, 20
>   Du – Brandgans   Fr – Bernache nonnette
>   Ge – Weisswangengans   Sw – Vitkindad gås

Identification: 23-27″. Quickly identified by *black and white plumage, conspicuous white face and forehead*; *black on neck extending down to* *breast*; lavender-grey upper-parts with bold white-edged black bars, greyish under-parts, white rump and black tail. Legs and small bill black. Flight in close ragged packs. Feeds nocturnally. Strongly gregarious. Distinguished from Brent by larger size, white face and more terrestrial habits; from Canada Goose by smaller size, white face, black breast and grey (not brown) upper-parts.

Voice: Distant flock sounds like pack of yapping lap-dogs. Usual note a rapidly repeated barking "*gnuk*."

Habitat: Seldom far inland, preferring salt marshes, grass fields near estuaries, tidal mud-flats, or small grass-topped islands. Breeds colonially, usually on ledges of steep Arctic cliffs, rocky river gorges and hill-sides, sometimes open tundra. Map below.

BRENT GOOSE *Branta bernicla*   pages 16, 20

    Du – Rotgans   Fr – Bernache cravant
    Ge – Ringelgans   Sw – Prutgås

Identification: 22-24″. *Smallest and darkest* of the "black geese" (near size of Mallard), with *dull black head, neck and breast*, dark grey-brown upper-parts, brilliant white "stern" and *small white fleck on side of neck* (sometimes looking almost like narrow collar, but absent in immature). Dark-bellied form *B. b. bernicla* has dark grey-brown belly; pale-bellied *B. b. hrota* has much paler under-parts, contrasting strongly with upper-parts (both may occur in same flock). More maritime than other geese. Strongly gregarious, feeding at water's edge along coast by day or night; rests on water at high tide; often "up-ends." Flight rapid, seldom in formation, usually in irregularly changing flocks. Distinguished from Barnacle and much larger Canada Geese by *all-black head*.

Voice: A soft, throaty "*rronk*" or "*rruk*," also various lesser conversational notes. Flock makes distinctive growling noise.

Habitat: Maritime outside breeding season, frequenting coasts and estuaries where *Zostera* weed abounds. Breeds sociably on high rocky tundra and islets off Arctic coasts. Map below.

← BARNACLE GOOSE
Winter vis. from high Arctic. Passage Baltic, Iceland. Vag. s. to Spain, Italy

BRENT GOOSE →
Winter visitor from high Arctic, Vagrant s. to Italy, Roumania

RED-BREASTED GOOSE *Branta ruficollis* pages 16, 21
    Du – Roodhalsgans   Fr – Bernache à cou roux
    Ge – Rothalsgans   Sw – Rödhalsad gås

Identification: 21-22″. Easily identified by contrasting *combination of black, white and chestnut plumage*. At a distance *white flank-stripe* is most conspicuous feature. Legs and very small bill blackish. Immature is paler, duller and browner, with indistinct white patch between bill and eye. Behaviour and flight similar to "grey geese," but is extremely quick and agile when feeding and seldom flies in regular chevron or line formation. Often associates with Lesser White-fronts.

Voice: A shrill, staccato, *"kik-wik,"* or *"kee-kwa"* and various rather squeaky conversational notes.

Habitat and Range: Normally winters on grassy steppes, roosting along sea coast. Breeds sociably on coastal tundra. Some winter in Hungary. Vagrant across Europe to Britain, France, Sweden.

GREY LAG GOOSE *Anser anser* pages 17, 21
    Du – Grauwe gans   Fr – Oie cendrée
    Ge – Graugans   Sw – Grågås

Identification: 30-35″. Two European races recognisable in the field: the British and W. European race *A. a. anser* has *thick orange* bill; the E. European race *A. a. rubrirostris* has *thick pink* bill and looks *paler* due to light feather edges. Both are further distinguished from other "grey geese" by *lack of black markings on bill, pinkish legs and feet, head and neck no darker than body, very pale grey fore-wings* and unbarred belly (but adults often have some black spots on breast). Immature has greyish-pink legs. In distant flight all "grey geese" look much alike, usually flying in chevrons or lines; all are gregarious outside breeding season and are normally diurnal, flighting to grazing grounds at dawn. Grey Lag is distinguished from adult White-fronted and Lesser White-fronted by larger size, pale head and neck, lack of white patch at base of bill and, at all ages, by pink (not orange) legs; from Bean and Pink-footed by head and neck being no darker than body, large orange bill (in W. Europe) without black markings and generally paler appearance.

Voice: Same nasal and reedy gabbling notes as domestic bird, *"aahng ung-ung,"* etc. Distant flock sounds rather like baaing of sheep.

Habitat: In winter on grasslands, arable fields near coast, marshes, estuaries. Breeds sociably on moors, marshes, reed-beds, boggy thickets, islets. Map p. 38.

WHITE-FRONTED GOOSE *Anser albifrons* pages 17, 21
    Du – Kolgans   Fr – Oie rieuse
    Ge – Blässgans   Sw – Bläsgås

Identification: 26-30″. Smaller and darker than Grey Lag. Adults distinguished from Grey Lag, Bean and Pink-footed by *bold white patch above the pink bill, orange legs and broad irregular black bars on belly*. Immature lacks dark bars on belly and white forehead, but

SEA DUCKS

● **LONG-TAILED DUCK** page 63
Male in summer: Needle tail; white face-patch.
Male in winter: Needle tail; pied pattern.
Female: Dark wings; white face; dark cheek-mark.

△ **HARLEQUIN** 62
Male: Dark; rusty flanks; harlequin pattern.
Female: Dark; face spots; small bill.

○ **SURF SCOTER** 62
Male: Black body; white patches on head and bill.
Female: Light face spots; no white on wing.

● **VELVET SCOTER** 59
Male: Black body; white wing-patch.
Female: Light face spots; white wing-patch.

● **COMMON SCOTER** 59
Male: All black: orange patch on bill.
Female: Dark body; light cheek; dark crown.

● **EIDER** 57
Male: White above; black below.
Female: Brown; heavily barred. See diagram.

○ **KING EIDER** 57
Male: Whitish fore-parts; black rear two-thirds;
orange shield. *Female:* See diagram below.

△ **STELLER'S EIDER** 58
Male: White head; chestnut under-parts; black spot.
Female: See diagram below.

EIDER ♀   KING EIDER ♀   STELLER'S EIDER ♀

FEMALE EIDERS can be told by their bills; long and sloping in the
Eider, with a long lobe extending to the forehead; stubbier in the
King Eider, with less lobing; no obvious lobes in the Steller's.

♂ Summer   ♂ Winter   LONG-TAILED DUCK   ♀ Winter

♂   HARLEQUIN   ♀

♂   SURF SCOTER   ♀

♂   VELVET SCOTER   ♀

♂   COMMON SCOTER   ♀

♂   EIDER   ♀

♂ KING EIDER   ♂ STELLER'S EIDER

♂ RED-BREASTED MERGANSER ♀

♂ GOOSANDER ♀

♂ SMEW ♀

♂ SHELDUCK ♀

♂ RUDDY SHELDUCK ♀

♂
Summer WHITE-HEADED DUCK ♀

Plate 12   37

SAWBILLS, SHELDUCKS, STIFFTAIL

SAWBILLS or fish-eating ducks have slender spike-like bills with toothed edges. They swim low in the water. SHELDUCKS are large and somewhat goose-like. STIFFTAILS are dumpy, with long tails, often cocked.

● RED-BREASTED MERGANSER   page 65
  Male: White collar; wispy crest; chestnut breast.
  Female: Crested head; *blended* throat and neck.

● GOOSANDER   65
  Male: Long white body; dark head; black back.
  Female: Crested; *sharply defined* throat and neck.

● SMEW   64
  Male: White, marked with black; white crest.
  Female: Chestnut cap; white cheeks; thin bill.

● SHELDUCK   44
  Chestnut belt encircling white body; red bill.
  Male has knob on bill; female is without knob.

○ RUDDY SHELDUCK   44
  Orange-chestnut body; pale head.
  Male with narrow black neck-ring; female without.

WHITE-HEADED DUCK   66
  Male: Dark body; white head; blue bill (in summer).
  Female: Light cheek crossed by dark line.
  Both sexes have swollen base to bill.

POSTURES OF DUCKS ON LAND

| *Marsh and pond ducks* (*Surface-feeders*) | *Estuary and sea ducks* (*Divers*) | *Sawbills* (*Divers*) | *Stifftails* (*Divers*) | *Shelducks* (*Surface-feeders*) |

combination of orange legs and lack of extensive black on bill are distinctive. Behaviour and normal flight like Grey Lag, though wing-beat is quicker and fore-wing brownish. Greenland race *A. a. flavirostris*, which winters mainly in Ireland and West Scotland, distinguishable in the field from typical race *A. a. albifrons* by its darker coloration, particularly on head and neck, and orange-yellow bill. See also Lesser White-fronted Goose.

Voice: Gabbling notes resemble those of other "grey geese," but are higher-pitched and quicker. Usual notes a cackling "*kow-lyow*," or "*lyo-lyok*," di- and trisyllabic.

Habitat: As Grey Lag, but seldom in stubble or potato fields. Usually breeds sociably in treeless tundra, open marshes, islets in rivers, etc. Map below.

LESSER WHITE-FRONTED GOOSE *Anser erythropus*

page 17

Du – Dwerggans	Fr – Oie naine
Ge – Zwerggans	Sw – Fjällgås

Identification: 21-26". General appearance resembles small White-fronted, but is distinguished by *much smaller, pinker bill, white forehead extending much higher on to crown* and tips of closed wings usually *extending beyond tail*. Usually looks darker than European White-fronted. At short range bright, swollen *yellow eye-ring* is sure mark. Immature lacks white base to bill and dark bars on belly, but has the yellow eye-ring. Behaviour and flight as in White-fronted, but wing-beats are faster.

Voice: Much squeakier than White-fronted. Most frequent notes "*kyu-yu*," or "*kyu-yu-yu*" (gander); "*kow-yow*" (goose).

Habitat: Much as White-fronted, but is a low-Arctic species and breeds at high altitudes only where range extends south, in dwarf birch and willow, around mountain lakes. In extreme north of Norway breeds at sea level. Map p. 39.

← GREY LAG
GOOSE
*Partial migrant.
Has bred Holland.
Feral in Norfolk*

WHITE-FRONTED
GOOSE →
*Winter vis. from
N. Russia, Green-
land. Few summer
Hungary (has
bred). Vag. Spain*

43

44

BEAN GOOSE   *Anser fabalis*   pages 17, 21
         Du – Rietgans   Fr – Oie des moissons
         Ge – Saatgans   Sw – Sädgås

Identification: 28–35″. Browner and *generally darker* than other "grey geese," pale feather margins appearing brighter. At a distance *head and rather long neck look dark*. No bars on under-parts. *Bill long and black, marked with orange-yellow*, occasionally with some white at base. Legs of adult *orange-yellow*; immature pale yellowish. Behaviour and flight as Grey Lag, but has dark fore-wing. Adult Pink-footed is slightly smaller, with smaller *pink and black* bill, *pink* legs and blue-grey upper-parts giving greater contrast to dark head and neck. (Pink-footed is sometimes considered as a race of the Bean.) Grey Lag is slightly larger and paler, especially on head and neck, with light grey fore-wings, white-tipped orange bill and *pink* legs. Adult White-fronted and Lesser White-fronted are smaller, with prominent white at base of bill and broadly barred bellies.

Voice: Less vocal than other "grey geese." A rich "*ung-unk*," lower and more reedy than similar call of Pink-footed.

Habitat: Winters inland, on grasslands near fresh water. Breeds in the Arctic among forest trees near rivers and lakes. Map below.

PINK-FOOTED GOOSE   *Anser brachyrhynchus*   pages 17, 21
         Du – Kleine rietgans   Fr – Oie à bec court
         Ge – Kurzschnabelgans   Sw – Spetsbergsgås

Identification: 24–30″. Distinguished from Bean and other "grey geese" by *pale blue-grey upper-parts* giving strong contrast with *very dark head and neck, small pink and black bill and pink legs*. (Pink-footed is sometimes considered as a race of the Bean.) During summer moult plumage varies greatly from blue-grey to brown-grey. *Blue-grey fore-wings conspicuous in flight*, though less so than in larger, paler Grey Lag, which lacks the blueness. Immature sometimes has paler legs, and in winter looks browner and often paler-necked than adult. Behaviour and flight as White-fronted. Distinguished from adult White-fronted and Lesser White-fronted by lack of white at base

← Lesser White-fronted Goose *Migratory. Vagr. s.w. to Italy, Spain, Britain*

Bean Goose → *Migratory. Vagr. Balearics, also Iceland*

45   46

DUCKS IN FLIGHT (See also Plate 15)

NOTE: Males only are analysed below. For females see text.

● **SHELDUCK**   page 44
   Black, white and chestnut pattern.

○ **RUDDY SHELDUCK**   44
   Pale cinnamon colour; large fore-wing patches.

● **MALLARD**   45
   Dark head; two white borders on speculum; neck ring.

● **PINTAIL**   50
   Needle tail; one white border on speculum; dark
   head.

● **WIGEON**   47
   Large white shoulder-patches; grey back.

● **SHOVELER**   51
   Heavy bill; striking blue shoulder-patches.

● **GADWALL**   47
   Grey-brown; white inner secondaries.

● **GARGANEY**   51
   Small; white head-streak; bluish shoulder-patches.

● **TEAL**   46
   Small, dark-winged; dark head; green speculum.

● **SMEW**   64
   White head and inner wing; black outer wing and
   mantle.

● **GOOSANDER**   65
   Sawbill shape; white body and inner wing.

● **RED-BREASTED MERGANSER**   65
   Sawbill shape; dark chest; white inner wing.

Sawbills (Smew, Goosander and Red-breasted Merganser) fly with bill, head, neck and body held in a horizontal line. (Compare with Divers, Plate 1.)

TUFTED DUCK

SCAUP

FERRUGINOUS DUCK ♂

POCHARD

RED-CRESTED
POCHARD

GOLDENEYE

LONG-TAILED
DUCK

HARLEQUIN

KING EIDER ♂

EIDER

VELVET SCOTER

SURF SCOTER

COMMON SCOTER

Plate 14 **41**

DUCKS IN FLIGHT (See also Plate 16)

NOTE: Males only are analysed below. Some females have similar wing patterns. (See text.)

of bill (though some white occurs occasionally) and by lack of black bars on belly; immature extremely difficult to distinguish from immature White-fronts unless leg colour and rounder head can be clearly seen, as bill patterns are very similar.

Voice: Two- and three-syllable honking notes are high-pitched, lacking cackling quality of White-fronted. A musical *"ung-unk,"* and characteristic *"wink-wink-wink,"* or *"king-wink."*

Habitat: As Grey Lag, but more frequently in arable fields. Breeds colonially among rocky outcrops on hill-sides and river gorges, also on open tundra. Map below.

SNOW GOOSE *Anser caerulescens* pages 16, 20

Du – Sneeuwgans	Fr – Oie des neiges
Ge – Schneegans	Sw – Snögås

Identification: 25-30″. Adult easily identified by *pure white plumage, with black-tipped wings.* Stout, dark pink bill and legs. Head often stained orange. Immature is brownish-grey above, greyish-white below, with dark grey bill and legs. Behaviour and flight as in "grey geese." Feeds freely with other species. "Blue Goose" of N. America, which has occurred in British Isles, is colour phase of this species; it is dusky blue-grey, with white head, neck and "stern" (sometimes also breast and belly); immature is all dusky with white chin-spot. Snow Goose is easily distinguished from all swans by *shorter neck and black primaries;* from flying Gannet by much smaller head and bill on longer neck. short rounded tail and broader wings.

Voice: An abrupt, harsh *"kaank";* also a deep *"zung-ung-ung"* conversational gabble.

Habitat and Range: As in "grey geese." Breeds colonially on open tundra and lake islands. Vagrant from N. America to Iceland, Britain, Ireland, many Continental countries from Norway to Greece.

MUTE SWAN *Cygnus olor* pages 16, 20

Du – Knobbelzwaan	Fr – Cygne tuberculé
Ge – Höckerschwan	Sw – Knölsvan

Identification: 60″. Same size as Whooper, larger than Bewick's. Dis-

← PINK-FOOTED GOOSE
Migratory. Vagr. to France, Italy, Yugoslavia, Baltic Provinces

MUTE SWAN →
Partial migrant. Vagrant Norway, and south to Spain

47

49

tinguished from both by *orange bill with black knob and base* (knob greatly enlarged in male in spring). Also, when swimming, by *gracefully curved neck, with bill pointing downward*. Immature browner than young Whooper, with knobless, greyish-pink bill and grey legs. *Readily assumes aggressive attitude*, with neck curved and wings arched over back. Is often domesticated. Flight powerful and direct, with neck outstretched; *wing-beats make distinctive loud singing note*. Sociable (sometimes in very large herds), except in breeding season.

Voice: Is not mute, though less vocal than other swans; makes various explosive and hissing noises.

Habitat: May occur anywhere. In truly wild state frequents remote marshes and lakes; in winter, on sheltered sea coasts. Map p. 42.

WHOOPER SWAN *Cygnus cygnus* pages 16, 20

Du – Wilde zwaan Fr – Cygne sauvage
Ge – Singschwan Sw – Sångsvan

Identification: 60″. *Lemon-yellow* base to black bill distinguishes Whooper from Mute, which has orange bill with black knob at base. Further distinguished by *stiffly erect neck* and frequent *bugle-call notes*; from Bewick's by long, flat profile to head, considerably larger size, yellow on bill *tapering forward to a point*, and different voice. Immature marked with ashy-brown, greyer than young Mute; bill pale pinkish with dusky tip. Behaviour and flight like Mute, but walks more easily, does not arch wings aggressively and wing-beats lack characteristic singing note. Usually in noisy herds, except in breeding season, when solitary. Flies in wavering oblique lines, or chevrons.

Voice: Noisiest of swans. Flight-call of flock a loud trumpeting or whooping chorus "*hoop-hoop-hoop*."

Habitat: Sea coasts, tidal waters, lakes, large rivers. Nests on islets in swamps or lakes, moorland bogs, Arctic tundra. Map below.

BEWICK'S SWAN *Cygnus bewickii* page 16

Du – Kleine zwaan Fr – Cygne de Bewick
Ge – Zwergschwan Sw – Mindre sångsvan

← WHOOPER SWAN
Mainly migratory.
Has bred Scotland.
Vagr. s. to Medit.

BEWICK'S SWAN →
Winter vis. from
N. Russia. Vag. s.
to Yugoslavia,
Italy

Identification: 48". *Considerably smaller and shorter in neck* than Mute and Whooper; chiefly resembles latter; distinguished by *shorter bill with smaller, more rounded area of yellow, rounded head* and much quieter voice. Immature resembles young Whooper, except in size. Behaviour and habitat like Whooper, but seldom flies in regular formation. Does not arch wings aggressively. Wing-beats lack characteristic singing note made by Mute.

Voice: Quieter than Whooper. Feeding herds make quiet musical babble. Map p. 43.

RUDDY SHELDUCK *Tadorna ferruginea* pages 37, 40, 48

Du – Casarca   Fr – Tadorne casarca
Ge – Rostgans   Sw – Rostand

Identification: 25". Distinguished by goose-like shape, *uniform orange-chestnut plumage with pale head*, smallish black bill and legs, black tail, black wing-feathers with green speculum. In flight, shows *very conspicuous white wing-coverts*. Male has narrow black collar. Female has almost white head. Usually in pairs. Flight resembles Shelduck's. Locally feral Egyptian Goose also has conspicuous wing-patches, but is greyer, with russet eye-patch.

Voice: A loud, nasal "*ah-onk*," and several other goose-like cries.

Habitat: Much more terrestrial than Shelduck. In winter frequents sandy lake-shores, river banks, fields and even arid steppes. Breeds in holes in dunes, cliffs, old trees and walls. Map below.

SHELDUCK *Tadorna tadorna* pages 37, 40, 48

Du – Bergeend   Fr – Tadorne de Belon
Ge – Brandente   Sw – Gravand

Identification: 24". A large, rather goose-like duck, appearing white and black at long range. Distinguished by contrasting greenish-black head and neck, white body with *broad chestnut band around fore-part* and dark stripe down centre of under-parts. Scapulars and primaries black, with green speculum. Legs pink; *bill red*, male's having

← RUDDY
    SHELDUCK
*Partial migrant.
Vagr. most Europe
n. to Iceland, Finland. Winters S.
Spain, ?Greece*

SHELDUCK →
*Partial migrant.
Has bred Finland.
Vagrant Iceland,
Faeroes, Hungary*

prominent knob. Juvenile is ashy-brown above, lacks chestnut breast-band and has whitish face and throat, pink bill, grey legs. Flight is goose-like, with slower wing-beats than most ducks. When resting on water may be confused with male Shoveler, which also has white-upper-breast and dark head, but latter is smaller, sits lower in water and has dark, spatulate bill.

Voice: Seldom vocal outside breeding season. A quick, nasal "*ak-ak-ak*," and a deeper, louder, "*ark, ark.*" Female with young has soft twanging note.

Habitat: Sandy and muddy coasts, occasionally inland. Breeds in rabbit burrows, etc., and on bushy commons. Map p. 44.

MALLARD *Anas platyrhynchos* pages 28, 40, 48

Du – Wilde eend   Fr – Canard colvert
Ge – Stockente   Sw – Gräsand

Identification: 23". Male has *glossy green head, narrow white collar, purplish-brown breast*, pale grey under-parts, white tail with curled black centre feathers, yellowish bill. Female is mottled brown, with brownish bill (often mottled orange at sides). Both sexes have broad purple speculum between two white bars (very conspicuous in flight), and orange legs. Male in eclipse resembles dark female, but with brighter speculum, darker crown and ruddier breast. Flight rapid, with shallow wing-beats. Female distinguished from Gadwall by larger size, browner coloration, *purple* speculum, less pointed wings, also sits lower in water; from female Pintail by heavier bill and head, thicker neck, white *both sides* of purple speculum, shorter whitish tail; from female Shoveler by larger size, much smaller bill, longer neck. See also male Red-breasted Merganser.

Voice: Male has quiet "*yeeb*"; female quacks loudly.

Habitat: Almost any water; in winter also on sea coasts and estuaries. Nests beneath undergrowth near water, occasionally in holes. Map below.

← MALLARD
Partial migrant

TEAL →
*Partial migrant.
Has bred Spain,
Portugal, Corsica,
Macedonia*

54   55

TEAL *Anas crecca* pages 28, 40, 48

Du – Wintertaling   Fr – Sarcelle d'hiver
Ge – Krickente   Sw – Kricka

Identification: 14″. Smallest European duck. Male has conspicuous *horizontal white stripe* on scapulars, *dark chestnut head with curving green eye-patch* and *creamy-buff patches* either side of black "stern." At a distance male looks like a *small grey duck with a dark head.* Both sexes have glossy green and black speculum and double wing-bar. Female speckled brown and buff; paler and spotted below; distinguished from similar female Garganey by lack of distinct face pattern and *larger, brighter green speculum.* Flight very rapid, in very compact flocks, usually low, often erratic. Male Green-winged Teal *A. c. carolinensis* (subsp.), accidental in Europe, has *vertical* white mark in front of wing, instead of horizontal bar above wing.

Voice: Very vocal. Male has short, low musical "*krrit*"; female, a high, harsh quack; feeding flock makes pleasant chuckling chorus of short nasal notes, like sound of child's toy squeaker.

Habitat: Reedy pools and streams. In winter, frequents marshes, occasionally estuaries and sea coasts. Breeds on moors, marshes, among bracken in woods, often far from open water. Map p. 45.

BLUE-WINGED TEAL *Anas discors* page 285

Du – Blauwvleugeltaling   Fr – Sarcelle soucrourou
Ge – Blauflügelente   Sw – Amerikansk Årta

Identification: 15″. Size of Garganey. Male distinguished by dark grey-brown head with *large white crescent in front of eye*; under tail-coverts black, bordered in front by *conspicuous white patch*; in flight. *pale, chalky-blue fore-wing* is brighter, less grey than Garganey's, similar to Shoveler's, but latter is easily distinguished by huge bill. Female resembles female Garganey, but has darker plumage, brighter blue fore-wing and a longer, rather straight bill; is indistinguishable from escaped Cinnamon Teal *A. cyanoptera.* Male's speculum green with white in front; female's duller. Male's bill black; female's dusky with paler base and edges.

Voice: Male has high squeaking note; female quacks faintly.

Habitat and Range: In winter frequents large marshes, rice-fields, small ponds. Breeds around fresh-water ponds. Vagrant from N. America to Britain, Ireland, Denmark, Holland, Italy.

BAIKAL TEAL *Anas formosa* page 285

Du – Siberische Taling   Fr – Sarcelle élégante
Ge – Gluckente   Sw – Gulkindad Kricka

Identification: 16″. Larger than Teal. Male has unmistakable *creamy side of head, crossed by black vertical mark from eye to chin*; crown, hind neck and chin black; bold green crescent edged white curving from eye to nape and round side of neck; long, drooping scapulars rufous, cream and black; pinkish breast, grey flanks, black stern, the three colours separated by *two vertical white stripes.* Female resembles female Teal, but distinguished by *bold whitish spot at base of bill* and broken supercilium above dark eye-stripe. Bill and rather long legs grey. Behaviour resembles Teal's, but flight less swift, less erratic.

Voice: More noisy than Teal. Male has curious deep chuckling notes "*wot-wot*" or "*proop.*" Female quacks like Teal.

Habitat and Range: Mainly a fresh-water duck, though occasionally seen at sea. Vagrant from Asia to Britain, France, Holland, Finland, Sweden, Belgium, Switzerland, Italy.

GADWALL *Anas strepera*   pages **28, 40, 48**

Du – Krakeend	Fr – Canard chipeau
Ge – Schnatterente	Sw – Snatterand

Identification: 20″. Smaller, slighter and with more abrupt forehead than Mallard, with which it often associates. Both sexes have *white patch on rear of wing*, conspicuous chiefly in flight. Male is greyish with chestnut wing-coverts, visible chiefly in flight, when *white belly contrasts with black tail-coverts*; the best mark on the water, at a distance, is the *black "stern" contrasting with the grey plumage*; bill grey, legs orange-yellow; in eclipse resembles female, but retains chestnut wing-coverts. Female resembles female Mallard and Pintail; distinguished from latter by shorter tail, from both by orange panels on sides of bill and *white wing-patch*. Flight like Mallard's, but wings are more pointed.

Voice: Female quacks loudly in falling diminuendo "*kaaak-kaaak-kak-kak-kak.*" Male has a low single note.

Habitat: Like Mallard, but less cosmopolitan and seldom occurs on sea coast. Map below.

WIGEON *Anas penelope*   pages **28, 40, 48**

Du – Smient	Fr – Canard siffleur
Ge – Pfeifente	Sw – Bläsand

Identification: 18″. Male distinguished by *chestnut head with yellow forehead*, grey body and pinkish breast; in flight *large white areas towards front of wings* and white belly and black "stern" are dis-

← GADWALL
*Partial migrant.
Has bred Spain,
Denmark. Vagrant
Norway, Finland,
Faeroes*

WIGEON →
*Partial migrant.
Has bred Holland,
Ireland. Few win-
ter Czecho.*

DUCKS OVERHEAD (See also Plate 13)

NOTE: Only males are analysed below. For females, see text.

● **SHELDUCK** page 44
Chestnut breast-band across white under-parts.

○ **RUDDY SHELDUCK** 44
Pale cinnamon body; white under wings.

● **MALLARD** 45
Dark head and chest; paler belly; neck-ring.

● **PINTAIL** 50
Small dark head; white breast; long thin neck; needle tail.

● **WIGEON** 47
Clean-cut white belly; dark pointed tail.

● **SHOVELER** 51
Dark head and belly; thick white neck; big bill.

● **GADWALL** 47
White belly; white inner secondaries.

● **GARGANEY** 51
Small size; pale under-parts; dark fore-parts.

● **TEAL** 46
Small size; white belly; dark head.

● **SMEW** 64
All-white below, except on wings and tail.

● **GOOSANDER** 65
Dark head; white body; white wing-linings.

● **RED-BREASTED MERGANSER** 65
Sawbill shape; dark breast-band.

SHELDUCK

RUDDY
SHELDUCK

♂

♂

MALLARD

PINTAIL

WIGEON

SHOVELER

GARGANEY

TEAL

♂

GADWALL

GOOSANDER

SMEW

RED-BREASTED MERGANSER

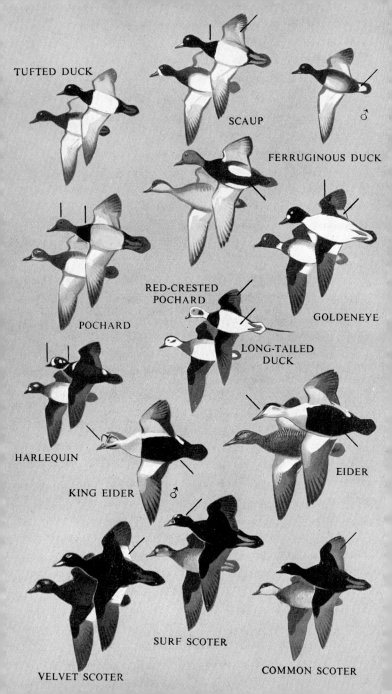

TUFTED DUCK

SCAUP

FERRUGINOUS DUCK

♂

RED-CRESTED
POCHARD

POCHARD

GOLDENEYE

LONG-TAILED
DUCK

HARLEQUIN

KING EIDER

♂

EIDER

VELVET SCOTER

SURF SCOTER

COMMON SCOTER

Plate 16 49

DUCKS OVERHEAD (See also Plate 14)

NOTE: Only males are analysed below. For females, see text.

● **SCAUP** page 56
    Black chest; white stripe showing through wing.

● **TUFTED DUCK** 56
    Similar to Scaup overhead, but less bulky.

○ **FERRUGINOUS DUCK** 55
    Mahogany fore-parts and flanks, framing white belly.

● **POCHARD** 55
    Chestnut head; black breast; grey belly.

● **RED-CRESTED POCHARD** 54
    Black under-parts; bold white flank-patches.

● **GOLDENEYE** 63
    Blackish wing-linings; white body.

● **LONG-TAILED DUCK** 63
    Uniform dark wings and breast; white belly and head.

△ **HARLEQUIN** 62
    Uniform dark colour; white spots; small bill.

○ **KING EIDER** 57
    White chest; black belly; blunt head.

● **EIDER** 57
    White chest; black belly; pointed head.

● **VELVET SCOTER** 59
    Black body; white secondaries.

○ **SURF SCOTER** 62
    Black body; white on head and bill.

● **COMMON SCOTER** 59
    Black body; silvery flight feathers.

tinctive; in eclipse resembles dark female, but distinguished by white shoulders. Female distinguished from Mallard by smaller size, much smaller bill, more rounded head, pointed tail and more rufous plumage; also by partly obscured green and black speculum and shorter-necked appearance. Feeds in shallows, on mud-flats and grazes around ponds, often resting on sea by day in compact flocks. Young male distinguished from young Gadwall by smaller bill, darker head and blackish speculum. See also American Wigeon.

Voice: Male has high whistling "*whee-oo*." Female has low purring note.

Habitat: Many maritime in winter, numbers also seen on fresh water. Breeds on moors, lake islands, marshes. Map p. 47.

AMERICAN WIGEON (BALDPATE) *Anas americana*

page 285

Du – Amerikaanse Smient	Fr – Canard siffleur d'Amérique
Ge – Nordamerikanische Pfeifente	Sw – Amerikansk Bläsand

Identification: 18-22". Male, unlike mainly grey Wigeon, is mostly *pinkish-brown*, with *broader creamy-white crown*, wide glossy green band from eye to nape and grey cheeks and upper neck. Female very similar to female Wigeon, but head and neck are *greyer*, contrasting with reddish brown chest. Male shows bold white wing-patches (in flight) as Wigeon, but axillaries in both sexes are *white*, whereas Wigeon's are dusky.

Voice: Male has whistling call "*wee, whee-oo*."

Habitat and Range: Habitat similar to Wigeon's. Vagrant from N. America to Britain, Ireland, Iceland, Holland, France.

PINTAIL *Anas acuta*

pages 28, 40, 48

Du – Pijlstaart	Fr – Canard pilet
Ge – Spiessente	Sw – Stjärtand

Identification: 22". A slender, long-necked, surface-feeding duck with a pointed tail. Male has chocolate-brown head and neck, with *conspicuous white streak* from white breast up each side of neck, and long, *needle-pointed tail*. Upper-parts and flanks grey. Male in eclipse and when young resembles female, but with darker upper-parts. Female distinguished from similar females of Mallard, Gadwall and Wigeon by slim shape, thin neck, more pointed tail, obscure speculum and grey bill; in flight, light border on rear of wing is useful detail. Only other duck with long tail is Long-tailed Duck which is smaller, with largely *white* head and is a maritime *diving* duck.

Voice: Seldom vocal. Male has a low whistle. Female has growling note and a low quack.

Habitat: Chiefly coastal in winter. As Wigeon in breeding season, but also nests in sand-dunes. Map p. 51.

GARGANEY *Anas querquedula*   pages 28, 40, 48
  Du – Zomertaling   Fr – Sarcelle d'été
  Ge – Knäkente   Sw – Årta

Identification: 15″. Only slightly larger than Teal, but with more slender neck, flatter crown and straighter bill. Male distinguished in flight by *pale blue-grey fore-wing*, sharply contrasting brown breast and white belly; easily identified when at rest by *conspicuous curving white streak from eye to nape*, also by long drooping black and white scapulars; in eclipse resembles female, but is always distinguishable by blue-grey shoulders. Female like female Teal, but identified by striped head pattern (particularly whitish supercilium and cheeks), paler shoulders and indistinct speculum. Behaviour and feeding habits more like Shoveler's than Teal's. Flight very rapid and agile.
Voice: Male makes peculiar dry rattling or grating noise. Female's quack is like female Teal's, but shorter.
Habitat: Much as Teal, but seldom on salt water. Breeds in long grass or rank vegetation near water. Map below.

SHOVELER *Anas clypeata*   pages 28, 40, 48
  Du – Slobeend   Fr – Canard souchet
  Ge – Löffelente   Sw – Skedand

Identification: 20″. Distinguished from all other ducks by *huge spatulate bill*. Male is largely black and white above, with green-glossed head, *chestnut belly and flanks*, white breast and pale blue patch on fore-wing. At rest or flying overhead male has unique pattern: *dark-white-dark-white-dark*. Female is mottled brownish, like Mallard, but has *blue shoulders* (so has male Garganey). On water sits very low in front, with bill pointing downwards. In flight-silhouette *wings appear set far back*.
Voice: Flight-note a deep "*tuk-tuk*." Male has low double quack; female's resembles Mallard's, though less loud.
Habitat: Less maritime than other surface-feeders. Usually in marshes and over-grown ponds. Breeds in water meadows, marshes, bushy commons. Map p. 54.

← PINTAIL
Partial migrant.
Has bred S. Spain,
France, Belgium,
Hungary

GARGANEY →
Mainly summer
visitor. Has bred
Ireland, Spain.
Vag. Norway, Fae-
roes

CRAKES, RAILS, COOTS, AND GALLINULES

- **WATER RAIL**   page 110
    Adult: Long red bill; barred flanks; white under tail.
    Juvenile: Dusky; mottled under-parts.

- **CORNCRAKE**   112
    Rusty-red wings; yellowish bill. Often darker than
    shown, with greyish cheeks and breast.

- **SPOTTED CRAKE**   111
    Recalls short-billed Rail; often darker than shown.
    Buff under tail-coverts; greenish legs; red base to bill.

- O **BAILLON'S CRAKE**   111
    No red on bill; legs brownish-flesh; bold bars on
    flanks. Upper-parts richer vinous-chestnut than
    shown, boldly streaked white.

- O **LITTLE CRAKE**   111
    Male: Legs green; no spots on breast; no dark bars
    on flanks; upper-parts olive-brown.
    Female: Buffish breast; green legs; both sexes have
    red spot on bill.

- **MOORHEN**   112
    Adult: Red bill; white flank-stripe and under tail.
    Juvenile: Brownish with yellowish-green bill.

- **COOT**   113
    Adult: White bill and shield.
    Juvenile: From Moorhen by larger size, no white on
    tail-coverts.
    Downy young: Orange-red head.

  CRESTED COOT   114
    Whitish bill and shield; red knobs often inconspicuous.

  PURPLE GALLINULE   113
    Deep purplish-blue; red legs; very large red bill.

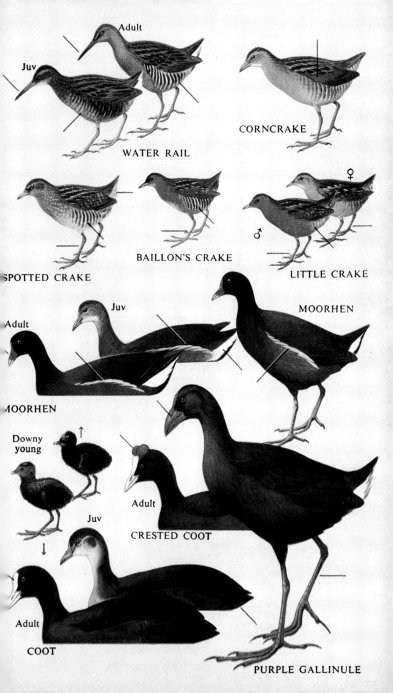

WATER RAIL

Adult

Juv

CORNCRAKE

BAILLON'S CRAKE

SPOTTED CRAKE

LITTLE CRAKE

♀

♂

MOORHEN

Adult

Juv

MOORHEN

Downy
young

CRESTED COOT

Adult

Juv

COOT

Adult

PURPLE GALLINULE

Typical

Pale

ROUGH-LEGGED
BUZZARD

BUZZARD

Dark

Pale

Typical

HONEY
BUZZARD

Adult

LONG-
LEGGED
BUZZARD

♂   ♀

Adult

Immature

SPARROW HAWK

GOSHAWK

Plate 18   53

BUZZARDS AND HAWKS
(See also Plates 22 and 24)

BUZZARDS have heavy bodies, short wide tails.

● **ROUGH-LEGGED BUZZARD**   page 76
    Dark belly; whitish tail with dark terminal band.

● **BUZZARD**   76
    Variable. Usually dark with blotched or barred under-
    parts. Tail usually as shown, sometimes almost un-
    barred cinnamon.

● **HONEY BUZZARD**   70
    Head smaller, tail longer than Buzzard's.
    Tail has broad black bands near base and at tip.

LONG-LEGGED BUZZARD   76
    Tail pale cinnamon, usually unbarred; base sometimes
    whitish.

ACCIPITERS (bird hawks) have small heads,
short wings, long tails.

● **SPARROW HAWK**   75
    Male: Small; under-parts closely barred red-brown.
    Female: Under-parts closely barred with grey.

○ **GOSHAWK**   74
    Adult: Large, barred; dark cheek; white supercilium.
    Juvenile: Brown, streaked; pronounced supercilium.

MARBLED TEAL *Anas angustirostris* page 28
    Du – Marmereend   Fr – Sarcelle marbrée
    Ge – Marmelente   Sw – Marmorand

Identification: 16″. Slightly larger than Teal with longer neck and bigger head. Distinguished by light and dark brown "marbled" or dappled plumage, with *dark patch or smudge through eye*. Looks uniform pale grey-brown at a distance, with dark eye-patch. No pattern in flight, except pale secondaries and white-tipped tail. Male has slight crest on nape. Juvenile is yellower below, with dark stripe through eye and two whitish spots on wing. Behaviour sluggish and retiring.

Voice: Male has a low wheezing croak; female a feeble quack.

Habitat and Range: A fresh-water species, preferring overgrown to open water. Nests near water, along stream banks, etc. Summer visitor S. Spain, breeds rarely S. France. Occasional Portugal. Vagrant to rest of S. Europe, N. to Germany, Czechoslovakia, Roumania.

RED-CRESTED POCHARD *Netta rufina* pages 29, 41, 49
    Du – Krooneend   Fr – Nette rousse
    Ge – Kolbenente   Sw – Rödhuvad dykand

Identification: 22″. A plump, large-headed diving duck, sitting high in the water. Male has *red bill, rich chestnut head* with paler erectile crown, dark brown upper-parts, black neck, breast and belly-stripe, with gleaming white flanks. In flight shows broad white band *almost full length of wing*. In eclipse resembles female, except for crest and red bill, which also distinguish it from smaller Pochard. Female is drab brown with *pale greyish cheeks contrasting with dark brown crown*; wing-bar dingy white. Female Common Scoter is only other brown duck with pale cheeks, but has stouter bill and no white on wing.

Voice: A grating "*kurr*," usually in flight.

Habitat: Large reedy fresh-water lakes, or brackish lagoons, seldom on sea. Breeds among vegetation on islands in lagoons. Map below.

← Shoveler
*Partial migrant.
Has bred Spain,
Switzerland*

Red-crested
Pochard →
*Partial migrant.
Has bred Belgium.
Vagrant Sweden,
Finland, Estonia*

POCHARD *Aythya ferina* pages 29, 41, 49
Du – Tafeleend Fr – Fuligule milouin
Ge – Tafelente Sw – Brunand

Identification: 18″. High crown and long, sloping profile to head. Male easily distinguished by *uniform dark chestnut head and neck*, contrasting with black breast and pale grey body. Black bill with pale blue band, grey wing-band and absence of white on wings separate male from Red-crested Pochard (red bill, white on wing). In eclipse resembles female, but is greyer above. Female has brown head and fore-parts; differs from female Scaup and Tufted by indistinct pale patch around bill and chin, bluish ring around bill, and grey (not white) wing-band. Seldom on land, resting on water by day and feeding at dawn and dusk. Dives freely. See also Wigeon.

Voice: Male has hoarse wheezing note. Female makes harsh growling noise. Flocks make quiet whistling chorus.

Habitat: Seldom on sea. Frequents large and small lakes, backwaters, etc. Breeds in dense reeds. Map below.

FERRUGINOUS DUCK *Aythya nyroca* pages 29, 41, 49
Du – Witoogeend Fr – Fuligule nyroca
Ge – Moorente Sw – Vitögd dykand

Identification: 16″. Smaller and more neatly built than Tufted. Both sexes have *rich, dark mahogany head, neck and breast*. White belly and wing-bar are often hidden when at rest. In distance can be confused (particularly the female) with female Tufted Duck, but is usually distinguishable by *white under tail-coverts* and, in flight, by *large curved white wing-bars*; never has white at base of bill. (Tufted occasionally shows white beneath tail, but when seen together Ferruginous sits higher in water and holds tail higher). Male has *white eyes*. Female duller, with brown eyes. Juvenile like female, but has mottled underparts; distinguished from somewhat similar female Pochard by darker, much more rufous appearance, brown flanks and white wing-bar.

← POCHARD
Partial migrant. Has bred Spain, Belgium, Switzerland, Iceland. Vagrant Faeroes

FERRUGINOUS →
DUCK
Partial migrant. Has bred Holland, Belgium. Vagrant Brit. Is., Sweden, Finland

Behaviour more active than Pochard, voice and habitat similar. Map p. 55.

TUFTED DUCK *Aythya fuligula*   pages 29, 41, 49

Du – Kuifeend	Fr – Fuligule morillon
Ge – Reiherente	Sw – Vigg

Identification: 17″. Black and white male can be confused with slightly larger Scaup, but is distinguished by *uniform black upper-parts and thin drooping crest*. In eclipse resembles dark female. Female is browner, with a rudimentary crest and sometimes a light patch at base of bill (female Scaup looks similar, but shows more white on face than Tufted, also paler upper-parts and larger bill). In flight Tufted and Scaup adults both show bold white bar almost full length of wing. See also Ferruginous Duck.

Voice: Male has very soft whistling courtship note. Female growls like female Pochard.

Habitat: Seldom on sea. Frequents large and small lakes, often joining tame ducks in parks. Breeds, often sociably, on lakes and ponds. Map below.

SCAUP *Aythya marila*   pages 29, 41, 49

Du – Toppereend	Fr – Fuligule milouinan
Ge – Bergente	Sw – Bergand

Identification: 19″. In distance male looks *black both ends and white in the middle*. Head, fore-parts and "stern" are black, *back pale grey*, flanks and under-parts white. Bill blue-grey. Distinguished from slightly smaller male Tufted by *grey back*, lack of crest and broader beam. In eclipse resembles female, but with greyish back and little or no white on face. Female distinguished from female Tufted by *bold white patch around base of bill and broader beam*. (Female and young Tufted often have pale patch, but never as large.) Young

← Tufted Duck
*Partial migrant.
Bred Switzerland
(regular summer),
France, Yugo.,
Albania, Bulgaria,
Roumania*

Scaup →
*Mainly migratory.
Bred Scotland,
Holland. Vagrant
Portugal, Sardinia,
Albania, Greece*

68

69

females of both species are very difficult to separate. Young male Scaup is distinguished by greyish back. In flight both sexes show bold white wing-bar, like Tufted. Flies in close irregular flocks or lines. Expert diver, often in rough sea.

Voice: Seldom vocal. Male has soft crooning courtship notes. Female has low harsh "*karr-karr*."

Habitat: Maritime except when breeding; usually in bays and estuaries. Breeds sociably on lake islands. Map p. 56.

MANDARIN *Aix galericulata* page 28

    Du – Mandarijneend   Fr – Canard mandarin
    Ge – Mandarinente   Sw – Mandarinand

Identification: 17″. Highly coloured male easily distinguished *by upstanding orange "sails"* on wings, ample chestnut "side-whiskers," and multi-coloured drooping crest. Female drab brownish-grey, with large whitish spots on breast and *bold white marks behind eye and around bill.* Male in eclipse and when immature resembles female, but with dark red, instead of blackish, bill.

Habitat: Usually on wooded inland waters and ornamental ponds. Artificially introduced into Europe and now breeding in feral state (in trees) in many regions, including some parts of England.

EIDER *Somateria mollissima* pages 36, 41, 49

    Du – Eidereend   Fr – Eider à duvet
    Ge – Eiderente   Sw – Ejder

Identification: 23″. Distinguished from all other ducks by large size, long heavy body, elongated profile of head and distinctive flight. Male is only duck with *black belly and white back*; breast white, tinged pinkish, whole fore-wing white, head white with black crown and pale green patches on nape; easily distinguished from male King Eider by white back and long profile of head. In protracted eclipse male very variable, patchy blackish with lighter breast and white forewings. Female is brown, *closely barred* with black (only eiders are so marked); distinguished from female scoters, with which eiders often associate, by warmer brown *barred* plumage; from female King Eider by flatter profile of head (see diagram p. 36). Young male at first somewhat like female, later developing chocolate head and white areas irregularly. Usually flies low, in single file, with head carried rather low.

Voice: Male has loud moaning "*coo-roo-uh*," second syllable rising and emphasised. Female has grating "*cor-r-r*."

Habitat: Strongly maritime, but also along rocky coasts. Breeds along coasts; locally inland around lakes, or on river islands. Map p. 58.

KING EIDER *Somateria spectabilis* pages 36, 41, 49

    Du – Koningseidereend   Fr – Eider à tête grise
    Ge – Prachteiderente   Sw – Praktejder

Identification: 22″. At distance male's *fore-parts appear white, rear-parts* *black* (no other duck gives this effect). Distinguished from Eider by *black back*, very different shape and colours of head. Crown and nape pearl grey, face tinged green; *short bill has large orange shield*; fore-wing has large white patch. Female distinguished from Eider by *less flat profile from forehead to stubby bill* (see diagram, p. 36) and considerably more rufous plumage; some females have unmarked throats, giving head contrasting effect not seen in Eider. In breeding plumage female has greyish head and behind neck, throat therefore looks darker; scapulars rusty brown with dark centres, giving stronger contrast than in female Eider. Young male has pale breast and dark brown head, amount of white varying as it acquires adult plumage. (Female Goldeneye also has dark brown head but is greyer bird, with square white wing-patches.)

Voice: As Eider, but male's crooning notes usually have accent on final syllable.

Habitat and Range: As Eider, but usually breeds fairly sociably by fresh-water ponds on tundra. In summer non-breeding N. Norway, Iceland. Winters on N. Norwegian coast S. to Arctic Circle, Faeroes, Iceland. Vagrant to S. Baltic, Denmark, Britain, Ireland, France, Italy, Hungary.

STELLER'S EIDER *Polysticta stelleri* page 36

Du – Steller's eidereend   Fr – Eider de Steller
Ge – Scheckente   Sw – Alförrädare

Identification: 18″. Male unmistakable, a black and white bird with *rufous-buff under-parts*, *white head* with black eye-patch and throat and emerald-green patch on nape. *Round black spot* on side of rufous breast is distinctive. *White fore-wing conspicuous in flight*. In eclipse looks like female except for wings. Female is more duck-like, with dark buffish plumage mottled brown; sides of head rufous; white wing-bar and purple speculum visible at short range. Juvenile and

← EIDER
Mainly res. Reach English Channel in winter. Annual Switzer., S. France. Vagrant s. to Spain, Italy

COMMON SCOTER →
Mainly migrant Summers coasts Denmark to Brit. Isles. Vag. E. Med., often Switz.

female easily distinguished from other eiders by much smaller size and *very different shape of small head and bill* (see diagram, p. 36).

Voice: Male's crooning notes resemble Eider's but are quieter. Female has growling note.

Habitat and Range: Winters along rocky northern coasts. Breeds on tundra. In winter N. Norway (may have bred) and northernmost Baltic. Vagrant to W. Europe, S. to England, France, Germany.

COMMON SCOTER *Melanitta nigra* pages 36, 41, 49
Du – Zwarte zeeëend Fr – Macreuse noire
Ge – Trauerente Sw – Sjöorre

Identification: 19″. Male is *the only entirely black duck*; black bill has bright orange-yellow ridge-patch and large black knob at base. Female and immature are dark brown with *whitish cheeks and throat, contrasting with dark crown* and mottled brownish-white under-parts; distinguished from female Red-crested Pochard (which also has pale cheeks but is not a sea-duck) by darker appearance, squat shape and *lack of wing-bar*; from female Velvet and Surf Scoters by different face pattern and by blackish (not reddish) feet, (female Velvet Scoter also has conspicuous white wing-bar in flight). Swims buoyantly, with sharply pointed tail often raised. Flight strong, usually in wavering lines or groups.

Voice: Male has variety of melodious, cooing notes and a rapid tittering cry. Female growls harshly.

Habitat: Chiefly maritime except in breeding season, but prefers quieter water than Velvet Scoter. Breeds around lakes on high moors or tundra. Map p. 58.

VELVET SCOTER *Melanitta fusca* pages 36, 41, 49
Du – Grote zeeëend Fr – Macreuse brune
Ge – Samtente Sw – Swärta
N.Am – White-winged Scoter

Identification: 22″. Heavily built, with swollen bill. Both sexes distinguished from smaller Common Scoter by *white wing-patch*, often hidden at rest, but conspicuous when wings are flapped. When diving, reddish feet are noticeable (Surf Scoter's also red, Common's black). Male has *small white patch below eye* and yellow sides to black bill. Female usually distinguishable from Common Scoter by two whitish patches on side of head (more pronounced in young birds); when these are absent, white on wings makes identification positive. Usually in small parties or singly, often with Eiders near shore.

Voice: Much less vocal than Common Scoter. Male's usual note a whistled "*whur-er.*" Female growls harshly.

Habitat: As Common Scoter, but often seen in rougher water. Breeding places vary from off-shore islands and open tundra to undergrowth in northern forests. Map p. 62.

HARRIERS AND KITES (See also Plate 23)

HARRIERS have small heads, long bodies, long wings, long tails.

● **MARSH HARRIER** page 89
Male: Grey on wings and tail; rufous below.
Female: Dark brown; pale crown and throat.
Juvenile: Like female, or with head nearly all dark.

● **MONTAGU'S HARRIER** 88
Male: Black bars across secondaries; greyish rump; rusty marks on under-parts.
Female: Slimmer than Hen Harrier; rump patch slightly narrower.

● **HEN HARRIER** 87
Male: Grey, with clear white rump-patch; no black bar across wing, but secondaries dark-tipped.
Female: Brown, streaked; white rump-patch.

△ **PALLID HARRIER** 88
Male: Paler than Hen Harrier, with white breast; no white rump-patch; no black wing-bar.
Female: Indistinguishable in field from Montagu's.

KITES are rather similar in shape to harriers, but have notched or forked tails.

△ **BLACK KITE** 71
Dusky; slightly forked tail.

● **RED KITE** 70
Rich rusty, with pale head; deeply forked tail.

BLACK-WINGED KITE 67
Black shoulders; white tail.

MARSH HARRIER

MONTAGU'S HARRIER

HEN HARRIER

PALLID HARRIER

RED KITE

BLACK KITE

BLACK-WINGED KITE

KESTREL ♂ ♀

LESSER KESTREL ♂

MERLIN ♂ ♀

PEREGRINE — Adult — Juv

LANNER

SAKER

HOBBY

ELEONORA'S FALCON — Dark form Adult — Pale form Adult

RED-FOOTED FALCON ♂ ♀

Plate 20   **61**

FALCONS (See also Plate 24)

FALCONS have rather large heads, broad shoulders, long pointed wings, longish tails.

● **KESTREL**   page 99
> *Male:* Rufous back; grey tail with black band.
> *Female:* Rufous upper-parts; barred.

△ **LESSER KESTREL**   98
> *Male:* From Kestrel by absence of spots on back; white wing-linings. Mediterranean. Gregarious.

● **MERLIN**   97
> *Male:* Small; dark blue-grey back.
> *Female:* Dark above and below; banded tail.

● **PEREGRINE**   95
> *Adult:* Slate back; whitish breast; heavy black "moustache".
> *Immature:* Brown, streaked; heavy "moustache."

LANNER   95
> Buff cap; dark brown back.

SAKER   95
> Whitish head; brown back and wings.

● **HOBBY**   96
> Like small Peregrine; streaked under-parts; rufous "trousers"; white neck-patch.

ELEONORA'S FALCON   97
> Longer-tailed than other falcons.
> *Dark phase:* Black with yellow feet.
> *Pale phase:* Suggests small immature Peregrine, but moustaches narrower and cere yellower (not bluish).

○ **RED-FOOTED FALCON**   98
> *Male:* Slaty; red feet; rusty under tail-coverts.
> *Female:* Rusty crown and belly; barred grey back.

SURF SCOTER *Melanitta perspicillata*   pages 36, 41, 49
Du – Brilzeeëend   Fr – Marcreuse à lunettes
Ge – Brillenente   Sw – Vitnackad svärta

Identification: 21″. Male distinguished at reasonable range from other scoters by *white patches on forehead and nape* and more massive *red, white and yellow* bill. Both sexes have reddish legs, like Velvet Scoter. Female and immature usually have two whitish patches on side of head, like female and young Velvet Scoters, but both adults and young are distinguished by *absence of white on wings*; female may have whitish patch on nape. (Female and young Common Scoters have contrasting pale cheeks and dark crowns.)   Rarely vocal.

Habitat and Range: Maritime and off-shore outside breeding season. Vagrant from N. America to Faeroes, British Isles, W. Europe from Finland to France.

HARLEQUIN *Histrionicus histrionicus*   pages 36, 41, 49
Du – Harlekijneend   Fr – Garrot arlequin
Ge – Kragenente   Sw – Strömand

Identification: 17″. A small, very dark, short-billed duck. Male has dark blue-grey plumage (looks black at distance) with *chestnut flanks and bizarre pattern of white spots and streaks* on head, neck and breast. Has same flight-silhouette as Goldeneye, but is *uniformly dark below*. In eclipse male distinguished from female by dark slate-grey upper-parts and lack of white on breast.   Female uniformly dark brown with mottled brown and whitish breast, *two indistinct white spots in front of eye, one bright spot behind eye*; distinguished from female Velvet and Surf Scoters by small size, small bill; easily confused with young Long-tailed which, however, are much whiter on belly. Swims buoyantly, jerking head constantly, often cocking tail. Likes to dive in rough surf.

Voice: Usually silent, but male has quiet whistle. Female croaks harshly.

← VELVET SCOTER
Mainly mig. Summer British, German coasts. Vagr. Iceland, Ireland, and s. to Med.

LONG-TAILED
DUCK →
Mainly migrant. Vagrant s. to Portugal, Sardinia, central Europe, Yugoslavia

Habitat and Range: Winters along steep coasts with plenty of submerged rocks. Breeds socially on islands in swift rivers, usually near rough water or waterfalls. Resident Iceland. Vagrant to Britain, Scandinavia, Germany, Italy.

LONG-TAILED DUCK *Clangula hyemalis* pages 36, 41, 49

Du – IJseend   Fr – Harelde de Miquelon
Ge – Eisente   Sw – Alfågel
N.Am – Old Squaw

Identification: Male 21″, including *long pointed tail-feathers*; female 16″. The only sea duck combining *white on body with uniform dark wings*; also distinguished by small round head and short bill. Male in winter boldly patterned with dark brown and white: head, neck, belly and scapulars white; breast, back and wings blackish-brown; large dark patch on side of neck; bill banded pink and black. Male in summer is mostly dark brown, with white belly and white patch around eye. Female in winter is dark above, white below, with brown breast-band; head white with blackish crown, *cheek-spot* and bill; normal length tail; in summer is darker, with head-pattern similar to male. Juvenile like female, but greyer, with brownish throat. Swims buoyantly, diving with agility in rough sea. Only other long-tailed duck is the larger, *dark-headed* Pintail, which is a coastal or inland surface-feeder.

Voice: Noisy. Male has lively call of about four high nasal notes, giving musical goose-like effect from distant flock. Female has low barking note.

Habitat: Mainly maritime except in breeding season. Nests on lake islands, in tundra, or among Arctic scrub. Map p. 62.

GOLDENEYE *Bucephala clangula* pages 29, 41, 49

Du – Brilduiker   Fr – Garrot à oeil d'or
Ge – Schellente   Sw – Knipa

Identification: 18″. Male strikingly black and white; neck and under-parts white, back and tail black with *boldly streaked scapulars*; head is black, "triangular" in shape, with short black bill. Distinguished by *large circular white spot between bill and eye*. Legs orange. In flight looks big-headed, short-necked, with conspicuous *square white wing-patches extending almost to front of wing*. In eclipse resembles female, but retains a blackish head and white chest. Female has mottled grey upper-parts with *chocolate brown, triangular head, a white collar and large square white wing-patches* (showing on closed wing, unlike Tufted and Scaup). Immature is browner, without collar. Rises from water more rapidly than other diving ducks. Wings make characteristic whistling noise. See also Scaup and Barrow's Goldeneye.

Voice: Usually silent. Male has harsh nasal double note. Female's hoarse notes resemble Scaup's.

Habitat: Coastal waters, often also on inland lakes. Breeds in holes in trees, rabbit burrows, etc., along river banks and around wooded lakes. Map below.

BARROW'S GOLDENEYE *Bucephala islandica* page 29

Du – IJslandse brilduiker   Fr – Garrot d'Islande
Ge – Spatelente   Sw – Islandsknipa

Identification: 21″. An Iceland species. Easily mistaken for Goldeneye, though larger and heavier. Look for *crescent-shaped* white patch in front of eye (Goldeneye has *round* white spot). Male shows greater amount of black on sides of body, but Goldeneye in eclipse can look similar, though never as jet-black on head and wings. Barrow's head is *glossed purple* instead of green and is of remarkable shape, with more abrupt forehead, low rounded crown, and distinct mane on nape. Scapulars boldly barred black and white. Female very like female Goldeneye, but larger, with shorter, deeper bill, more abrupt forehead and slightly ragged nape. Behaviour, voice and habitat as in Goldeneye. Resident in Iceland. Accidental Germany, Spain, Scandinavia, Faeroes.

SMEW *Mergus albellus* pages 37, 40, 48

Du – Nonnetje   Fr – Harle piette
Ge – Zwergsäger   Sw – Salskrake

Identification: 16″. Much smaller, more duck-like and shorter-billed than other "saw-bills". Male looks *uniformly white with conspicuous black eye-patch*; at short range small drooping black and white crest is visible, also narrow black lines across fore-parts and above scapulars; flanks pale grey, back black; in flight looks darker above, with conspicuous black and white wings; in eclipse white wing-patches are larger than female's. Female is smaller and greyer, with slightly crested *chestnut cap and white cheeks and throat*. Immature has brownish-white wing-patches. See females of Red-crested Pochard, and Common Scoter, which also have brown and white heads; see also winter Slavonian and Black-necked Grebes.

← GOLDENEYE
Mainly migratory. Has bred England, Switz., Czecho., Rumania, Albania. Vagrant Spain, Portugal, Iceland

SMEW →
Migratory. Has bred Roumania. Vagrant Ireland, Portugal

Voice: Usually silent. Male has weak whistling note. Female's notes as female Goosander's.

Habitat: Lakes, reservoirs and rivers, occasionally in estuaries and along coasts. Nests in hollow trees near water. Map p. 64.

RED-BREASTED MERGANSER *Mergus serrator*

pages 37, 40, 48

Du – Middelste zaagbek   Fr – Harle huppé
Ge – Mittelsäger   Sw – Småskrake

Identification: 23″. Smaller than Mallard, with rakish form, very narrow red bill and legs, as in larger Goosander. Distinguished from latter by more conspicuous wispy *double crest*. The greenish-black head is separated from *dark chestnut breast-band by wide white collar*; flanks grey; wing pattern resembles Goosander's, but with two narrow black lines across the white patch. Female distinguished from very similar female Goosander by *brownish*-grey upper-parts, diffuse white chin-patch, more conspicuous and ragged crest, duller head *blending* into whitish neck. More maritime than Goosander; both may occur on same lake or river.

Voice: Usually silent; male has rasping disyllabic courtship note. Female as female Goosander.

Habitat: Chiefly maritime outside breeding season. Breeds in heather, vegetation among rocks, etc., by wooded lakes or rivers, on islands in sea lochs and in tundra. Map below.

GOOSANDER *Mergus merganser*

pages 37, 40, 48

Du – Grote zaagbek   Fr – Harle bièvre
Ge – Gänsesäger   Sw – Storskrake
N.Am – American Merganser

Identification: 26″. Long-bodied and rakish. Larger and longer than Mallard, with very narrow red bill and feet. Male has *pinkish-white breast and under-parts*, black back, *glossy greenish-black head*; easily identified in flight by white body and wings, with black head and primaries; distinguished from smaller and darker Red-breasted

← RED-BREASTED MERGANSER
Partial migrant. Has bred Holland

GOOSANDER →
Partial migrant. Has bred Roumania. Vagrant to Ireland, Mediterranean

Merganser by lack of wispy crest and by uniform whitish breast, flanks and under-parts. Female has *crested chestnut head*, blue-grey upper-parts and flanks, white under-parts and a *square white wing-patch* conspicuous in flight; distinguished from very similar female Merganser by *sharp division* of chestnut fore-neck from white chest and blue-grey upper-parts. Flight silhouette distinctively "long-drawn."

Voice: Usually silent. Male has low croaking note; female a guttural "*karr*."

Habitat: Winters on large rivers, lakes, reservoirs. Breeds in hollow trees, holes in peat banks, etc., usually among trees near water, also beyond tree limit in north. Map p. 65.

WHITE-HEADED DUCK *Oxyura leucocephala*   page 37
          Du – Witkopeend   Fr – Erismature à tête blanche
          Ge – Ruderente   Sw – Kopparand

Identification: 18″. The only "stiff-tail" duck in Europe apart from regionally feral Ruddy Duck. Identified by large head, plump body and long, stiff, pointed tail which is often cocked *vertically* to show white under tail-coverts. Male's bill, swollen at base, is *brilliant pale blue* in courtship season. Male has conspicuous *white head* with narrow black crown, black neck, brownish body. Female is darker, with dark cap, and pale cheek *crossed by a dark line*; also has swollen base to bill, which helps to distinguish from "escaped" female Ruddy Duck. Behaviour grebe-like. Flight whirring, usually low over water, with characteristic silhouette of big head, stocky body, small uniform dark wings and long pointed tail (looking like projecting feet). Pintail and Long-tailed Ducks have long but flexible tails, smaller heads and thinner necks.

Habitat: Reedy inland waters and brackish lagoons, Nests among reeds and aquatic vegetation near water. Map p. 67.

KITES, BUZZARDS, HAWKS, EAGLES, HARRIERS, VULTURES: Accipitridae

Kites have long, angular wings, forked tails, buoyant, gliding flight. Sexes similar. Tree nesting.

Buzzards have broad wings, broad rounded tails and relatively smaller heads and bills than eagles. Usually seen circling and soaring. Sexes similar. Tree and cliff nesting.

Hawks are smaller, with short, rounded wings and long tails. Cruise swiftly among trees at low altitudes and chase or pounce on prey. Females much larger than males. Tree nesting.

Eagles have prominent, projecting heads, unusually deep bills; long, broad-ended wings: soaring, majestic flight. Sexes similar. Tree or cliff nesting.

Harriers are slim, with long, slightly angled wings and long tails flight usually low and wavering, with wings held in shallow "V." Ground or reed nesting.

Vultures are very large, eagle-like, with huge wing-spans, short tails and naked heads (except Bearded). Sexes similar. Cliff or tree nesting.

Exceptions to these groupings are Osprey and Short-toed Eagle.

OSPREY   *Pandion haliaetus*   page 68

Du – Visarend	Fr – Balbuzard pêcheur
Ge – Fischadler	Sw – Fiskgjuse

Identification: 20-23″. No other eagle-like birds (except Short-toed Eagle) have contrast of *dark upper-parts and snow-white under-parts*, with dusky breast-band. Has slightly crested *white head, with broad black patch through eye*. Wings long, narrow and *decidedly angled*; under-surfaces are white *with black carpal patches* and rows of small dark spots. Tail barred. Hovers heavily above water and *plunges feet first for fish*. Usually perches on dead tree, or rock, near water.

Voice: A short, cheeping whistle, sometimes slightly declining.

Habitat: Invariably near water; lakes, large rivers, or sea coasts. Nests on small remote islands, rocky cliffs, trees, ruins, occasionally on sandy or rocky ground. Breeds in scattered groups in some localities. Map below.

BLACK-WINGED KITE   *Elanus caeruleus*   page 60

Du – Grijze wouw	Fr – Elanion blanc
Ge – Gleitaar	Sw – Svartvingad glada

Identification: 13″. A small, stumpy hawk, with long wings and shortish forked tail, which is sometimes held erect. Head whitish, *upper-parts pale blue-grey*, with *whitish tail and black "shoulders."* Primaries grey above, but black beneath, in sharp contrast to pure white under-parts. Eyes dark red. Immature grey-brown above, white below, tinged with rufous and lightly streaked with brown. Behaviour not at all kite-like;

← WHITE-HEADED
DUCK
*Partial migrant.
Vagr. n. to France,
Holland, Germany*

OSPREY →
*Mainly summer
vis. Has bred
Switz., Austria,
Italy, N. Greece.
Vagrant Iceland,
Faeroes, Ireland*

EAGLES AND OSPREY OVERHEAD

● **GOLDEN EAGLE**   page 82
Much larger than Buzzard, with different silhouette.
Immature: "Ringed" tail with white base; large
white patches at base of primaries and outer
secondaries.
Adult: Almost uniformly dark. When upper side is
seen, golden feathers on head and wing-coverts are
diagnostic.

○ **WHITE-TAILED EAGLE**   86
Immature: From adult Golden by more wedge-shaped
tail, huge bill and vulturine wing-shape. Paler than
Golden, often streaked with white and brown on
under-parts.
Adult: White tail.

● **OSPREY**   67
White head, clear white belly, black "wrist" patches.

SPOTTED EAGLE Immature (*after P. J. Hayman*)
NOTE: all head-on silhouettes show gliding, not soaring, attitudes.

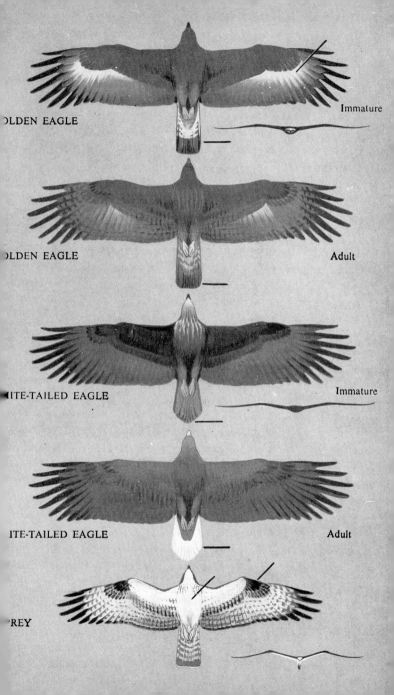

GOLDEN EAGLE   Immature

GOLDEN EAGLE   Adult

WHITE-TAILED EAGLE   Immature

WHITE-TAILED EAGLE   Adult

OSPREY

BUZZARD

ROUGH-LEGGED BUZZARD

HONEY BUZZARD

LONG-LEGGED BUZZARD

BONELLI'S EAGLE
Adult

BONELLI'S EAGLE
Juvenile

BOOTED EAGLE
Light phase

BOOTED EAGLE
Dark phase

SHORT-TOED EAGLE

Plate 22   69

BUZZARDS AND SMALL EAGLES OVERHEAD
(See also Plate 18)

 BUZZARDS are bulky, with broad wings and broad tails. They soar and wheel high in the open sky. Certain of the eagles are similar in outline to buzzards, but usually have proportionately longer wings.

● **BUZZARD**   page 76
Variable, usually dark; short-necked; secondaries and tail usually with numerous narrow bars.

● **ROUGH-LEGGED BUZZARD**   76
Dark belly; whitish tail with broad black band at tip; black "wrist patches" on pale wing-linings.

● **HONEY BUZZARD**   70
Head more projecting, tail longer than Buzzard's, with broad black bands near base. Note bars across all flight-feathers.

LONG-LEGGED BUZZARD   76
Tail pale rusty, usually without bars; rufous wing-linings.

BONELLI'S EAGLE   77
Adult: Silky white under-parts; dark wings.
Juvenile: Rufous wing-linings have dark edges.

BOOTED EAGLE   77
Buzzard size; longer tail.
Light phase: White wing-linings; dark flight-feathers.
Dark phase: Dark; pale at base of primaries and tail.

SHORT-TOED EAGLE   87
White under-parts and under-wings usually contrast strikingly with dark upper breast. Some birds lack dark breast-band. Owl-like head.

hovers slowly on long wings, flies slowly, like miniature harrier, or more quickly on sharply angled wings. Feeds on mice, large insects, etc. Often crepuscular.

Voice: A weak, whistling *"gree-er."*

Habitat and Range: Cultivated areas with scattered trees, or woodland glades, forest edges, etc. Nests fairly low in trees. Resident Portugal, perhaps Spain. Vagrant in W. Europe, N. to Holland, Germany, Czechoslovakia and in Mediterranean countries.

HONEY BUZZARD　　*Pernis apivorus*　　　　　　pages 53, 69

　　　Du – Wespendief　　　　　　Fr – Bondrée apivore
　　　Ge – Wespenbussard　　　　　Sw – Bivråk

Identification: 20-23″. Flight silhouette very different from Buzzard's and Rough-legged Buzzard's in having *narrow-based* broad wings, *longer* tail and *smaller* (*pigeon-like*) *head on longer neck*; tail has *dark terminal band and two narrower bands nearer base*; markings on under-parts and beneath dark-edged wings are brighter. Plumage very variable. Upper-parts dark brown, head greyish; under-parts heavily scolloped with dark brown, sometimes completely brown. Immature often has creamy marking on head; under-parts streaked. Soars and hovers less than Buzzard; when gliding, *wings droop very slightly*, with up-turned tips. Feeds on larvae of wasps and bees, sometimes mice, small birds, eggs.

Voice: A high, squeaky *"kee-er,"* quite unlike Buzzard's mewing; also a rapid *"kikiki."*

Habitat: Open glades or outskirts of woods. Usually builds on old nest of crow. Map below.

RED KITE　　*Milvus milvus*　　　　　　　　pages 60, 72

　　　Du – Rode wouw　　　　　　Fr – Milan royal
　　　Ge – Roter Milan　　　　　　Sw – Glada

Identification: 24″. Easily distinguished by *long, deeply forked chestnut tail*, narrow, strongly angled wings, with *large whitish patches* on under-

← Honey
　Buzzard
*Summer visitor.
Prob. breeds Eng-
land. Vag. Iceland,
Faeroes, Ireland*

Red Kite →
*Partial migrant.
Has bred Norway,
Denmark. Vagrant
Scotland, Ireland,
Finland*

sides of black primaries, red-brown upper-parts with pale edges to feathers, dark-streaked rufous under-parts and *streaked whitish head.* Immature is paler, with brownish head. Effortless soaring flight resembles Buzzard's, but silhouette is unmistakably different and normal flight much more buoyant. Partial to carrion, but also preys on animals as large as rabbits, and small birds. Distinguished from Black Kite by more deeply forked tail, more rufous plumage and more slender silhouette.

Voice: A high, Buzzard-like mewing *"hi-hi-heea."*

Habitat: Usually in wooded hills, but also locally in lowlands and open country with scattered trees. Nests in trees, occasionally on old crow's nest. Map p. 70.

BLACK KITE *Milvus migrans*   pages 60, 72

Du – Zwarte wouw	Fr – Milan noir
Ge – Schwarzer Milan	Sw – Brun glada

Identification: 22″. Resembles Red Kite, but easily distinguished by *much less forked tail* which can look almost straight-ended in flight, slightly smaller size and *much darker plumage*; upper wing-coverts have paler panel from base of wing to carpal joint; is also more sociable and frequently seen over inland waters. Faint whitish patches beneath wings of immature resemble Red Kite's, but are absent in adults. Flight and feeding habits like Red Kite's but also feeds on dead fish. Where numerous, flocks quickly gather on carrion. When gliding holds wings level, not in shallow "V" like Marsh Harrier, which see.

Voice: Very noisy in breeding season. A thin, quavering, gull-like squeal, sometimes followed by a chatter.

Habitat: In western range usually near lakes or rivers, in areas with woods or scattered trees. In S. and E. of range more frequently in drier localities and in villages. Nests, often sociably, in trees, occasionally on old nest of crow. Map below.

← BLACK KITE
Mainly summer visitor. Has bred Sweden. Vagrant Britain, Denmark, Holland, Belgium

GOSHAWK →
Mainly resident; extends Holland in winter. Has bred England. Vagrant Ireland, Scotland

HARRIERS AND KITES IN FLIGHT
(See also Plate 19)

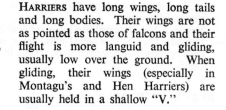

HARRIERS have long wings, long tails and long bodies. Their wings are not as pointed as those of falcons and their flight is more languid and gliding, usually low over the ground. When gliding, their wings (especially in Montagu's and Hen Harriers) are usually held in a shallow "V."

● **MARSH HARRIER**   page 89
Male: Contrasting grey wing-patches and tail.
Female: Dark; pale crown and pale shoulders.

● **MONTAGU'S HARRIER**   88
Male: Dark bar on wing; greyish rump.
Female: From Hen Harrier by slimmer build and slightly smaller rump-patch.

● **HEN HARRIER**   87
Male: Dark tips to secondaries (not shown) form narrow bar; white rump.
Female: Streaked brown; white rump.

KITES are rather similar in shape to harriers, but have notched or forked tails. They are buoyant gliders, making great use of their flexible tails.

△ **BLACK KITE**   71
Dusky; slightly forked tail; nearly uniform wings below.
Note: Easily confused with some dark Marsh Harriers.

● **RED KITE**   70
Rusty; deeply forked tail; distinctive wing-pattern.

MARSH
HARRIER

♂

♀

MONTAGU'S
HARRIER

♂

♀

HEN
HARRIER

♂

♀

RED KITE

BLACK KITE

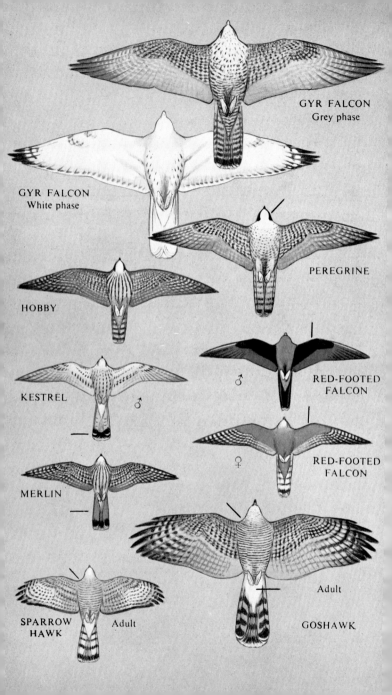

GYR FALCON
Grey phase

GYR FALCON
White phase

PEREGRINE

HOBBY

KESTREL ♂

RED-FOOTED
FALCON ♂

MERLIN

RED-FOOTED
FALCON ♀

SPARROW
HAWK   Adult

GOSHAWK
Adult

Plate 24   73

FALCONS AND ACCIPITERS OVERHEAD
(See also Plates 18 and 20)

FALCONS have long, pointed wings, long tails. Their wing-strokes are strong, rapid but shallow.

○ **GYR FALCON**   page 94
Grey phase: Larger than Peregrine; broader wing-bases; no contrasting face pattern.
White phase: White as a Snowy Owl.

● **PEREGRINE**   95
Falcon shape; face pattern; size near that of Crow.

● **HOBBY**   96
Like small Peregrine; tail shorter; wings Swift-like.

● **KESTREL**   99
Small, slim; black band near tip of tail. Hovers.

● **MERLIN**   97
Smaller than Kestrel; darker, more compact.

○ **RED-FOOTED FALCON**   98
Male: Very dark; red feet; rusty under tail-coverts.
Female: Rusty wing-linings; unmarked rusty belly.

ACCIPITERS (bird hawks) have short, rounded wings and long tails. In flight they alternate several rapid wing-beats with a short glide; they also soar.

● **SPARROW HAWK**   75
Under-parts barred with rusty (male), or grey (female).

● **GOSHAWK**   74
Very large; under-parts barred with grey; conspicuous white under tail-coverts.

GOSHAWK   *Accipiter gentilis*   pages 53, 73
> Du – Havik   Fr – Autour des palombes
> Ge – Habicht   Sw – Duvhök

Identification: 19-24″. Female much larger than male. Resembles *very large female Sparrow Hawk* but with broad-based wings, which, however, often look pointed except when soaring. Upper-parts dark, with *whitish stripe* above and behind eye; under-parts whitish, closely barred with dark brown and with *conspicuous white under tail-coverts*. Juvenile paler above, with buffish under-parts, boldly marked, with dark-brown, drop-shaped streaks. Dashes after birds, doubling among trees with extreme agility. Hunting flight among trees is fast and low, with a few rapid wing-beats and long glides. See female Sparrow Hawk.

Voice: A short, Buzzard-like cry and a chattering "*gig-gig-gig.*"

Habitat: Woods (especially coniferous) often near open country. Builds large nest, or adopts old nests of other birds, in secluded wood. Map p. 71.

LEVANT SPARROW HAWK   *Accipiter brevipes*
> Du – Balkansperwer   Fr – Epervier à pieds courts
> Ge – Kurzfangsperber   Sw – Balkanhök

Identification: 13-15″. Female often difficult to distinguish from female Sparrow Hawk, but male is distinctive. Both sexes have *white under-surfaces to wings with dark wing-tips* and red-brown (not yellow) eyes; wings longer than Sparrow Hawk's. Male larger than male Sparrow Hawk (disparity between sexes is less), has *clear blue-grey on nape, mantle and upper wing-surfaces*; under-parts can look almost white, but usually have buff towards wing-roots contrasting with white lower wing-surfaces; cheeks greyish (not rufous), with buff on sides of neck. Female greyer above than female Sparrow Hawk, with brown spots on throat. Immature has large brown spots on very white under-parts.

Voice: A shrill "*keeveck*" (very unlike Sparrow Hawk).

Habitat: Much as Sparrow Hawk, though more often in the open and in deciduous woods. Map below.

← Levant
  Sparrow Hawk
Mainly summer visitor. Vagrant Czechoslovakia and Italy

Sparrow
  Hawk →
Partial migrant. Vagrant Iceland, Faeroes

SPARROW HAWK *Accipiter nisus* pages 53, 73

Du – Sperwer Fr – Epervier d'Europe
Ge – Sperber Sw – Sparvhök

Identification: 11-15″. Female much larger than male. Distinguished from other small birds of prey by combination of *short rounded wings and long tail*. Adults have closely barred under-parts and long yellow legs. Male has dark slate-grey upper-parts with rufous cheeks and whitish spot on nape, under-parts finely barred with red-brown, tail boldly banded with grey and dark brown. Female has blackish-brown upper-parts, with white stripe above and behind eye and whitish under-parts finely barred with dark brown. Female looks like Goshawk, but latter is larger, with relatively shorter tail and white under-tail coverts. Immature like brown female, but is more boldly and irregularly barred below. Hunts by cruising just above hedges, or through woodlands and pouncing on small birds and other animals. Normal flight consists of a few rapid wing-beats between long glides. See also Levant Sparrow Hawk.

Voice: Has large vocabulary in breeding season: a loud, rapid *"kek-kek-kek,"* *"keeow,"* *"kew,"* etc.

Habitat: Chiefly woodlands and farm-lands, with coppices, plantations, etc. Nests in spruce or other conifer in mixed woods, occasionally in tall bushes, thickets, etc. Map p. 74.

FALCONS
Pointed Wings, Narrow Tail

HARRIERS
Long Wings, Long Tail

BUZZARDS
*Broad Wings
Broad Rounded Tail*

ACCIPITERS
(Bird Hawks)
Short Rounded Wings, Long Tail

BASIC FLIGHT SILHOUETTES

ROUGH-LEGGED BUZZARD *Buteo lagopus* pages 53, 69
  Du – Ruigpootbuizerd   Fr – Buse pattue
  Ge – Rauhfussbussard   Sw – Fjällvråk
              N.Am – Rough-legged Hawk
Identification: 20-24″. Normally distinguished from Buzzard by *longer, narrower wings, white tail with broad dark terminal band*; usually much whiter beneath wings and on under-parts, with dark belly; head looks pale. *Conspicuous dark carpal patches beneath pale wings and dark tips to primaries are distinctive.* Legs feathered whitish to base of toes (Buzzard has unfeathered yellow tarsi). Immature resembles young Buzzard, but has some white on tail. Behaviour, voice and flight are similar, but hunts close to ground and *hovers frequently*, on slowly beating wings, pouncing on prey. Feeds chiefly on rabbits and small rodents, occasionally birds. See also Honey Buzzard and Booted Eagle.
Habitat: Usually barren open country and mountain slopes, also marshes and sand-dunes. Nests on cliff ledges, or on ground in high tundra. Map p. 77.

LONG-LEGGED BUZZARD *Buteo rufinus* pages 53, 69
  Du – Arendbuizerd   Fr – Buse féroce
  Ge – Adlerbussard   Sw – Örnvråk
Identification: 24-26″. Extremely difficult to distinguish from occasional very similar form of Buzzard. Has similar wide variation of plumage, from rich rufous brown, with broadly streaked creamy under-parts, to rare melanistic form with very dark brown under-parts. Adult's head is usually *pale* and the tail *unbarred, often cinnamon*, but Buzzards, particularly *B. b. vulpinus* of E. Europe, often have similar tails with scarcely detectable barring. In flight, looks conspicuously whitish below, except for dark wing-tips, carpal patches and thighs. Immature inseparable from young Buzzard.
Habitat and Range: Dry, open plains and steppes; locally in mountains. Nests on ground, occasionally in isolated tree. A few breed in Greece. Vagrant to W. Europe, N. to Denmark, more regular in S.E. Europe.

BUZZARD *Buteo buteo* pages 53, 69
  Du – Buizerd   Fr – Buse variable
  Ge – Mäusebussard   Sw – Ormvråk
Identification: 20-22″. Buzzards may be identified by flight silhouette (*broad wings, ample rounded tails and very short necks*). Adults very variable, generally dark brown, mottled with white below. Amount of white on under-parts and beneath wings varies, but is rarely as pronounced as in Rough-legged. Distinguished from latter by *narrowly barred* brown and grey tail with broad dark terminal band, inconspicuous dark carpal patches beneath wings, and unfeathered yellow tarsi. Soars circling for hours, on broad motionless wings, with tips of primaries up-curved and tail widely spread; wings held straight,

slightly raised; short neck gives distinctive *blunt appearance* unlike eagles', whose heads project. Flight rather heavy. Hovers occasionally. Hunts by pouncing from low altitude on small animals, beetles, rarely small birds; also fond of carrion. Often seen in small groups. See also Honey Buzzard.

Voice: A high, plantive mewing *"pee-oo,"* often long-drawn; also a short croaking note.

Habitat: Secluded rocky coasts, moors, plains, mountain slopes, cultivated and wooded regions. Nests on róck ledges, in trees and on broken ground. Map below.

BOOTED EAGLE *Hieraaetus pennatus*   page 69
    Du – Dwergarend   Fr – Aigle botté
    Ge – Zwergadler   Sw – Dvärgörn

Identification: 18-21″. A Buzzard-size, long-tailed eagle. Dimorphic; light-phase most plentiful. *White below, with dark flight-feathers and uniform pale cinnamon-buff tail,* which is longish and square-ended. Seen from above, body and wing-coverts are buffish, flight-feathers darker. Dark-phase birds less distinctive, a rich, uniform dark brown *except for pale tail.* Soars on level wings held slightly forward; wing-beats *quicker* than Buzzard's, flight more graceful and rapid, often weaving among trees. Feeds on small birds and other animals.

Voice: Usual notes, a thin, high *"keee,"* with downward inflection, and various chattering cries.

Habitat: Deciduous and pine forests, near clearings for hunting. Seldom far from trees. Breeds in tall trees. Map p. 78.

BONELLI'S EAGLE *Hieraaetus fasciatus*   page 69
    Du – Havikarend   Fr – Aigle de Bonelli
    Ge – Habichtsadler   Sw – Hökörn

Identification: 26-29″. Upper-parts dark brown, almost black on wing-tips, paler on nape, usually showing whitish patch on back. Longish tail has half-dozen faint bars and a *broad dark terminal band.* Seen from below, the narrowly streaked, *silky white or creamy under-*

← ROUGH-LEGGED BUZZARD
Migratory. Vagr. Iceland, Ireland and s. to Mediterranean, Malta

BUZZARD →
Partial migrant. Re-established in N. Ireland

93   95

parts contrast with the *long, dark, narrow wings*, distinguishing adult from all other eagles. Juvenile has rusty head, closely streaked rufous-brown under-parts and closely barred tail. Second-year birds are confusing, almost uniform brown; under-parts lose rufous tinge, but are not yet white. Behaviour aggressive. Hunts rabbits, birds, etc. Flight rapid and dashing; stoops on prey like falcon.

Voice: Recalls Goshawk; a chattering "*kie, kie, kikiki.*"

Habitat: Rocky mountainous country, but seldom at great altitudes; descends to plains and deserts in winter. Nests on precipitous rock-face, occasionally in tree. Map below.

TAWNY EAGLE *Aquila rapax* page 83

Du – Steppenarend	Fr – Aigle ravisseur
Ge – Raubadler	Sw – Stäppörn

Identification: 26-31″. Adults almost uniform dark brown, with indistinct grey bars on short, rounded tail. Very easily confused with adult Lesser Spotted, but Tawny often has rusty-yellow patch on nape and *never* has the white on upper tail-coverts of some (not all) Lesser Spotteds. Juvenile is "café au lait" coloured, with blackish primaries and shows two pale wing-bars in flight. Behaviour very sluggish, often perching for long periods on ground and usually flies close to ground; seldom soars, but when doing so holds wings slightly flexed. Feeds on carrion, frogs, etc. Adults distinguished from Golden Eagle by smaller size, smaller head and bill and smaller, only faintly barred tail, without broad dark terminal band; from Imperial by *dark crown* and smaller size. Steppe Eagle *A. r. nipalensis* (an accidental straggler from Asia) is indistinguishable in the field from Tawny and is probably conspecific.

Voice: Usual note a high "*kow, kow, kow.*"

Habitat and Range: Open bushy plains or steppes. Nests on ground on small mound. Vagrant to Mediterranean countries.

← BOOTED EAGLE
Mainly summer vis. Vagrant Italy, Germany, Czecho., Switzerland

BONELLI'S
EAGLE →
Mainly resident. Vagrant Belgium, Holland, Germany, Austria, Hungary, Bulgaria

SPOTTED EAGLE *Aquila clanga*   pages 68, 83
Du – Bastaardarend   Fr – Aigle criard
Ge – Schelladler   Sw – Större skrikörn

Identification: 26-29″. Adults very dark purplish-brown, slightly paler below; a little white often visible on upper tail-coverts. When soaring does so on *straight-edged wings* (not held forward), which *droop slightly from carpal joints when gliding*; *seventh* spread primary just discernible; rather short, slightly rounded tail; *small head with small bill* projects conspicuously on slender neck; Wings proportionately broader than Golden's. See distinctions from Lesser Spotted. Immature has *copious, large whitish spots* on upper-parts and noticeable white, often in "V," at base of tail; in flight, shows two pale bands on wings. Behaviour sluggish.

Voice: Like shrill yapping of small dog: "*kyak, kyak, kyak*."

Habitat: A tree-loving species; usually near inland lakes, rivers, marshes. Nests in forest tree or bush. Map below.

LESSER SPOTTED EAGLE *Aquila pomarina*   page 83
Du – Schreeuwarend   Fr – Aigle pomarin
Ge – Schreiadler   Sw – Mindre skrikörn

Identification: 24-26″. Very similar to Spotted, though slighter in shape; often a little paler on crown and wing-coverts. Upper tail-coverts may be marked with a little white; immature has fewer and smaller white spots and usually has a rusty patch on nape. Can be separated in flight by narrower *base* to tail, narrower wings *held slightly forward* and *sixth* primary just discernible. Has similar droop to wings when gliding. Hovers occasionally.

Voice: Less vibrant than Spotted's, a thin "*kyeep, kyeep*."

Habitat: Often found near water, though to lesser extent than Spotted. Frequents remote wooded country, with open ground accessible for hunting. Nests in tree. Map below.

← SPOTTED EAGLE
Mainly sum. vis. Annual Sweden. Vag. w. to Brit Is., Portugal; few winter S. and W. France, Greece

LESSER SPOTTED EAGLE →
Mainly summer. May nest Austria. Vag. Finland; w. to Denmark, Spain

PIGEONS AND DOVES

THE TERMS "PIGEON" AND "DOVE" are loosely used and often interchangeable, but for the most part "pigeon" refers to the larger species, "dove" to the smaller.

● **WOOD PIGEON** page 17
Large; white wing-patches; white neck-patch.

● **STOCK DOVE** 17
Short black bars on secondaries; grey rump.

● **ROCK DOVE** 17
White rump; two bold black wing-bars.
The various domestic pigeons are descendants of this
species and many still closely resemble it.

● **TURTLE DOVE** 17
Slender; rufous back; deeply rounded, white-tipped
tail.

● **COLLARED DOVE** 17
White beneath end half of tail; black collar. The
domestic Barbary Dove (*S. risoria*) is very similar, but
is creamy-buff instead of vinous-grey and has pale,
not dark, primaries.

*Domestic pigeons (descended from Rock Dove) show great variety of
colour and pattern.*

WOOD PIGEON

ROCK DOVE

STOCK DOVE

TURTLE DOVE

COLLARED DOVE

GREAT
BUSTARD

♂

LITTLE
BUSTARD

♀

♂

HOUBARA
BUSTARD

Sexes
similar

BLACK-BELLIED
SANDGROUSE

PIN-TAILED
SANDGROUSE

STONE CURLEW

PALLAS'S
SANDGROUSE

Plate 26   81

BUSTARDS, SANDGROUSE AND STONE CURLEW

BUSTARDS are large-bodied, long-legged birds of the open plains.
SANDGROUSE are plump, dove-like desert birds with pointed tails.

△ **GREAT BUSTARD**   page 114
　　Very large size; head and neck pale grey (no black);
　　White on wing extends to primaries.

○ **LITTLE BUSTARD**   115
　　Male: Black and white neck pattern; shows much
　　white in flight.
　　Female: Streaked brown head and neck.

△ **HOUBARA BUSTARD**   115
　　Silhouette recalls hen turkey with longish tail.
　　Long black and white feathers drooping from neck.

BLACK-BELLIED SANDGROUSE   175
　　Black belly; tail less elongated than in other sand-
　　grouse; blackish wing-linings.

PIN-TAILED SANDGROUSE   176
　　White belly and under-wings; long needle-pointed
　　tail.

△ **PALLAS'S SANDGROUSE**   176
　　Black belly; long needle-pointed tail; pale wing-
　　linings.

● **STONE CURLEW**   150
　　Hunched attitude; large pale eyes; broad light bar
　　on closed wing.

IMPERIAL EAGLE   *Aquila heliaca*   page 83
    Du – Keizerarend   Fr – Aigle impérial
    Ge – Kaiseradler   Sw – Kejsarörn

Identification: 31-33″.   A large, rather heavy-looking eagle with
blackish-brown plumage and a pale yellowish crown and nape (almost
white in old birds).   Usually has *a few pure white feathers on scapulars.*
Tail rather square-cut and shorter than Golden's, with 5-7 grey bars.
When soaring, wings held *straight*, not in shallow "V" or forward;
upper surfaces uniformly dark (unlike adult Golden).   Immature varies
from yellowish-brown to mottled blackish-brown according to age;
normally shows dark streaking and has ochreous or pale rufous crown.
Adult of Spanish form *A. h. adalberti* has conspicuous *pure white
shoulders*, showing in flight as short white band along leading edge of
wing.   Immature is pale yellowish-brown with darker tail and flight-
feathers;   fairly distinct pale patch in centre of wing and on lower
back;   but distinguished from rather similar Tawny by bold streaking
on under-parts.   Behaviour sluggish.   See also Tawny and Golden.
Voice: A quick, barking, "*owk-owk-owk.*"
Habitat: Plains, steppes and marshes.   Builds huge conspicuous nest
in isolated tall tree.   Map below.

GOLDEN EAGLE   *Aquila chrysaetos*   pages 68, 83
    Du – Steenarend   Fr – Aigle royal
    Ge – Steinadler   Sw – Kungsörn

Identification: 30-35″.   Large size, majestic gliding and soaring flight
with occasional wing-beats, broadly spread up-curved primaries and
ample, squarish tail are characteristic.   Plumage of adult uniformly dark,
except for *golden tinge* on head, nape and across upper surface of
secondary coverts.   Immature birds show *conspicuous* white at base of
primaries and secondaries and have *white tail with broad dark terminal
band*, the white diminishing with age.   Hunts by quartering mountain-

← IMPERIAL
EAGLE
*Part. migrant. Has
bred Austria. Vagr.
to Poland, Germ.,
Italy, France*

GOLDEN EAGLE →
*Mainly res., ex-
tending E. Europe
in winter. Vagr.
Holland, Belgium.
Recently bred Ire-
land*

Adult

TAWNY

Adult

GOLDEN

Adult

SPOTTED

Immature

Immature

LESSER SPOTTED

Adult

Spanish Form

Adult

Eastern Form

Adult

IMPERIAL

EAGLES

WADERS IN FLIGHT
(See also Plate 33)

● SNIPE   page 143
> Long bill held downwards; pointed wings; whitish rim to tail; zig-zag flight.

○ GREAT SNIPE   144
> Slightly bulkier than Snipe; more white on corners of tail; more direct flight.

● JACK SNIPE   144
> Smaller than Snipe; shorter bill; no white on tail; rises silently, with less zig-zagging.

● WOODCOCK   142
> Long bill; rounded wings; dead-leaf colour.

○ DOWITCHER (both species)   142
> Snipe bill; long narrow white patch on back; white on rear edge of wing.

● GREENSHANK   136
> Long white patch up back to shoulders; no white wing-stripe.

● REDSHANK   136
> White rump; broad white stripe on rear edge of wing.

● SPOTTED REDSHANK   135
> *Winter:* Pattern similar to Greenshank, but white patch narrower; legs project.

● GREEN SANDPIPER   138
> Very dark above; white rump; blackish under-wing.

● WOOD SANDPIPER   138
> From Green Sandpiper by less white on tail and rump; paler under-wing.

○ CREAM-COLOURED COURSER   150
> Sandy buff; black primaries above and below.

○ PRATINCOLE   151
> Tern-like; tail forked, white at base.

GREAT SNIPE

SNIPE

JACK SNIPE

WOODCOCK

DOWITCHER

ENSHANK

REDSHANK

GREEN
SANDPIPER

SPOTTED
REDSHANK

CREAM-COLOURED COURSER

PRATINCOLE

WOOD SANDPIPER

DUNLIN
Autumn

PURPLE
SANDPIPER

KNOT
Winter

CURLEW
SANDPIPER
Autumn

Winter

SANDERLING

COMMON
SANDPIPE

LITTLE
STINT

Immature

RED-NECKED
PHALAROPE

TEMMINCK'S
STINT

PECTORAL
SANDPIPER

GREY
PHALARO
Winter

STONE CURLEW

♀
(Reeve)

RUFF

♂
Summer

Plate 28   85

WADERS IN FLIGHT
(See also Plate 34)

● **DUNLIN**   page 129
  Autumn: Brownish-grey; near size of Sanderling, but darker, with less conspicuous wing-stripe.

● **PURPLE SANDPIPER**   128
  Slaty-brown; white lateral tail-coverts.

● **KNOT**   130
  Winter: Stocky; greyish with light barred rump.

● **CURLEW SANDPIPER**   129
  Autumn: Suggests elegant Dunlin, but rump white.

● **SANDERLING**   130
  Pearly grey. Has most conspicuous wing-stripe of any small wader.

● **COMMON SANDPIPER**   139
  Identify by very short wing-stroke (giving a stiffly-bowed appearance when gliding).

● **LITTLE STINT**   127
  Very small; narrow wing-stripe; grey sides of tail.

● **TEMMINCK'S STINT**   127
  From Little by greyer colour, white sides of tail.

● **RED-NECKED PHALAROPE**   147
  Immature: Stripey; bold wing-bars; needle bill.

● **GREY PHALAROPE**   146
  Winter: Sanderling-like, but wing-stripe less contrasting; bill thicker than Red-necked Phalarope's.

● **PECTORAL SANDPIPER**   128
  Dark brown, with faint narrow wing-bar; tail pattern like Dunlin's.

● **STONE CURLEW**   150
  Double white wing-bar.

● **RUFF**   131
  Male has ruff on neck in summer; very variable; oval white patches almost join at base of tail.

sides and pouncing on Ptarmigan, hare, etc., from very low altitude. When soaring, holds wings well forward and in shallow "V." Distinguished in flight from young White-tailed Eagle by longer, squarer tail, and less rectangular wing-shape; when perched, by less bulky appearance and, at close range by smaller bill and feathered tarsi. Variations of immature plumage can cause confusion with Imperial, Spotted, Lesser Spotted and Tawny Eagles. Apart from size, boldly projecting head and more ample tail prevent confusion with soaring Buzzard.

Voice: Has very occasional yelping "*kya*" and a few whistling notes.
Habitat: Barren mountain-sides, locally also mountain forests, sea cliffs and plains. Nests on rocky ledge, sometimes in tree. Map p. 82.

WHITE-TAILED EAGLE *Haliaetus albicilla* page 68

Du – Zeearend	Fr – Pygargue à queue blanche
Ge – Seeadler	Sw – Havsörn

N.Am – Gray Sea Eagle

Identification: 27-36″. A very bulky eagle with *huge, broad, blunt-ended wings and heavy, projecting head*. Adult distinguished by *short wedge-shaped white tail*, pale brownish head and heavy yellow bill. Immature has blackish-brown head, tail and bill, but is readily distinguishable from Golden Eagle by tail being much shorter and wedge-shaped (not full and squared, nor with largely white base of immature Golden). Tarsi are unfeathered. Soars on straight wings, giving vulture-like silhouette. Catches fish on surface, in low cruising flight, occasionally plunging for them; catches mammals as large as weakling roe-deer, birds as large as ducks; also eats carrion.

Voice: A creaking "*kri, kri, kri,*" and a lower, barking "*kra.*"
Habitat: Rocky coasts, or remote inland waters. Nests on cliff-face, or on top of rocky pinnacle, in large trees, occasionally on ground. Map below.

← WHITE-TAILED EAGLE
W. to dotted line in winter. Has bred Czecho., Austria. Vag. W. Europe

SHORT-TOED EAGLE →
Summer visitor. Has bred Denmark, Germany. Vagrant Finland, Sweden

SHORT-TOED EAGLE *Circaetus gallicus* page 69
Du – Slangenarend   Fr – Circaète Jean-le-Blanc
Ge – Schlangenadler   Sw – Ormörn

Identification: 25-27″. Larger than Osprey. Under-parts and beneath wings *nearly uniform white except for dark upper-breast and throat* (dark markings occasionally lacking). Seen closely, under-surfaces of wings have lines of small dark spots. Has *round* owl-like head, small bill and large orange eyes. Upper-parts grey-brown, with blackish primaries. Rather long tail has 3-4 indistinct dark bars. Juvenile browner below, with dark bars. Flight is powerful, wings level when soaring; hovers frequently, with legs dangling. Feeds on snakes, lizards, frogs, etc. See also Honey Buzzard.

Voice: Rather noisy. A harsh, plaintive *"jee,"* a rather weak *"ok, ok, ok,"* or *"mew-ok."*

Habitat: Mountain slopes and gorges, secluded woodlands, plantations, marshy plains, coastal dunes. Nests in tree. Map p. 86.

HEN HARRIER *Circus cyaneus* pages 60, 72
Du – Blauwe kuikendief   Fr – Busard Saint-Martin
Ge – Kornweihe   Sw – Blå kärrhök
N.Am – Marsh Hawk

Identification: 17-20″. Distinguished from very similar Montagu's by *more conspicuous white on rump*, also, when seen together, by slightly heavier build (particularly in female), slightly broader wings and tail. Ash-grey male distinguished by *white rump, blackish trailing edge to secondaries* (Montagu's has two black bars in centre of wing) and unstreaked belly and thighs. Female and immature have dark brown upper-parts and broadly streaked buffish under-parts. Juvenile distinguished from young Montagu's by *streaked under-parts*. Flight distinctive, usually very low, gliding buoyantly with wings held in shallow "V." See also Pallid Harrier.

Voice: A high chattering *"ke-ke-ke"*; also a long wailing *"pee-e."*

← HEN HARRIER
*Partial migrant.
Has bred England,
Denmark.
Vagrant Iceland*

PALLID →
HARRIER
*Part. migrant. Has
bred Sweden, Ger-
many, Vag. Brit-
ain, W. Europe n.
to Finland*

Habitat: More varied than Montagu's. Nests on ground on moors, in swamps, thickets, or crops. Map p. 87.

PALLID HARRIER *Circus macrourus* page 60

Du – Steppenkuikendief   Fr – Busard pâle
Ge – Steppenweihe   Sw – Stäpphök

Identification: 17-19″. Male looks strikingly white about head and under-parts, with pale blue-grey tail and wings and contrasting primaries *forming small black wedge on wing-tip.* Distinguished from pale male Hen Harrier by *grey* instead of pure white rump, *white* instead of grey breast and sides of head, less black on wing-tips and *lack of dark trailing edge to secondaries;* from pale male Montagu's by paler grey upper-parts, *lack of black wing-bars and unstreaked white under-parts and thighs.* Female and first-winter birds not distinguishable in the field from those of Montagu's, but juvenile distinguished from young Hen Harrier by unstreaked rufous under-parts. Behaviour as Montagu's. Female's cry *"preee-pri-pri-pri"* is distinctive. **Habitat:** As Hen Harrier, but also in dry steppes, open plains and hill country with sparse trees. Map p. 87.

MONTAGU'S HARRIER *Circus pygargus* pages 60, 72

Du – Grauwe kuikendief   Fr – Busard cendré
Ge – Wiesenweihe   Sw – Mindre kärrhök

Identification: 16-18″. Slightly smaller and slimmer than Hen Harrier, *with narrower, more pointed wings and noticeably more buoyant flight.* Female closely resembles Hen Harrier, though usually with less white on rump. Male distinguished from Hen Harrier by greyish instead of pure white rump, *narrow black wing-bars in centre of wing and brown streaks on belly and thighs.* Immature like female, but with unstreaked rich rufous under-parts. Behaviour like Hen Harrier's. See also Pallid Harrier.

← MONTAGU'S HARRIER
Mainly summer vis. Has bred Scot., Ireland, Switz. Irreg. Czecho. Vagrant Norway

MARSH HARRIER →
Partial mig. Has bred Wales, Ireland. Vag. Faeroes, Norway

Voice: Querulous "*kek-kek-kek*," more shrill than Hen Harrier's chatter.

Habitat: Marshes, fens, moors with clumps of trees, or agricultural land. Where numerous, nests in wet vegetation, or on dry heaths, occasionally in cornfields. Map p. 88.

MARSH HARRIER *Circus aeruginosus* pages 60, 72

Du – Bruine kuikendief Fr – Busard des roseaux
Ge – Rohrweihe Sw – Brun Kärrhök

Identification: 19-22″. Distinguished from other harriers by larger size, heavier build, *broader wings* and *absence of white on rump*. Has low, quartering flight, with occasional wing-beats and long, wavering glides, with wings in shallow "V." Plumage variable. Adult male distinguished from other harriers by *dark mantle and secondary wing-coverts*, contrasting with grey tail and secondaries; streaked buffish head, nape and breast and rich brown under-parts. Female and immature male usually lack grey and are fairly uniform dark chocolate-brown with *pale heads and shoulders* (females sometimes are all-dark, suggesting Black Kite). First-winter birds are dark chocolate brown with *bright creamy* crown and throat. Hunts by pouncing from low altitude into reeds, etc.

Voice: A high, Lapwing-like "*quee-a*" and variants.

Habitat: Almost invariably fens, swamps and marshes, with large areas of dense reeds. Builds large nest in reed-bed usually surrounded by water. Map p. 88.

EGYPTIAN VULTURE *Neophron percnopterus* page 91

Du – Aasgeier Fr – Percnoptère d'Egypte
Ge – Schmutzgier Sw – Smutsgam

Identification: 23-26″. Much smaller than other vultures. Has distinctive flight-silhouette, with *long, straight-edged but pointed black and white wings* and wedge-shaped *white* tail. Head and throat of adults have *bare yellow skin*, above a shaggy whitish ruff. Plumage dingy

← EGYPTIAN
VULTURE
*Summer visitor.
Vagr. n. to Britain,
Denmark and
E. Prussia*

BEARDED
VULTURE →
*Mainly resident.
Recently a few
summering E. Alps.
Has bred Sicily*

white, with contrasting blackish primaries. Bill is *thinner* than in other vultures. Immature varies according to age from dark brown to dirty whitish, with brownish head and ruff. Although not very sociable, occasionally two or three will join Griffons at carcase to eat what the much larger birds leave. Scavenges for offal. See White Stork, which has rather similar flight-pattern.

Habitat: As Griffon, but also frequents village refuse dumps; nests on cliffs. Map p. 89.

BEARDED VULTURE, (LAMMERGEIER) *Gypaetus barbatus*
page 91

Du – Lammergier   Fr – Gypaète barbu
Ge – Bartgeier   Sw – Gamörn

Identification: 40-45″. Distinguished from other vultures by distinctive flight-silhouette, more like huge falcon than vulture, with *long, narrow, angled wings and long diamond-shaped dark tail.* Adults have greyish-black upper-parts, wings and tail, mainly *buff* head with conspicuous broad black patch slanting forward from eye to prominent bunch of black bristles below bill. Under-parts yellowish-orange, vivid orange on breast, contrasting with dark wings. Immature has dark head and neck. Less sluggish than other vultures. Normally solitary.

Voice: Has a thin, querulous cry "*quee-er.*"

Habitat: Remote mountain ranges. Nests in caves on precipices. Map p. 89.

BLACK VULTURE *Aegypius monachus*   page 91

Du – Monniksgier   Fr – Vautour moine
Ge – Mönchsgeier   Sw – Grågam

Identification: 39-42″. In size and flight-silhouette very like Griffon, but distinguished by larger head, deeper, more massive bill and *longer, slightly wedge-shaped tail* (which however is often worn down and can resemble Griffon's); also by *uniform sooty-brown* plumage (looks black at a distance). Seen from above, *wing-coverts are darker* than flight feathers; seen from below lack typical barring of Griffon. Neck bare bluish-pink skin, above *brown* ruff. Behaviour and voice like Griffon's. Usually rather solitary.

Habitat: Remote mountains and plains. Nests in trees, very occasionally on ledge on cliff-face. Map p. 94.

GRIFFON VULTURE *Gyps fulvus*   page 91

Du – Vale gier   Fr – Vautour fauve
Ge – Gänsegeier   Sw – Gåsgam

Identification: 38-41″. Distinguished from other vultures by flight-silhouette: very long, broad wings with widely spread primaries forming rounded ends *and very short, dark, squared tail*; under-sides of wings have pale bars from axillaries towards carpal joint; small head is sunk well back into ruff. Sandy plumage contrasts with dark wing and tail feathers. Head and neck covered with white down. Ruff is

GRIFFON

BLACK

BEARDED

EGYPTIAN

EGYPTIAN

BEARDED

GRIFFON

BLACK

VULTURES

LARGE WADERS IN FLIGHT
(See also Plate 22)

● **AVOCET**   page 145
   Black and white pattern above; thin upturned bill.

○ **BLACK-WINGED STILT**   page 145
   White below; wings black above and below;
   extremely long trailing pink legs.

● **OYSTERCATCHER**   118
   White wing-bands and rump; black head; orange
   bill.

● **WHIMBREL**   141
   Decurved bill; broad stripes on crown.
   Both Whimbrel and Curlew are brown with whitish
   rump, but former is smaller and neater.

● **CURLEW**   140
   Very long decurved bill; no bold stripes on crown.

● **BAR-TAILED GODWIT**   140
   Long slightly upturned bill; barred greyish tail; no
   wing-stripe.

● **BLACK-TAILED GODWIT**   139
   Very long bill; bold white rump and wing-stripe;
   broad black tail-band.

OYSTERCATCHERS

AVOCET

BLACK-WINGED
STILT

WHIMBREL

OYSTERCATCHER

CURLEW

BAR-TAILED GODWIT

BLACK-TAILED GODWIT

RINGED
PLOVER

LITTLE
RINGED
PLOVER

KENTISH
PLOVER

Summer

GREY PLOVER

GOLDEN
PLOVER
Northern form
Summer

Winter
above

above

Winter
below

below

GOLDEN
PLOVER
Winter

DOTTEREL
Summer

Summer

TURNSTONE
Summer

LAPWING

Plate 30   93

PLOVERS AND TURNSTONE IN FLIGHT
(See also Plate 31)

● **RINGED PLOVER**   page 119
   Prominent wing-bar; dark tail with white borders.

● **LITTLE RINGED PLOVER**   119
   From Ringed Plover by voice and lack of wing-bar.

● **KENTISH PLOVER**   120
   Sandy-brown above; white sides of tail.

● **GREY PLOVER**   122
   Summer: Black under-parts; white on wings and rump.
   Winter: Black axillaries; white on wings and rump.

● **GOLDEN PLOVER**   121
   Summer: Black under-parts; no white above.
   Winter: Lack of pattern above and below.

● **DOTTEREL**   121
   White face; light breast-bar; dark under-parts; belly paler in winter.

● **LAPWING**   123
   Black and white; very broad, rounded wings.

● **TURNSTONE**   126
   Harlequin pattern.

A   B   C   D

TYPICAL FLIGHT PATTERNS
A *No wing-stripe, no tail-pattern.*
B *No wing-stripe, white rump and tail.*
C *Wing-stripe, dark rump and tail.*
D *Wing-stripe, white rump and tail.*

pale buffish in adult, brown in juvenile. Sociable when roosting and feeding. See also Black Vulture.

Voice: Croaking and whistling notes, in breeding season only.

Habitat: Ranges over all types of country, but normal habitat is mountainous. Breeds sociably in caves, or on ledges. Map below.

FALCONS: Falconidae

Falcons have long, pointed wings and longish tails. Flight fast, with rapid wing-beats and glides. Large falcons kill their prey by stooping on it at terrific speed. Sexes sometimes similar. Tree, cliff and ground nesting.

GYR FALCON *Falco rusticolus*   page 73
    Du – Giervalk   Fr – Faucon gerfaut
    Ge – Gerfalke   Sw – Jaktfalk

Identification: 20-22″. Distinguished in flight from Peregrine by larger size, slightly longer tail, *broader wing-bases*, slightly blunter wing-tips and slower wing-beats. When perched, *considerably paler, more uniform coloration* and absence of, or only vestigial, moustachial stripe, are noticeable. Some individuals of the Greenland race (*F. r. candicans*) look almost totally white, except for dark primaries. (Snowy Owl is larger-headed, round-winged.)

Voice: Usually silent. Occasional call notes and a high, yapping chatter are slightly lower-pitched than similar notes of Peregrine.

Habitat: Wild rocky open country, sea-coasts and islands. Locally also around edges of coniferous forests. Breeds on rocky cliff faces. Map 95.

← BLACK
VULTURE
Mainly res. ?Extinct Roumania. Vagr. cent. Europe, n. to Denmark, Baltic Provinces

GRIFFON
VULTURE →
Partial migrant. Vagrant n. to British Isles., Denmark, Finland

111   112

SAKER *Falco cherrug* page 61
Du – Saker Valk   Fr – Faucon sacre
Ge – Würgfalke   Sw – Tatarfalk

Identification: 18″. Distinguished from Peregrine by *earth-brown* (not slate-blue) upper-parts and wings, with buffish emarginations, *whitish crown and nape streaked with dark brown*, narrow, indistinct moustachial streak, white under-parts lightly spotted or streaked (not barred) with brown. Wings broader than Peregrine's. Immature has more closely streaked crown and under-parts than adult, particularly on flanks. Very bold and ferocious, attacking prey far larger than itself. Frequently used for falconry. See also Lanner.

Habitat: Open plains, semi-deserts and deserts. Usually nests high in large tree, occasionally among rocks. Map below.

LANNER *Falco biarmicus* page 61
Du – Lanner Valk   Fr – Faucon lanier
Ge – Feldeggsfalke   Sw – Slagfalk

Identification: 17″. Looks like pale Peregrine; distinguishable at close quarters by *buff or sandy crown*, small black moustachial stripe (not broad and lobe-shaped like Peregrine's), whitish ear-coverts and *very lightly spotted* (not barred) whitish under-parts. Immature is darker above than adult and much more heavily marked below. Less bold than Peregrine, preying on smaller birds; looks more slender in flight, which is less rapid. See also Saker.

Voice: A shrill "*kri, kri, kri*," during breeding season.

Habitat: Cliffs, ruins, rocky mountain slopes, extending to stony plains and semi-desert. Nests among rocks, sometimes in trees. Map p. 96.

PEREGRINE *Falco peregrinus* pages 61, 73
Du – Slechtvalk   Fr – Faucon pèlerin
Ge – Wanderfalke   Sw – Pilgrimsfalk
N.Am – Duck Hawk

← Gyr Falcon
Mainly resident. Winter vagr. s. to British Is., Portugal, Italy; fairly regular Faeroes

Saker Falcon →
Mainly migrant. Vagrant w. to E. Prussia, Sweden, France, Italy

Identification: 15-19". Distinguished as a falcon by *long pointed wings, slightly tapered tail,* and rapid pigeon-like flight, but with shallower wing-beats, broken by long glides. Identified as this species by *crow-size* and when perched, by *heavy, black, lobe-shaped "moustaches."* Male has blackish crown, slate-grey upper-parts contrasted with buffish-white under-parts, narrowly barred with black. Female considerably larger and often darker. Juvenile dark brown above, with streaked (not barred) buffish under-parts. Hunts by stooping on prey almost vertically at terrific speed, with wings nearly closed. Feeds chiefly on birds up to size of pigeon, grouse, etc. See also Gyr Falcon and Hobby.
Voice: Has wide range of notes during breeding season: a repeated *"we-chew,"* a high, chattering *"kek-kek-kek,"* a short *"kiack,"* a thin squeal, etc.
Habitat: Open wild country, cliffs, mountains, moors; in winter, also marshes, locally high spires and towers. Breeds on steep cliffs, mountain crags, etc., sometimes on buildings. Map below.

HOBBY   *Falco subbuteo*   pages 61, 73
Du – Boomvalk   Fr – Faucon hobereau
Ge – Baumfalke   Sw – Lärkfalk

Identification: 12-14". The most aerial of the falcons, with dashing flight like Peregrine's, but wings look longer and *tail shorter* (suggesting large Swift). Preys on swallows, larks, etc., and, particularly at dusk, on flying insects. When perched looks slender and compact, *with chestnut on thighs and beneath tail*; pointed "moustaches" are narrower than Peregrine's and *under-parts more heavily streaked (not barred).* Juvenile blackish-brown above, more heavily streaked below and lacking chestnut on thighs and below tail. Distinguished from Kestrel by longer, narrower, more back-swept wings, moustachial stripe, chestnut on thighs and beneath tail. See also Red-footed Falcon.
Voice: A clear, repeated *"kew,"* or *"ket,"* and a rapid *"kikiki,"* often with varying pitch.
Habitat: Downs and commons with scattered trees, coppices, light

← LANNER FALCON
*Mainly resident.
(?) breeds Spain.
Vagrant Portugal,
Southern France,
Roumania*

PEREGRINE →
*Partial migrant.
Vagrant Faeroes*

115   116

woodlands. Breeds in trees, in old nests, particularly of crow family. Map below.

ELEONORA'S FALCON *Falco eleonorae* page 61

Du – Eleonora's valk   Fr – Faucon d'Eléonore
Ge – Eleonorenfalke   Sw – Eleonorafalk

Identification: 15″. About size of Peregrine but more slender. In silhouette resembles *long-tailed* Hobby. Dimorphic. Dark form is *uniform dark brown* with paler streaks on breast; occasionally all-black. Light form has paler slate or dark brown upper-parts, buff or creamy breast heavily streaked with black. Under-parts increasingly rufous towards tail. Cere pale lemon or whitish. Stoops like Peregrine on small birds, hawks for insects like Hobby (particularly at dusk) and hovers occasionally like Kestrel. Gregarious. See also Red-footed Falcon.

Voice: A harsh *"keya,"* sometimes repeated rapidly.

Habitat and Range: Rocky Mediterranean islands and sea cliffs. Migratory, breeding mainly in late summer on Greek islands, Sardinia, Balearics. Vagrant to S. France, Sicily, Spain.

MERLIN *Falco columbarius* pages 61, 73

Du – Smelleken   Fr – Faucon émerillon
Ge – Merlin   Sw – Stenfalk
N.Am – Pigeon Hawk

Identification: 10½-13″. A very small falcon, dashing after prey at low altitude over open country. Flight buoyant and erratic, with occasional short glides. Male slate-blue above, with *broad black terminal band on tail and heavily rufous-striped under-parts.* Female larger, with dark brown upper-parts and barred brown and creamy tail. No moustachial stripe. Sparrow Hawk has short rounded (not pointed) wings. Kestrel has chestnut upper-parts, slimmer tail.

Voice: Male has quick high chatter *"ki-ki-ki-ki."* Female has lower chatter and a slow, plaintive *"eep-eep."*

← HOBBY
Summer visitor. Occasional Norway. Vagrant Ireland

MERLIN →
Partial migrant.

Habitat: Open, hilly and marshy moors, sea cliffs and sand-dunes. Breeds on ground among heather, coarse grass, or on sand, or in trees in old nests of crows. Map p. 97.

RED-FOOTED FALCON *Falco vespertinus* pages 61, 73

Du – Roodpootvalk   Fr – Faucon kobez
Ge – Rotfussfalke   Sw – Aftonfalk

Identification: 12″. A small, gregarious falcon with long wings reaching nearly to tip of short tail, and *bright reddish-orange bill, eye-patches and legs*. Males, usually outnumbering females, are uniform blackish-grey with chestnut under tail-coverts. Female has rufous crown, sandy under-parts, short dark moustachial stripe, barred grey upper-parts and tail. Juvenile resembles brownish young Hobby, with paler, more closely barred upper-parts and tail, *pale forehead* and less boldly streaked buff under-parts. Hovers like Kestrel, but with body at steeper angle. Hunts flying insects until late dusk; takes grasshoppers, small rodents, etc., from ground. See also Hobby, Merlin, Kestrel and Lesser Kestrel.

Voice: A shrill "*kikikiki*," higher than Kestrel's cry.

Habitat: Open plains dotted with scrub and coppices, edges of woods, and around farmsteads. Breeds colonially in old nests of Rooks, Magpies, etc. Map below.

LESSER KESTREL *Falco naumanni* page 61

Du – Kleine torenvalk   Fr – Faucon crécerellette
Ge – Rötelfalke   Sw – Rödfalk

Identification: 12″. Looks like small, brightly-coloured Kestrel; distinguishable by *more fearless, noisier behaviour* and *sociable nesting*. Flight more supple than Kestrel's and tail more slender, particularly at base; hovers seldom but glides frequently. Male has *unspotted* bright chestnut-red upper-parts, and bluer head and tail than Kestrel; female and juvenile more similar to Kestrels. Viewed overhead, wings

← RED-FOOTED FALCON
Summer vis. Has bred Austria, Ger., Finland, Sweden. Vag. w. to Spain, Brit. Is., Norway

LESSER KESTREL →
Summer visitor. Vagrant Britain, Ireland, Denmark, Germany, Czecho., Switzerland

and tail look very pale, with black edges; viewed from above, secondaries show large slate-blue patch; claws are white (Kestrel's are black). Feeds chiefly on flying insects.

Voice: Much more vocal and varied than Kestrel. Usual notes, a chattering *"chet-che-che,"* and a plaintive, rising *"wheee."*

Habitat: Frequents old buildings, rocky gorges, etc., but usually hunts over open country. Breeds in colonies in holes in high walls, roofs, crevices in cliffs, often among pigeons, sparrows, etc. Map p. 98.

KESTREL *Falco tinnunculus*   pages 61, 73
    Du – Torenvalk   Fr – Faucon crécerelle
    Ge – Turmfalke   Sw – Tornfalk

Identification: 13½″. Pointed wings, slim tail, mark it as a falcon; small size and *habit of protracted hovering*, as this species. Male has *spotted chestnut* upper-parts, warm buff under-parts with scattered black spots. Head, rump and tail grey, latter with broad black band near white tip. Female has rusty brown upper-parts, barred instead of spotted, and rusty barred tail. Perches on trees, telegraph poles, rocks, etc. Flies with rapid wing-beats, occasional short glides and frequent periods of hovering, head to wind; slants steeply down to catch mice, beetles, etc. See Merlin, Lesser Kestrel and Sparrow Hawk for differences.

Voice: A shrill repeated *"kee, kee, kee,"* and a more musical double note *"kee-lee."* Usually silent outside breeding season.

Habitat: Moors, coasts, farm-lands, open woodlands, locally cities. Breeds in old nests of crows, Magpies, etc., and on cliffs, buildings, occasionally in split trees. Map below.

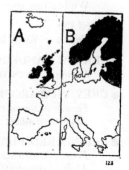

← KESTREL
*Partial migrant.
Vagrant Iceland,
Faeroes*

RED GROUSE(A) →
*Resident Britain,
Ireland. (Intro-
duced Belgium).*

WILLOW
GROUSE(B) →
*Resident contin-
ental Europe*

WADERS (See also Plate 30)

● **RINGED PLOVER**   page 119
  Band across breast; yellow legs and base of bill.

● **LITTLE RINGED PLOVER**   119
  Smaller than Ringed Plover; flesh legs; white line
  above black on forehead.

● **KENTISH PLOVER**   120
  Black on sides of breast only; black legs; unbroken
  supercilium.

● **GREY PLOVER**   122
  Summer: Black below; silvery above.
  Winter: Stout shape; grey above.

● **GOLDEN PLOVER**   121
  Summer: Black below, dark above; broad white side
  stripe. (Southern form has less black.)
  Winter: Less stout than Grey; golden-brown above.

● **LAPWING**   123
  Long wispy crest; black breast; iridescent back.

● **TURNSTONE**   126
  Summer: "Tortoiseshell" back; distinctive face.
  Winter: Dark breast-band; orange legs.

○ **CREAM-COLOURED COURSER**   150
  Sandy; bold eye-stripes; long creamy legs.

● **DOTTEREL**   121
  White stripe over eye; russet flanks; black belly.

● **DUNLIN**   129
  Summer: Rusty back; black patch on belly.

● **CURLEW SANDPIPER**   129
  Summer: Decurved bill; rufous plumage.

● **GREY PHALAROPE**   146
  Female in summer: Rufous below; white cheeks.
  Male in summer: Duller.

● **RED-NECKED PHALAROPE**   147
  Female in summer: Red neck; white throat.
  Male in summer: Duller.

KENTISH PLOVER

RINGED PLOVER

LITTLE RINGED PLOVER

Winter

Winter

Winter

Southern form Summer

Summer

GOLDEN PLOVER

Northern form Summer

GREY PLOVER

Juv

LAPWING

Winter

TURNSTONE

Summer

DUNLIN

Summer

CREAM-COLOURED COURSER

Summer

DOTTEREL

CURLEW SANDPIPER

Summer

♂

♀ Summer

GREY PHALAROPE

♂

♀ Summer

RED-NECKED PHALAROPE

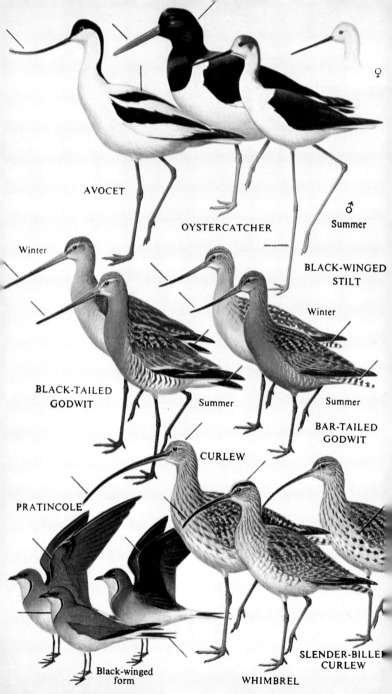

AVOCET

OYSTERCATCHER

♀

♂

Summer

BLACK-WINGED
STILT

Winter

Winter

BLACK-TAILED
GODWIT

Summer

Summer

BAR-TAILED
GODWIT

CURLEW

PRATINCOLE

Black-winged
form

WHIMBREL

SLENDER-BILLED
CURLEW

Plate 32   **101**

LARGE WADERS
(See also Plate 29)

● **AVOCET**   page 145
   Upturned bill; black and white back.

● **OYSTERCATCHER**   118
   Large size; black head; orange-red bill.

○ **BLACK-WINGED STILT**   145
   Black above; white below; very long pink legs.

● **BLACK-TAILED GODWIT**   139
   Summer: Chestnut breast; long straight bill; black
   tail and flank-bars.
   Winter: Grey; long straight bill; black tail.

● **BAR-TAILED GODWIT**   140
   Summer: Shorter legs than Black-tailed; more
   upturned bill; barred tail; rufous to belly.
   Winter: Grey-brown.

○ **PRATINCOLE**   151
   Rather tern-like; forked tail; white rump; light
   throat-patch.

△ **BLACK-WINGED PRATINCOLE**   151
   Like Pratincole, but *black* beneath wings, not rufous.

● **CURLEW**   140
   Very long, decurved bill; no head-stripes.

● **WHIMBREL**   141
   Decurved bill; striped crown.

  SLENDER-BILLED CURLEW   141
   Bill size close to Whimbrel's, but crown more like
   Curlew's. Note heart-shaped spots on sides.

GROUSE: Tetraonidae

Plump, chicken-like, chiefly ground-dwelling birds, without the long tails of pheasants. Tarsi and often the toes are feathered. Sexes sometimes similar. Ground nesting.

WILLOW GROUSE/RED GROUSE *Lagopus lagopus* page 157
    Du – Moerassneeuwhoen   Fr – Lagopède des saules
    Ge – Moorschneehuhn   Sw – Dalripa
            N.Am – Willow Ptarmigan

Identification: 15-16″. A stout, short-winged, blackish-tailed bird, with rufous-brown plumage. Like all game-birds, flight is rapid, with alternate whirring wing-beats and gliding on down-curved wings; when flushed, looks back in flight. Willow (N. Europe) and Red *L. l. scoticus* (Brit. Is.) now regarded as conspecific.

Willow Grouse and Ptarmigan both have white wings and are often indistinguishable except by voice and habitat. Both very variable, but Willow has darker rufous breeding plumage; at short range *stouter bill* is obvious. In autumn, Willow becomes patchy white and brown; Ptarmigan becomes grey above. In winter, where ranges overlap, a white grouse with black tail and unmarked white head may be male or female Willow, or female Ptarmigan; if it has *black face-patch* it is male Ptarmigan (see diagram p. 157).

Red Grouse is dark rufous-brown *with darker brown wings*. Summer plumage paler than winter, female paler and smaller than male. Irish race yellower than British. Distinguished from female Black Grouse (Greyhen) by smaller size, more rufous colour and unforked tail; from summer Ptarmigan by dark wings and belly.

Voice: Willow crows a rapid "*kowk, ok, ok, ok,*" often preceded by a quiet "*ow . . . ow. . . .*" Red has similar loud crowing call; during breeding season a strident "*go-bak, bak-bak-bak.*"

Habitat: Willow inhabits moors, heather, with willow, birch and juniper scrub, at lower altitudes than Ptarmigan; nests in scrub. Red prefers moors and peat-bogs with crowberry and cranberry, descending in autumn to lower levels and stubble fields; nests among heather and rough grass. Maps p. 99.

PTARMIGAN *Lagopus mutus*   page 157
    Du – Sneeuwhoen   Fr – Lagopède des Alpes
    Ge – Alpenschneehuhn   Sw – Fjällripa
            N.Am – Rock Ptarmigan

Identification: 14″. A grouse of the high mountain slopes, which at all seasons shows *white wings* and white belly. Small red wattle over eye; feet feathered white. In breeding plumage male has richly mottled blackish-brown upper-parts, breast and flanks; female is tawnier. In autumn male's upper-parts, breast and sides are grey, closely marked with black and white, belly mainly white; female is yellowish-grey and looks darker than male. In winter both sexes are *pure white with exception of black tail* (which is largely hidden at rest by white tail-coverts) but male has *black mark from bill through eye*—a clear distinction from Willow Grouse (see diagram p. 157). At short range Ptarmigan's bill looks more slender than Willow Grouse's; both species are very variable, with three distinct changes of plumage.

Voice: A low, harsh croak; alarm a repeated grating, crackling sound; during display male has brief crowing "song."

Habitat: Barren stony mountain slopes (usually higher than Willow Grouse), except when driven down by weather; breeds at lower levels in Arctic. Nests in shelter of rock or clump of vegetation. Map below.

HAZEL HEN *Tetrastes bonasia*   page 164

  Du – Hazelhoen   Fr – Gelinotte des bois
  Ge – Haselhuhn   Sw – Järpe

Identification: 14". A woodland species. Typical grouse-shape, but with longish tail and slightly crested crown. In flight both sexes show *conspicuous black band on grey tail.* Upper-parts greyish to rusty-brown (greyest in north of range, more rufous in south), richly spotted and barred black and brown. Broad white bands down side of throat and across scapulars. Under-parts whitish, closely marked with brown, more heavily on flanks. Male has *conspicuous black throat, broadly bordered with white.* Female has whitish throat. Perches freely in trees.

Voice: A high, whistling "*tsissi-tseri-tsi, tsi, tsi, tsiu.*"

Habitat: Mixed hill woodlands and thickets, particularly among aspen and birch; locally also in wooded plains. Map below.

BLACK GROUSE *Lyrurus tetrix*   page 164

  Du – Korhoen   Fr – Tétras lyre
  Ge – Birkhuhn   Sw – Orre

Identification: Male 21", female 16". Male (Blackcock) easily dis-

← Ptarmigan
Resident

Hazel Hen →
Mainly resident

tinguished by glossy *blue-black* plumage with *lyre-shaped tail*, conspicuous *white under tail-coverts and white wing-bar*. Female (Greyhen) distinguished from Red Grouse by larger size and *less rufous plumage*; from female Capercaillie by smaller size and *less boldly barred plumage*; from both by narrow, pale wing-bars and forked tail (neither easy to observe). Both sexes have scarlet wattle above eye. Male in autumn eclipse looks dingy, mottled above, with white throat; tail lacks distinctive shape until full grown. Usually flies higher than Red Grouse with longer glides; longer neck and tail give distinctive silhouette. Perches freely in trees. Confusing hybrids with Capercaillie, Red Grouse and Pheasant occur occasionally.

Voice: Male has a deliberate, sneezing "*tchu-shwee.*" Song at "lek" (display ground) a rapid, protracted, musical chorus of pigeon-like or bubbling notes.

Habitat: Near trees bordering moors, marshy ground with rushes and scattered trees, peat-mosses, rocky heather-covered hills, plantations, etc. Nests on ground. Map below.

CAPERCAILLIE *Tetrao urogallus* page 164

Du – Auerhoen	Fr – Grand Tétras
Ge – Auerhuhn	Sw – Tjäder

Identification: Male 34″, female 24″. A huge grouse-like bird. Male distinguished from all other game-birds by *very large size, dark colouring and ample tail*. General coloration grey, with rich brown wing-coverts, glossy blue-green breast, shaggy "beard," whitish bill and scarlet skin over eye; under-parts and tail boldly marked with white. White carpal-patch conspicuous during display. Female may be confused with female Black or Red Grouse, but is much larger, with broad tail and *rufous patch on breast* contrasting with paler under-parts. Usually seen on ground in coniferous forests in summer; in trees in winter. Flight usually brief, with alternate spells of quick wing-beats and long glides; bursts out of cover noisily. Hens may hybridise with Blackcock.

Voice: Male at display ground has guttural retching call; female, a

← BLACK GROUSE
Resident

CAPERCAILLIE →
Resident

Pheasant-like "*kok-kok*." Male's song is quiet, beginning with "*tik-up, tik-up, tik-up*" accelerating rapidly and ending with a "pop" (like withdrawing a cork), followed by a short phrase of grating, whispering notes.

Habitat: Coniferous hilly woodlands. Nests among undergrowth at foot of pine, or in scrub on open high ground. Map p. 104.

PARTRIDGES AND PHEASANTS:
Phasianidae

Chicken-like terrestrial birds, with unfeathered legs. Pheasants have long, sweeping tails (females shorter). Partridges and Quail are much smaller, more rotund, with very short tails. Sexes similar. Ground nesting.

ROCK PARTRIDGE *Alectoris graeca*   page 157
      Du – Steenpatrijs   Fr – Perdrix bartavelle
      Ge – Steinhuhn   Sw – Stenhöna

Identification: 13″. Indistinguishable at long range from Red-legged Partridge and Chukar. Best identified by *distinctive voice*. White throat-patch is slightly larger, with black lower border *clean-cut*, instead of merging into upper breast; forehead is ash-grey; upper-parts are grey-brown instead of brown.

Voice: Call note, a Nuthatch-like "*whit-whit-whit*"; alarm an explosive "*pitchi-i*"; song (spring and autumn) a staccato "*tchertsi-ritt-chi*," with many variants.

Habitat: Stony and rocky slopes and lightly wooded high ground, descending to lower altitudes in winter. Nests among rocks. Map p. 106.

CHUKAR *Alectoris chukar*
Identification: 13″. Very similar to Rock Partridge; best distinguished by *clucking or cackling voice*, like *barnyard fowl*. Lores are *white* (black in Rock); black "mask" is *narrower* and broken; throat more

ROCK PARTRIDGE   CHUKAR

buff, less grey; centre of gorget *flecked* (not clean-cut); flank-bars bolder and fewer; upper-parts browner.

Habitat and Range: Similar habitat to Rock Patridge, but also in more arid regions. Breeds E. Greece, E. Bulgaria, Aegean.

BARBARY PARTRIDGE *Alectoris barbara* page 157

Du – Barbarijse patrijs   Fr – Perdrix gambra
Ge – Felsenhuhn   Sw – Klipphöna

Identification: 13″. At long range looks paler and pinker than Red-legged Partridge and at short range is easily identified by broad *chestnut* collar, speckled with whitish and by *blue-grey* "face," throat and upper breast. "Inflamed" pink eye-ring. Broad buffish streak behind eye; upper-parts pinkish brown, with slate-blue scapulars, broadly margined with crimson. Under-parts resemble Red-legged, flanks boldly barred with grey, black, white and chestnut. Legs reddish.

Voice: Noisy at dawn and dusk. A rapid *"kakelik"* and a slower *"chuk, chuk, chuk, chukor, chukor."*

Habitat and Range: Scrub-covered hillsides, wadis, semi-deserts with a certain amount of water and cover. Resident Gibraltar, Sardinia.

RED-LEGGED PARTRIDGE *Alectoris rufa* page 157

Du – Rode patrijs   Fr – Perdrix rouge
Ge – Rothuhn   Sw – Rödhöna

Identification: 13½″. At distance can be confused with Partridge, but adult easily distinguished by *long white stripe above eye, black-bordered white gorget,* lavender flanks *heavily barred chestnut-black-white,* chestnut crown and red bill and legs. Juvenile is very like young Partridge. Voice is very different; runs more swiftly than Partridge; flocks are less compact. See also Rock, Chukar and Barbary Partridges.

Voice: Usual note of male *"chuck, chuck-er,"* or a slow harsh *"tschreck . . . tschreck . . .";* when flushed, calls *"kuk-kuk."*

Habitat and Breeding: Much as Partridge. Although often on marshy

← ROCK
  PARTRIDGE
  Resident

RED-LEGGED
PARTRIDGE →
  Resident

129

131

ground, normally prefers dry localities, sandy soil, chalk downs, stony wastes. Map p. 106.

PARTRIDGE   *Perdix perdix*   page 157
  Du – Patrijs   Fr – Perdrix grise
  Ge – Rebhuhn   Sw – Rapphöna
    N.Am – Hungarian Partridge

Identification: 12″. Like all the partridges, a rotund, chicken-like bird, with short rounded wings and short rufous tail; flies low and rapidly, with alternate spells of whirring wing-beats and gliding on deeply arched wings. Easily confused with larger Red-legged Partridge, but distinguished by *pale orange-chestnut "face,"* grey neck and breast. Male has *conspicuous dark chestnut horse-shoe mark on lower breast* (female shows trace of similar mark, juvenile is streaky); upper-parts streaked with buff, flanks barred with chestnut. Walks in crouched attitude, squatting when alarmed and running swiftly with head well up in preference to flight. Much shorter-tailed than young Pheasant. Much larger and less sandy than Quail. See also Red-legged Partridge.
Voice: A penetrating, grating *"krrr-ic,"* or *"kar-wic,"* repeated rapidly when excited.
Habitat: Farm-lands, pastures, waste-land, moors, sand-dunes, etc. Nests well hidden in hedge bottoms, in growing corn, etc. Map below.

QUAIL   *Coturnix coturnix*   page 157
  Du – Kwartel   Fr – Caille des blés
  Ge – Wachtel   Sw – Vaktel

Identification: 7″. Looks like tiny Partridge. Usually first identified by male's *distinctive voice.* General colour *sandy, strongly streaked* with whitish-buff and black above, paler below, with light and dark streaks (not bars) on flanks. Crown dark brown, with creamy stripe down centre and a long creamy stripe above eye. Male has blackish stripes on throat. Female has unmarked buff throat and closely spotted breast. Flight is slower and usually much briefer than Partridge's. Very difficult to flush in breeding season.

← Partridge
Resident

Quail →
*Partial migrant.
Irreg. most Britain.
Formerly bred
Finland.   Occas.
winters north to
Britain*

Voice: Ventriloquial. Characteristic trisyllabic call of male has accent on first syllable: a repeated *"whic, whic-ic."* Female has wheezing double note *"queep . . . queep."* Heard day and night.

Habitat: Seldom seen in open. Frequents and breeds in rough pastures, crops, grass tussocks, etc. Map p. 107.

PHEASANT   *Phasianus colchicus*   page 164
    Du – Fazant   Fr – Faisan de chasse
    Ge – Fasan   Sw – Fasan

Identification: Male 30-35″, female 21-25″. A familiar game-bird with a *long, pointed tail*. Male highly coloured, with glossy dark green head, scarlet wattles around eyes and short ear-tufts. Plumage very variable owing to variety of introduced stock, but usually has *white neck-ring*. Female soberly mottled buff and blackish, with shorter but still lengthy tail. Runs swiftly to cover rather than taking wing. Flight strong (take-off noisy), but seldom long sustained or high.

Voice: Crowing male has strident double note *"korrk-kok,"* usually followed by brief whirr of wing-flapping. Female has thin whistling note on taking off.

Habitat: Woodland borders, park-land, farm-land, shrubberies, reeds. Nests on ground, beneath low vegetation and bracken. Map p. 109.

BUTTON-QUAILS: Turnicidae

ANDALUSIAN HEMIPODE   *Turnix sylvatica*   page 157
    Du – Vechtkwartel   Fr – Turnix d'Andalousie
    Ge – Laufhühnchen   Sw – Springhöna

Identification: 6″. A small, Quail-like bird, very likely to be confused with Quail, when flushed. Crown dark, with buffish centre stripe; sides of head and throat pale buffish, with small dark speckles. Chief distinction from Quail is the *bright orange-rufous patch* on the breast and the *bold black spotting* on the sides. Eye-ring and eye are pale blue. Sexes similar. Extremely shy. Difficult to flush. Runs swiftly in zig-zag. Flight reluctant, low and rapid. Solitary or in pairs.

Voice: A very distinctive *"crooo,"* increasing in intensity, resembling distant lowing of cattle; heard particularly at dawn and dusk; when calling often "blows itself up" like a ball. Also quiet whistling notes.

Habitat and Range: Sandy plains with palmetto scrub, brush-covered wastes, extensive low thickets, stubble and sugar-beet fields. Nests in dense vegetation. Breeds very locally in S. and N.E. Spain, S. Portugal.

CRANES: Gruidae

Large, stately terrestrial birds, superficially resembling storks. Inner secondaries much elongated, drooping over the tail. Long neck and legs extended in flight. Usually migrate in "V" or line formation. Voices trumpet-like. Sexes similar. Ground nesting.

CRANE *Grus grus* page 8

Du – Kraanvogel	Fr – Grue cendrée
Ge – Kranich	Sw – Trana

Identification: 45″. Distinguished from storks and herons by much elongated inner secondaries, forming *drooping blackish "tail."* General colour slate-grey, with *curving white stripe* on side of head and neck, contrasting with black face and throat. At short range *red crow*n is visible. Bill is shorter than in storks and herons. Immature has brown head and upper-parts, lacking the white head-pattern of adult and with much less bushy "tail." Behaviour extremely shy. Walks slowly and gracefully. When suspicious stretches upright, with long neck erect. Very rarely perches on trees. Flight slow but powerful, neck and legs extended, wing-tips square-ended. Migrating flocks assume "V" or line formations. (Storks usually fly in shapeless flocks.)

Voice: A strident, trumpeting "*kr-rooh*" and a quieter guttural "*kr-r-r*"; various grating and hissing notes.

Habitat: In winter, avoids wooded regions, occurring on river banks, lagoons, fields and steppes. Breeds on ground in wet bogs, lightly wooded swamps, reed-beds, etc. Map below.

DEMOISELLE CRANE *Anthropoïdes virgo* page 8

Du – Jufferkraan	Fr – Demoiselle de Numidie
Ge – Jungfernkranich	Sw – Jungfrutrana

Identification: 38″. Easily distinguished from Crane by much smaller size (stands 12″ shorter) and by *large crest-like tuft of white feathers behind each eye* and much smaller bill. Plumage mostly ashy blue-grey, with black on lores, much of neck, elongated breast feathers and wing-quills. Black-tipped inner secondaries much elongated, drooping right over tail, but *without Crane's bushy effect.* Flight as Crane, with neck extended; not distinguishable at high altitude unless both together, when smaller size and shriller voice are discernible.

← PHEASANT
Resident

CRANE →
*Migrant.
Vagrant Faeroes,
British Isles*

Voice: A loud, musical trumpeting, noticeably higher-pitched than Crane's.

Habitat and Range: Open plains and high plateaux, visiting fresh water regularly in hot weather. Nests on dry ground. Formerly bred Roumania. Vagrant to S. Europe, northwards to Germany, Denmark, Sweden.

RAILS, CRAKES AND COOTS:
Rallidae

Rails and crakes are compact, skulking marsh birds, more often heard than seen; wings short and rounded; tails short and often cocked; flight usually brief and reluctant, with legs and long toes dangling. Moorhens and coots have stout bodies, small heads and long toes for walking on aquatic vegetation; heads often jerked while swimming. Sexes usually similar. Reed or ground nesting.

WATER RAIL *Rallus aquaticus* page 52

Du – Waterral   Fr – Râle d'eau
Ge – Wasserralle Sw – Vattenrall

Identification: 11″. Difficult to observe; usually identified by *very distinctive voice*. Distinguished from all the "crakes" by *long red bill*. Upper-parts olive brown, patterned with blackish feather-centres; face, throat and breast dark blue-grey; *flanks conspicuously barred black and white*; under tail-coverts *whitish*; legs pinkish-brown. Juvenile has mottled under-parts. Nervous and skulking behaviour as Corncrake, but occasionally perches on bushes in open.

Voice: A hard, persistent "*gep . . . gep . . . gep . . .*"; a diminishing series "*krui, krui, krui*" and an astonishing variety of groaning, grunting, squealing and purring notes, including a sharp "*kik, kik, kik*" which can be confused with other crakes. Often heard at night.

Habitat: Dense aquatic vegetation, reed and osier beds, sewage-farms,

← WATER RAIL
Partial migrant

SPOTTED CRAKE →
*Part. migrant. Occ.
winter n. to Britain.
Vagrant Ireland
(has bred). May
breed Spain*

overgrown ponds, ditches, river banks. Nests among reeds or sedges above shallow water. Map p. 110.

SPOTTED CRAKE *Porzana porzana* page 52

Du – Porceleinhoen   Fr – Marouette ponctuée
Ge – Tûpfelsumpfhuhn   Sw – Småfläckig sumphöna

Identification: 9″. Body near size of Water Rail, but bill much shorter. Very difficult to observe, but voice is distinctive. Resembles small, dark Corncrake, with *dark* olive-brown upper-parts *streaked and spotted with white* and short *dark brown* (not chestnut) wings. Legs greenish. Bill yellowish with red base. Breast grey, with white speckles. Jerks tail when suspicious, revealing *conspicuous buff under tail-coverts*. Solitary and largely crepuscular. Little and Baillon's are much smaller, with barred under tail-coverts.

Voice: A high, whipping "*whitt . . . whitt . . . whitt*," long repeated on the same note. Male also has monotonous hard ticking note "*tchick-tchuck*," recalling Snipe's clock-like note.

Habitat: Rather less aquatic than Baillon's or Little Crakes. Swamps and fens, overgrown ditches, margins of ponds, rivers, etc. Nests in boggy locations. Map p. 110.

LITTLE CRAKE *Porzana parva* page 52

Du – Klein waterhoen   Fr – Marouette poussin
Ge – Kleines Sumpfhuhn   Sw – Liten sumphöna

Identification: 7½″. Little and Baillon's Crakes are very similar in appearance, voice and habitat and can seldom be seen closely. Both are *much smaller* than Spotted Crake. Male Little differs from male Baillon's in having *olive-brown upper-parts, no white streaks on wing-coverts* (only indistinct pale flecks on mantle) and *lack of black bars on flanks*, though rest of under-parts are slate-grey and under tail-coverts are barred like Baillon's. Females easily separated, Little having *buff* under-parts (not grey) and a *whitish throat*. Both sexes have green bill *with red base*. Legs *green* (Baillon's are dull flesh coloured). Juveniles of both species resemble female Little, but young Little is less heavily barred below than young Baillon's. Behaviour and flight as Spotted Crake. See Baillon's.

Voice: A sharp "*quek, quek, quek*," gradually dropping in scale and accelerating to a short trill. Call-note an explosive "*kirrook*."

Habitat: As Spotted, but with fondness for high *Phragmites* reeds and lagoons with floating vegetation. Map p. 112.

BAILLON'S CRAKE *Porzana pusilla* page 52

Du – Kleinst waterhoen   Fr – Marouette de Baillon
Ge – Zwergsumpfhuhn   Sw – Dvärgsumphöna

Identification: 7″. Smaller than Starling. Both sexes resemble male Little Crake, but when seen well (which rarely occurs) distinguished by smaller size (the smallest European crake), *rufous upper-parts, boldly and closely etched with white, strongly barred black and white* *flanks, dull flesh legs* and green bill *without* red base. (Little Crake is olive-brown above.) In flight narrow white edge to first primary is a further distinction. Males of both species have slaty blue-grey face, throat and under-parts and barred black and white under tail-coverts. Juveniles very similar (resembling Little Crake), though under-parts of Baillon's are often more strongly barred and upper-parts have more distinct pale markings. Behaviour as Little Crake. See also Spotted Crake.

Voice: Easily confused with Little Crake, but Baillon's is a quicker, more jarring trill, sometimes with 2-4 slower introductory notes.

Habitat: Usually prefers lower, denser vegetation and smaller pools than Little Crake, in swamps, fens and overgrown ponds. Map below.

CORNCRAKE   *Crex crex*   page 52

Du – Kwartelkoning	Fr – Râle de genêts
Ge – Wachtelkönig	Sw – Kornknarr

Identification: 10½". Difficult to observe. Presence usually indicated by male's *distinctive rasping voice*. Looks *short-necked*. Plumage *yellowish-buff*, marked with blackish above; greyish on head and breast; flanks and under tail-coverts barred with chestnut. *Chestnut wings conspicuous in flight.* Behaviour solitary, crepuscular and very skulking, hiding in long grass. Distinguished from all other crakes by larger size and buffer appearance.

Voice: In breeding season male has penetrating and persistent call, a rasping, disyllabic *"rerrp-rerrp"* (often written *"crex-crex"*), usually at night, but often also by day.

Habitat: Frequents and nests in meadows, lush vegetation, crops. Map p. 113.

MOORHEN   *Gallinula chloropus*   page 52

Du – Waterhoen	Fr – Poule d'eau
Ge – Teichhuhn	Sw – Rörhöna
N.Am – Florida Gallinule	

← Little Crake
*Summer visitor.
Has bred Sweden,
Holland, ?Spain.
Vag. w. to Brit. Is.*

Baillon's
Crake →
*Summer visitor.
Vag. n. to Britain
(has bred), Ireland,
Faeroes. May
breed Denmark,
Sweden*

Identification: 13". A stout blackish bird of pond margins. Distinguished from Coot by smaller size, *bold irregular white streak along flanks and conspicuous white under tail-coverts* with black centre stripe. Legs green, with red "garter" above joint. Red frontal shield and bill, latter with yellow tip. Juvenile dark grey-brown, with whitish belly, greenish brown bill and frontal shield. Jerks tail when nervous. Swims buoyantly with jerking head. Dives occasionally. Rises from water by pattering along surface. Flight usually low, legs dangling. Often feeds in flocks in winter.

Voice: A harsh, penetrating *"kr-r-rk,"* or *"kittick,"* etc.

Habitat: Ponds, slow streams, marshes, tarns, sewage farms and meadows, even farmyards. Nests in reeds and bushes near water, occasionally in trees and old nests of other species. Map below.

PURPLE GALLINULE *Porphyrio porphyrio* page 52

Du – Purperkoet Fr – Poule sultane
Ge – Purpurhuhn Sw – Purpurhöna

Identification: 19". Upper-parts rich, dark *blue-purple*, glossed with turquoise on throat and breast; under tail-coverts *pure white*. *Very deep bill,* frontal shield, legs and eyes are *bright red*. Much larger and heavier-bodied than Coot, *with longer legs*. Juvenile is dusky bluish-slate, with grey throat and sides of head. Climbs among reeds; seldom in open. Easily distinguished in flight by long, dangling *red* legs. Coot is uniform blackish, with white frontal shield and grey legs; Moorhen is much smaller, has green legs.

Voice: A weird, hooting shriek.

Habitat and Range: Swamps with extensive reed-beds, borders of lakes fringed with dense cover. Nests in reeds, cane-brakes, etc. Breeds in S. Spain, Sardinia. Vagrant to N. France, Norway, Czechoslovakia, Austria.

COOT *Fulica atra* page 52

Du – Meerkoet Fr – Foulque macroule
Ge – Blässhuhn Sw – Sothöna

← CORNCRAKE
*Summer visitor.
Has wintered n. to
England, Ireland.
Vagrant Iceland*

MOORHEN →
*Partial migrant.
Vagrant Iceland,
Faeroes*

Identification: 15″. A stout, slaty-black water bird with jet-black head. Distinguished from Moorhen by larger size, bulkier body and *conspicuous white frontal shield and bill*; also by lack of white stripe across flanks and of white on under tail-coverts. In flight shows narrow white edge to secondaries. Legs green, with large "scalloped" toes, projecting in flight like long "tail." Juvenile dusky-grey, with white throat and upper breast, sometimes confused with young Great Crested Grebe. Stays closer to water than Moorhen and "plop-dives" frequently for food, staying submerged up to half a minute. Gregarious in winter. Distinguished at long range when swimming with ducks by rounded back and small head. Flight is laboured, alighting on water with big splash. Patters along surface when taking off.

Voice: A loud, short "*tewk*"; also various disyllabic calls "*kt-kowk*," etc., and a hard, explosive "*skik*."

Habitat: Usually prefers larger areas of open water than Moorhen. Packs occur on reservoirs and salt-water in winter. Nests among reeds and other aquatic vegetation. Map p. 115.

CRESTED COOT *Fulica cristata*   page 52
    Du – Knobbelmeerkoet   Fr – Foulque à crête
    Ge – Kammblässhuhn   Sw – Kamsothöna

Identification: 16″. Closely resembles Coot, but distinguished at short range by *prominent red knobs* above each side of bluish-white frontal shield and *distinctive voice*. Lacks white on secondaries. Legs bluish-grey. Behaviour, flight and habitat as Coot, with which it mingles, but is more shy and keeps closer to cover.

Voice: Usual note a loud, almost human "*hoo, hoo*."

Range: Resident S. Spain, extending to Portugal in winter. Vagrant to France, Sardinia, Italy, Sicily.

BUSTARDS: Otididae

Chiefly terrestrial, frequenting grassy steppes and extensive cultivated fields. Gait a stately walk. Behaviour very shy, crouching or running swiftly at first sign of danger. Flight is powerful, wings broad, bodies stout. Ground nesting.

GREAT BUSTARD *Otis tarda*   page 81
    Du – Grote trap   Fr – Outarde barbue
    Ge – Grosstrappe   Sw – Stortrapp

Identification: 40″. Female 30″. Easily distinguished by *very large size, stout body and long thick neck and legs*. Head and neck *pale grey* (male has long "moustaches" of whitish bristles), upper-parts rich buff barred with black, under-parts white with rich chestnut breast; female less stout, lacking breast-band. In flight wings look *chiefly white*, with widely spread black tips; neck and legs are extended;

wing-beats slow, regular, but powerful. Walks sedately, with head erect. Exceptionally shy. Usually in small flocks, females predominating; in breeding season males remain in flocks. Distinguished from other bustards by much larger size and lack of black on neck.

Voice: In breeding season has occasional gruff bark.

Habitat: Frequents and breeds on open treeless plains, grassy steppes, extensive fields of corn, maize, etc. Map below.

LITTLE BUSTARD *Otis tetrax* page 81

Du – Kleine trap   Fr – Outarde canepetière
Ge – Zwergtrappe   Sw – Småtrapp

Identification: 17″. Less than half size of Great Bustard. Extreme shyness makes observation difficult. Male in breeding plumage distinguished by *bold black and white neck*; upper-parts and crown finely vermiculated sandy-buff, with blue-grey face; under-parts white. Female is paler above, streaked and barred with black, buffish-white below, with barred breast and flanks, no distinctive markings on face or neck. Behaviour as Great Bustard, but runs readily and hides by crouching flat. Flight very swift, recalling grouse; male has rapid whistling wing-beats, *Looks chiefly white in flight*, with bold black wing-tips; flies much higher than Great Bustard. Usually in small flocks, but large groups occur in autumn. See also Houbara.

Voice: A short "*dahg*," or "*kiak*," and a snorting "*ptrrr*," or "*prett*", which carries considerable distance.

Habitat: Grassy plains, large fields of corn, clover and other crops. Map p. 118.

HOUBARA BUSTARD *Chlamydotis undulata* page 81

Du – Kraagtrap   Fr – Outarde houbara
Ge – Kragentrappe   Sw – Kragtrapp

Identification: 25″. Size between Great and Little Bustards, in shape resembling female turkey. Neck and rufous tail noticeably long. Both sexes distinguished at all seasons by *tufts of long black and white feathers*

← Coot
*Partial migrant.
Sometimes breeds
Iceland*

Great
Bustard →
*Mainly resident,
extending range in
winter. Vagrant
north to Brit. Is.;
Sweden, Finland,
south to Greece*

WADERS (See also Plate 27)

● **SNIPE**   page 143
Long straight bill; striped crown and mantle.

○ **GREAT SNIPE**   144
Larger but stouter-billed; white on tail-corners.

● **JACK SNIPE**   144
Smaller than Snipe; bill shorter; centre crown dark;
pointed tail lacks white.

● **WOODCOCK**   142
Stout; long bill; barred crown; barred under-parts.

○ **LONG-BILLED DOWITCHER**   134
Snipe-like bill; long white rump; short legs.
Winter: Grey. *Summer:* Rusty.

● **GREEN SANDPIPER**   138
Dark above, with square white rump; dark legs.

● **WOOD SANDPIPER**   138
Paler and browner than Green Sandpiper; legs paler,
yellowish at times; slender form.

△ **MARSH SANDPIPER**   136
Like tiny, delicate Greenshank, with very long legs,
needle-like bill. White up back extends to shoulders.

○ **LESSER YELLOWLEGS**   137
Long, bright yellow legs; white rump; fine bill.

● **RUFF**   131
Male (spring): Extraordinary ruff; very variable.
Male (autumn): Brownish "scaly" upper-parts.
Female (Reeve): Like small autumn male.

● **GREENSHANK**   136
Greenish legs; white rump and back; pale head.

● **REDSHANK**   136
Long orange-red legs; reddish base of bill.

● **SPOTTED REDSHANK**   135
Adult (summer): Blackish; dark red legs.
Adult (winter): Much paler than Redshank; white up
back; longer bill.

SNIPE

GREAT SNIPE

JACK SNIPE

Summer

Winter

LONG-BILLED DOWITCHER

WOODCOCK

GREEN SANDPIPER

WOOD SANDPIPER

♂ Summer

♂ Autumn

RUFF

♂

MARSH SANDPIPER

LESSER YELLOWLEGS

♀ (Reeve)

GREENSHANK

REDSHANK

Summer

Winter

SPOTTED REDSHANK

GREY PHALAROPE — Winter

COMMON SANDPIPER

PURPLE SANDPIPER — Winter

RED-NECKED PHALAROPE — Winter

DUNLIN — Winter

CURLEW SANDPIPER — Autumn

KNOT — Winter

SANDERLING — Winter

TEREK SANDPIPER

KNOT — Summer

PECTORAL SANDPIPER

BAIRD'S — Summer

WHITE-RUMPED — Winter

BUFF-BREASTED

LITTLE STINT — Summer — Autumn

TEMMINCK'S STINT — Summer — Winter

BROAD-BILLED SANDPIPER

Plate 34 117

SMALL WADERS (See also Plate 28)

● **COMMON SANDPIPER** page 139
Smudge on sides of breast; "bobs" tail.

● **GREY PHALAROPE** 146
Winter: Eye-patch; less fine bill; grey back.

● **RED-NECKED PHALAROPE** 147
Winter: Eye-patch; needle-like bill; striped back.

● **DUNLIN** 129
Winter: Slightly curved bill; streaky breast and flanks.

● **PURPLE SANDPIPER** 128
Portly; slaty; yellow legs and base to bill.

● **SANDERLING** 130
Winter: Whitish; black "shoulders"; short bill.
Summer: Rusty above and on breast; white belly.

● **KNOT** 130
Winter: Stout, grey; light feather edgings; short legs.
Summer: Rufous under-parts; relatively short bill.

● **CURLEW SANDPIPER** 129
Autumn: Grey; decurved bill; white rump.

△ **TEREK SANDPIPER** 139
Upturned bill; short yellow legs; "bobs" tail.

● **PECTORAL SANDPIPER** 128
Sharp division on breast; striped back; dark cap.

△ **BAIRD'S SANDPIPER** 316
Buffish breast; scaly back; small bill; black legs.

○ **BUFF-BREASTED SANDPIPER** 131
Under-parts rich buff; small head; yellow legs.

○ **WHITE-RUMPED SANDPIPER** 128
Winter: Differs from Curlew Sandpiper by shorter
legs, shorter straight bill, smaller white rump.

● **LITTLE STINT** 127
Summer: Tiny; rusty; legs black; very small bill.
Autumn: Light "V's" on back; whitish breast.

● **TEMMINCK'S STINT** 127
Greyer than Little; legs olive or yellowish; no "V's."

○ **BROAD-BILLED SANDPIPER** 134
Kinked, broad-based bill; double eye-stripes; short
legs.

drooping down each side of neck, which can be displayed conspicuously or partly hidden; short black and white crest; large eyes. Upper-parts pale vermiculated sandy-buff, under-parts white, with greyish throat. In flight shows uniform sandy mantle and wing-coverts, black flight-feathers with bold white patch near base of primaries, but much less white than Great or Little Bustards. Wing-beats slow; wings long and comparatively narrow.

Habitat and Range: Bare stony or sandy steppes, or semi-desert. Also occurs in corn and other crops. Vagrant to Britain and most of Continental Europe.

OYSTERCATCHERS: Haematopodidae

OYSTERCATCHER   *Haematopus ostralegus*   pages 92, 101
     Du – Scholekster   Fr – Huitrier pie
     Ge – Austernfischer   Sw – Strandskata

Identification: 17″. A large *pied* shore-bird with a *long orange-red bill and stout pink legs*. Has black head, breast and upper-parts contrasting with pure white under-parts. Bill flattened laterally, often slightly up-tilted. Broad white wing-bar, white rump, black and white tail, conspicuous in flight. Non-breeders have a white band across throat. Very noisy. Flocks rest on islets and sand-bars between tides; feed among rocks and on mud-flats. Flight strong, with shallow wing-beats.

Voice: A loud "*pic, pic, pic.*" Alarm, a strident "*kleep, kleep.*" Song, a long piping trill, beginning slowly, varying in volume and pace.

Habitat: Mainly sea-shores, islands, estuaries. Locally inland on grass. Usually breeds on sea-shores, locally inland by lakes and streams in northern Britain, occasionally far from water. Map below.

← LITTLE
BUSTARD
Part. migrant. Has bred Germ., Hung., Vag. n. to Brit. Is., Scand., Finland

OYSTER-
CATCHER →
Partial migrant. wintering south of dotted line. Vagr. central Europe and Med. Islands

PLOVERS: Charadriidae

Wading birds, more compactly built, thicker-necked and more boldly patterned than sandpipers; bills are shorter and stouter, eyes larger. Distinctive tilting action when feeding. Plumage patterns in flight, and call-notes, are important in identification. Many species summer on coasts south of breeding range. Sexes usually similar. Ground nesting.

RINGED PLOVER *Charadrius hiaticula*   pages 93, 100
    Du – Bontbekplevier   Fr – Grand Gravelot
    Ge – Sandregenpfeifer   Sw – Större strandpipare
Identification: 7½". A plump, lively little shore-bird, with a *broad black band* across its white breast and *orange legs* (which often look black when muddy). Behaviour active, running with brief pauses, *tilting* distinctively to pick up food. Upper-parts hair-brown with white collar, black mark through eyes and *prominent white forehead*. Bill orange with black tip. White wing-bar conspicuous in flight. Immature scaly-brown above, without black on head; blackish-brown breast-band often incomplete (resembling Kentish); legs yellowish; tail white-tipped. Flight rapid, with regular wing-beats.
Voice: A melodious "*too-li,*" or "*coo-eep.*" Song begins slowly, becoming a trilling repetition of the phrase "*quitu-weeoo.*"
Habitat: Sandy and muddy shores, visiting inland waters, etc., on migration. Breeds on beaches, among dunes, salt marshes, locally inland on tundra, sandy ground and dry stream-beds. Map below.

LITTLE RINGED PLOVER *Charadrius dubius*   pages 93, 100
    Du – Kleine plevier   Fr – Petit Gravelot
    Ge – Flussregenpfeifer   Sw – Mindre strandpipare
Identification: 6". Resembles small Ringed Plover, but distinguished by *lack of white wing-bar*, flesh-coloured or yellowish legs (not orange,

← Ringed
    Plover
*Partial migrant.
Has bred Czech.
May winter S.
France*

Little Ringed
    Plover →
*Summer visitor.
Vagrant Ireland,
Scotland*

151   152

but colour not reliable when muddy), *different voice* and usually different habitat; also by white line *above* black forehead-band. At short range *yellow eye-ring* can be seen. Juvenile often has incomplete brown gorget, giving resemblance to Kentish Plover, but is distinguished by pale flesh legs and lack of wing-bar.

Voice: A high, piping "*tee-u*". Trilling song rather like Ringed Plover's, but lacks its richness, chiefly repetition of "*tree-a, tree-a*."

Habitat: Freshwater localities, particularly flooded gravel pits and gravelly river islands; on coasts in winter. Breeds on gravel or sand shores of inland waters, locally on coasts. Map p. 119.

KENTISH PLOVER *Charadrius alexandrinus* pages 93, 100

Du – Strandplevier Fr – Gravelot à collier interrompu
Ge – Seeregenpfeifer Sw – Swartbent strandpipare
N.Am – Snowy Plover

Identification: 6¼″. Distinguished from Ringed and Little Ringed Plovers by paler upper-parts, less plump form, *blackish bill and legs*, narrower dark patch through eye and *small dark patch* each side of upper-breast (instead of complete black band). Narrower white wing-bar recalls Ringed Plover, but upper-parts are paler and dark tail shows more conspicuous white at sides. Male has narrow white supercilium, blackish patch on front of *rufous* crown. Female is paler, with brownish instead of black patches on sides of breast and lacks black on crown. Juvenile can be confused with young Ringed and Little Ringed, which have incomplete breast-bands and yellowish or flesh-coloured, not black, legs. Leg-action much faster when running than Ringed.

Voice: A soft "*wit-tit-tit*," a fluty "*poo-eet*," or "*po-it*." Alarm, "*kittup*." Song, a long trill, beginning slowly and accelerating.

Habitat: Mainly coastal. Frequents and nests on shingle, or mixed sand and mud beaches, dry mud-flats. Map p. 121.

GREATER SAND PLOVER *Charadrius leschenaultii*

page 285

Du – Woestijnplevier Fr – Gravelot mongol
Ge – Wüstenregenpfeifer Sw – Ökenpipare

Identification: 8½″. Dun-brown above, white below, with *heavy tern-like black bill* and dark olive legs. Male in breeding plumage has *broad rusty breast-band, black ear-coverts and narrow black band across white forehead*; fore-crown and nape pale cinnamon (no white neck-ring). Female has paler, more diffuse breast-band and grey in place of black on head. In winter sexes similar, but male retains faint traces of black on head and shows broad white supercilium. Immature has pale fringes to feathers of upper-parts and rusty fringes on breast.

Voice: A musical, whistling "*peeph*." Less vocal than most plovers.

Habitat and Range: Frequents sandy coasts and coastal mud-flats. Vagrant from Central and W. Asia, to Sweden, Germany, Greece.

DOTTEREL   *Eudromias morinellus*   pages 93, 100
    Du – Morinelplevier   Fr – Pluvier guignard
    Ge – Mornellregenpfeifer   Sw – Fjällpipare

Identification: 8½″. Male smaller. Very tame. Distinguished by *white band* between brown breast and *orange-chestnut under-parts*, and blackish crown with very broad *white eye-stripes*, joining in distinctive "V" on nape. Belly black. Winter adults and juveniles are paler, with indistinct markings and ash-brown breasts. In overhead flight the white throat, pectoral band and tail-coverts contrast sharply with dark breast and black belly; in winter, markings are less clear, but the eye-stripes and pectoral band are always diagnostic though sometimes difficult to see. Has "chunky," short-tailed appearance in flight. Legs yellowish.

Voice: A repeated, soft *"titi-ri-titi-ri,"* becoming a rapid trill.

Habitat: Stony heights and tundra; on migration on lowland heaths, coastal fields. Breeds on bare high ground. Map below.

GOLDEN PLOVER   *Pluvialis apricaria*   pages 93, 100
    Du – Goudplevier   Fr – Pluvier doré
    Ge – Goldregenpfeifer   Sw – Ljungpipare

Identification: 11″. Distinguished in all plumages by dark upper-parts *richly spotted with gold.* Northern birds in summer usually have *jet-black face and under-parts*, cleanly divided by broad white stripe from forehead, down neck (almost meeting at breast) and down sides to flanks. Southern birds are much less clean-cut, with partly obscured black face and under-parts and the white *blurred and yellowish.* In winter, face and under-parts whitish, mottled golden-brown on breast. No wing-bar, but tail and rump are *uniform with rest of upper-parts*, and centre and base of under-surfaces of wings are *white.* Can be confused in juvenile plumage with Grey.

Voice: Call-note (usually in flight) a clear liquid *"tlui"*; alarm, a melancholy *"tlu-i."* Song, in display flight, a varied rippling trill, embodying repeated phrases *"toori," "tirr-peeoo,"* etc.

Habitat: Hilly and lowland moors, and, in winter, also fields, sea-shores and estuaries; nests among heather. Map p. 122.

← Kentish
   Plover
*Partial migrant.
Vagrant British
Isles, Estonia*

Dotterel →
*Migrant. Formerly
bred N. England.
Vagrant Ireland,
Faeroes*

LESSER GOLDEN PLOVER *Pluvialis dominica*

Du – Aziatische Goudplevier   Fr – Pluvier doré asiatique
Ge – Sibirischer Goldregenpfeifer   Sw – Arktisk Ljungpipare

Identification: 10″. Smaller and more slightly built than Golden, with *longer legs*, relatively larger head and narrower wings extending well beyond tail when closed. Distinguished in all plumages by *dusky-buff under wings and grey axillaries* (Golden has white under wings). Adult in summer shows more black on upper- and under-parts, flanks usually lacking white borders. Immature recalls Dotterel of same age; has whiter face and supercilium and buffer under-parts than immature Golden.

Voice: A quiet, musical *"pu,"* an emphatic *"klee-eet"* and other multi-syllabic cries recalling Golden.

Habitat and Range: On migration as Golden. Breeds on Arctic tundra. Vagrant to Britain and western Europe.

GREY PLOVER *Pluvialis squatarola*   pages 93, 100

Du – Zilverplevier   Fr – Pluvier argenté
Ge – Kiebitzregenpfeifer   Sw – Kustpipare
N.Am – Black-bellied Plover

Identification: 11″. In breeding plumage, *black below and whitish above.* Resembles no other wader except Golden Plover, but distinguished in any plumage by heavier build and bill, larger eyes, *conspicuous black axillaries* ("wing-pits") contrasting with whitish under-surfaces of wings and by *whitish wing-bar, rump and tail.* Adults in summer have upper-parts spangled with *whitish* (not gold); in winter, upper-parts are more uniform brownish-grey, under-parts look whiter than Golden Plover's; immature is yellowish, can be confused with Golden Plover. Has dejected, hunched appearance.

Voice: Call-note a plaintive, *trisyllabic*, slurred whistle *"tlee-u-ee."*

Habitat: Chiefly coastal mud-flats, sandy beaches and shores. Breeds on Arctic tundra. Map below.

← GOLDEN
PLOVER
*Partial migrant.
Formerly bred
Holland*

GREY PLOVER →
*Winter vis. from
n. Non-breeders
summer on coasts.
Also inland on
passage. Vagrant
to Iceland*

KILLDEER   *Charadrius vociferus*   page 285
    Du – Killdeerplevier   Fr – Gravelot à double collier
    Ge – Keilschwanzregenpfeifer Sw – Skrikstrandpipare
Identification: 10″. Superficially resembles Ringed Plover, but is very
much larger and has *two* black breast-bands. Long rufous tail has
black sub-terminal band with white tips. In flight shows a *golden-
rufous rump, long, wedge-shaped tail* and strong white wing-bars. Bill
slender and black; legs pale flesh.
Voice: Usually noisy; a loud, insistent and repeated "*kill-dee*," or
"*kill-deea*"; also a plaintive "*dee-ee*," with rising inflection.
Habitat and Range: Usually seen on ploughed fields and pastures, on
which it also breeds (like an American counterpart of the Lapwing);
in winter also frequents sea-shore. Vagrant from N. America to
Britain, Ireland, France, Faeroes, Iceland.

SOCIABLE PLOVER   *Vanellus gregarius*   page 285
    Du – Steppenkievit   Fr – Pluvier sociable
    Ge – Steppenkiebitz   Sw – Stäppvipa
Identification: 11½″. A rather large, long-legged plover. Looks pinkish-
grey in distance, but at close range *black crown contrasts with broad
white supercilia joining in "V" at nape*. In flight the *white secondaries,
black primaries and white tail with broad black sub-terminal band* are
conspicuous. In summer, cheeks and lower throat warm buff, breast
and back pinkish-grey, belly shading to *dark chestnut, contrasting with
white under-tail coverts* in flight. In winter, head and belly markings
are less distinct and breast has some dark streaking. Immature looks
like brownish winter adult, but under-parts buffish with stronger
streaking. Flight recalls Lapwing, but wings are narrower and less
rounded.
Voice: In winter a shrill, short whistle and a harsh rasping "*etch-etch-
etch*," sometimes becoming a long chatter.
Habitat and Range: Open sandy or grassy plains, wastelands near
upland cultivation; also occurs near coasts. Breeds in steppe. Vagrant
from Asia across Central and S. Europe to Spain, Britain, Ireland
Denmark, Finland.

LAPWING   *Vanellus vanellus*   pages 93, 100
    Du – Kievit   Fr – Vanneau huppé
    Ge – Kiebitz   Sw – Tofsvipa
Identification: 12″. Typical of farming country. A large iridescent
greenish-black and white plover, distinguished by a *long wispy crest* and
black breast contrasting with pure white under-parts and cheeks; also
by distinctive voice and, in flight, by *broad, very rounded wings*. Tail
white, with broad black terminal band and chestnut under tail-coverts.
Flight often wildly erratic, with slow, "flapping" wing-beats and headlong plunges during acrobatic display-flight. Gregarious, often in
huge, straggling flocks in winter.

SKUAS

Skuas are dark, hawk-like sea-birds which pursue other birds in a piratical manner. All show a white flash on the wing. Adults of the three smaller species have elongated central tail feathers (see drawing). Arctic and Pomarine occur in light, intermediate and dark phases; the tail points are sometimes broken off. Immatures have stubbier central tail feathers and are difficult to separate.

● **GREAT SKUA** page 151
Dark, heavily-built; large wing-patches; blunt tail.

● **ARCTIC SKUA** 152
Pointed central tail-feathers.

● **POMARINE SKUA** 152
Blunt (and partially twisted) central tail-feathers; broad wing-bases; scalloped flanks and under wings.

○ **LONG-TAILED SKUA** 153
Very long, flexible, pointed central tail-feathers; narrow wings; complete white collar.

Arctic

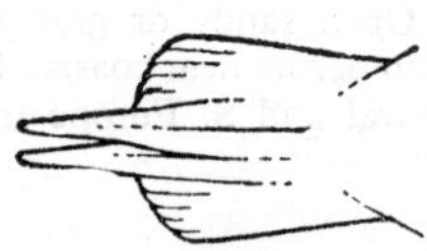

Long-tailed

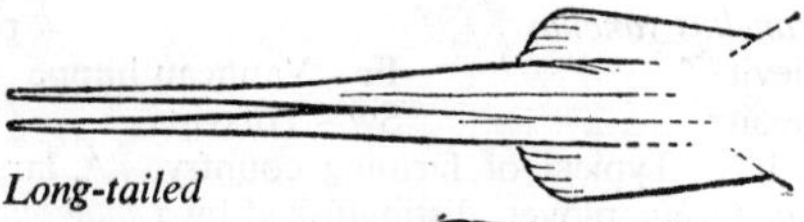

Pomarine

Tails of Skuas (Adults)

GREAT
SKUA

ARCTIC
SKUA
Light phase

ARCTIC SKUA
Dark phase

Intermediate
phase

ARCTIC
SKUA
Juvenile

POMARINE SKUA
Dark phase

POMARINE SKUA
Light phase

LONG-TAILED
SKUA

Winter   BLACK GUILLEMOT   Summer

Immature

Winter   PUFFIN   Summer

Winter   LITTLE AUK   Summer

Immature

Winter   RAZORBILL   Summer

Winter   BRÜNNICH'S GUILLEMOT   Summer

"Bridled" form

Winter   GUILLEMOT   Summer

Plate 36   125

AUKS

Auks are bustling black and white sea-birds with stubby necks. They have a whirring flight and a straddle-legged look when about to land.

● **BLACK GUILLEMOT**   page 174
  Winter: Mottled off-white body; large white patches.
  Summer: Black body; pointed bill; large white wing patches.

● **PUFFIN**   174
  Winter: Triangular bill; dusky cheeks.
  Immature: Smaller bill; dusky cheeks.
  Summer: Triangular, coloured bill; whitish cheeks.

● **LITTLE AUK**   172
  Starling size; stubby bill; "neck-less" form.

● **RAZORBILL**   173
  Adult: Heavy head; deep bill with white mark.
  Immature: Smaller bill, with curved ridge.

△ **BRÜNNICH'S GUILLEMOT**   173
  Thicker bill than Guillemot.
  Winter: Dark cap to below eye.
  Summer: Light mark on gape.

● **GUILLEMOT**   173
  Winter: Black line on white cheek.
  Summer: Slender bill; dark head.
  "Bridled" form: White eye-ring and white line.

| PUFFIN | RAZORBILL | GUILLEMOT | BLACK GUILLEMOT |

Voice: A loud, nasal *"peese-weet,"* or a longer *"pee-r-weet,"* with variants.

Habitat: Farmlands, sewage farms, marshes and mud-flats. Breeds on arable land, moors, marshes, etc. Map below.

SPUR-WINGED PLOVER   *Vanellus spinosus*   page 285

Du – Sporenkievit   Fr – Vanneau éperonné
Ge – Spornkiebitz   Sw – Sporrvipa

Identification: 10½″. Very striking *black and white* appearance. Slightly crested, jet-black crown, *black centre of throat*, breast and under-parts. Cheeks, neck and under tail-coverts white. Upper-parts dun brown with drooping dark-edged scapulars. Wings and tail strongly patterned black and white, with small spur on bend of wing. Behaviour resembles Lapwing's.

Voice: Usual note, a noisy *"zac-zac-zac."*

Habitat and Range: Open ground and marshes, often saline. A North African and Asiatic species, breeding in N.E. Greece, probably Bulgaria. Vagrant to Malta.

TURNSTONE   *Arenaria interpres*   pages 93, 100

Du – Steenloper   Fr – Tournepierre à collier
Ge – Steinwälzer   Sw – Roskarl

Identification: 9″. A robust shore bird with *"tortoiseshell"* plumage. Short *orange* legs and a stout, pointed, black bill. In summer, upper-parts are rich chestnut and black, head black and white, under-parts white with *broad dark breast-band*. In winter, "tortoiseshell" replaced by dusky brown, with white throat. See Plate 30 for unique flight-pattern. Turns over stones and shells when seeking food.

Voice: A quick, staccato *"tuk-a-tuk"* and a long rapid trill.

Habitat: Winters along rocky or pebbly coasts. Usually breeds on exposed rocky ground on coastal islands, but in Arctic also occasionally on river islands. Map below.

← LAPWING
Partial migrant

TURNSTONE →
Migrant. Non-breeders summer in winter-range Passage through most of Europe. May winter Greece

SANDPIPERS, GODWITS, CURLEWS, SNIPE: Scolopacidae

Legs longish, or very long; wings usually pointed and angular; bills long and slender; plumages often differ in summer and winter. Wing-bars, rump and tail patterns important diagnostically. Many species summer on coasts south of breeding range, some occurring in large flocks. Sexes similar. Usually ground nesting.

LITTLE STINT *Calidris minuta*   pages 85, 117
　　　Du – Kleine strandloper　　　Fr – Bécasseau minute
　　　Ge – Zwergstrandläufer　　　Sw – Småsnäppa
Identification: 5¼". Smallest common wader. Distinguished from Dunlin by *straight short bill* and smaller, neater appearance. Adult in summer has rufous upper-parts and crown, rufous-tinged and streaked breast, white supercilium and belly. In winter has cold grey upper-parts and whiter neck and breast. Immature like pale summer adult with cleaner breast and two distinctive pale "V's" on back. In flight shows narrow wing-bar and white *sides* to rump, like Dunlin. See also Temminck's, summer Sanderling, and Semi-Palmated (Accidentals p. 316).
Voice: A sharp "*tit*," or "*tirri-tit-tit*." Song, a long undulating trill.
Habitat: On passage, much as Dunlin. Breeds in coastal marshes and on tundra, among willow scrub, etc. Map below.

TEMMINCK'S STINT *Calidris temminckii*   pages 85, 117
　　　Du – Temminck's strandloper　　Fr – Bécasseau de Temminck
　　　Ge – Temminckstrandläufer　　Sw – Mosnäppa

← LITTLE STINT
Migrant. Passage most Europe. Few winter north to Britain. Vagrant Faeroes

TEMMINCK'S STINT →
Migrant. Has bred England, Scotland. Passage most Eur. Vagrant Ireland

164

165

Identification: 5½″. Distinguished from similar Little Stint by *more uniform, grever appearance* above and on breast, different voice and different behaviour. In flight, shows an inconspicuous white wing-bar and white on outer tail-feathers (Little Stint shows grey). At short range *pale greenish or brownish legs* are also diagnostic (Little Stint's are black). When flushed, "towers" like Snipe. See also Common Sandpiper.

Voice: A short trilling *"tirrr"* and a clear, prolonged tittering, in display flight and from ground.

Habitat: Seldom on sea-shore. On passage frequents wet marshes, lakes with vegetation, occasionally saltings and estuaries. Breeds among low vegetation on tundra, shores and islets. Map p. 127.

WHITE-RUMPED SANDPIPER *Calidris fuscicollis* page 117
Du - Bonaparte's strandloper   Fr - Bécasseau de Bonaparte
Ge - Weissbürzelstrandläufer   Sw - Piplärksnäppa

Identification: 7″. A small, streaked sandpiper, more slender than Dunlin, with a *neat curved white patch on upper tail-coverts* contrasting with dark tail. Upper-parts rufous in spring with dark feather-centres; greyer in autumn. Immature resembles autumn adult, but has rufous and whitish feather-margins. In flight shows thin, obscure whitish wing-bar. Distinguished from Curlew Sandpiper by smaller size, shorter, *straight* bill and smaller white rump-patch.

Voice: A thin, mouse-like *"jeet."*

Habitat and Range: Beaches, mud-flats. A vagrant from North America to British Isles, Holland.

PECTORAL SANDPIPER *Calidris melanotos* pages 85, 117
Du - Gestreepte strandloper   Fr - Bécasseau tacheté
Ge - Graubruststrandläufer   Sw - Tuvsnäppa

Identification: 7½″. A little larger than Dunlin, smaller than Knot. Crown, neck and upper-parts streaked black and rusty brown, with buff snipe-like *stripes down back.* Rich brown cap and ear-coverts contrast with long, creamy supercilium and chin. Neck and breast closely streaked, *ending abruptly against pure white of lower breast.* When alert, neck looks longer than in most similar shore-birds (more like small Reeve). *Legs ochre.* Flight erratic when flushed, showing virtually no wing-bar and very dark centre tail-feathers. See also Sharp-tailed and Baird's Sandpipers (Accidentals, p. 316).

Voice: A reedy *"trrip, trrip."*

Habitat and Range: Occurs on passage on grassy mud-flats and marshes, occasionally on sea-shores. Autumn visitor from N. America to Britain, Ireland. Vagrant to Iceland, Norway, Sweden, France.

PURPLE SANDPIPER *Calidris maritima* pages 85, 117
Du - Paarse strandloper   Fr - Bécasseau violet
Ge - Meerstrandläufer   Sw - Skärsnäppa

Identification: 8¼″. Size between Dunlin and Knot. Distinguished by rock-haunting habits, stocky build and, in winter, by *very dark head, breast and upper-parts*, contrasting with white belly and scolloped flanks; in summer upper-parts look paler, light rufous emarginations giving patterned effect. Has white throat and "spectacles." Tame behaviour usually permits sight of *short yellow legs and yellow base to bill.* Shows narrow white wing-bar and secondary edges. Feeds among rocks.

Voice: When flushed, a short *"tritt, tritt,"* or a piping *"weet-wit."*

Habitat: In winter frequents rocky coasts and off-shore islets. Breeds on hill-sides in tundra. Map below.

DUNLIN *Calidris alpina*   pages 85, 100, 117
    Du – Bonte strandloper   Fr – Bécasseau variable
    Ge – Alpenstrandläufer   Sw – Kärrsnäppa
              N.Am – Red-backed Sandpiper

Identification: 7″. Commonest British shore-bird. Distinguished in summer by *large black patch on lower breast*; upper-parts and crown *chestnut*, streaked black; upper breast white, finely streaked. Bill fairly long, slightly down-curved at tip. In winter, streaked brownish-grey above, white below, with finely streaked greyish breast and flanks. White wing-bar and white *sides* of rump and tail fairly conspicuous in flight. (Sanderling in winter is larger, with whiter plumage and a brighter wing-bar; Curlew Sandpiper in winter, though more graceful, with longer legs and whiter under-parts, is best distinguished by its conspicuous white rump.) Feeding attitude is "hunched up."

Voice: A short, high, nasal *"tree."* Song, a purring trill.

Habitat: Sea-shores, estuaries, also inland waters, sewage-farms, etc. Breeds near water on high moors, bogs, salt marshes. Map below.

CURLEW SANDPIPER *Calidris ferruginea*   pages 58, 100, 117
    Du – Krombekstrandloper   Fr – Bécasseau cocorli
    Ge – Sichelstrandläufer   Sw – Spovsnäppa

← PURPLE
  SANDPIPER
Part. migrant. Non-breeders south to Britain. Vagrant to Austria, Switz., Italy, Portugal

DUNLIN →
Part. migr. Passage all Europe. Non-br. summer in winter-range. Has bred Holland

168   169

Identification: 7½″. In breeding plumage mainly brick-red, resembling much larger Knot; crown and upper-parts richly marked black and chestnut; sides of head, neck and under-parts *bright brick-red* with some mottling; white rump partly obscured by blackish tips. In winter, looks very similar to Dunlin, with which it associates; best distinguished by *white rump*, which is conspicuous in flight (Dunlin's has dark centre); also by longer legs and neck, more elegant, upright carriage, clearer breast (washed rosy-buff in immature), brighter supercilium, different voice and *more slender, longer, evenly down-curving bill*. Shape of bill is not always diagnostic, as Dunlin's is sometimes similar.
Voice: A very distinctive, liquid *"chirrip."*
Habitat and Range: On passage, as Dunlin. Breeds in E. Arctic Asia. Non-breeders summer in Italy. On passage throughout Europe; in winter occasionally N. to British Isles.

KNOT *Calidris canutus* pages 85, 117
    Du – Kanoetstrandloper   Fr – Bécasseau maubèche
    Ge – Knutt   Sw : Kustsnäppa
Identification: 10″. *Noticeably stocky and short in neck, bill and legs.* In summer, upper-parts strongly mottled chestnut and black; head and under-parts *russet* (Curlew Sandpiper is similar in coloration, but is much smaller, longer in leg and has longer, curved bill). In winter is nondescript "scaly" ash-grey above, whitish below. Identified in flight by large size, *uniform pale rump and tail* and pale wing-bar. (Dunlin and Sanderling in flight have blackish centre to their rumps and sharper wing-bars, and are much smaller.) Often in *densely packed flocks*.
Voice: A low *"nut"*; flight-call a whistling *"twit-wit."*
Habitat: Frequents sandy and muddy sea-shores, occasionally on inland waters. Breeds on high Arctic barrens. Map p. 131.

SANDERLING *Calidris alba* pages 85, 117
    Du – Drieteenstrandloper   Fr – Bécasseau sanderling
    Ge – Sanderling   Sw – Sandlöpare
Identification: 8″. A plump, small, extremely active, whitish bird which races after the retreating waves like a clockwork toy. In flight *long white stripe on dark wing* contrasts more boldly than in other small shore-birds. Dark tail has white sides. In summer, upper-parts, head and breast chestnut, speckled blackish, contrasting with pure white belly. (See also Little Stint and Baird's Sandpiper.) In winter, is *whitest of the small waders*; head and under-parts white; upper-parts pale grey with dark "shoulder-patch"; distinguished from much slimmer winter phalaropes by lack of dark eye-patch and different behaviour. Bill and legs black. Distinguished in winter from darker Dunlin by smaller size, *much bolder wing-bar and stouter, straight bill*; in summer also by *paler upper-parts and lack of black patch on belly*. Immature chequered black and white above, with pinkish-buff head and breast.
Voice: A short *"twick,"* or *"quit."*

Habitat: Winters on sandy beaches; a few occur inland on passage.
Breeds on stony Arctic tundra. Map below.

RUFF *Philomachus pugnax*   pages 85, 116
 Du – Kemphaan   Fr – Chevalier combattant
 Ge – Kampfläufer   Sw – Brushane

Identification: 11¼″; female 9″. Male unmistakable in breeding
plumage, with *enormous erectile ruff and ear-tufts* in various combina-
tions of black, white, purple, chestnut, buff, giving thick-necked
appearance in flight. Female (Reeve) and male in winter have bold
"scaly" dark and sandy upper-parts, buff breast, no ruff or ear-tufts.
Adults in early or late breeding plumage are brown above, with copious
dark mottling around breast, contrasting sharply with pale chin and
white belly. In winter resembles Redshank, but distinguished by shorter
bill, "scaly" plumage, *dark tail with conspicuous oval white patch each
side* (occasionally joined), lack of white on secondaries and more erect
stance. Legs vary from grey-brown to green or orange. Juvenile resembles Reeve, but with more richly marked upper-parts and pinkish-
buff breast; can be very puzzling.
Voice: A low "*chut-ut*"; has occasional deep guttural gobbling note, at
display mounds, where sexually promiscuous.
Habitat: In winter and on passage on inland marshes, lake shores,
occasionally estuaries. Breeds on northern tundra; in southern range
in water meadows and marshes. Map p. 134.

BUFF-BREASTED SANDPIPER *Tryngites subruficollis* page 117
 Du – Blonde strandloper   Fr – Bécasseau rousset
 Ge – Grasläufer   Sw – Prärielöpare

Identification: 8″. Recalls immature Ruff, but smaller. Has distinctive
*small round head on long neck, pale eye-ring, short bill and chrome-
yellow legs.* Upper-parts like Ruff, but lacks black or white markings
above tail; no wing-bar. Face and under-parts rich clear buff, often

← KNOT
*Winter vis. Nonbr.
summer W. Europe.
Passage coasts
most Europe ex-
cept S.E.*

SANDERLING →
*Winter vis. Non-
breeders often
summer coasts W.
Europe. Passage
most Europe*

171
172

GULLS (ADULT)

IN IDENTIFYING GULLS, look for wing-patterns and colour of legs.

● **GREAT BLACK-BACKED GULL** page 161
Large size; black back and wings; flesh legs.

● **LESSER BLACK-BACKED GULL** 159
Size of Herring Gull; legs usually yellow or orange.
Northern form: Darker (blackish back).
Southern form: Paler (dark grey).

● **GLAUCOUS GULL** 160
Size of Great Black-backed Gull; white primaries;
heavy head and bill.

◉ **ICELAND GULL** 160
Size of Herring, but head and bill smaller; white
primaries.

○ **IVORY GULL** 166
Size of Kittiwake; all white; black legs.

● **HERRING GULL** 159
Grey back and wings; black on wing-tips; flesh legs.

● **COMMON GULL** 161
Smaller than Herring; greenish-yellow bill and legs.

● **KITTIWAKE** 162
Solid black "dipped in ink" wing-tips; black legs.

AUDOUIN'S GULL 162
Heavy red bill with black band; legs olive; primaries
graded from grey bases to black tips.

● **LITTLE GULL*** 155
Rounded wings are blackish below.

● **SABINE'S GULL*** 162
Black outer primaries; white triangle; forked tail.

● **BLACK-HEADED GULL*** 155
Long wedge of white on primaries; red bill and legs.

◉ **MEDITERRANEAN GULL*** 154
White primaries; extensive black hood.

△ **SLENDER-BILLED GULL** 158
Wings as Black-headed, but long bill drooping.
* *Adults in winter lose the black heads, which then resemble immatures*
(Plate 38).

GLAUCOUS

GREAT
BLACK-BACKED

ICELAND

hern
m

LESSER
BLACK-BACKED

IVORY

HERRING

KITTIWAKE

COMMON

SABINE'S

below

above
LITTLE

OUIN'S

above

ow

ACK-HEADED

MEDITERRANEAN

SLENDER-BILLED

GREAT
BLACK-BACKED

GLAUCO
First win

LESSER
BLACK-BACKED

Second winter

GLAUCO
Second wi

HERRING

First winter

HERRING

Second wint

COMMON

KITTIWAKE

BLACK-HEADED

SABINE'S

MEDITERRANEAN

LITTLE

Plate 38 133

GULLS (IMMATURE)

● **GREAT BLACK-BACKED GULL** page 161
Large size; more contrast between chequered back and under-parts than in young Herring Gull.

● **LESSER BLACK-BACKED GULL** 159
Indistinguishable at first from young Herring; but second winter birds have dark saddle (not shown).

● **GLAUCOUS GULL** 160
First winter: Pale coffee, with whitish primaries.
Second winter: Very white throughout.
(Iceland Gull has same sequence of plumages.)

● **HERRING GULL** 159
Streaked muddy-brown in first winter, becoming whiter below and greyer above with age.

● **COMMON GULL** 161
Smaller size; shorter bill. From second-winter Herring by distinct black band on white tail.

● **KITTIWAKE** 162
Dark diagonal band across wing; dark neck-bar.

● **BLACK-HEADED GULL** 155
Dark spots on cheek; white on primaries.

● **SABINE'S GULL** 162
Forked tail and adult's wing-pattern; no dark diagonal bar as in Kittiwake; grey crown, cheeks.

● **MEDITERRANEAN GULL** 154
From Common by narrower tail-band and whitish inner primaries.

● **LITTLE GULL** 155
Wing pattern as in immature Kittiwake; wings more rounded; lacks dark bar on nape.

fading to whitish on belly.   Under-surfaces of wings white, scalloped
with blackish.   Very tame.
Voice: A low, trilled *"pr-r-r-reet"* and a clicking *"tik."*
Habitat and Range: Dry fields with very short grass, in preference to
shores. A vagrant from N. America. Recorded chiefly in British Isles;
also Heligoland, Denmark, Holland, France.

BROAD-BILLED SANDPIPER   *Limicola falcinellus*   page 117
Du – Breedbekstrandloper   Fr – Bécasseau falcinelle
Ge – Sumpfläufer   Sw – Myrsnäppa

Identification: 6½″. Smaller than Dunlin, with disproportionately short
legs and long bill with heavy base and kinked tip. Distinguished in
breeding plumage by *very dark upper-parts*, with bold Jack Snipe-like
creamy streaks on back; *bold double supercilium forking behind eye*,
giving head a distinctive *striped appearance*; at rest, *copper edges* of
secondaries can be conspicuous; streaked breast contrasts with white
under-parts. Looks very dark in flight, with very slight wing-bar. In
winter, is greyish above, with streaked breast, very like Dunlin, but
upper fork of eye-stripe is sometimes indistinct and has blackish patch
at carpal joint on closed wing. Less active than most small shore-
birds.
Voice: A deep, trilling *"chr-r-eek."*
Habitat: On passage, usually in salt-marshes, mud-flats, sewage farms,
less often on sea-shore. Nests in tussocks in wet bogs and morasses.
Map below.

LONG-BILLED DOWITCHER   *Limnodromus scolopaceus*
pages 84, 116

Identification: 11½″. A bulky, short-tailed bird of snipe-like proportions.
In any plumage recognised by the combination of long, *snipe-like bill*
and white back, rump and tail. The white extends *up the back* in a
long point. Might be mistaken for Greenshank, but legs are much

← Ruff
*Bred England, Aus-
tria. Vag. Iceland.
Passage   Faeroes.
Irreg. winter n. to
Holland*

Broad-billed
Sandpiper →
*Summer vis. Pass-
age Denmark,
Italy   eastwards.
Vagr. Brit. Is.,
France*

shorter and wings have white stripe on rear margin. In summer plumage has breast washed with cinnamon-red. Feeds with "sewing-machine" motion, rapidly jabbing its long bill perpendicularly into the mud. Hard to separate from Short-billed *L. griseus* (Accidentals p. 317), but is larger, bill is longer, closed wings do not reach tail-tip and under tail-coverts are *barred* (not spotted). See I.C.T. Nisbet, *British Birds* 1961: p. 343-57.

Voice: Long-billed Dowitcher: a long, shrill *"keeek,"* repeated when flushed in a long rippling trill. Short-billed Dowitcher: a rapid triple *"kut-kut-kut"* recalling Lesser Yellowlegs.

Habitat: Long-billed on passage usually in muddy fresh-water pools with marginal vegetation. Short-billed on open coastal mud-flats.

SPOTTED REDSHANK *Tringa erythropus*   pages 84, 116

   Du – Zwarte ruiter   Fr – Chevalier arlequin
   Ge – Dunkler Wasserläufer   Sw – Svartsnäppa

Identification: 12″. Distinguished in summer from all other waders by *sooty-black plumage*, speckled with white on upper-parts, looking at a distance darker below than above. Long white streak up rump and back; tail barred. In winter, looks more like Redshank, but distinguished by *lack of wing-bar*, longer and thinner bill, longer legs projecting well beyond tail in flight, and *cleaner ash-grey upper-parts* copiously spotted with white. Legs dark red in summer, orange in winter. Voice is very distinctive. When seen with Redshank, Spotted has more upright stance with longer neck and is more active in feeding. See also Greenshank.

Voice: A loud, distinctive *"tchuit,"* and a scolding *"chick-chick-chick."*

Habitat: As Redshank. Breeds in open areas in northern forests. Map below.

← SPOTTED REDSHANK *Migr. Nonbreeders summer south to Italy. At times winters Holland, S. France, Hungary*

REDSHANK → *Partial migrant*

REDSHANK *Tringa totanus*   pages 84, 116

Du – Tureluur   Fr – Chevalier gambette
Ge – Rotschenkel   Sw – Rödbena

Identification: 11″. Distinguished in flight by conspicuous *white hind edges of dark wings and white back and rump*; when perched, by long *orange-red* legs. Bill long, reddish, with black tip. Upper-parts strongly marked with black and grey. Tail barred black and white. Under-parts closely streaked and speckled. Juvenile buffer above, with orange-yellow legs; sometimes confused with Lesser Yellowlegs (which see). Behaviour suspicious and noisy; when uneasy, often "bobs." See also Spotted Redshank.

Voice: When flushed, a volley of high-pitched notes. Usual call a musical, down-slurred *"tleu-hu-hu."* Alarm, an incessant yelping *"teuk."* Song has various repeated musical phrases, notably *"taweeo."*

Habitat: Marshes, moors, saltings, water-meadows, sewage-farms. Winters on estuaries and mud-flats. Nests in tussock. Map p. 135.

MARSH SANDPIPER *Tringa stagnatilis*   page 116

Du – Poelruiter   Fr – Chevalier stagnatile
Ge – Teichwasserläufer   Sw – Dammsnäppa

Identification: 9″. Slender and long-legged, in winter plumage recalling Greenshank, but distinguished, apart from size, by *very fine straight bill, white face and forehead* and proportionately longer, spindly, greenish legs. In summer, feathers on mantle have black centres with buffish edges, giving *boldly spotted effect*. In flight, shows dark and white pattern similar to Greenshank's, but *feet project farther beyond tail*. Voice is quite different. Movements noticeably more graceful than Greenshank's.

Voice: Usual notes (none very loud), *"tew," "teea," "chik," "chik-cleuit,"* etc., and a twittering trill.

Habitat: Seldom on sea-shore. Winters around inland waters and marshes. Breeds (occasionally in small groups) on grassy borders of lakes and on marshy steppes. Map p. 137.

GREENSHANK *Tringa nebularia*   pages 84, 116

Du – Groenpootruiter   Fr – Chevalier aboyeur
Ge – Grünschenkel   Sw – Gluttsnäppa

Identification: 12″. Distinguished from Redshank by whiter face and under-parts, *lack of white on wing*, longer greenish legs, which project well beyond tail in flight. Also by slightly larger size, very slightly up-turned blackish bill and *extensive white up back*. In winter upper-parts are paler and greyer. See also Spotted Redshank, Lesser Yellow-legs and Marsh Sandpiper.

Voice: A ringing *"tew-tew-tew,"* less shrill than Redshank; a repeated scolding *"tyip,"* etc. Song a mellow, repeated *"tew-i."*

Habitat: As Redshank. Breeds on moors or in patches of grass or heath in forest, usually not far from water. Map p. 137.

GREATER YELLOWLEGS *Tringa melanoleuca* page 285
    Du – Grote Geelpootruiter   Fr – Grand Chevalier à pattes jaunes
    Ge – Grosser Gelbschenkel   Sw – Stor Gulbena
Identification: 13-15″. About one third larger than very similar Lesser. Best distinction is *relatively longer, stouter bill* which is usually *slightly up-curved* (like Greenshank's); stouter and longer than Redshank's. Looks much like Greenshank though more spotted above and lacking the long white wedge up lower back (the whitish rump is lightly speckled). Rather stout, rich yellow legs; bill black with olive base. Immature in winter is whiter below and on rump.
Voice: A 3-4 syllable "*heu-heu-heu*," very like Greenshank, but louder, higher and more ringing than Lesser Yellowlegs.
Habitat and Range: Outside breeding season usually on grassy marshes, around pools and on coastal mud-flats. Vagrant from N. America to Britain, Ireland, Iceland.

LESSER YELLOWLEGS *Tringa flavipes* page 116
    Du – Kleine Geelpootruiter   Fr. – Petit Chevalier à pattes jaunes
    Ge – Gelbschenkel   Sw – Gulbena
Identification: 10″. Slightly smaller than Redshank; delicate proportions recall Wood Sandpiper, but is larger, with longer, more slender bill and longer *bright yellow legs*. No white on wings. Square white rump-patch *not extending up back* distinguishes it from Redshank and Greenshank. White supercilia meet on forehead. Greater Yellowlegs is larger, with longer, more up-curved bill.
Voice: A soft whistle of one, two or occasionally three notes, "*cu,*" or "*cu-cu.*"
Habitat and Range: Frequents mud-flats, marshes, margins. A vagrant from North America, chiefly to British Isles; recorded Holland, Denmark.

← Marsh
Sandpiper
Summer vis. Has bred Austria, Hungary. Passage w. to Italy, Poland. Vag. n. to Finland, w. to England, Spain

Greenshank →
Migr. Nonbreeders summer s. to Italy. Vag. Iceland

GREEN SANDPIPER *Tringa ochropus*   pages 84, 116
Du – Witgatje   Fr – Chevalier culblanc
Ge – Waldwasserläufer   Sw – Skogssnäppa

Identification: 9″. Larger and stouter than Wood or Common Sandpipers. Easily distinguished in flight by *blackish* beneath wings (Wood Sandpiper has buffish-white) and by *blackish upper-parts*, contrasting strongly with *brilliant white rump*, most of tail and under-parts. Neck and breast streaked greyish-brown, particularly on sides. No wing-bar. Tail barred with black near tip. In summer, upper-parts are speckled with whitish-buff, but much less boldly than in Wood Sandpiper (though juveniles are more speckled); faintly speckled in winter. Legs greenish and do not project beyond tail. Behaviour shy and solitary. "Bobs" head and tail. Flight rapid, with jerky, snipe-like wing-beats.

Voice: When flushed, a ringing *"weet, tluitt, weet-weet."* Song, a medley of high, fluty trilling *"titti-looi, titti-looi,"* etc.

Habitat: Outside breeding season on marshes, sewage-farms, lakes and streams, seldom on sea-shore. Breeds in swampy forest regions, often in old nests in trees. Map below.

WOOD SANDPIPER *Tringa glareola*   pages 84, 116
Du – Bosruiter   Fr – Chevalier sylvain
Ge – Bruchwasserläufer   Sw – Grünbena

Identification: 8″. A delicately built sandpiper. Distinguished in summer by dark olive-brown upper-parts, *closely spotted with white*; head, neck and breast finely streaked; bold whitish supercilium. In flight, *whitish rump and buffish-white beneath wings* contrast with upper-parts less boldly than in Green. No wing-bar. In winter, white speckles are faint, giving resemblance to Green Sandpiper, but latter is stouter and blacker, with contrasting white on rump and tail and has blackish beneath wings. Legs are long, yellow or yellowish-green.

Voice: Habitually noisy; parties making high liquid trilling. When

← GREEN
SANDPIPER
*Migrant. Has bred
England, Scotland,
Holland. Passage
Scotland, Ireland*

WOOD
SANDPIPER →
*Mig. Bred Holland.
Pass w. to Brit.,
Portugal. Vag.
Ireland, Faeroes*

flushed, a shrill *"chiff-chiff-chiff."* Also a rising, liquid, *"tlui."* Song embodies a musical *"tleea-tleea-tleea,"* in high song-flight.

Habitat: On passage frequents marshes, sewage-farms, lake shores, etc. breeds in fairly open ground near water in northern forest regions, and on tundra. Map p. 138.

COMMON SANDPIPER   *Tringa hypoleucos*   pages 85, 117
Du – Oeverloper   Fr – Chevalier guignette
Ge – Flussuferläufer   Sw – Drillsnäppa

Identification: 7¾". Distinguished by *olive-brown upper-parts* (faintly speckled with black in summer), brown rump and tail with white sides, white under-parts, faintly streaked on neck and breast. Has characteristic low flight over water, with rapid, *shallow* wing-beats alternating with brief glides on *down-curved wings* showing conspicuous white wing-bar. Also distinguished by *constant bobbing of head and tail* and by shrill voice. Runs among riverside stones. Distinguished from other sandpipers by combination of small size, dark upper-parts *and dark rump.* See also Temminck's Stint.

Voice: When flushed, a shrill piping *"twee-see-see."* Song, a high, rapid *"titti-weeti, titti-weeti."*

Habitat: Clear-running rivers, hill streams and lakes; on passage at sewage-farms, estuaries, etc. Breeds on banks of streams and lakes, river shingle bars, etc. Map p. 140.

TEREK SANDPIPER   *Xenus cinereus*   page 117
Du – Terek strandloper   Fr – Bargette de Térek
Ge – Terekwasserläufer   Sw – Tereksnäppa

Identification: 9". Distinguished by long, dark, *noticeably up-curved bill and bright orange legs.* In winter, crown and upper-parts pale greyish; in summer browner, with two broad, irregular black stripes converging down back. Under-parts white, with faint streaks on neck and breast. In flight, pale rump and white rear edge of wings are conspicuous. "Bobbing" action strengthens similarity to large, short-legged Common Sandpiper.

Voice: Rather noisy. A fluty *"dudududu,"* or piping *"twita-wit-wit-wit."* In breeding season, a variety of melodious notes, some recalling Whimbrel.

Habitat and Range: Occurs along shores of large rivers, saltings, coastal flats. Breeds in marshes among willow scrub, also on islets. Sometimes breeds Finland. Vagrant to Britain and most W. European countries.

BLACK-TAILED GODWIT   *Limosa limosa*   pages 92, 101
Du – Grutto   Fr – Barge à queue noire
Ge – Uferschnepfe   Sw – Rödspov

Identification: 16". A tall, upstanding wader. Distinguished from

Bar-tailed by longer, *straighter* bill, *longer legs* trailing well beyond tail in flight, *broad white wing-bar and bold black band* on pure white tail. In summer, head and breast are chestnut, flanks and belly white with blackish bars. Winter plumage more like dark Bar-tailed, but wing and tail pattern are unchanged. Juvenile has rufous-buff neck and breast.

Voice: Flight-call a clear "*reeka-reeka-reeka*"; most frequent notes at breeding grounds a rapid, tittering "*tiu-i-tiu*" and a nasal "*quee-it.*"

Habitat: In winter, estuaries, marshes; on passage, inland lakes and sewage-farms. Nests in water meadows, bogs, moors and dunes. Map below.

BAR-TAILED GODWIT *Limosa lapponica* pages 92, 101
Du – Rosse grutto Fr – Barge rousse
Ge – Pfuhlschnepfe Sw – Myrspov

Identification: 15″. Bar-tailed is slightly smaller than Black-tailed and distinguished by lack of white wing-bar, *closely barred tail*, more upturned bill, dull white rump and *considerably shorter legs*, which barely project beyond tail in flight. In summer, male looks rich reddish-chestnut, particularly about head, neck and breast; female is much duller. In winter, both look strikingly pale, with mottled grey upper-parts, whitish under-parts; in distance, colour is not unlike Curlew's. Juvenile has more strongly streaked buffish breast.

Voice: Usually silent outside breeding season. Flight-note a harsh "*kirrik*"; alarm, a shrill "*krick.*"

Habitat: Usually coastal. Often seen in winter in dense packs at water's edge. Breeds on swampy peat moss, in marshes near or beyond tree limits. Map p. 141.

CURLEW *Numenius arquata* pages 92, 101
Du – Wulp Fr – Courlis cendré
Ge – Grosser Brachvogel Sw – Storspov

← COMMON SANDPIPER *Mainly summer visitor. Has bred Holland.*

BLACK-TAILED GODWIT → *Migrant. Has bred Scotland, Faeroes, Spain, Switzerland*

Identification: 21-23". Largest European wader. Easily recognised by *very long*, *down-curved bill* and distinctive voice. Plumage greyish or buffish-brown, closely streaked; whitish rump extends to lower back. Flight strong and rather gull-like, with measured beat; flocks usually fly high, in lines or chevrons. Whimbrel is smaller, with shorter curved bill and boldly striped crown. See also Slender-billed Curlew.
Voice: A pure, ringing *"cour-li,"* or *"crwee," "croo-ee."* Song is loud, slowly delivered and remarkably liquid, embodying long bubbling trill. Sings almost all the year.
Habitat: Mud-flats and estuaries. Occurs inland during migration. Nests on moors, marshes, meadows, sand-dunes. Map below.

SLENDER-BILLED CURLEW *Numenius tenuirostris*   page 101
Du – Dunbekwulp	Fr – Courlis à bec grêle
Ge – Dünnschnabel-Brachvogel	Sw – Smalnäbbad spov

Identification: 16". Smaller and slimmer than Curlew, slightly longer-billed than Whimbrel. A pale, Whimbrel-size bird, uniformly chequered above, without striations but with *distinctive spots on breast and flanks* (spots heart-shaped, but look round at distance). Crown *finely* streaked, giving capped appearance above white supercilium. Distinguished in flight by combination of *snow-white under-parts and rump*, pale tail and contrast between dark primaries and pale, barred secondaries. Flight recalls Curlew, but can be very swift and erratic.
Voice: Resembles Curlew's *"cour-lee,"* but shorter and less deep; alarm, a sharp *"kew-ee."*
Habitat and Range: In winter as Curlew. Breeds in marshy steppes. Occurs on passage in Balkans and Italy. Vagrant to W. Mediterranean and N. to Germany.

WHIMBREL *Numenius phaeopus*   pages 92, 101
Du – Regenwulp	Fr – Courlis corlieu
Ge – Regenbrachvogel	Sw – Småspov

← BAR-TAILED
GODWIT
*Migr. Nonbreeders
summer coasts
Britain, W. Europe.
Vagrant Iceland.
Irreg. winter
Greece*

CURLEW →
*Partial migrant.
Non-breeders sum-
mer on coasts s. to
Mediterranean*

Identification: 16″. Smaller than Curlew. Distinguished by neater appearance, darker, more contrasting upper-parts, relatively shorter bill more kinked than curved, and *boldly striped crown*. Call is entirely different. Wing-beats are quicker. See also Slender-billed Curlew. Hudsonian Whimbrel *N. p. hudsonicus* (a N. American race, accidental Iceland, Scotland, Ireland, Spain), lacks the white rump and is darker.
Voice: An even tittering of about seven whistling notes. Song resembles the fluty, bubbling part of Curlew's song.
Habitat: As Curlew. In breeding season frequents boggy moors; nests among heather and rough grass on moors and islands. Map below.

UPLAND SANDPIPER *Bartramia longicauda*

Du – Bartram's strandloper Fr – Bartramie à longue queue
Ge – Bartrams Uferläufer Sw – Höglandssnäppa

Identification: 11″. A large, streaked, buffish-brown wader, near size of Ruff, with graceful, slender appearance. The general brown coloration, rather short bill (shorter than head), comparatively small-headed, thin-necked appearance, *long wings, rather long tawny tail* and habit of holding wings elevated upon alighting, are helpful points (under-wing surfaces are strongly barred). See also Pectoral Sandpiper.
Voice: A mellow whistle in flight, "*kip-ip-ip-ip*."
Habitat and Range: Extensive fields, burnt ground, etc. (not sea-shores). A vagrant from North America. Has been recorded chiefly in British Isles; also Denmark, Germany, Holland, Italy, Malta.

WOODCOCK *Scolopax rusticola* pages 84, 116

Du – Houtsnip Fr – Bécasse des bois
Ge – Waldschnepfe Sw – Morkulla

Identification: 13½″. A rather solitary woodland species. Perfect "dead leaf" camouflage and retiring habit make observation difficult. Distinguished from Snipe by larger, stouter form, thicker bill, *more rounded wings, finely barred* buffish under-parts and *transverse black*

← WHIMBREL
Migr. Nonbreeders summer British, W. Europe coasts. Passage also inland. Occ. winters north to Brit. Is.

WOODCOCK →
Partial migrant. Passage Faeroes. Prob. annual Iceland

bars on back of head and neck. Passes day in thick shelter, taking wing with distinctive swishing sound (but without calling), quickly dropping to cover again. Flight usually rapid and dodging. In flight looks stout, short-tailed and "neckless," with bill pointing downward at an angle. Crepuscular.

Voice: During slow display flight (known as "roding") above trees, at dawn and dusk, male has soft, croaking *"orrrt-orrrt"*; also a high, sneezing *"tsiwick."*

Habitat: Well wooded regions, particularly with wet, over-grown rides and patches of evergreen. Usually nests at foot of tree. Map p. 142.

SNIPE *Gallinago gallinago*   pages 84, 116

     Du – Watersnip   Fr – Bécassine des marais
     Ge – Bekassine   Sw – Enkelbeckasin
           N.Am – Wilson's Snipe

Identification: 10½" A secretive, tight-sitting, brown marsh bird, with a long straight bill. Difficult to observe closely, but quickly identified by characteristic *zig-zag flight and hoarse rasping cry when flushed.* Much larger than shorter-billed Jack Snipe, near size of Great Snipe but less bulky, smaller than Woodcock. Black and rufous back *strongly striped* with golden-buff. Tail shows a *little* white on outer edges and tips (adult Great Snipe shows *conspicuous* white corners, Jack Snipe none; young Great Snipe also shows none and is difficult to distinguish in the field from Snipe except by behaviour). Stripes on head are *lengthways* (Woodcock's are *across*). Long, slender bill carried downwards in flight. Flies in small parties, or "wisps."

Voice: When flushed, a dry, rasping *"schaap."* Song, a rhythmic monotonously repeated *"chic-ka."* In oblique dives during display-flight, a vibrating sound (so-called drumming) is produced by the widely spread outer tail-feathers, like rapidly repeated *"huhuhuhuhu."*

Habitat: Marshes, water-meadows, sewage-farms, boggy moors, etc. Nests in coarse grass or rushes, occasionally in heather. Map below.

← Snipe
Partial migrant

Great Snipe →
*Summer visitor.
Occ. summer in
Austria. Vagrant
west to Ireland*

GREAT SNIPE *Gallinago media*   **pages 84, 116**
     Du – Poelsnip   Fr – Bécassine double
     Ge – Doppelschnepfe   Sw – Dubbelbeckasin
Identification: 11″. Distinguished on the ground with difficulty from
Snipe by deeper-chested, *darker and more barred appearance* and
shorter bill with deeper base. More easily distinguished in flight, when
adults show *much more white on outer tail-feathers*. Juveniles not
separable. Flight is slower and heavier and usually direct (not twisting),
with wings more bowed; *usually rises silently*; bill held more horizontally.
Voice: An occasional brief croak. Males at display grounds in spring
indulge in remarkable bubbling chorus singing.
Habitat: Except in breeding season often frequents drier localities
than Snipe—stubble fields, bracken-covered heaths, etc. In breeding
season usually in marshy country, banks of rivers, etc. Map p. 143.

JACK SNIPE *Lymnocryptes minima*   **pages 84, 116**
     Du – Bokje   Fr – Bécassine sourde
     Ge – Zwergschnepfe   Sw – Dvärgbeckasin
Identification: 7½″. Smallest snipe. Difficult to observe on the ground,
but quickly distinguished from Snipe by *smaller size, relatively much
shorter bill and slower, more direct flight* (though it may dodge a little
occasionally). Breaks cover at last moment and drops again quickly,
instead of "towering" after wild zig-zag flight, like Snipe. *Usually
silent when flushed.* At short range lack of buff centre-stripe on crown,
brighter stripes contrasting with purplish gloss on back, *lack of white
on tail* and of barring on flanks, are further distinctions from Snipe.
Voice: Muffled throbbing note, like sound of galloping horse, delivered in display-flight and on ground.
Habitat: As Snipe. Breeds in wet swamps and bogs. Map below.

← Jack Snipe
*Migrant, May
breed Holland, N.
Germany. Vagrant
Faeroes, Iceland*

Black-winged
Stilt →
*Summer vis. Has
bred Austria n. to
N. Germany, Eng-
land. Vag. Ireland
n. to Sweden*

STILTS AND AVOCETS: Recurvirostridae

BLACK-WINGED STILT *Himantopus himantopus* pages 92, 101
    Du – Steltkluut   Fr – Echasse blanche
    Ge – Stelzenläufer   Sw – Styltöpare
Identification: 15". Unmistakable. In flight, *grotesquely long pink legs* project nearly 7 inches beyond tail. *Black upper-parts contrast with gleaming white under-parts.* Male in summer has black back to head; female has white head and neck (sometimes mottled black) and dark brown mantle and wings. Juvenile and winter adults have dusky markings on head and neck. *Black under-surfaces of narrow, sharply pointed, triangular wings conspicuous in flight.* Gait, a deliberate long-paced walk, often wading deeply. Behaviour nervous and very noisy.
Voice: A very shrill, yelping *"kyik, kyik, kyik."*
Habitat: Wet marshes, lagoons, flood-waters. Breeds colonially, building nest in shallow water, or on tussock or mud. Map p. 144.

AVOCET *Recurvirostra avosetta*   pages 92, 101
    Du – Kluut   Fr – Avocette
    Ge – Säbelschnäbler   Sw – Skärfläcka
Identification: 17" Unmistakable. Identified by *long, slender, up-curved* bill, contrasting *black and white* plumage and long, *lead-blue* legs. Immature birds more or less suffused with brownish. In flight legs project well beyond tail. Gait, a graceful, fairly quick walk; feeds in shallows with side-to-side sifting motion of head, but also wades deeply; swims readily and "up-ends" like duck.
Voice: A high, fluty *"kleep,"* or *"kloo-it."*

← AVOCET
Partial mig. Bred Ireland, Belgium. Vag. Switzerland, E. Baltic, Norway, Faeroes, Iceland
GREY
PHALAROPE →
Summer vis. Passage/winter coasts W. Europe. Vag. elsewhere (not Balkans)

Habitat: Exposed mud-flats, estuaries and sand-banks. Breeds colonially among scrub and tussocks near shallow water, on sand-banks, low islands in river deltas and in brackish lagoons. Map p. 145.

PHALAROPE SWIMMING

PHALAROPES: Phalaropidae

Small swimming waders, with slender bills and lobed feet. Females larger and brighter than males. Ground nesting.

GREY PHALAROPE *Phalaropus fulicarius*   pages 85, 100, 117
     Du – Rosse franjepoot   Fr – Phalarope à bec large
     Ge – Thorshühnchen   Sw – Brednäbbad simsnäppa
             N.Am – Red Phalarope

Identification: 8″. Phalaropes are dainty birds, *conspicuously tame, swimming habitually and buoyantly*, often far out at sea. When feeding on shallow water they "spin" characteristically. Females larger and brighter than males. In summer, Grey Phalarope has *dark chestnut under-parts* (blackish at a distance), *white face, dark crown, yellow bill*; upper-parts have bold snipe-like pattern; white wing-bar conspicuous in flight. In winter, pale blue-grey above, with white head and under-parts, resembling Sanderling, but distinguished by *dark mark through eye*, long-bodied appearance and different behaviour. Very like Red-necked Phalarope in autumn, but is slightly larger, paler and less streaked above; distinguished at short range by thicker, shorter bill; in flight by less contrasting white on grey wings. Bill is black, some-times yellowish at base; legs horn, grey or black; yellow webs on toes are diagnostic when visible.

Voice: A shrill "*whit*," or "*prip*," resembling Sanderling.

Habitat: Pelagic outside breeding season, but occurs occasionally on passage on coasts and inland waters. Breeds on tundra around pools or coastal lagoons. Map p. 145.

RED-NECKED PHALAROPE   *Phalaropus lobatus*

pages 85, 100, 117

Du – Grauwe franjepoot   Fr – Phalarope à bec étroit
Ge – Odinshühnchen   Sw – Smalnäbbad simsnäppa

Identification: 7″. Similar in habits to Grey Phalarope, but distinguished in breeding plumage by smaller size, *white throat* and under-parts, with *bright orange patch down side of neck* (less evident in male). In autumn, distinguished by *darker*, more streaked upper-parts, *more brightly contrasting white wing-bar on darker wing*; at short range also by *needle-fine* bill. Bill, legs and feet blackish, *never showing yellow*. Immature resembles winter adult, but with much darker crown and upper-parts. Distinguished from winter Sanderling by characteristic dark mark through eye, much finer bill, and swimming habit.

Voice: Similar to Grey, but lower-pitched.

Habitat: As Grey Phalarope. Breeds in small scattered groups in wet marshes, lake shores and river islands. Map below.

WILSON'S PHALAROPE   *Phalaropus tricolor*   page 285

Du – Wilson's Franjepoot   Fr – Phalarope de Wilson
Ge – Wilsons Wassertreter   Sw – Wilsons Simsnäppa

Identification: 9″. A fairly large, dark-winged phalarope, with *no wing-bar* and a *white rump*. Breeding female has broad neck-stripe from black eye-stripe through rich chestnut on neck to paler chestnut along back; crown, hind-neck and back pale grey; under-parts white with reddish suffusion on front of neck. Male is duller, with dark crown and back. In winter, sexes alike, pale grey-brown above, the unstreaked breast and flanks gleaming white; sides of head and neck mainly white, sometimes with dark mark through eye. Black bill *longer than in other phalaropes*, needle-fine; legs black in summer, often yellowish in winter. In flight shows white rump and tail like Yellowlegs, but easily distinguished by actions, unspotted plumage and shorter legs. Very active, running on mud with lurching gait, darting bill from side to side.

Voice: A nasal, grunting *"aangh"* and a Yellowlegs-like *"chu"* in flight

← RED-NECKED PHALAROPE
Summer vis. Vagr. or passage. England, most Europe

STONE CURLEW →
Part. mig. At times winters England, Vag. Ireland, Scotland, Denmark, Sweden, Estonia

200

202

TERNS

TERNS ARE MORE SLENDER in build, narrower of wing and more graceful in flight than gulls. Bills are more slender and sharply pointed, usually held downward towards the water. Tails are usually forked. Most terns are whitish, with black caps in summer.

● **SANDWICH TERN**   page 168
    Pale; long slender black bill, yellow tip; shaggy head;
    white tail.

○ **GULL-BILLED TERN**   168
    Stout, stubby black bill; neat cap; grey tail.

○ **CASPIAN TERN**   168
    Large size; huge scarlet bill.
    Dusky under-side of primaries.

● **COMMON TERN**   169
    Look for semi-transparent wing-patch (see text).
    Adult in summer: Bill orange-red with black tip.
    Juvenile: White forehead; dark "shoulders."

● **ROSEATE TERN**   170
    Adult in summer: Bill largely black; whiter than
    Common Tern; long tail streamers.
    Juvenile: Paler "shoulders"; more flecking on wings
    than Arctic.

● **ARCTIC TERN**   170
    Adult in summer: Bill blood-red to tip; greyer than
    Common Tern.
    Juvenile: Very similar to Common, but with stronger
    black flecking on wings.

A   *Roseate Tern. Whitest of three; tail extends well beyond short wings.*
B   *Common Tern. Tail does not extend beyond wing-tips.*
C   *Arctic Tern. Greyer; shorter legs; tail slightly longer than Common's.*

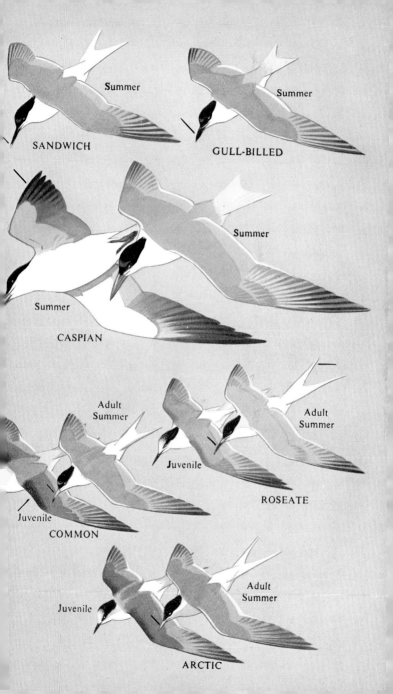

SANDWICH Summer

GULL-BILLED Summer

CASPIAN Summer Summer

COMMON Adult Summer Juvenile

ROSEATE Adult Summer Juvenile

ARCTIC Juvenile Adult Summer

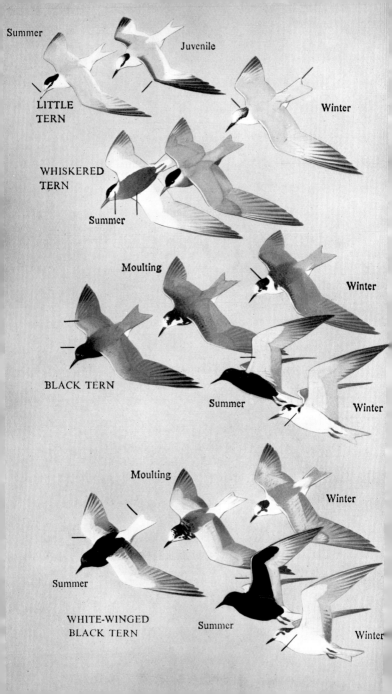

Summer

Juvenile

LITTLE
TERN

Winter

WHISKERED
TERN

Summer

Winter

Moulting

Winter

BLACK TERN

Summer

Winter

Moulting

Winter

Summer

WHITE-WINGED
BLACK TERN

Summer

Winter

Plate 40   149

TERNS

With the exception of the Little Tern, the species shown on this plate are "marsh terns." See also Plate 41.

● **LITTLE TERN**   page 171
    Adult in summer: Small; yellow bill; white forehead.
    Juvenile: Small; black fore-edge of wing.

○ **WHISKERED TERN**   167
    Adult in summer: Dusky belly; white cheek.
    Winter: Paler than Black Tern and larger; less black
    on nape; mantle and rump uniform grey.

● **BLACK TERN**   166
    Adult in summer: Black body and head; grey wings.
    Winter: From White-winged Black by dark mark on
    side of neck; dark band along fore-wing (not shown);
    no contrast between mantle and rump.

○ **WHITE-WINGED BLACK TERN**   167
    Adult in summer: Black body and head; black wing-
    linings. White wing-coverts; white tail.
    Winter: Like Black, but lacks dark mark on neck and
    dark band along fore-wing. Unlike Whiskered or
    Black, whitish rump contrasts with grey mantle.

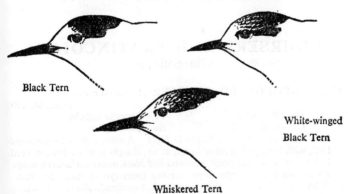

Black Tern

White-winged
Black Tern

Whiskered Tern

HEADS OF MARSH TERNS IN WINTER

Habitat and Range: Less aquatic than other phalaropes, usually seen on muddy shore or in shallows. Vagrant from N. America to Britain, Ireland.

THICK-KNEES: Burhinidae

STONE CURLEW   *Burhinus oedicnemus*   pages 81, 85
   Du – Griel   Fr – Oedicnème criard
   Ge – Triel   Sw – Tjockfot

Identification: 16″. A large, rather ungainly bird, distinguished from all other waders by round-headed appearance *with large yellow eyes*. Has short, stout, yellow and black bill, long, heavy, pale yellow legs and streaked sandy brown and white plumage. Shows conspicuous wing-pattern in flight, with *two bold whitish bars* (one fairly conspicuous on closed wing). Runs furtively with head low and body hunched. Rests on horizontal tarsi, flattening itself with head on ground to hide. Flight usually low, with deliberate wing-beats and occasional long glides, but may be erratic in flock evolutions at dusk.
Voice: A wailing, Curlew-like *"coo-ree,"* or a high, shrill *"kee-rrr-eee,"* the middle syllable dropping. Chiefly vocal in evening.
Habitat: Frequents and breeds on stony, sandy and chalky open ground, bare downs, heaths, etc., with scant vegetation, occasionally among scattered pines, marshes, etc., increasingly in cultivation. May occur in winter on sea coasts. Map p. 147.

COURSERS AND PRATINCOLES: Glareolidae

CREAM-COLOURED COURSER   *Cursorius cursor*

                                                          pages 84, 100
   Du – Renvogel   Fr – Courvite isabelle
   Ge – Rennvogel   Sw – Ökenlöpare

Identification: 9″; looks larger in flight. A slim, *pale sandy-coloured* bird, with long, *pale creamy legs*, a short, sharply pointed down-curved bill, *very conspicuous black primaries* and *black* under-surfaces of wings. Broad *black and white stripe* curving from eye to pale grey nape. Behaviour plover-like, running swiftly but spasmodically and crouching to escape detection. Flight rapid, with regular beats of distinctively black wings. Easily distinguished from pratincoles by paler appearance, longer whitish legs, prominent eye-stripe and short rounded tail.
Voice: Call-note a barking *"praak-praak."*
Habitat and Range: A desert-haunting species, occurring as vagrant

on sandy beaches, dunes, etc., in most European countries, N. to British Isles, Scandinavia, Finland.

PRATINCOLE *Glareola pratincola*   pages 84, 101
    Du – Vorkstaartplevier   Fr – Glaréole à collier
    Ge – Brachschwalbe   Sw – Vadaresvala
Identification: 10″. Looks unusual, perched or flying. Has long pointed dark wings and *deeply forked black tail with white base*, black legs and short, slightly down-curved bill. Upper-parts olive-brown, under-parts buffish with white belly and *black-bordered creamy throat-patch*. In winter, throat-patch has indistinct border. Juvenile has a broad breast-band of dark brown streaks. Has rapid, tern-like flight. On take-off or landing can show chestnut wing-pits, but they normally look black in flight. Outer halves of upper wing-surfaces darker than inner. See also Black-winged Pratincole and Cream-coloured Courser. Large noisy flocks hawk for flying insects. Gregarious and often crepuscular.
Voice: Noisy in flight. Call-note a hard, rather tern-like, "*kyik,*" or a chattering "*kitti-kirrik-kitik-tik.*"
Habitat: Sun-baked mud-flats, with low vegetation, marshes, plains, often near water. Breeds colonially. Map p. 153.

BLACK-WINGED PRATINCOLE *Glareola nordmanni* page 101
    Du – Steppenvorkstaartplevier   Fr – Glaréole à ailes noires
    Ge – Schwarzflügelige Brachschwalbe Sw – Svartvingad vadaresvala
Identification: 10″. Very difficult to distinguish from Pratincole owing to rare opportunities for seeing black wing-pits, which can only be noted with certainty when bird takes off or lands. Upper-parts and wings almost uniformly dark, *lacking white edges to secondaries.* Wing-pits of both species look black in flight; intermediate forms occur and they may be conspecific. Behaviour, flight, voice and habitat much as Pratincole. On passage S.E. Europe. Vagrant to Britain, Ireland, Norway.

SKUAS: Stercorariidae

Large, rather hawk-like sea-birds with dark plumage and narrow, angled wings. Centre tail-feathers usually elongated in adults. Plumage very variable and confusing, occurring in light, intermediate and dark phases; but all show flash of white on the wing created by white wing-quills. Behaviour piratical, chasing other birds until they disgorge. Settle freely on water. Sexes similar. Ground nesting.

GREAT SKUA *Stercorarius skua*   page 124
    Du – Grote Jager   Fr – Grand Labbe
    Ge – Grosse Raubmöwe   Sw – Storlabb
            N.Am – Skua

Identification: 23″. Larger and stockier than Herring Gull. **Plumage** fairly uniformly dark, rustier below. Distinguished in flight from all other adult skuas and from immature gulls by heavier build, *short tail*, stout hooked black bill and very *conspicuous* white patch across base of primaries. Wings broad and rounded, *not pointed* as in other skuas. Legs blackish. Juvenile has less white on wings. Normal flight gull-like, but dashing and hawk-like in pursuit of other birds, which it forces to disgorge and occasionally kills. Solitary outside breeding season. Settles frequently on water.

Voice: When attacking, a guttural *"tuk-tuk"*; also a harsh, nasal *"skeerrr"* and a deep barking *"uk-uk-uk."*

Habitat and Range: Pelagic and coastal waters. Breeds in scattered colonies on moors near sea, Iceland, Faeroes, Shetlands and Orkneys; also N. Scotland. Mainly migrant, in winter extending south over Atlantic and western North Sea to S. Spain (and beyond). Vagrant Scandinavia, Finland, Central Europe and Mediterranean, east to Jugoslavia.

POMARINE SKUA *Stercorarius pomarinus* page 124

Du – Middelste jager   Fr – Labbe pomarin
Ge – Mittlere Raubmöwe   Sw – Bredstjärtad labb
N.Am – Pomarine Jaeger

Identification: 20″, including 2″ tail projection. Smaller than Great Skua, larger, *heavier* and deeper breasted than Arctic and Long-tailed. Adults distinguished by elongated but *blunt and twisted* centre tail-feathers, giving very thick-ended appearance in flight; but projections may be broken short. Occurs in light and dark forms. Light form has blackish face and cap, yellowish white cheeks and collar, white under-parts, barred flanks and wing-tips and usually a dark breast-band. Dark form is fairly uniform dark brown. Both forms have whitish patches on upper and lower wing-surfaces, but not as white as in Great Skua. Immature uniformly mottled dark brown and buffish, heavily barred below, without tail elongations; indistinguishable in the field from young Arctic and Long-tailed, except by larger size, much heavier build and broader, more rounded wings.

Voice: A harsh, quick *"which-you."*

Habitat and Range: Chiefly off-shore, but also pelagic. Breeds in small widely scattered colonies on Russian tundra. On passage W. European coasts and Baltic. Vagrant to central Europe and Mediterranean.

ARCTIC SKUA *Stercorarius parasiticus* page 124

Du – Kleine jager   Fr – Labbe parasite
Ge – Schmarotzerraubmöwe   Sw – Labb
N.Am – Parasitic Jaeger

Identification: 18″, including 3″ tail projection. Smaller and slighter than Pomarine, larger and heavier than Long-tailed. Distinguished by

elongated but *straight and pointed* centre tail-feathers; Pomarine's are blunt and twisted; Long-tailed's are usually much longer and thinner. Bill more slender than Pomarine's. Light form has blackish cap, contrasting with yellowish-white cheeks and hind-neck, dark brown upper-parts, white under-parts, usually with dusky breast-band. Intermediate forms pale brown below, with varying whitish-buff sides of head. Dark form is uniform blackish-brown. Immature light form is closely barred and mottled above and below. See Pomarine for similarities. Behaviour piratical, chasing other sea-birds until they disgorge. Normal flight steady and graceful, otherwise hawk-like and dashing. Adults and particularly immatures show white flash on wing.
Voice: Higher than Great Skua's; also a nasal, squealing "*eee-air*"; alarm, "*ya-wow*" repeated.
Habitat: Off-shore and pelagic waters, occurring occasionally in large numbers on coasts on migration. Breeds colonially on tundra and moors. Map below.

LONG-TAILED SKUA *Stercorarius longicaudatus*   page 124
    Du – Kleinste jager   Fr – Labbe à longue queue
    Ge – Kleine Raubmöwe   Sw – Fjällabb
                 N.Am – Long-tailed Jaeger
Identification: 20-22″, including 5-8″ tail projection. Distinguished from pale form of commoner Arctic Skua by smaller size, lighter build and usually *much longer, thinner, very flexible centre tail feathers* (but streamers may be broken short in both species). Long-tailed is much whiter on breast than Arctic, lacking breast-band and has *more clean-cut black cap, contrasting with broad white collar* and pale back; cheeks are cleaner yellow; bill *black* (not brown); legs *grey* (not black); also has less white on wings. The uniform dark brown form apparently unknown in recent years. Immature usually indistinguishable from young Arctic, but is greyer and has little, if any, white on wings. When swimming, erect neck and long cocked tail are characteristic. Flight more buoyant and graceful than other skuas.

← Pratincole
*Summer visitor.
Vagrant n. to British Isles, Denmark*

Arctic Skua →
Mainly summer vis. Few winter n. to N. Sea. Prob. regular passage cent. Europe. Med.

204   208

Voice: Seldom vocal. At breeding grounds a shrill *"kreee."*
Habitat: More pelagic than Arctic Skua. Breeds in widely scattered colonies on high tundra and stony fells. Map below.

GULLS AND TERNS: Laridae

Gulls are long-winged sea-birds; some are seen regularly over land. Mostly white, with grey or black backs and wings. More robust, wider-winged and longer-legged than terns, walking readily. White-headed species often have dusky streaks on heads in winter; dark-hooded species have mainly white heads in winter, more or less mottled with brown. Sexes similar. Ground or cliff nesting.

Terns are slender, narrower-winged than gulls and more graceful in flight; bills more slender, sharply pointed, often carried downward in flight; tails forked. Most terns are whitish, with black caps; in winter, foreheads are white. Usually hover and plunge for fish. Poor walkers. Sexes similar. Ground or pond nesting.

MEDITERRANEAN GULL *Larus melanocephalus* pages 132, 133
    Du – Zwartkopmeeuw   Fr – Mouette mélanocéphale
    Ge – Schwarzkopfmöwe   Sw – Svarthuvad mås
Identification: 15½″. Larger and stouter than Black-headed. Adult distinguished at all seasons by *white primaries without black tips* and *heavier, droop-tipped bill*. Legs and bill *rich red*, latter crossed by dark band. In summer, head is *really black* (not brown), hood extending well down nape, with striking white broken eye-ring. In winter, head resembles winter Black-headed. Immature easily confused with young Common Gull, but black tail-band is narrower; wings have whitish patch extending to inner primaries. Sub-adult has black on outer primaries. Behaviour as Black-headed.

← LONG-TAILED
  SKUA
Summer vis. Passage Brit. Is., Iceland, Baltic. Vag. cent. Europe, Med.

MEDITERRANEAN
    GULL →
Part. mig. Has bred Holland, Estonia. Annual England, Switz. Vag. Scot., Ireland

Voice: Deeper and more wailing than Black-headed.
Habitat: As Black-headed, but less often seen inland. Breeds on islets in lagoons and lakes. Map p. 154.

BONAPARTE'S GULL *Larus philadelphia* page 285
Du – Kleine Kokmeeuw Fr – Mouette de Bonaparte
Ge – Bonaparte-Möwe Sw – Bonapartes mås

Identification: 12½″. Smaller than Black-headed, which it resembles in white fore-wing with black tips to primaries, but has *thinner, black bill* and, in summer, a dark, *slate-coloured* "hood." In winter, head resembles Black-headed. Best field-mark at all ages is *white undersides to primaries* (Black-headed's are dark greyish in adult, dusky in first-winter birds). Adult legs *orange* (not red); dusky in juvenile. Juvenile looks like small juvenile Black-headed, but black patches near tips of inner primaries and secondaries form prominent dark trailing edge. *Flight noticeably buoyant and tern-like.*
Voice: Rather silent, but has occasional rasping cry.
Habitat and Range: Habitat much as Black-headed. Nests near coasts in spruce forest belt. Vagrant from N. America to Britain, Ireland, Iceland, France, Holland, Heligoland.

LITTLE GULL *Larus minutus* pages 132, 133
Du – Dwergmeeuw Fr – Mouette pygmée
Ge – Zwergmöwe Sw – Dvärgmås

Identification: 11″. The smallest gull. When perched, looks like tiny Black-headed. Distinguished, apart from size, by *jet-black* (not dark brown) head, the black coming well down the nape; also by *absence of black* on upper surfaces of *rather rounded wings.* Distinguished from Black-headed in flight by contrasting *blackish under-surfaces* of *wings.* Bill dark red in summer, blackish in winter. Legs red. In winter, adults have head markings like Black-headed, but differences in size and wings are obvious. Sub-adult has white under-surfaces of wings, a black-tipped tail and a transverse dark bar across fore-wing to black primaries, forming a *bold zig-zag pattern* in flight (young Kittiwake has similar zig-zag but a dark nape patch and a slightly forked, not rounded, tail); when perched, wing shows a *broad horizontal dark stripe.* Immature looks *almost solid blackish above*, with a broad whitish patch along centre of closed wing. Behaviour as Black-headed, but feeds in tern-like flight from surface of water. See also Sabine's Gull.
Voice: A rather low "*kek-kek-kek*" and a repeated "*kay-ee.*"
Habitat: As Black-headed. Nests in small scattered colonies, often with terns or other gulls, usually around inland marshes. Map p. 158.

BLACK-HEADED GULL *Larus ridibundus* pages 132, 133
Du – Kokmeeuw Fr – Mouette rieuse
Ge – Lachmöwe Sw – Skrattmås

Identification: 15″. A smallish, active gull, frequently seen inland. Dis-

HEADS OF TERNS

THE BILLS OF TERNS are the key features in their recognition. All terns in breeding season have *black caps*. By late summer they begin to get the white foreheads typical of winter plumage.

● **BLACK TERN** page 166
  Summer: Black head.
  Winter: "Pied" head (see text).

○ **WHITE-WINGED BLACK TERN** 167
  (see plate 40).

○ **WHISKERED TERN** 167
  Summer: Dusky throat, white cheeks.
  Winter: See text.

● **LITTLE TERN**
  Summer: Small size; yellow bill; white forehead. 171
  Immature: Small size (see text).

● **COMMON TERN** 169
  Summer: Bill orange-red, black tip.
  Winter: Black patch from eye around nape.

● **ARCTIC TERN** 170
  Summer: Bill blood-red, no black tip.
  Winter: Similar to Common Tern (see text).

● **ROSEATE TERN** 170
  Summer: Bill mostly black (some have considerable red at base).
  Winter: Longer than Common Tern (see text).

○ **GULL-BILLED TERN** 168
  Summer: Bill stout and black.
  Winter: Black ear-patch; bill stout and black.
  Juvenile: Gull-like (see text).

● **SANDWICH TERN** 168
  Summer: Crested; bill black with yellow tip.
  Winter: Similar, with white forehead.

○ **CASPIAN TERN** 168
  Summer: Large size; large scarlet bill.
  Winter: Large scarlet bill; streaked forehead.

Winter Summer

BLACK

Winter Summer

WHISKERED

Immature Summer

LITTLE

Winter

Summer

COMMON

Winter

Summer

ARCTIC

Winter

Summer

ROSEATE

GULL-BILLED

Winter Summer

Winter

Summer

SANDWICH

Winter Summer

Winter CASPIAN Summer

RED GROUSE ♂

RED GROUS ♀

♂ Winter

♂ Summ

♀ Summer

PTARMIGAN

RED-LEGGED PARTRIDGE below

♂ Summer

♂

WILLOW GROUSE

PARTRIDGE

QUAIL

ANDALUSIA HEMIPODE

PARTRIDGES WITH RED LEGS

ROCK →
← RED-LEGGED

BARBARY

Plate 42 157

GAME BIRDS

● **RED GROUSE** page 102
Dark rufous plumage; dark wings; dark tail.
Female less rufous, more barred.

● **PTARMIGAN** 102
Winter: White, with black tail.
Summer: White wings; grey or brown body; black tail.

WILLOW GROUSE 102
Winter: From male Ptarmigan, see drawing below.
Summer: Rufous; white wings; black tail.
Lower altitudes than Ptarmigan.

● **PARTRIDGE** 107
Rufous tail; rusty head.
Male with dark horseshoe mark on belly.

Red legs and rufous tails (conspicuous only in flight) characterise the following three partridges. Best separated by their neck-patterns.

● **RED-LEGGED PARTRIDGE** 106
Necklace black, breaking into short streaks.

ROCK PARTRIDGE 105
Necklace black, clean-cut. (See Chukar, p. 105)

BARBARY PARTRIDGE 105
Necklace red-brown, with white spots; grey face.

● **QUAIL** 107
Small; sandy brown; striped head.

ANDALUSIAN HEMIPODE 108
Quail-like; bright rufous patch on breast; bold spots on sides of breast.

PTARMIGAN ♂   WILLOW GROUSE ♂ *and* ♀
Note the black face-patch on the male (not female) Ptarmigan in winter.
Both sexes of Willow Grouse lack this, but have thicker bills.

tinguished in flight by *pure white leading edges of pointed wings*. Under-surfaces of primaries dark grey. Slender crimson bill and legs. In summer, head is *chocolate-brown*; in winter, white with blackish marks before and behind eye. Immature has patterned brown upper-parts and crown and a black-tipped white tail, but still shows characteristic white leading edge to wing; head pattern as winter adult; bill yellowish with dark tip; legs dark yellowish. Flight more agile than in larger gulls; often follows plough. Adult Common Gull is slightly larger, and is distinguished at all seasons by greenish bill and legs, and by different wing and head patterns. See also Mediterranean, Slender-billed, Little and Sabine's.

Voice: Noisy in breeding season. Usual notes, a harsh "*kwarr*," a short "*kwup*," etc.

Habitat: Common inland and on coast, rarely far from land. Frequents lakes, sewage-farms, harbours, farm-lands. Breeds colonially on marshes, moors, shingle banks, lake islands. Map below.

SLENDER-BILLED GULL *Larus genei* page 13

Du – Dunbekmeeuw   Fr – Goéland railleur

Ge – Dünnschnäblige Möwe   Sw – Smalnäbbad mås

Identification: 17″. Can be confused with Black-headed owing to *similar wing-pattern*, but has longer neck, longer, wedge-shaped tail and usually *distinctively down-tilted head and bill*. Bill longer, more pointed but heavier than Black-headed's; looks black, though actually dark red. Legs dark red. In breeding plumage head and neck *pure white*. Under-parts have faint rosy tinge. Immature more like adult than in other gulls, but has black terminal bar on tail; grey smudge usually visible on ear-coverts; pale brown markings on upper-parts fainter than in young Black-headed; legs dirty yellowish.

Habitat: Coastal waters and estuaries. Nests in small groups or colonies, sometimes among terns, on dry mud-banks, islands in lagoons, in marshes, along river banks. Map p. 159.

← LITTLE GULL
*Partial migrant.
Vagrant Ireland,
Iceland, Faeroes,
Norway*

BLACK-HEADED
GULL →
Partial migrant

2/2   2/3

LESSER BLACK-BACKED GULL *Larus fuscus* pages 132, 133
Du – Kleine mantelmeeuw Fr – Goéland brun
Ge – Heringsmöwe Sw – Silltrut

Identification: 21″. About size of Herring Gull; smaller than Great Black-backed from which (apart from size, which is often difficult to judge) distinguished in summer by *yellow* legs; but in winter some adults and near-adults have flesh or pallid legs. British form *L. f. graellsii* has slate-grey upper-parts; Scandinavian *L. f. fuscus* is as black as Great Black-backed. Juvenile and first-year birds are mottled dark brown, with blackish bills and brownish-flesh legs, usually indistinguishable from young Herring Gull. Older immature birds have progressively darker backs, whiter heads and under-parts, yellower legs and bills.

Voice: Like deep-toned Herring Gull.

Habitat: As Herring Gull, but more frequent inland and out at sea. Nests colonially on inland moors and bogs, grassy sea islands, cliff tops. Map below.

HERRING GULL *Larus argentatus* pages 132, 133
Du – Zilvermeeuw Fr – Goéland argenté
Ge – Silbermöwe Sw – Grâtrut

Identification: 22″. Commonest coastal gull. Looks rather like Common, with similar *black and white wing-tips*, but is much larger, paler above and has a heavier yellow bill with a red spot and *flesh-pink legs* (except in Mediterranean form *L. a. michahellis* and eastern Scandinavian form *L. a. omissus* which have *yellow* legs and *darker backs*). Best distinguished from adult Lesser Black-backed (which see) by *paler* grey upper-parts; Glaucous and Iceland Gulls have no black on wings. Juvenile uniform brown with darker primaries and tail and blackish bill, indistinguishable from young Lesser Black-backed. Second-year bird has greyer back and whiter base to tail, with darker tip.

Voice: A repeated, strident *"kyow"*; anxiety note when breeding, a dry *"gah-gah-gah"*; also varied mewing, barking and laughing notes.

← SLENDER-
BILLED GULL
Partial migrant.
Vagrant England

LESSER BLACK-
BACKED GULL →
Mainly migrant.
Non-breeders
Greece

Habitat: Coasts, estuaries, also waters and fields often far inland. Breeds, usually colonially, on rocky cliffs, islands, beaches, occasionally in marshes. Map below.

ICELAND GULL *Larus glaucoides* page 132

Du - Kleine burgemeester   Fr – Goéland à ailes blanches
Ge - Polarmöwe   Sw – Vitvingad trut

Identification: 22″. Closely resembles Glaucous, but is distinguished at all ages by smaller si·e and *less heavy bill* (slighter than Herring Gull's). Build recalls Common Gull. Breeding adult also distinguished at short range by *reddish* eye-ring. Plumages of young as in Glaucous, but *at least half* of bill is black in first winter. Wings look noticeably long in flight, which is more rapid and more buoyant than Glaucous Gull. See also smaller Ivory Gull. Considered by some to be conspecific with Herring Gull. Winter visitor (from high Arctic) to North Scandinavia, Iceland, Faeroes, Shetland, Orkney and Hebrides. Vagrant south to Italy.

GLAUCOUS GULL *Larus hyperboreus* pages 132, 133

Du - Burgemeester   Fr – Goéland bourgmestre
Ge - Eismöwe   Sw – Vittrut

Identification: 25-29″. Glaucous and Iceland Gulls are "white-winged" gulls, easily confused. Adults have very pale grey mantle, *pure white primaries*, flesh-pink legs and yellow bill with red spot. Glaucous is usually distinguished by *larger size* and *heavier bill* than Iceland or Herring. Breeding adult also distinguished at short range by *lemon-yellow* eye-ring. First-year bird is pale creamy brown with dark-tipped bill; wing-tips are paler than rest of wing; tail has no dark tip. Second-year birds look uniformly white, the mantle becoming progressively greyer.

Voice: Resembles Herring Gull's, but usually shriller.

Habitat: As Great Black-backed. Breeds colonially above and below sea cliffs, on stacks and islands in Arctic. Map below.

← HERRING GULL *Partial migrant. Winters coasts and to less extent inland all Europe exc. where waters freeze*

GLAUCOUS GULL → *Partial migrant. Vagrant s. to Mediterranean*

GREAT BLACK-BACKED GULL *Larus marinus* pages 132, 133

Du – Mantelmeeuw   Fr – Goéland marin
Ge – Mantelmöwe   Sw – Havstrut

Identification: 27″. Much larger than Herring and Lesser Black-backed. Distinguished in breeding season from latter (apart from size) by *whitish-pink legs* and deeper voice. Adult is *almost black* above, not slate-grey as in British Lesser Black-backed, though Scandinavian Lesser Black-backed is also blackish. Bill is more massive than in Lesser Black-backed. Juvenile has more chequered, clearer-cut markings than young Herring, with paler head and under-parts, latter becoming progressively whiter and mantle darker in second and third years. Behaviour fiercely predatory.

Voice: Usual note a curt, deep *"owk."*

Habitat: Off-shore waters, coasts and estuaries. Locally inland in winter. Breeds either singly or colonially, sometimes with Lesser Black-backed, on rocky coastal islands, moors, also cliffs and lake islands. Map below.

COMMON GULL *Larus canus* pages 132, 133

Du – Stormmeeuw   Fr – Goéland cendré
Ge – Sturmmöwe   Sw – Fiskmås
N.Am – Short-billed Gull

Identification: 16″. Adult Common and Herring look rather alike, with pale grey upper-parts and black wing-tips with white spots, but Common is much smaller and longer-winged, with more delicate *greenish-yellow bill and legs*. Herring Gull's legs are pale flesh (yellow in Mediterranean and eastern Scandinavian forms) and its heavier yellow bill has a red spot; its back is also paler. In winter, head more strongly streaked with grey than Herring. Immature distinguished from second-year Herring Gull by *clean-cut black band on white tail* (see picture, p. 133). Juvenile largely grey-brown, with blackish bill and flesh-brown legs. See also Kittiwake (same size) and Black-headed (smaller).

← GREAT BLACK-BACKED GULL
Part. mig. Winter and nonbreeders coasts s. to dotted line; inland S. Sweden, Britain; vag. elsewhere

COMMON GULL →
Partial migrant

Voice: Much higher and shriller than Herring Gull's.

Habitat: As Herring Gull, but more often inland. Breeds colonially on moors, hill-sides and around lochs. Map p. 161

AUDOUIN'S GULL *Larus audouinii* page 132

Du – Audouin's meeuw   Fr – Goéland d'Audouin
Ge – Korallenmöwe   Sw – Rödnäbbad trut

Identification: 19½". Size near Herring Gull, but of slighter build and with *narrow* wings. Bill is *heavy, angular, coral-red with black subterminal band and yellow tip*; yellow difficult to see at long range, when bill looks dark and short. Legs dark olive-green. Eye dark, with red rim. In flight, primaries are *graded from grey bases to black tips* (not "dipped in ink" like Kittiwake's), with only inconspicuous white spot on outer primary. Seen from below, white tips visible on several primaries. Immature has pale grey crown and neck with small dark mark behind eye and pale brownish upper-parts. Behaviour as Herring Gull.

Voice: A weak but harsh "*gi-errk*."

Habitat: A deep-sea species. Locally around islands, occasionally along rocky mainland coasts. Nests colonially on sloping cliffs or among rocks on small Mediterranean islands. Map p. 163.

SABINE'S GULL *Larus sabini* pages 132, 133

Du – Vorkstaartmeeuw   Fr – Mouette de Sabine
Ge – Schwalbenmöwe   Sw – Tärnmås

Identification: 13". The only European gull with a quite strongly *forked tail* (young Kittiwake's is only very slightly forked). *Black outer primaries and broad white triangle behind them, contrasting with grey wing-coverts*, provide unmistakable flight pattern. In summer, head has slate-grey hood, bordered below by narrow black collar; head is mottled dusky white in winter. Bill rather short, black, with yellow tip. Legs grey. Juvenile is grey-brown above, with similar flight pattern, but white tail is broadly tipped with black. Feeds chiefly in buoyant flight from surface of water. Sometimes confused in flight with immature Little Gull or immature Kittiwake, but distinguished by more forked tail and *lack of dark bar* on wing-coverts.

Voice: Has a grating tern-like cry.

Habitat and Range: Northern coastal waters and, in breeding season, also on Arctic tundra. Breeds on swampy islets in tundra and along low-lying coasts. Occurs annually in British Isles, occasionally Iceland, Faeroes and coasts of W. Europe. Vagrant Switzerland and Baltic.

KITTIWAKE *Rissa tridactyla* pages 132, 133

Du – Drieteenmeeuw   Fr – Mouette tridactyle
Ge – Dreizehenmöwe   Sw – Tretåig mås

Identification: 16". An open-sea species. Slighter than Common Gull. Distinguished by "*dipped-in-ink*" black wing-tips, usually blackish legs, unmarked yellow bill and more bounding flight. Dark eye gives distinctive gentle appearance. Mantle and wings slightly darker than in

Common, remainder of plumage pure white. Immature distinguished from young Common by grey mantle, white head and under-parts, *black band across back of neck and broad black band along closed wing*; in flight shows *conspicuous dark band diagonally across wing, giving zig-zag effect*, and black-tipped, slightly forked tail; immature Little Gull has similar flight pattern but is much smaller, with squared tail and no neck-band; see also Sabine's. Picks food off surface and plunges like tern.

Voice: Noisy only at breeding grounds. A loud *"kitti-wa-ak,"* or *"kaka-week,"* with rising inflection.

Habitat: Usually well out at sea, often at northern fishing grounds: rare inland. Breeds in close colonies on steep cliff-faces and in sea caves; locally on buildings. Map below.

ROSS'S GULL *Rhodostethia rosea* page 285

Du – Rose Meeuw	Fr – Mouette de Ross
Ge – Rosenmöwe	Sw – Rosenmås

Identification: 12½". Breeding adult unmistakable, pale grey above, otherwise all-white tinged with pale rose and with *narrow black collar* and *small, delicate black bill*. Feet red. Tail graduated. Wings long and *without black* (except for outer web of first primary), projecting well beyond tail at rest. In winter, head tinged greyish with some dark mottling around eye; pink on plumage usually faint. Immature back and crown grey; forehead white; sides of head mottled; tail has dark terminal band; slight dusky breast-band; contrasting wing-pattern (with black-ended inner primaries) recalls young Sabine's, but latter has wholly white inner primaries, lighter back and forked tail.

Voice: Variable; high-pitched and more melodious than most gulls; typical calls are *"a-wo, a-wo,"* and *"claw"*, or *"cliaw."*

Habitat: Migrants frequent sea coasts and coastal lagoons. Seen regularly perched on ice floes and glacier edges, seldom swimming. Breeds in swampy Arctic tundra. Vagrant from N.E. Siberia to Britain, France, Holland, Iceland, Faeroes, Norway, Denmark, Germany, Sardinia.

← AUDOUIN'S GULL
Resident.(?) breeds S. Spain. Vagrant in Mediterranean away from breeding areas

KITTIWAKE →
Part. mig. Winters s. to dotted line. Vag. Baltic, cent. Europe, Greece

GAME BIRDS

● **PHEASANT**   page 108
    Male: Highly-coloured; very long tail; usually a
    neck-ring.
    Female: Large, brown; long pointed tail.

● **BLACK GROUSE**   103
    Male (Blackcock): Glossy black; lyre-shaped tail;
    white wing-bar.
    Female (Greyhen): Large, brown; long notched tail
    (notch not always evident).

● **CAPERCAILLIE**   104
    Male: Very large size; dusky coloration; broad fan
    tail.
    Female: Large, brown; fan tail.

HAZEL HEN   103
    Partridge-size; fan tail with wide black band. Colour
    phases vary from rufous to grey, tending towards
    rufous in south of range, grey in north.

        ♂   ♂   ♂
PHEASANT   BLACK GROUSE   CAPERCAILLIE

See also illustrations of other game birds, Plate 42.

♀
PHEASANT

♂
PHEASANT

♀
(Greyhen)
BLACK GROUSE

♂
(Blackcock)
BLACK GROUSE

♀
CAPER-
CAILLIE

HAZEL HEN

♂
CAPERCAILLIE

Dark-breasted form

Light-breasted form

SNOWY

BARN

SHORT-EARED

SCOPS

LONG-EARED

EAGLE

Plate 44   165

OWLS

MAINLY NOCTURNAL birds of prey, large headed, with large eyes
facing front, facial discs, and moth-like, noiseless flight.

○ SNOWY OWL   page 184
  Large, white; big yellow eyes.

● BARN OWL   183
  Heart-shaped face, or round "monkey" face; no
  breast streaks; dark eyes.
  Light-breasted form: White breast.
  Dark-breasted form: Tawny breast.

● SHORT-EARED OWL   186
  Yellowish brown; strongly streaked; marshes.

○ SCOPS OWL   186
  Marbled grey-brown; small head; erect "ears" when
  alarmed.

● LONG-EARED OWL   185
  Slender; mottled rusty-brown; erects long "ears"
  when alarmed.

△ EAGLE OWL   184
  Huge; "eared"; rusty, with streaks and bars.

See also illustrations of other owls, Plate 45.

IVORY GULL   *Pagophila eburnea*   page 132

       Du – Ivoormeeuw   Fr – Goéland sénateur
       Ge – Elfenbeinmöwe   Sw – Ismås

Identification: 17½″. Distinguished by striking *all-white plumage*, *short black legs* and, when perched, by plump, densely-feathered, *pigeon-like* appearance. Head small and rounded. Bill rather short, yellowish, with grey base and reddish tip. Eye-ring red, eye large and black. Immature has irregular grey "smudges" on face and chin, grey bill, a *sprinkling of black spots* on upper-parts (sometimes also on under-parts), small black tips to primaries, narrow black terminal band on tail. Wings noticeably long when closed; flight buoyant, almost tern-like. Seldom alights on water. Much larger Glaucous and Iceland Gulls also have unmarked white primaries and grey backs, but have pinkish legs. Beware occasional albino Common Gulls and Kittiwakes.

Voice: Harsh shrill cries *"kee-er,"* etc., are tern-like.

Habitat and Range: An Arctic species usually seen on fringe of pack-ice, but wanders south occasionally in winter. Breeds colonially on more or less ice-bound rocky cliffs and ground. Occasional Iceland, Faeroes, N. Scandinavia. Vagrant S. to Britain, N. France, Italy.

BLACK TERN   *Chlidonias niger*   pages 149, 156

       Du – Zwarte stern   Fr – Guifette noire
       Ge – Trauerseeschwalbe   Sw – Svarttärna

Identification: 9½″. Black, White-winged Black and Whiskered are small marsh terns with generally dark breeding plumage and distinctively *dipping* feeding-flight. Black is only tern with *all-blackish-grey* breeding plumage, except for conspicuous *white under tail-coverts*. During moult looks mottled and patchy. In winter has white forehead, neck and under-parts, with small blackish patch on sides of breast in front of wings. Immature like winter adult but with darker "saddle." Bill black, slender, almost as long as head. See Whiskered and White-

← BLACK TERN
Summer vis. Bred Norway, Finland; Greece(?). Passage Brit. Is. Vagrant Faeroes, Iceland

WHITE-WINGED
BLACK TERN →
Summer vis. Has bred France, Belg., Ger. Passage w. to Spain. Vagr. Brit. Is., Den., Sweden

---

winged Black Terns for winter and immature comparisons. Flies back
and forth over water, dipping erratically to pick insects off surface, but
very rarely plunges.
Voice: Seldom vocal. Usually a rather squeaky "*kitt*" or "*kreek*."
Habitat: Inland waters, also coastal on passage. Breeds in scattered
colonies, building floating nest in shallows of marshes and lagoons.
Map p. 166.

WHITE-WINGED BLACK TERN *Chlidonias leucopterus*
pages 149, 156

Du – Witvleugelstern   Fr – Guifette leucoptère
Ge – Weissflügelseeschwalbe   Sw – Vitvingad tärna

Identification: 9¼". Unmistakable in summer, with startling *black plumage and conspicuous white wing-coverts and tail*; further distinguished from Black by *white tail* and *black* (not pale grey) under wing-coverts. Adult in winter distinguished from Black by *absence of dark patches on breast*, less black on crown, stouter build and steadier flight; from Whiskered by *complete* white collar, paler rump and squarer tail. Immature distinguished from young Black by *contrasting* dark brown "saddle" and pale grey wings; from young Whiskered by *uniform* dark "saddle" and clear white rump. Bill red in summer, blackish in winter; shorter and stubbier than Black or Whiskered. Behaviour, voice and habitat resemble Black Tern, with which it frequently associates throughout the year. Map p. 166.

WHISKERED TERN *Chlidonias hybrida*   pages 149, 156

Du – Witwangstern   Fr – Guifette moustac
Ge – Weissbartseeschwalbe   Sw – Skäggtärna

Identification: 9¾". In summer, distinguished from Black Tern and White-winged Black Tern by *white cheeks and sides of neck*, contrasting with black crown and *dark grey under-parts*; in flight, *white beneath*

← WHISKERED
TERN
*Summer vis. Has
bred Holl., Switz.,
Ger., Poland. Vag.
Brit. Is., Belgium*

GULL-BILLED
TERN →
*Summer vis. Bred
Germany, England;
prob S.Italy. Vag.
cent. Europe, Ire-
land, Scand.*

wings and white under tail-coverts are fairly conspicuous. Looks very much paler than other "black" terns; but forked tail, flight and plunging for food recall Common Tern. Winter adult distinguished from Black by paler upper-parts, *absence of dark patches on sides of breast* and *less black on crown*; from White-winged Black by *greyish* (not white) on nape, longer bill and uniform upper-parts. Immature distinguished from young Black by *variegated* "saddle" contrasting with pale wings, absence of breast-patches; from young White-winged Black by *pale grey* (not white) rump and longer bill. Bill dark red in summer, blackish in winter, as long as head and deeper than other marsh terns.

Voice: A rasping *"ky-ik"* and other disyllabic notes.

Habitat: Like Black, but prefers deeper waters. Map p. 167.

GULL-BILLED TERN *Gelochelidon nilotica*   pages 148, 156
   Du – Lachstern   Fr – Sterne hansel
   Ge – Lachseeschwalbe   Sw – Sandtärna

Identification: 15″. Resembles Sandwich Tern both in summer and winter plumage, but distinguished by *"swollen," much shorter wholly black bill* and much less forked *grey* tail; in flight is broader-winged and heavier-bodied. Legs black, noticeably longer than in other terns. Black cap is lost in winter, head becoming much whiter than in Sandwich. Juvenile has buffish crown with dark patch around eye. Behaviour much as other terns, but *habit of hawking for insects over land* is certain distinction from Sandwich; seldom plunges into water.

Voice: A throaty, rasping *"kaywuck,"* or *"za-za-sa,"* quite distinct from Sandwich Tern's higher note.

Habitat: Salt marshes, sandy coasts and inland waters. Breeds colonially on sandy shores and islets in saline lagoons. Map p. 167.

CASPIAN TERN *Hydroprogne tschegrava*   pages 148, 156
   Du – Reuzenstern   Fr – Sterne caspienne
   Ge – Raubseeschwalbe   Sw – Skräntärna

Identification: 21″. Almost as big as Herring Gull; distinguished by large black cap, forked tail and *heavy, bright orange-red bill.* Black cap extends just below eye, but in winter looks greyish, darkest around eye. Juvenile like winter adult with brownish mottling on upper-parts. Looks gull-like in flight, much less buoyant than other terns, but is quickly identified by huge bill; dark under-surfaces of primaries are conspicuous. See also Royal Tern (Accidentals p. 317).

Voice: A loud, deep, corvine *"kraa-uh,"* or *"kaah."*

Habitat: Chiefly coastal, but occurs also on lakes and large rivers. Breeds singly or colonially on sandy coasts or islands. Map p. 169.

SANDWICH TERN *Sterna sandvicensis*   pages 148, 156
   Du – Grote stern   Fr – Sterne caugek
   Ge – Brandseeschwalbe   Sw – Kentsk tärna
            N.Am – Cabot's Tern

Identification: 16″. Distinguished by rather large size, long wings, short forked tail and *long black bill with yellow tip*. Legs black. Underparts may have pinkish tinge, like Roseate, but latter's very long tail streamers and bright red legs are distinctive. *Elongated feathers at back of crown* erected when excited, giving shaggy appearance; in winter, crown is chiefly white, with streaky black crest; may assume winter plumage while still breeding. Immature looks very white, with much less forked tail and can lack yellow on bill, causing confusion with Gull-billed. Flight more gull-like than in smaller terns.

Voice: Noisier than most terns. A strident, rasping *"kirrink"* (higher-pitched than rather similar note of Gull-billed), or *"kirr-kit."*

Habitat: Almost exclusively maritime. Nests in crowded colonies on sandy or shingle beaches, rocky or sandy islands, occasionally on shores of inland waters. Map below.

COMMON TERN *Sterna hirundo* pages 148, 156

Du – Visdiefje Fr – Sterne pierregarin
Ge – Flusseeschwalbe Sw – Fisktärna

Identification: 14″. Common, Arctic and Roseate are easily confused and their usual differences are seldom completely reliable. In summer, Common usually distinguishable at short range by *black tip to orange-red bill* (Arctic's is wholly blood-red, Roseate's is mainly black). In winter, Common's bill is blackish with red base (Arctic's and Roseate's are wholly blackish). All three have red legs in summer, but when perched together Arctic usually shows noticeably shorter legs; in winter, Common's legs are still reddish (Arctic's are blackish, Roseate's orange-red). Common's tail streamers *do not project beyond closed wing-tips* (Arctic's project slightly, Roseate's go far beyond wings). In winter and immature plumage all three have incomplete black caps, with white foreheads, but Common has darker "shoulder" patches. In overhead flight Arctic's primaries are *all semi-transparent*; in Common only innermost four make *light patch* behind wing angle.

← CASPIAN TERN
*Migrant. Has bred
Denmark, S. Baltic
Yugosla. Sardinia.
Vag. most Europe,
Brit. Is., Faeroes*

SANDWICH
TERN →
*Mainly summer
visitor, locally on
marked coasts.
Has bred Estonia.
Vagrant Norway,
Czecho., Switz.*

Voice: Noisy and varied. A long, grating *"kree-errr"* with downward inflection, *"kirri-kirri"* and a chattering *"kikikikik."*
Habitat: Coastal and some inland waters, beaches and islands. Breeds colonially on beaches, sand-dunes and islands. Map below.

ARCTIC TERN *Sterna paradisea* pages 148, 156

Du – Noordse stern   Fr – Sterne arctique
Ge – Küstenseeschwalbe   Sw – Silvertärna

Identification: 15″. Distinguished from Common Tern by *wholly blood-red bill* (wholly blackish in winter, and tip may still be black in spring); when perched, usually by *shorter legs*. Under-parts and neck usually greyer than in Common and Roseate, often showing by contrast a *white streak below the black cap*. Tail streamers usually project *a little* beyond the wing-tips when perched, but never as far as in Roseate. See Common Tern for detailed comparison between the three species.
Voice: As Common Tern, but whistled *"kee-kee,"* with rising inflection, said to be characteristic.
Habitat and Breeding: As Common Tern, but more maritime and more frequently on rocky off-shore islets. Map below.

ROSEATE TERN *Sterna dougallii* pages 148, 156

Du – Dougall's stern   Fr – Sterne de Dougall
Ge – Rosenseeschwalbe   Sw – Rosentärna

Identification: 15″. Distinguished in mixed flock with Common or Arctic by very different voice, *much whiter* appearance and shorter wings. Bill *black* with red base in summer, all-black in winter. Rosy tinge on breast visible in spring, but soon disappears. Sandwich also often has pinkish tinge, but Roseate is easily distinguished by *red legs* and long tail streamers. When perched, tail streamers extend *far beyond* wing-tips; in Common and Arctic they seldom project. Juvenile just distinguishable from young Common and Arctic by bolder markings on crown and upper-parts. Behaviour as in Common Tern, but flight is more buoyant, with shallower wing-beats.

← COMMON TERN
Summer visitor

ARCTIC TERN →
  Summer visitor.
  Vagrant central
  and S. Europe

Voice: A long rasping "*aaak*," a soft, very characteristic "*chu-ick*" and a long angry chattering "*kekekekek*," like Common or Arctic.
Habitat and Range: As Common Tern, but exclusively maritime. Nests sociably with Common or Arctic Terns, on islets, occasionally on beaches. Summer visitor, breeding very locally to Britain from Clyde and Tay southwards, also on coasts of Ireland and off Brittany. Has bred S. France. Vagrant on coasts of W. Europe north to Sweden and east to Italy, also Switzerland, Austria.

SOOTY TERN

SOOTY TERN   *Sterna fuscata*

Du – Bonte stern	Fr – Sterne fuligineuse
Ge – Russseeschwalbe	Sw – Sottärna

Identification: 16″. No other tern on the European list is *black above and white below* (adult at all seasons). Crown, back, wings and tail black; under-parts, cheeks and patch on forehead white; bill long and black; feet black. The much smaller Black Tern is blackish-grey above, never completely black, and has a slightly forked grey tail. The Sooty has a very deeply forked black tail with white outer margins. Immature is sooty-brown above, flecked with white on back, grey-brown below. See also Bridled Tern (Accidentals, p. 318).
Voice: A nasal "*ker-wacky-wack*."
Habitat and Range: Oceanic, breeding on islands in warm southern oceans. A vagrant to England, Wales, France, Germany, Italy.

LITTLE TERN   *Sterna albifrons*   pages 148, 156

Du – Dwergstern	Fr – Sterne naine
Ge – Zwergseeschwalbe	Sw – Småtärna
N.Am – Least Tern	

Identification: 9¼″. Easily distinguished from other terns by *diminutvei size*, black-tipped *yellow bill, yellow legs and white forehead*, the last contrasting sharply in summer with black crown and black stripe through eye. In winter back of crown is ash-grey merging to black at nape. Immature resembles winter adult but has darker bill and legs. Tail streamers are short. In flight, wings are relatively narrower, *wing-beats quicker* and periods of hovering before diving longer, than in other terns.

Voice: A high rasping *"kree-ik,"* a sharp repeated *"kitt"* and a rapid chattering *"kirri-kirri-kirri."*

Habitat: Sand and shingle beaches, occurring inland on migration. Breeds in small scattered colonies on beaches; on Continent also on shores of lakes and rivers. Map below.

AUKS: Alcidae

Black and white salt-water diving birds with short necks, very short, narrow wings, and legs set far back. Flight is whirring, large feet jutting out sideways before alighting. Carriage usually upright when standing. Sexes similar. Cliff or hole nesting.

LITTLE AUK *Plautus alle* page 125
  Du – Kleine alk   Fr – Mergule nain
  Ge – Krabbentaucher   Sw – Alkekung
      N.Am – Dovekie

Identification: 8″. Smallest winter sea-bird. Not much larger than Starling. Easily distinguished by *chubby, "neckless" form and very short bill.* In summer, head and upper breast blackish-brown and upper-parts black; narrow white wing-bar; white under-parts. In winter, ear-coverts, throat and upper breast become dirty white.

Voice: Noisy at breeding grounds. A high, shrill chatter.

Habitat and Range: Off-shore to pelagic. Occasionally "wrecked" on shore during severe gales. Breeds in vast colonies, in holes among rocks, on high Arctic sea-cliffs, locally among mountains. Nests N. Iceland. Partial migrant. In winter extends south from Arctic to North Sea and N. Atlantic; irregular English Channel; vagrant Finland and south to Mediterranean, east to Italy.

← LITTLE TERN
Summer vis. Vag.
Finland, Norway

RAZORBILL →
Part. mig., leaving
N. Baltic; winters
s. to dotted line.
Vagr. cent. Europe

RAZORBILL *Alca torda*   page 125

    Du – Alk   Fr – Petit pingouin

    Ge – Tordalk   Sw – Tordmule

            N.Am – Razor-billed Auk

Identification: 16″. Black above, white below. Distinguished from Guillemot by rather heavy head, short thick neck and *laterally compressed bill*, crossed midway by a conspicuous *white line*. Looks more squat than Guillemot when swimming and usually carries pointed tail *cocked up*. Both species have curved white bar on closed wing and conspicuous white rear edge to wings in flight. Throat and sides of head of adult are white in winter. Juvenile has smaller bill, without white stripe; young Guillemot has longer, more pointed bill and distinctive black line running back from eye. Sociable, perching upright or horizontally, on ledges with Guillemots.

Voice: A weak whirring whistle and a protracted querulous growling, at breeding grounds.

Habitat: Spends most of time in coastal and off-shore waters. Breeds in colonies, usually with Guillemots, on sea cliffs. Map p. 172.

GUILLEMOT *Uria aalge*   page 125

    Du – Zeekoet   Fr – Guillemot de Troïl

    Ge – Trottellumme   Sw – Sillgrissla

            N.Am – Common Murre

Identification: 16½″. Distinguished from Razorbill by *slender pointed bill and thinner neck*. Upper-parts of northern race *U. a. aalge* usually look as black as Razorbill's, though head is browner; but southern *U. a. albionis* is dark chocolate-brown in summer, grey-brown in winter. Fairly frequent "Bridled" form (not separate species) has narrow white eye-ring and a white line extending back from eye. In winter, sides of head and throat are white, as in winter Razorbill, but with conspicuous *black line* from eye across ear-coverts. Behaviour like Razorbill, but in flight head and neck look thinner and longer and tail shorter. See also Brünnich's Guillemot.

Voice: Very noisy in breeding season. A long, harsh *"arrrr,"* or *"arra."*

Habitat: As Razorbill. Breeds in dense colonies on ledges on steep cliff-faces and on flat tops of isolated stacks, often with Razorbills and Kittiwakes. Map p. 174.

BRÜNNICH'S GUILLEMOT *Uria lomvia*   page 125

    Du – Kortsnavelzeekoet   Fr – Guillemot de Brünnich

    Ge – Dickschnabellumme   Sw – Spetsbergsgrissla

            N.Am – Brünnich's Murre

Identification: 16½″. Closely similar to Guillemot, but distinguished at close range at all seasons by *noticeably shorter and thicker bill* (but much less deep than Razorbill's) and by *narrow pale line along sides of bill*. In winter also by black of crown extending *well below eye*, without dark stripe through ear-coverts. Young Razorbill may be confused with Brünnich's Guillemot, but its bill is more stubby and rounded. Flight, behaviour and voice as Guillemot.

Habitat: As Guillemot, but roams farther out to sea in winter. Breeds Iceland, winters S. to Norway, occasionally Faeroes. Vagrant on coasts S. to British Isles, N. France, also Austria, Czechoslovakia.

BLACK GUILLEMOT *Cepphus grylle* page 125
    Du – Zwarte zeekoet   Fr – Guillemot à miroir
    Ge – Gryllteiste   Sw – Tobisgrissla
Identification: 13½″. Much smaller than Guillemot. Easily distinguished in summer by *all-black plumage, with large white wing-patch and bright red feet.* In winter, under-parts are white, black portions of upper-parts closely mottled with white. Juvenile darker above than winter adult, with whites indistinctly mottled with brown. Behaviour as Guillemot, but is usually seen in very small numbers. In summer and at distance on water might be confused with Velvet Scoter, which is much larger and shows only small white bar on closed wing and *white on rear* (not front) of wing in flight. See also winter grebes.
Voice: Very distinctive—a weak, whistling cry, occasionally becoming a trilling twitter, during which brilliant vermilion gape is conspicuous.
Habitat: Stays closer to shore than other guillemots, often among rocky, even well-wooded, islands. Nests singly or in small scattered groups, in holes or under boulders on rocky shores, cliff-ledges, islands. Map below.

PUFFIN *Fratercula arctica* page 125
    Du – Papegaaiduiker   Fr – Macareux moine
    Ge – Papageitaucher   Sw – Lunnefågel
Identification: 12″. Easily distinguished in summer by *triangular, red, blue and yellow laterally-flattened bill*, stumpy big-headed form, black and white plumage and *bright orange feet*. In winter, bill is somewhat

← GUILLEMOT
Part. mig., leaving N. Baltic; winters coasts s. to Spain. Vag. Finland, Austria; in Med. e. to Malta

BLACK
GUILLEMOT →
Mainly res. Winter s. to dotted line. Vagrant Holland, Belgium, France

smaller, but still recognisably Puffin-shaped; cheeks greyer. Juvenile has much smaller, blackish bill, but shows typical Puffin face-pattern (see illustration). In flight looks distinctively big-headed. Perches upright, but rests horizontally.

Voice: Usually silent, but has long growling notes *"ow,"* or *"arr,"* at breeding site.

Habitat: Coastal and off-shore waters. Breeds colonially in rabbit or shearwater burrows, or in holes excavated in turf, on cliffs or grassy islands. Map below.

SANDGROUSE: Pteroclidae

Plump, pigeon-like terrestrial birds, with very short, feathered legs and toes. Wings and tails long and pointed. Flight very rapid. Gait mincing and dove-like. Habitat usually deserts and arid ground. Noisy. Ground nesting.

BLACK-BELLIED SANDGROUSE *Pterocles orientalis*   page 81
        Du – Zwartbuikzandhoen   Fr – Ganga unibande
        Ge – Sandflughuhn   Sw – Ringflyghöna

Identification: 14″. Larger and bulkier than Pin-tailed. Distinguished even at a distance by less elongated tail and *very conspicuous black belly*. Male has sandy-grey head, greyish upper-parts speckled with orange, orange wing-coverts and secondaries, chestnut throat with black patch below, pinkish-grey breast, crossed with a narrow black band. Female is sandy, closely spotted on head and upper-parts, throat is yellow with a blackish patch, breast warm ochreous, closely spotted with black and crossed below with a black band.

Voice: Usual note a deep *"churr-rur-rur."*

Habitat and Range: Semi-desert, or undulating stony country. Nests on ground. Resident Spain, Portugal. Vagrant to Italy, Malta, Greece, Germany.

← Puffin
Summer visitor to land. Vagrant eastward to Adriatic, also Hungary

242

PIN-TAILED SANDGROUSE *Pterocles alchata* page 81
Du – Witbuikzandhoen Fr – Ganga cata
Ge – Spiessflughuhn Sw – Långstjärtad flyghöna

Identification: 12½″. On ground resembles squat, pale Partridge, but quickly distinguished by long, needle-pointed centre tail-feathers; in flight also by long, sharply pointed wings and "neckless" silhouette. Smaller than Black-bellied and Pallas's. Distinguished from both (particularly in flight) by *white belly* and *white under-wing with black tip.* Male in breeding plumage has upper-parts boldly spotted with lemon-yellow on dark grey-brown, chestnut wing-coverts, grey crown, orange-yellow face, *black chin and throat,* broad chestnut breast-band. Female has yellowish upper-parts, finely barred with black and lavender; throat and under-parts white, with two or three narrow black bands across the breast. Male in winter resembles female, but lacks lavender barring. Rapid flight recalls Golden Plover; flocks usually much larger than Black-bellied, often executing massed evolutions. See Black-bellied, Pallas's, and Spotted (Accidentals p. 318).

Voice: A loud, croaking "*cata, cata,*" usually in flight.

Habitat and Range: Dry, dusty plains, high stony plateaux, sun-baked mud-flats, and edges of marismas. Nests on ground. Resident S. France, Spain, Portugal. Vagrant to Italy, Sicily, Malta.

PALLAS'S SANDGROUSE *Syrrhaptes paradoxus* page 81
Du – Steppenhoen Fr – Syrrhapte paradoxal
Ge – Steppenhuhn Sw – Stäpphöna

Identification: 14-16″. Distinguished by long, needle-pointed centre tail-feathers (longer than Pin-tailed) and conspicuous *black patch* on belly (less extensive than in Black-bellied). Male has orange head and throat, with curved grey mark from eye down side of neck; barred sandy upper-parts; pale greyish breast and primaries. Female has narrow black border to throat-patch and black spots on crown and neck, which lack orange. See Black-bellied and Pin-tailed.

Voice: Flocks very noisy. Usual notes "*kerki,*" or "*kerkerki.*"

Habitat and Range: Sandy semi-desert regions. During periodic irruptions into Europe, usually occurs on sandy coasts, stubble-fields, etc. Nests on ground. Has occurred sporadically throughout Europe, W. to Britain (where it has bred, also in Denmark) and has reached Ireland, Faeroes. Last big invasion 1908.

PIGEONS AND DOVES: Columbidae

Plump, fast-flying birds, with small heads and characteristically deep, crooning voices. The terms "pigeon" and "dove" are loosely used and interchangeable, but in a general way "pigeon" refers to the larger species with ample, squared or rounded tails, "dove" to the smaller, more slender species with longer, graduated tails. Sexes similar. Tree or hole nesting.

WOOD PIGEON *Columba palumbus*   page 80
    Du – Houtduif   Fr – Pigeon ramier
    Ge – Ringeltaube   Sw – Ringduva

Identification: 16″. Larger than other pigeons, with *broad white band across wing* (conspicuous in flight) and glossy green and purple on vinous neck, with *white patch each side*. Juvenile lacks neck markings. Often roams in huge flocks in winter. Mingles freely with town pigeons and Stock Doves. "Explodes" noisily from trees when alarmed. See also Stock and Rock Doves.

Voice: Muffled cooing song, a repeated phrase of five notes, "*cooo-coo, coo-coo, cu,*" accented on first syllable, last one abrupt.

Habitat: Occurs almost anywhere, including town centres, but not otherwise in treeless regions or extreme north. Nests in trees, hedges, old nests, etc. Map below.

STOCK DOVE *Columba oenas*   page 80
    Du – Holenduif   Fr – Pigeon colombin
    Ge – Hohltaube   Sw – Skogsduva

Identification: 13″. Rather *smaller and darker* than Wood Pigeon, from which easily distinguished in flight or when perched by *absence of white on wings and neck*. Upper-parts bluer grey. Glossy green patch on side of neck. Two short broken black wing-bars. Juvenile lacks green on neck. Behaviour like Wood Pigeon, with which it often associates in winter, but less gregarious and flight is more rapid. Rock Dove has distinctive whitish rump and two very broad black wing-bars; but some feral domestic pigeons have rumps like Stock Dove.

Voice: Distinguished from Wood Pigeon's by more monotonous delivery: "*ooo-roo-oo,*" etc., the first syllable being emphasised.

Habitat: As Wood Pigeon, but prefers more open park-land with old trees, also cliffs, sand-dunes, etc. Nests in holes in old trees, rocks, rabbit burrows, buildings, etc. Map p. 178.

WOOD PIGEON →
Partial migrant. Vagrant to Iceland, Faeroes

246

ROCK DOVE *Columba livia* **page 80**

  Du – Rotsduif   Fr – Pigeon biset
  Ge – Felsentaube   Sw – Klippduva

Identification: 13″. The ancestor of the familiar "domestic pigeon." Distinguished from Stock Dove and much larger Wood Pigeon by *whitish rump, two broad black bands right across secondaries, and white beneath wings*. Tail has black terminal band, usually with some white on outer feathers. Plumage blue-grey, paler on back, with glossy green and lilac on sides of neck. Domestic varieties vary from typical ancestral form to white, tan and blackish varieties. Flight faster than Wood Pigeon's and usually low.

Voice: Song indistinguishable from domestic pigeon's "*oo-roo-coo.*"

Habitat: Usually in small numbers around rocky sea cliffs and adjacent fields. On Continent also locally around inland cliffs. Nests in crevices or caves among rocks. Domestic forms abundant in cities and farms, nesting in buildings. Map below.

COLLARED DOVE *Streptopelia decaocto* **page 80**

  Du – Turkse tortel   Fr – Tourterelle turque
  Ge – Türkentaube   Sw – Turkduva

Identification: 11″. Distinguished from Turtle Dove by *impression of longer tail*, uniform *pale* dusty-brown upper-parts and narrow black half-collar at *back* of neck. From below, *white terminal half of black tail* is diagnostic; from above, closed tail looks uniform with upper-parts. Head and under-parts paler and greyer, with vinous-pink flush, particularly on breast. Blackish primaries contrast with rest of plumage. Eyes red. Barbary Dove *S. risoria* (often domesticated) is rather similar but has paler creamy-buff plumage and lacks contrasting dark primaries.

Voice: A deep, "*coo-cooo, coo,*" usually accented on second syllable (*S. risoria* usually accents first syllable). Flight call, a nasal "*kwurr.*"

Habitat: Mainly towns and villages. Usually nests in trees; locally on buildings. Map p. 179.

← STOCK DOVE
Partial migrant

ROCK DOVE →
Resident. Feral birds extend to Arctic circle in Finland

PALM DOVE *Streptopelia senegalensis*   page 284
    Du – Palmtortel   Fr – Tourterelle du Sénégal
    Ge – Palmtaube   Sw – Palmduva

Identification: 10¼″. A smallish dove with a *frontal* neck-ring. Head and neck vinous-pink, with *broad, speckled black and copper collar at base of fore-neck*; chin paler, belly and under tail-coverts white; upper-parts dark rufous, with greyish rump; *pale blue-grey wing-coverts are conspicuous in flight*; tail blackish, with broad white tips to outer feathers; legs and eye-ring crimson. Sexes similar, immature duller.

Voice: A rapidly repeated "*coo*," each series of notes ascending and descending.

Habitat and Range: Widespread in and around towns and villages in parts of Africa and S.W. Asia, nesting in thorn bushes, small trees and on buildings. Now breeds in European as well as Asiatic Turkey.

TURTLE DOVE *Streptopelia turtur*   page 80
    Du – Tortelduif   Fr – Tourterelle des bois
    Ge – Turteltaube   Sw – Turturduva

Identification: 11″. Smaller than other common pigeons; recognised by much more slender shape and *well graduated black tail with white edges*. Upper-parts *sandy-rufous* with black centres to feathers; black and white striped patch on side of neck; soft pinkish throat and breast. Juvenile lacks neck-patches and vinous tinge. Usually in pairs or small parties. Flight swift and direct, wing action more jerky than Wood Pigeon's. See also Collared, Palm, and Rufous (Accidentals p. 319).

Voice: Softer and "sleepier" than that of other pigeons: a repeated, almost purring, "*roor-r-r.*"

Habitat: Open bushy country with uncut hedges and small woods. Nests in bushes, thickets, orchards, etc. Map below.

← COLLARED
DOVE
Resident, but range extended n.w. enormously in last few years. Vagrant Finland

TURTLE DOVE →
Summer visitor. Vag. n. to Iceland, Finland

OWLS

MOST OWLS ARE NOCTURNAL and therefore seldom seen well unless discovered at their daytime roosts. It is particularly important to learn their voices, which are described in the text. None of the following species has "ear tufts."

● **TAWNY OWL**   page 190
    Heavily built; streaked breast; black eyes; rufous
    or grey plumage.

● **LITTLE OWL**   187
    Small; spotted above; low frowning "eyebrows."

PYGMY OWL   187
    Hawfinch-size; small headed; jerks up tail.

▲ **HAWK OWL**   190
    Heavy black facial "frames"; barred under-parts,
    long tail.

○ **TENGMALM'S OWL**   186
    From Little Owl by larger head, broad "eye-brows,"
    whiter face, more heavily outlined facial discs.

URAL OWL   191
    Very large, streaked; unlined face; small dark eyes.

GREAT GREY OWL   191
    Very large, grey; large round head; lined face; small
    yellow eyes.

See also illustrations of other owls, Plate 44.

Grey phase

LITTLE

PYGMY

Rufous phase

Juvenile

TAWNY

HAWK

TENGMALM'S

Adult

URAL

GREAT GREY

ROLLER

HOOPO[E]

BEE-EATER

KINGFISHE[R]

CUCKOO

CUCKOO
Rufous phas[e]
(♀ onl[y]

GREAT SPOTTED
CUCKOO

NIGHTJAR

RED-NECKED NIGHTJ[AR]

Plate 46 181

ROLLER, BEE-EATER, HOOPOE, KINGFISHER, CUCKOOS AND NIGHTJARS

○ **ROLLER** page 198
    Blue-green head and breast; chestnut back.

○ **BEE-EATER** 195
    Yellow throat; blue-green breast; chestnut and yellow above.

● **HOOPOE** 198
    Black and white wing-pattern; erectile fan crest.

● **KINGFISHER** 194
    Stumpy; brilliant blue-green back.

● **CUCKOO** 182
    Grey head and upper breast; barred under-parts. *Rufous phase of female* (rare): Barred above and below.

△ **GREAT SPOTTED CUCKOO** 182
    Crest; long white-edged tail; creamy below, spotted above.

● **NIGHTJAR** 192
    "Dead leaf" camouflage above, closely barred below.

△ **RED-NECKED NIGHTJAR** 193
    Distinguished from Nightjar by rustier upper-parts, more white on throat, heavier head, different voice.

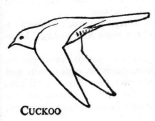

CUCKOO

NIGHTJAR

CUCKOOS: Cuculidae

Rather slim, long-tailed, slender-winged birds, with two toes forward and two behind. Brood-parasitic in nesting. Sexes similar.

CUCKOO *Cuculus canorus*   page 181
    Du – Koekoek   Fr – Coucou gris
    Ge – Kuckuck   Sw – Gök
Identification: 13″. Long-tailed, rather sharp-winged; in flight some-times confused with Sparrow Hawk (which has broad, *rounded* wings). *Call-note is unmistakable.* Upper-parts and throat blue-grey; under-parts whitish, barred dark grey; tail long, rounded, slate-grey, spotted and tipped with white. Legs yellow. Juvenile is variable; upper-parts either red-brown strongly barred (suggesting female Kestrel), or grey-brown with faint bars; both forms have barred buffish-white under-parts and white patch on nape. Rufous females, similar to red-brown juvenile, occur occasionally. Flight direct, gliding before alighting. Solitary outside breeding season.
Voice: A mellow, penetrating "*cuc-coo,*" sometimes single or treble notes; also a deep "*wow-wow-wow.*" Female has long, bubbling note.
Habitat: Edges of woodlands, bushy commons, etc., also in treeless areas, locally on open high ground. Polyandrous and brood-parasitic; individual birds usually parasitising only one species, laying single egg in each nest. Map p. 183.

GREAT SPOTTED CUCKOO *Clamator glandarius*   page 181
    Du – Kuifkoekoek   Fr – Coucou-geai
    Ge – Häherkuckuck   Sw – Skatgök
Identification: 15½″. Easily distinguished by *conspicuous crest*, "capped" appearance, long graduated dark grey tail with *bold white edging*, brown upper-parts *boldly spotted with white*. Under-parts and sides of head creamy-white, yellowish on throat. Bright orange orbital ring. Juvenile has blackish head, no crest, *rich chestnut* primaries. Conspicuous and noisy when breeding, often perching on fences; Magpie-like in some attitudes. Flight fairly strong and direct. Sociable.
Voice: A chattering, tern-like "*kittera, kittera, kittera,*" followed by gobbling notes; a harsh, rising "*zhree*" (recalling Azure-winged Mag-pie), a crow-like "*kark*" of alarm, etc.
Habitat and Range: Outskirts and glades of woods, olive groves, bushy plains with occasional trees. Brood-parasitic, eggs usually laid in nests of crow family, particularly Magpie; often lays several eggs in same nest. Summer visitor to Spain, Portugal, S. France, perhaps Bulgaria, Yugoslavia. Vagrant to S. Europe, N. to Finland, Germany, Denmark and British Isles.

YELLOW-BILLED CUCKOO *Coccyzus americanus*
Du – Geelsnavelkoekoek   Fr – Coulicou à bec jaune
Ge – Gelbschnabelkuckuck   Sw – Gulnäbbad regengök

Identification: 12″. Smaller, slimmer and more dove-like than Cuckoo; dull brown above and whitish below. Distinctive marks are *yellow* lower mandible, *large white spots* at the tips of the dark tail feathers and *rufous* in the wings, conspicuous in flight. See also Black-billed Cuckoo (Accidentals, p. 319).

Voice: A rapid, throaty "*ka-ka-ka-ka-ka-kow-kow-kowp-kowp-kowp*" (slower towards end).

Habitat and Range: Copses, thickets, woodlands. A vagrant from N. America, to British Isles, Iceland, France, Belgium, Denmark, Italy.

BARN OWLS: Tytonidae

BARN OWL *Tyto alba*   page 165
Du – Kerkuil   Fr – Chouette effraie
Ge – Schleiereule   Sw – Tornuggla

Identification: 13½″. A long-legged, very pale owl, with a white face. *Pale golden-buff upper-parts*, finely speckled; *unstreaked white under-parts*. Eyes black. No ear-tufts. Nocturnal, but occasionally hunts by day. Perches upright, when "knock-kneed" long legs and large head are distinctive. Flight wavering and, at dusk, distinctly ghostly. Feeds chiefly on small rodents. Dark-breasted form *T. a. guttata* of N. and E. Europe is darker above and rich buff below.

Voice: A long, wild shriek. Hissing, snoring and yapping notes also occur.

Habitat: Very partial to human habitation, breeding in farm buildings, church towers, ruins, etc. Also frequents parks with old timber, occasionally cliffs. Map below.

← Cuckoo
Summer visitor.
Vagrant Iceland,
Faeroes

Barn Owl →
Mainly resident.
Vagrant north. to
Finland

OWLS: Strigidae

Largely nocturnal birds of prey, with large heads, flattened faces forming "facial discs," and forward-facing eyes. Half-hidden hooked bills and powerful claws. Flight noiseless. Some species have conspicuous feather-tuft "ears." Most owls have large eyes and closely feathered feet. Sexes usually similar. Nest in holes, old nests, or on ground.

SNOWY OWL *Nyctea scandiaca*   page 165
  Du – Sneeuwuil   Fr – Chouette harfang
  Ge – Schneeule   Sw – Fjälluggla

Identification: 21–26″. A *very large, white, round-headed* owl, flecked or barred with dusky brown; some much whiter than others; males whiter than females. Chiefly diurnal and solitary. Glides slowly, or dashes swiftly after passing birds. Takes prey up to size of Arctic Hare and Eider. Perches in open on post, rock, haystack, dune, or other low vantage point. Irrupts from Arctic every four years or so. Distinguished from white Gyr Falcon by larger, rounder head, rounded wings and less vigorous flight; from White-breasted Barn Owl by much larger size, white upper-parts and *yellow eyes.*

Voice: Usually silent. Flight notes when breeding, a repeated loud "*krow-ow,*" or a repeated "*rick.*"

Habitat: Arctic tundra and barren hills. During irruptions frequents open country, dunes, marshes, sea and lake shores, etc. Nests on mossy hummocks in tundra. Map below.

EAGLE OWL *Bubo bubo*   page 165
  Du – Oehoe   Fr – Hibou grand-duc
  Ge – Uhu   Sw – Berguv

Identification: 26–28″. Largest European owl (twice the size of Long-

← SNOWY OWL
See map, but range variable. Partial mig., irregular Scotland. Vag. s. to France, Austria, Yugoslavia

EAGLE   OWL →
Mainly resident. Vagrant Britain, Holland, Denmark

eared Owl), with *prominent ear-tufts*, broadly streaked tawny breast, *large orange eyes*. Upper-parts tawny, mottled with dark brown. Kills prey up to size of Hare and Capercaillie. Hunts at dawn and dusk, roosting in cleft rocks or hollow trees, or perched upright on branch close to tree trunk. Solitary.

Voice: A deep, but brief *"ooo-hu,"* second syllable falling slightly, sometimes followed by a quiet, guttural chuckling.

Habitat: Rocky promontories in forests, crags, mountain sides and open steppes. Breeds in hollow among rocks and scrub, in hollow trees, or old nests of birds of prey. Map p. 184.

LONG-EARED OWL *Asio otus* page 165

Du – Ransuil	Fr – Hibou moyen-duc
Ge – Waldohreule	Sw – Hornuggla

Identification: 14″. Only medium-size owl with *long ear-tufts*. Upper-parts freckled and mottled buff and grey-brown; under-parts buff, boldly marked with dark streaks and with fine cross-barring. Distinguished from bulbous-headed Tawny by angular head, long ear-tufts (when visible), more slender body and *orange-yellow* (instead of black) eyes. In flight, wings and tail look longer than Tawny's; wing-beats are very deep. Short-eared is stockier, with much shorter ear-tufts. Roosts by day in thick foliage, or in upright elongated posture on branch, close to tree trunk. Feeds on small mammals, birds and insects. Locally roosts in small parties in autumn or winter.

Voice: A low, sighing *"oo-oo-oo,"* much more moaning than cry of Tawny. Several yelping and wailing notes and wing clapping also occur. Normally silent outside breeding season.

Habitat: Coniferous forests, also small coppices of conifers, locally in deciduous woods. Breeds in old nests, and occasionally on ground in wood, or on moorland. Map below.

← LONG-EARED OWL
In Finland to c. 68°N. in Lemming years. Partial migrant. Annual Iceland, Faeroes

SHORT-EARED OWL →
Partial migrant. Has bred Ireland, Switz., Hungary. Occas. Faeroes

258   259

SHORT-EARED OWL *Asio flammeus*   page 165
    Du – Velduil   Fr – Hibou des marais
    Ge – Sumpfohreule   Sw – Jorduggla
Identification: 15″. Hunts at dusk and in daylight in open country, when *pale tawny body with boldly streaked under-parts* is distinctive. Has rather long, barred wings, with dark patch on under-side at carpal joint, conspicuous when flying overhead; Long-eared has rather similar patch, but Short-eared also shows darkish carpal patch on upper surface of wing. Distinguished from perched Long-eared Owl by tawnier colour, scarcely visible ear-tufts, "fiercer" expression and lack of cross-barring on under-parts. Perches chiefly on ground, with body held at distinctive inclination. Flight low and rolling, with frequent periods of gliding on slightly raised wings; occasionally flies very high. Sometimes seen in parties, during rodent "plagues."
Voice: A high sneezing bark "*kee-aw.*" Song, a repeated, deep "*boo-boo-boo,*" usually during circling display flight. Wing clapping also occurs.
Habitat: Open marshy country, sand-dunes, moors. Breeds on ground among heather, sedges, clumps of marram grass, etc. Map p. 185.

SCOPS OWL *Otus scops*   page 165
    Du – Dwergooruil   Fr – Hibou petit-duc
    Ge – Zwergohreule   Sw – Dvärguv
Identification: 7½″. Identified by combination of very small size and *ear tufts* (latter not always conspicuous). Plumage closely vermiculated and speckled grey-brown. Has smaller, less flat head than Little Owl and is slimmer, with more tapered shape and longer tail. *Monotonous song* is very distinctive. Chiefly nocturnal. Feeds chiefly on insects.
Voice: Usual note a soft, penetrating, persistently repeated "*pew,*" closely resembling voice of Midwife Toad, which often causes confusion.
Habitat: Trees near human habitation, plantations, gardens, etc.; also among old buildings. Nests in holes, occasionally in old nests of other birds. Map p. 187.

TENGMALM'S OWL *Aegolius funereus*   page 180
    Du – Ruigpootuil   Fr – Chouette de Tengmalm
    Ge – Rauhfusskauz   Sw – Pärluggla
              N.Am – Boreal Owl
Identification: 10″. Slightly larger than Little Owl, but distinguished by more erect posture, larger, *much more rounded head, with deeper facial discs* (not flattened over eyes as in Little Owl). Has *blacker borders* to facial discs, broader white eyebrows, *chocolate-brown* coloration, and white, well-feathered legs and feet, crown finely spotted (not streaked) with white. Juvenile almost uniform mahogany-colour with broad white eyebrows. Strictly nocturnal except in Arctic. Roosts by day in conifers. Flight wavering, not dipping like Little Owl.
Voice: A fairly rapid phrase of 3-6 similar, high, but musical notes,

"poo-poo-poo," etc., the final note often diminishing in emphasis, sometimes accelerating almost to a trill.

Habitat: Coniferous forests in mountainous regions, locally in mixed woods. Winters in valleys and lowlands. Nests in woodpecker holes, or natural holes in trees. Map below.

LITTLE OWL *Athene noctua* page 180

Du – Steenuil	Fr – Chouette chevêche
Ge – Steinkauz	Sw – Minervauggla

Identification: 8½″. Distinguished by *small size* and *squat, flat-headed appearance.* Upper-parts dark brown, closely spotted and barred with white. Under-parts whitish, broadly streaked with dark brown. Flattened head and face and yellow eyes give fierce, frowning expression. Often seen in daylight. Perches upright on telegraph poles, fences, etc. Bobs and bows when suspicious. Flight low and rapid, *deeply undulating.* Feeds chiefly on insects and small rodents, less often on small birds. See also Tengmalm's Owl.

Voice: A shrill rather plaintive *"kiu,"* a sharp, barking *"werro,"* etc.

Habitat: Varied, but usually fairly open farming country and stony waste land. Nests in holes in trees, especially pollarded willows, and in rocks, buildings, burrows. Map p. 190.

PYGMY OWL *Glaucidium passerinum* page 180

Du – Dwerguil	Fr – Chouette chevêchette
Ge – Sperlingskauz	Sw – Sparvuggla

Identification: 6½″. Smallest European owl—smaller than Starling. Distinguished by *very small size* and relatively small head. Upper-parts dark brown, spotted with whitish-buff; grey-white under-parts streaked with blackish; whitish face with small yellow eyes beneath short white "eyebrows." Tail closely barred brown and whitish, *frequently elevated or jerked upward.* Behaviour bold and active. Partly diurnal. Hunts and kills small birds in flight. Little Owl is much larger and paler, with flattened crown. See also Tengmalm's.

← Scops Owl
*Partial migrant.
Vag. British Isles,
Holland, Denmark,
Sweden, Iceland*

Tengmalm's
Owl →
*Part. resident. At
times numerous in
winter Den. (has
bred). Vagrant w.
to Britain, Spain*

WOODPECKERS AND WRYNECK

● **LESSER SPOTTED WOODPECKER**   page 203
Sparrow-size; closely barred back.

MIDDLE SPOTTED WOODPECKER   202
Resembles juvenile Great Spotted, but black face-
marks not joined. No black border to red cap.

● **GREAT SPOTTED WOODPECKER**   201
Large white scapular patches, black crown. Juvenile
has red crown.

SYRIAN WOODPECKER   201
Like Great Spotted, but white cheek lacks bar.

WHITE-BACKED WOODPECKER   203
White lower back; barred wings.

THREE-TOED WOODPECKER   204
White back; barred flanks; black cheeks.
Male has yellow cap.

BLACK WOODPECKER   200
Crow-size; black; flaming red crown.

● **GREEN WOODPECKER**   199
Greenish back; yellow rump; dark face with broad
pointed "moustaches." Juvenile spotted.

GREY-HEADED WOODPECKER   200
Grey head with narrow black "moustaches."
Male only has red cap.

● **WRYNECK**   199
Long tail; Nightjar-like pattern.

LESSER   MIDDLE   GREAT   WHITE-
SPOTTED   SPOTTED   SPOTTED   BACKED

LESSER SPOTTED

MIDDLE SPOTTED

SYRIAN

Juvenile

GREAT SPOTTED

BLACK

WHITE-BACKED

THREE-TOED

Juvenile

WRYNECK

GREEN

GREY-HEADED

CRESTED LARK

SKY LARK

WOOD LARK

♂ Summer

Immature

SHORE LARK

SHORT-TOED LARK

THEKLA LARK

CALANDRA LARK

LESSER SHORT-TOED LARK

Immature

WHITE-WINGED LARK

♂ Winter

BLACK LARK

DUPONT'S LARK

Plate 48 189

LARKS

STREAKED, MAINLY BROWN ground birds with
aerial songs. They somewhat resemble pipits
(Plate 58) but are heavier, broader-winged.

● **SKY LARK** page 208
  Crested; streaked; white edge to longish tail.

● **WOOD LARK** 208
  From Sky Lark by short tail without white edge;
  supercilia meet across nape; black and white mark
  on wing-edge.

△ **CRESTED LARK** 207
  Long crest; short tawny-edged tail; buff beneath
  rounded wings.

● **SHORE LARK** 207
  "Horns"; black patches on face and breast.
  Immature: Suggestion of adult pattern.

  THEKLA LARK 207
  Very like Crested, but with darker plumage; more
  clearly marked breast; grey beneath wings.

△ **CALANDRA LARK** 205
  Large; heavy bill; large neck-patch; whitish rear
  edges to dark wings.

○ **SHORT-TOED LARK** 205
  Small; pale; clear breast; small neck-spot.

△ **LESSER SHORT-TOED LARK** 205
  Small; grey-brown; finely streaked breast.

△ **WHITE-WINGED LARK** 206
  Rusty crown; white wing-patch (see Snow Bunting).

  BLACK LARK 206
  Black; in winter "scaled" with white.

  DUPONT'S LARK 204
  Thin curved bill; conspicuous eye-stripe.

Voice: Very vocal. A whistling *"keeoo," "kitchick,"* etc. Song, a monotonously repeated Bullfinch-like *"whee . . . whee . . . whee . . ."*
Habitat: Mature secluded forests, usually coniferous, in mountainous regions. Nests in hollow trees, and woodpecker holes. Map below.

HAWK OWL *Surnia ulula*   page 180
    Du – Sperweruil   Fr – Chouette épervière
    Ge – Sperbereule   Sw – Hökuggla
Identification: 14-16″. Distinguished from other owls by *long tail* and rather short, pointed wings, which give hawk-like silhouette in flight, and by *closely-barred* under-parts. Face whitish, *heavily bordered with black*. Crown and upper-parts blackish-brown, barred with white. Hunts chiefly by day. Perches conspicuously on tree-top or telegraph pole, often in un-owl-like, *inclined posture* and frequently jerks tail. Flight recalls Sparrow Hawk, usually low, sweeping upward to perch. Often bold and indifferent to man.
Voice: A chattering *"kikikiki,"* more like hawk than owl.
Habitat: Coniferous forests and open birch scrub. Breeds in shelter of broken tree-top, in hollow trees, old nests of hawks, etc. Map p. 191.

TAWNY OWL *Strix aluco*   page 180
    Du – Bosuil   Fr – Chouette hulotte
    Ge – Waldkauz   Sw – Kattuggla
Identification: 15″. *Mottled and streaked, large round head, black eyes, no ear-tufts.* Upper-parts vary from warm brown to tawny or greyish. Under-parts buffish-brown with bold dark streaks. Facial discs grey-brown. Strictly nocturnal. Feeds chiefly on small rodents, birds, insects, etc. Distinguished from Long-eared by heavier build, black eyes and absence of ear-tufts; from Short-eared by darker, less buff appearance and black eyes; from Barn Owl by larger size and much darker appearance, particularly of face and under-parts.

← Little Owl
Resident. Vagrant S. Sweden (has bred), Scotland, Ireland

Pygmy Owl →
Mainly resident. Vagrant Denmark, Holland, Belgium

Voice: A shrill *"ke-wick."* Song, a deep musical *"hoo-hoo-hoo,"* followed at an interval by a long, tremulous *"oo-oo-oo-oo."*

Habitat: Mature woods, parks, large gardens. Nests in hollow trees, old nests of large birds, occasionally in buildings and rabbit burrows. Map below.

URAL OWL *Strix uralensis* page 180

Du – Oeraluil   Fr – Chouette de l'Oural
Ge – Habichtskauz   Sw – Slaguggla

Identification: 24″. Resembles very large, *pale, long-tailed* Tawny. General colour greyish-white, broadly streaked with dark brown; wings and rather long, well-rounded tail are boldly barred. Head rounded, without ear-tufts. Facial discs greyish-white *without lines.* Eyes *blackish-brown.* Behaviour much as Tawny Owl. Great Grey is larger, with *yellow* eyes and heavily lined facial discs. Tawny is much smaller and darker, with larger eyes.

Voice: A rather high, barking *"wow . . . wow . . . wow . . ."* at irregular intervals, and a harsh *"kawveck."*

Habitat: Mixed woods, coppices and forests. Nests in fractures of broken-off trees, occasionally in old nests of birds of prey. Map p. 192.

GREAT GREY OWL *Strix nebulosa* page 180

Du – Laplanduil   Fr – Chouette lapone
Ge – Bartkauz   Sw – Lappuggla

Identification: 27″. Near size of Eagle Owl, but easily distinguished by *grey colour, very round head without ear-tufts* and longer tail. Plumage dusky grey, irregularly marked with dark and white on upper-parts and broadly streaked below. Facial discs very large and heavily lined; *dark patch on chin*; *eyes noticeably small and yellow.* In flight shows distinctive pale band across base of primaries. Ural Owl is somewhat smaller and browner, with *dark* eyes and *unlined* facial discs.

Voice: A deep-toned, booming *"hu-hu-hoo,"* often rising and repeated at regular intervals; also a high, shrill *"ke-wick"*; both calls not unlike Tawny's.

← HAWK OWL
Partial migrant.
Almost annual E.
Prussia. Vag. s. to
Britain, Switzer-
land, North Yugo-
slavia, Roumania

TAWNY OWL →
Resident

Habitat and Range: Dense northern coniferous forests. Lays in old nests of large birds of prey. Resident in Arctic Norway, Sweden, Finland. In "invasion" years, extends S. over much of Scandinavia, Finland, Estonia, occasionally E. Prussia.

NIGHTJARS: Caprimulgidae

Nocturnal insectivorous birds, with large eyes, huge gapes, tiny bills and feet, long wings and ample tails. Plumage beautifully camouflaged with "dead leaf" pattern. Usually pass day immobile, on ground or perched lengthways along branch. Sexes similar. Ground nesting.

NIGHTJAR *Caprimulgus europaeus*   page 181

Du – Nachtzwaluw   Fr – Engoulevent d'Europe
Ge – Ziegenmelker   Sw – Nattskärra

Identification: 10½". Best known for remarkable nocturnal *churring song*. General appearance elongated, grey-brown, closely speckled and barred with dark brown and buff, affording perfect camouflage. Broad head is flattened, with very small bill and very large gape. Wings and tail are long. Male has three white spots near wing-tips and conspicuous white tips to outer tail-feathers. Spends day crouched motionless along (occasionally across) branch, or on ground. Feeds on wing at night, pursuing moths in floating, erratic and silent flight. Loud "wing-clapping" is frequent during breeding season. See also Red-necked and Egyptian Nightjars.

Voice: Flight call, a soft nasal "*goo-ek*"; alarm, a high "*quick-quick-quick.*" Song, at night, a loud, rapid churring, *rising and falling* and sustained for as long as five minutes, sometimes "running down" with a few clucking notes. Beware similar noise of Mole Crickets.

Habitat: Moors, commons, open woodland glades with bracken and sand-dunes. Lays eggs on bare ground. Map below.

← URAL OWL
*Mainly resident.
To dotted line in
winter. Vag. Italy,
Hungary*

NIGHTJAR →
*Summer visitor.
Vagrant Iceland,
Faeroes*

RED-NECKED NIGHTJAR *Caprimulgus ruficollis* page 181
  Du – Moorse nachtzwaluw   Fr – Engoulevent à collier roux
  Ge – Rothalsziegenmelker   Sw – Rödhalsad nattskärra
Identification: 12″. Looks very similar to the Nightjar, but distinguished by somewhat larger size, *heavier head, sandy-rufous collar and larger white throat-patch.* In flight looks more rufous and heavier than Nightjar; *both* sexes show more conspicuous white marks on primaries and on outer tail-feathers.
Voice: Far-carrying song consists of single, or usually double incessantly repeated notes, "*kutuk-kutuk-kutuk,*" etc., like hard rapping on hollow wood, up to 100 notes per minute.
Habitat and Range: Pine-woods, bushy, semi-desert regions and pine-clad hillsides. Lays eggs on bare ground. Summer visitor Spain, and Portugal. Has bred S. France. Vagrant to Sicily, Malta, Britain.

EGYPTIAN NIGHTJAR *Caprimulgus aegyptius*
  Du – Egyptische nachtzwaluw   Fr – Engoulevent d'Egypte
  Ge – Ägyptischer Ziegenmelker   Sw – Ökennattskärra
Identification: 10″. *Much paler* and noticeably sandier than Nightjar, appearing almost uniform in flight, though plumage is finely pencilled. Neither sex has well-defined white spots on wings or tail, though webs of inner primaries are whitish.
Voice: Said to churr like Nightjar.
Habitat and Range: A desert species, of casual occurrence in Malta and Sicily. Has been recorded Heligoland, England.

SWIFTS: Apodidae

Essentially aerial. Slim, with long, scythe-like wings and short tails. Flight extremely rapid. Sexes similar. Hole nesting.

PALLID SWIFT *Apus pallidus*   page 196
  Du – Vale gierzwaluw   Fr – Martinet pâle
  Ge – Fahlsegler   Sw – Blek tornsvala
Identification: 6½″. With practice can be distinguished in silhouette from Swift by slightly broader head and less neat outline. Looks paler grey-brown; has larger area of whitish on throat; slight pale mottling visible on flanks; upper-surfaces of secondaries paler than rest of wing. Wing-beats less rapid than Swift's. Behaviour, voice and habitat as Swift, with which it often associates. Map p. 194.

SWIFT *Apus apus*   page 196
  Du – Gierzwaluw   Fr – Martinet noir
  Ge – Mauersegler   Sw – Tornsvala
Identification: 6½″. Distinguished from all swallow family by *long, scythe-shaped wings; sooty, blackish plumage,* with whitish chin (seldom

visible); short, forked tail. Sociable and exclusively aerial in habit. Flight very rapid and distinctive, on extremely quickly-beaten, stiffly-held wings. Noisy during breeding season, when screaming groups chase wildly around roof-tops. See also Alpine and Pallid Swifts.

Voice: A shrill, prolonged, piercing screech; also a rapid chirruping at nest or roosting hole.

Habitat: Aerial. May occur anywhere, but especially in areas with suitable nesting sites. Usually nests in buildings under eaves, occasionally in rocky cliffs; in holes in trees in N. Europe. Map below.

ALPINE SWIFT *Apus melba*   page 196
      Du – Alpengierzwaluw   Fr – Martinet alpin
      Ge – Alpensegler   Sw – Alpseglare

Identification: 8¼", with 21" wing-span. *Much larger*, paler and browner than Swift, with *white under-parts and brown breast-band*. Size is conspicuous when seen together. Very distinctive voice. Behaviour and flight like Swift, but often glides with wings deeply depressed. Sociable. See also Needle-tailed Swift (Accidentals p. 319).

Voice: Has loud, rising and falling, trilling flight-call, like distant cry of falcon and quite unlike Swift; usually in chorus while wheeling around nesting places.

Habitat: Chiefly in high, rocky mountainous regions, locally also along sea-cliffs and among old buildings. Builds cup-shaped nest in cleft rocks, natural crevices and beneath rafters. Usually nests in colonies. Map p. 195.

KINGFISHERS: Alcedinidae

KINGFISHER *Alcedo atthis*   page 181
      Du – IJsvogel   Fr – Martin-pêcheur
      Ge – Eisvogel   Sw – Kungsfiskare

← PALLID SWIFT
Summer visitor.
Vagrant Malta

SWIFT →
Summer visitor.
Vagrant Iceland,
Faeroes

Identification: 6½″. Unmistakable. Brilliant *iridescent blue and emerald green upper-parts*, white throat and neck-patch, *chestnut cheeks and under-parts, long dagger-shaped bill.* Head large, body stumpy, wings and tail short, feet small and bright red. Perches alertly, with frequent nervous "bobbing" action of head and tail, plunging into water after small fish or insects, occasionally hovering before plunging. Normal flight low, direct and very rapid. Solitary.
Voice: A high, piping *"chee,"* or *"chee-kee,"* repeated rapidly when excited. Infrequent song, a short trill, of similar quality to call-notes.
Habitat: Streams, rivers, canals, lakes. In winter also sea coast and tidal marshes. Nests in holes bored in stream banks, sometimes far from water. Map below.

BEE-EATERS: Meropidae

BEE-EATER *Merops apiaster*   page 181

Du – Bijeneter   Fr – Guêpier d'Europe
Ge – Bienenfresser   Sw – Biätare

Identification: 11″. Unmistakable. *Vivid colours,* long curved bill and projecting middle tail-feathers are conspicuous even at long range. Both sexes have *chestnut and yellow upper-parts,* blue-green primaries and tail, *blue-green under-parts* with *brilliant yellow throat.* Juvenile lacks long middle tail-feathers. Behaviour essentially gregarious; often perches on telegraph wires. Flight graceful, with gliding turns on level wings.
Voice: Very distinctive. Usual note a liquid but far-carrying and constantly repeated *"prruip."*
Habitat: Prefers open bushy country with a few trees, telegraph poles, etc., but also occurs in woodland glades. Breeds colonially in holes bored in cuttings, sand-pits, river banks, occasionally in level ground. Map p. 198.

← ALPINE SWIFT
*Summer visitor.
Has bred Germany.
Vagrant Brit. Is.,
Belgium, Holland,
Denmark, Czecho.*

KINGFISHER →
*Partial migrant,
Vagrant Norway,
and Malta*

273   274

SWIFTS, SWALLOWS AND MARTINS

SWALLOW   HOUSE MARTIN   SAND MARTIN

SWALLOW   HOUSE MARTIN   RED-RUMPED SWALLOW   SAND MARTIN

SWIFT

PALLID SWIFT

ALPINE SWIFT

HOUSE MARTIN

SWALLOW

RED-RUMPED SWALLOW

SAND MARTIN

CRAG MARTIN

MAGPIE

NUTCRACKER

AZURE-WINGED
MAGPIE

ALPINE CHOUG

JAY

CHOUGH

GOLDEN ORIOI

SIBERIAN
JAY

♀

♂

♂
Spring

Juvenile

Winter

Adult

SPOTLESS STARLING

STARLING

ROSE-
COLOURED
STARLING

Plate 50 197

MAGPIES, NUTCRACKER, CHOUGHS, JAYS, ORIOLE AND STARLINGS

ROLLERS: Coraciidae

ROLLER *Coracias garrulus*   page 181
   Du – Scharrelaar   Fr – Rollier d'Europe
   Ge – Blauracke   Sw – Blåkråka
Identification: 12″. A heavy Jay-like bird with a powerful bill. Plumage
is *pale azure-blue, with bright chestnut back, vivid blue wings with black
borders* (in flight), greenish-blue tail with brown centre feathers.
Behaviour rather shrike-like, pouncing from exposed perch or over-
head wires on passing insects. Flight Jackdaw-like, gliding occa-
sionally; "tumbles" from considerable height during nuptial display.
Voice: A loud, deep, corvine *"kr-r-r-r-ak,"* or *"krak-ak,"* and a harsh
chatter.
Habitat: Mature forests and fairly open country with a few trees.
Breeds in old hollow trees, holes in banks, ruins, etc. Map below.

HOOPOES: Upupidae

HOOPOE *Upupa epops*   page 181
   Du – Hop   Fr – Huppe fasciée
   Ge – Wiedehopf   Sw – Härfågel
Identification: 11″. Unmistakable. Both sexes have pale pinkish
brown plumage, *boldly barred black and white wings and tail,* long
black-tipped *erectile crest* (which is usually depressed) and long curved
bill. Feeds chiefly on ground in open. Flight lazy and undulating, with
distinctive, slow "open-and-shut" action of rounded wings.
Voice: A low, far-carrying *"poo-poo-poo"*; also several mewing notes
and a quiet chattering alarm.

← BEE-EATER
*Summer visitor.
Has bred Britain,
Belg., Den., Germ.,
Switzer. Vagrant
Ireland, Europe n.
to Sweden, Finland*

ROLLER →
*Summer visitor.
Vagrant n. to Brit.
Is., Iceland, Nor-
way, Finland*

275

276

Habitat: Open woodlands, orchards, park-lands, etc. Winters in more open bushy country. Nests in holes in old trees, occasionally in ruins. Map below.

WOODPECKERS: Picidae

Chisel-billed birds, with powerful feet (usually two toes front, two rear), remarkably long tongues, and short, stiff tails which act as props in climbing tree trunks. Flight usually strong, but undulating. Most males have some red on head. Nest in holes excavated in trees.

WRYNECK *Jynx torquilla*   page 188
    Du – Draaihals   Fr – Torcol fourmilier
    Ge – Wendehals   Sw – Göktyta

Identification: 6½". Although related to woodpeckers, appearance and attitudes are rather passerine. At a distance looks *uniform grey-brown, with paler under-parts*; at short range vermiculated plumage resembles Nightjar's. Upper-parts and long, rounded tail closely patterned grey, brown and buff. Under-parts buffish, closely chequered with grey-brown. Feet like woodpecker's: two toes forward, two behind. Crown feathers erectile. More often heard than seen. Feeds on ground, hopping with raised tail; perches across branches, but clings like woodpecker to tree trunks. Flight undulating, looking rather like long-tailed lark.

Voice: A nasal, repeated *"kyee kyee,"* louder and less shrill than Lesser Spotted Woodpecker's call, resembling distant Hobby.

Habitat: Gardens, orchards, parks, hedgerows with trees. Nests in natural holes in trees, masonry, nest boxes, etc. Map below.

GREEN WOODPECKER *Picus viridis*   page 188
    Du – Groene specht   Fr – Pic vert
    Ge – Grünspecht   Sw – Gröngöling

← HOOPOE
Mainly summer visitor. Has bred Britain, Sweden, Finland. Annual Ireland. Vagrant Iceland, Faeroes

WRYNECK →
Mainly summer visitor. Vagrant to Ireland, Scotland, Iceland, Faeroes

Identification: 12½″. A large woodpecker with *dull green upper-parts*, pale grey-green under-parts, crimson crown, *conspicuous yellowish rump and lower back*. Sides of head and moustachial stripe are black; male has crimson centre to very broad moustachial stripe. Juvenile is paler, distinctly spotted and barred. Frequently feeds on ground, at ants' nests. Hops heavily, in upright position. Flight deeply undulating, with long wing-closures between each upward bound. See also Grey-headed.
Voice: A very loud ringing "laugh." Very seldom drums.
Habitat: Deciduous woods, parks, farm-lands, commons with scattered trees. Nests in holes bored in trees. Map below.

GREY-HEADED WOODPECKER *Picus canus*   page 188

     Du – Kleine groene specht   Fr – Pic cendré
     Ge – Grauspecht   Sw – Gråspett

Identification: 10″. Easily mistaken for rather small, greyish Green Woodpecker, but distinguished by *grey head and neck* with thin black stripe through eye and *narrow* black moustachial stripe. Male has bright crimson forehead (not crown). Female lacks red. Juvenile is browner and has flanks barred with brown; young males show some crimson on forehead. Behaviour as Green Woodpecker. Spanish race of Green has little black on face and greyish coloration and can therefore be confused with Grey-headed.
Voice: Call notes resemble Green Woodpecker's, but "laughing" song is much less harsh and becomes *progressively deeper and slower*. Drums for long periods in spring.
Habitat: As Green Woodpecker, but also occurs locally in deciduous mountain forests up to tree limits. Less often in coniferous woods. Map below.

BLACK WOODPECKER *Dryocopus martius*   page 188

     Du – Zwarte specht   Fr – Pic noir
     Ge – Schwarzspecht   Sw – Spillkråka

Identification: 18″. Largest European woodpecker (big as a Rook),

← GREEN
     WOODPECKER
Resident. Vagrant N. Norway, Ireland

GREY-HEADED
     WOODPECKER →
Resident. Vagrant Lapland, Denmark

with *uniform black plumage*. Male has slightly crested crimson crown; female has crimson confined to patch on back of head. Eyes pale yellow. Bill pale. Flight heavy and undulating.

Voice: A loud, whistling "*kleea*" and a high, grating "*krri-krri-krri-krri.*" Song, usually in flight, a strident, ringing "*choc-choc-choc,*" recalling Green Woodpecker, but usually slower and shorter. Drums occasionally and very loudly.

Habitat: Mature coniferous forests in northern and mountainous regions and in beech woods. Excavates very large oval nest-hole, sometimes at considerable height. Map below.

GREAT SPOTTED WOODPECKER *Dendrocopos major*
page 188

Du – Grote bonte specht	Fr – Pic épeiche
Ge – Buntspecht	Sw – Större hackspett

Identification: 9″. Considerably smaller than Green, but much larger than Lesser Spotted, from which it is distinguished by black back with *large white shoulder patches* and *crimson under tail-coverts*. (Upper-parts of Lesser Spotted give closely barred impression.) *Unbroken black bar across white cheek*. Under-parts are unstreaked white, with *sharply defined* red below tail. Male (not female) has crimson nape-patch, but immatures of both sexes have *entire crown crimson*. Seldom feeds on ground, but often on bird-tables. See also White-backed, Middle Spotted and Syrian Woodpeckers.

Voice: A very loud, sharp "*tchick*" or "*kik,*" much louder and more frequent than similar call of Lesser Spotted. Both sexes drum very rapidly on resonant dead branches.

Habitat: More a woodland and garden bird than Green, but also in pine-woods in north. Map below.

SYRIAN WOODPECKER *Dendrocopos syriacus*   page 188

Du – Syrische bonte specht	Fr – Pic syriaque
Ge – Blutspecht	Sw – Syrisk hackspett

Identification: Very similar to Great Spotted (large white shoulder

← BLACK
   WOODPECKER
Mainly resident.
Vagrant Denmark

GREAT SPOTTED
   WOODPECKER →
Mainly resident.
Vagrant Iceland,
Faeroes, Ireland

patches and black cap), but *lack of black cheek-bar gives white-faced appearance*. Tail shows less white than Great Spotted, but wings show more white. Under tail-coverts are paler crimson than in Great Spotted. Juveniles, because of their red caps, may be confused with Middle Spotted, but have reddish collar and black moustachial stripe joining bill.

Voice: Softer than Great Spotted: a quiet "*chig*," "*kirrook*" (not unlike Moorhen) and a song recalling Middle Spotted.

Habitat: Chiefly around villages and near cultivation. Map below.

MIDDLE SPOTTED WOODPECKER *Dendrocopos medius*
page 188

<table>
<tr><td>Du – Middelste bonte specht</td><td>Fr – Pic mar</td></tr>
<tr><td>Ge – Mittelspecht</td><td>Sw – Mellanspett</td></tr>
</table>

Identification: 8½". Can be confused with Great Spotted and Syrian, which are only other European woodpeckers with *white shoulder patches*. Distinguished by slightly smaller size, conspicuous and slightly crested light crimson crown without any black edging; *conspicuous white sides to head* have very narrow black moustachial stripe, but no black-eye stripe; whole head looks pale; white underparts with heavily streaked flanks *merge gradually* into rose-pink on belly (instead of contrasting sharply with crimson under tail-coverts as in Great Spotted). Wings boldly barred black and white, with narrower white shoulder patches than Great Spotted. Female is duller, with paler crimson crown. See also Syrian.

Voice: Resembles Great Spotted's quick chatter, but is slightly lower in pitch and the first note is usually higher: "*ptik-teuk-teuk-teuk-teuk*." In spring has slow, nasal cry, "*wait . . . wait . . .*" repeated in descending or ascending scale. Drums rarely.

Habitat: Usually in hornbeam and beech forest, in high branches. Excavates nest hole high up in deciduous tree. Map below.

← Syrian Woodpecker *Mainly resident. Extending range north-west*

Middle Spotted Woodpecker → *Mainly resident. Vagrant Holland (has bred), Belg., Portugal, Finland*

WHITE-BACKED WOODPECKER *Dendrocopos leucotos*

page 188

Du – Witrugspecht	Fr – Pic à dos blanc
Ge – Weissrückenspecht	Sw – Vitryggig hackspett

Identification: 10″. Larger, more slender-looking than Great Spotted and with paler head. Distinguished by combination of *uniform black back and shoulders and white or barred rump*. Male has whitish forehead and scarlet crown extending to nape. Under-parts white, boldly streaked with black on flanks, *merging into* pink under tail-coverts. Wings boldly barred black and white, *without white shoulder patches*. Female has black crown. Juveniles show trace of red on crown and under tail-coverts. Three-toed is only other European woodpecker with white rump, but is much smaller and is white from nape to rump.

Voice: Infrequent notes resemble Great Spotted's, but are quieter.

Habitat: Hilly deciduous woods with plenty of old rotting trees; locally in dense coniferous forests; around towns in winter. Nests in holes bored in rotted trees. Map below.

LESSER SPOTTED WOODPECKER *Dendrocopos minor*

page 188

Du – Kleine bonte specht	Fr – Pic épeichette
Ge – Kleinspecht	Sw – Mindre hackspett

Identification: 5¾″. Smallest European woodpecker. Distinguished from all other "pied" woodpeckers by *sparrow-size, closely barred* black and white upper-parts and *absence of any red on under tail-coverts*. Forehead, cheeks and under-parts whitish, with a few dark streaks on flanks. Male has dull crimson crown; female's is whitish; juveniles show some crimson on crown and have browner under-parts. Behaviour retiring; spends most of time in small upper branches, *fluttering among twigs*.

Voice: A repeated, high "*pee-pee-pee*," not unlike Wryneck's call, but weaker and less ringing. Also a rather weak "*tchick*," resembling cry of Great Spotted. Drums less powerfully than Great Spotted.

Habitat: Old orchards and open woodlands. Map below.

← WHITE-BACKED
WOODPECKER
Resident.

LESSER SPOTTED
WOODPECKER →
*Resident. Vagrant
Denmark*

THREE-TOED WOODPECKER *Picoides tridactylus* page 188

Du – Drieteenspecht   Fr – Pic tridactyle
Ge – Dreizehenspecht   Sw – Tretåig hackspett

Identification: 8¾″. About size of Great Spotted, with large head. Feet have only three toes. Distinguished from all other European woodpeckers by *complete lack of crimson markings* (even in male), nearly all-black wings, *broad whitish stripe down back from nape to rump* and black cheeks. Male has *yellow* centre to crown; female's is black, with whitish forehead. Under-parts white, *barred with black* on flanks. Juveniles are greyer, with white backs considerably mottled with black. White-backed Woodpecker also has white, but its upper back is black and it has rosy under tail-coverts and white bars on wings. Less active than other woodpeckers, passing long periods at one spot.

Voice: Seldom vocal, but resembles weak Great Spotted; sometimes a chattering "*kek-ek-ek-ek.*" Drums occasionally, rather slowly.

Habitat: Mountain and Arctic forests, with preference for burnt tracts. Nests in holes bored in trees and telegraph poles. Map below.

LARKS: Alaudidae

Mostly streaked brown ground-birds, with running gait. Fine singers, often high in air. Sexes similar (except Black Lark). Ground nesting.

DUPONT'S LARK *Chersophilus duponti* page 189

Du – Dupont's leeuwerik   Fr – Sirli de Dupont
Ge – Dupont-Lerche   Sw – Smalnäbbad lärka

Identification: 7½″. An extremely secretive species, distinguished by rufous appearance, *long slender, down-curved bill* and absence of white on wings; outer tail-feather white; pale eye-stripe is conspicuous. Rarely seen on wing, except in spring song-flight, when it soars to great height; on landing *runs remarkably swiftly* to hide in thickest available cover; stands very slim and erect.

← THREE-TOED
    WOODPECKER
*Resident. Vagrant
Italy*

SHORT-TOED
    LARK →
*Summer visitor.
Vagrant n. to Fair
Isle, Ireland, Ice-
land, and central
Europe to Czecho.*

287

289

Habitat and Range: Semi-desert, with wild thyme, scrub, etc. Vagrant to Mediterranean Europe, from Malta westwards.

SHORT-TOED LARK *Calandrella cinerea* page 189
Du – Kortteenleeuwerik   Fr – Alouette calandrelle
Ge – Kurzzehenlerche   Sw – Korttålärka

Identification: 5½". Paler and much smaller than Sky Lark. Buffish above, with bold dark streaks; *unstreaked* buffish-white below; *small blackish patches* on sides of neck (often difficult to see). No crest, but slightly *darker "cap."* Short, pointed yellowish bill. Juvenile has a few spots on breast. Flight low and undulating. See also Lesser Short-toed Lark.

Voice: A short, dry chirrup, "*tchi-tchirrp*," recalling House Sparrow; anxiety note, "*tee-oo*." Song, chiefly in high, steeply *rising and falling* flight, a simple phrase of about eight high-pitched notes, repeated at short intervals, and long sustained.

Habitat: Open sandy or stony wastes, dry mud-flats with *Salicornia*, steppes and fields. Nests on ground. Map p. 204.

LESSER SHORT-TOED LARK *Calandrella rufescens* page 189
Du – Kleine kortteenleeuwerik   Fr – Alouette pispolette
Ge – Stummellerche   Sw – Dvärglärka

Identification: 5½". Distinguishable at short range from Short-toed, with which it may occur, by *finely streaked upper breast*. Crown as mantle, not "capped." Lacks dark neck patches and is generally darker, greyer and less rufous.

Voice: Has short, characteristic note "*prrit*" which also occurs in song. Song is more melodious, imitative and continuous than Short-toed, but has similar character; sings in rising spiral, or high circling flight.

Habitat and Range: As Short-toed, but also especially dry edges of marshes. Summer visitor, breeding S. Spain. Vagrant to British Isles, Malta, Italy, Heligoland.

CALANDRA LARK *Melanocorypha calandra* page 189
Du – Kalanderleeuwerik   Fr – Alouette calandre
Ge – Kalanderlerche   Sw – Kalanderlarak

Identification: 7½". Distinguished by large size, heavy build, *stout yellowish-horn bill and bold black half-collar on each side of neck*. Buffish breast lightly streaked with brown. In flight, tips of secondaries form *conspicuous white rear edges* to large *triangular* wings, which look *very dark below*. No crest. Juvenile more buffish; neck-patches partly obscured. Flight very buoyant. See also White-winged Lark and female Black Lark; also Bimaculated Lark (Accidentals p. 320).

Voice: A nasal chirrup "*kleetra*." Song similar to Sky Lark's, but louder, with frequent interjections of mimicry and trilling; sings in high circling flight, often diving silently last few hundred feet to ground.

Habitat: Stony waste-lands, farm-lands and steppes. Nests on ground. Map below.

WHITE-WINGED LARK *Melanocorypha leucoptera*　　　page 189
　　　Du – Witvleugelleeuwerik　　　Fr – Alouette leucoptère
　　　Ge – Weissflügellerche　　　Sw – Vitvingad lärka
Identification: 7″. Distinguished from other larks by *broad white wing-patch*, reaching hind edge, very conspicuous in flight; from Calandra also by lack of black neck-patches and narrower wings. Tawny upper parts have dark streaks; chestnut on crown, wing-coverts and tail; whitish under-parts and wing-pits, with lightly spotted buffish throat and breast. White outer web of longest primary visible on closed wing. Female has streaked brown crown. See also Snow Bunting.
Voice: Song said to resemble short version of Sky Lark's, delivered during brief soaring flights and from ground.
Habitat and Range: Mainly arid grass-steppes. Nests on ground. On passage and in hard winters in E. Roumania and S.E. Poland. Vagrant across Europe W. to Britain, and S. to Malta.

BLACK LARK *Melanocorypha yeltoniensis*　　　page 189
　　　Du – Zwarte leeuwerik　　　Fr – Alouette nègre
　　　Ge – Mohrenlerche　　　Sw – Svart lärka
Identification: 7½″. Male unmistakable: large and *black* with pale sandy margins to feathers which, in winter, partly obscure the black. Bill short and stout, yellow with black tip. Female very like *pale* Calandra but distinguished by *absence of black neck-patches.* Neither sex has white on wings or tail.
Voice: Has clear, piping call-note. Song resembles short spasms of Sky Lark's.
Habitat and Range: Grassy or bushy steppes, often near water, also on deserts; closer to cultivation and road-sides in winter. Vagrant in winter to central Europe, W. to Belgium, Holland, Heligoland.

← CALANDRA
LARK
Mainly resident.
Vagrant to Britain,
Norway, Finland

SHORE LARK →
Mainly migratory.
Passage Baltic.
Vagrant most other
parts of Europe

SHORE LARK   *Eremophila alpestris*   page 189
> Du – Strandleeuwerik   Fr – Alouette hausse-col
> Ge – Ohrenlerche   Sw – Berglärka
> N.Am – Horned Lark

Identification: 6½″. Easily distinguished from all other larks by *pale yellow face and throat, bold black breast-band and cheeks*. Pinkish-brown above, whitish below. Male has black band across crown and *small black "horns."* Female has less black. Juvenile appears spotted and duller. Adult head markings partly obscured in winter.

Voice: Clear, pipit-like, or wagtail-like: *"tsee-ree," "tsee-titi,"* etc. Song, tinkling, irregular and high-pitched, often long-sustained, sometimes high in air in manner of Sky Lark.

Habitat: Winters on coast on shingle strands, salt-marshes and adjacent stubble-fields. Breeds above tree limit in dry tundra. Map p. 206.

CRESTED LARK   *Galerida cristata*   page 189
> Du – Kuifleeuwerik   Fr – Cochevis huppé
> Ge – Haubenlerche   Sw – Tofslärka

Identification: 6¾″. Plumper and rather paler than Sky Lark. Distinguished by *long upstanding crest*, rather long, slightly curved bill and short tail with dark centre and *buff* sides. Upper-parts variable sandy- or grey-brown, less strongly streaked than Sky Lark; under-parts creamy-buff, streaked on breast; *in flight shows orange-buff under wings*. Juvenile more spotted above, with shorter crest. Distinguished from Sky Lark and Wood Lark by long narrow crest and absence of white on broad, very rounded wings and short tail. "Floppy" flight. See also very similar Thekla Lark.

Voice: A liquid *"twee-tee-too,"* rising and falling, or a shrill *"quee-tee."* Song less musical and shorter than Sky Lark's; usually in short repeated phrases, delivered from ground, low perch and in flight.

Habitat: Generally flat grassy or arid country; often near habitation, dusty mule-tracks, road-sides, etc. Breeds on ground. Map p. 208.

THEKLA LARK   *Galerida theklae*   page 189
> Du – Thekla leeuwerik   Fr – Cochevis de Thékla
> Ge – Theklalerche   Sw – Lagerlärka

Identification: 6¼″. Distinguishable in the field from Crested Lark only if the two can be compared at short range, where they occur together. Thekla is always slightly smaller, slightly greyer above, paler below with narrower, *less smudgy* breast-markings; *grey* (not buff) beneath wings; bill is smaller, looks stouter.

Voice: Song similar to Crested, but *often sings from bush-tops* and trees.

Habitat and Range: Shows some preference for dry, stony hill-sides with low, bushy vegetation and dunes with some cover. Occurs up to higher altitudes. Resident in Portugal, S. and E. Spain, Balearics; perhaps S. France.

WOOD LARK *Lullula arborea* page 189
Du – Boomleeuwerik Fr – Alouette lulu
Ge – Heidelerche Sw – Trädlärka

Identification: 6″. Distinguished from Sky Lark by smaller size, *very short tail without white sides, conspicuous white eye-stripes joining on nape* behind and below rounded crest, finer bill and distinctive voice. Has characteristic dark mark near bend of wing. Soars in wide spirals during song flight, finally plunging with closed wings almost to ground. Perches on trees. See also Tree Pipit.

Voice: A melodious "*toolooeet.*" Song less varied, less sustained and less powerful than Sky Lark's, but more melodious, consisting of short phrases interspersed with a liquid trilling "*lu-lu-lu-lu*"; from perch, ground, or in song-flight.

Habitat: Edges of woods, hill-sides with a few trees, sandy heaths, etc. Winters in fields. Nests on ground. Map below.

SKY LARK *Alauda arvensis* page 18
Du – Veldleeuwerik Fr – Alouette des champs
Ge – Feldlerche Sw – Sånglärka

Identification: 7″. Upper-parts brown, strongly streaked blackish; under-parts buffish-white with boldly streaked breast. *Longish tail with conspicuous white on outer feathers.* Hind margins of long, pointed wings show whitish in flight. Short, rounded crest often prominent. Walks in crouched position. Flight strong and slightly undulating, with alternate spells of wing-beats and "shooting" with closed wings; soars and hovers in song-flight. See also Wood and Crested Larks.

Voice: A clear, liquid "*chir-r-up.*" Song, a high-pitched, musical out-pouring, *very long sustained*, in hovering and ascending or descending flight; occasionally from ground or low perch.

Habitat: Moors, fields, marshes, sand-dunes. Nests on ground. Map p. 209.

← CRESTED LARK
*Mainly resident.
Vagrant England,
Finland*

WOOD LARK →
*Partial migrant.
Has bred Ireland.
Vagrant Scotland*

SWALLOWS AND MARTINS:
Hirundinidae

Slim, streamlined form and graceful flight are distinctive. Forked tails, long pointed wings and short bills with very wide gapes. Insect food caught in flight. Sexes similar. Build mud nests on rocks or buildings, except Sand Martin.

SAND MARTIN *Riparia riparia*   page 196
    Du – Oeverzwaluw   **Fr** – Hirondelle de rivage
    Ge – Uferschwalbe   **Sw** – Backsvala
             N.Am – Bank Swallow
Identification: 4¾″. Smallest European swallow. Distinguished by *earth-brown* upper-parts, white under-parts with *brown breast-band*. Strongly gregarious. Feeds chiefly over water. Flight more flitting, less swooping, than Swallow's. See also Crag Martin.
Voice: A dry "*tchrrip*"; alarm, a short "*brrit*." Song, a weak twittering.
Habitat: Open country with ponds, rivers, etc. Nests socially, in tunnels bored in sand and gravel pits, river banks, cliffs. Map below.

CRAG MARTIN *Hirundo rupestris*   page 196
    Du – Rotszwaluw   Fr – Hirondelle de rochers
    Ge – Felsenschwalbe   Sw – Klippsvala
Identification: 5¾″. At a distance can be confused with Sand Martin, but distinguished by stockier build and *dark wedge on under-wing from wing-pit*; under-parts dingy white, *without breast-band*, duskier on belly and under tail-coverts; at short range also by *white spots near tip of spread tail*. Alpine Swift is very much larger, with white under-parts and dark breast-band.

    ← Sky Lark
    Partial migrant.
    Vagrant Iceland

    Sand Martin →
    Summer visitor.
    Vagrant Faeroes

Voice: Not very vocal: a rather weak *"chich,"* or *"tchrrri."*
Habitat: Mountain gorges and rocky inland and coastal cliffs. Builds open half-cup shaped mud nest in cleft rocks or caves in cliff-face, occasionally with House Martins. Map below.

SWALLOW *Hirundo rustica* page 196
Du – Boerenzwaluw   Fr – Hirondelle de cheminée
Ge – Rauchschwalbe   Sw – Ladusvala
N.Am – Barn Swallow

Identification: 7½". Distinguished by *long tail streamers*. Has *dark metallic blue upper-parts*, chestnut-red forehead and throat, *dark blue lower throat*, remainder of under-parts creamy white. Juvenile much duller with shorter streamers. Flight swooping and graceful. Gregarious, though less so when breeding. House Martin has white throat and rump, no tail streamers. Sand Martin and Crag Martin are brown above, with no tail streamers. Swift is uniformly dark. See also Red-rumped Swallow.
Voice: A high *"tswit,"* becoming a rapid twitter when excited. Alarm, a high *"tswee."* Song, a pleasant, weak mixture of rapid twittering and warbling notes.
Habitat: Open cultivated country with farms, meadows, ponds, etc. Builds open mud and straw nest on rafters or ledges in cow sheds, stables, etc., locally in chimneys. Map below.

RED-RUMPED SWALLOW *Hirundo daurica* page 196
Du – Roodstuitzwaluw   Fr – Hirondelle rousseline
Ge – Rötelschwalbe   Sw – Rostgumpsvala

Identification: 7". Distinguished immediately by *buff rump, chestnut nape and eye-stripe*, buff throat and under-parts, without dark gorget patch. Crown and back dark metallic blue, wings and forked tail blackish. Lacks Swallow's white tail markings and has rather thicker streamers and *blunter* wing-tips and more lethargic flight. Distinguished from House Martin by buffish, instead of white, rump and under-parts.

← Crag Martin
Partial migrant

Swallow →
*Summer visitor.
Has bred Iceland
and Faeroes*

300   301

211

Voice: Has distinctive rough, thin, flight-call. Alarm "*keer*." Song resembles Swallow's, but is less musical.
Habitat: Sea and inland cliffs; less partial to cultivated areas than Swallow, but in flat country usually frequents bridges and buildings. Builds nest like House Martin's, but with spout-shaped entrance, in caves, cleft rocks, under bridges, etc. Map below.

HOUSE MARTIN *Delichon urbica* page 196
      Du – Huiszwaluw   Fr – Hirondelle de fenêtre
      Ge – Mehlschwalbe   Sw – Hussvala
Identification: 5″. The only European swallow with a *pure white rump*. Under-parts white; head, back, wings and tail blue-black. Tail is short and forked, and without streamers. Short legs and feet are feathered white. Behaviour like Swallow's, but more sociable, nesting in close colonies. Flight less swooping, more fluttering than Swallow's, and often flies higher. See also White-rumped Swift (Accidentals p. 319).
Voice: A clear "*tchirrip*" or "*tchichirrip*"; alarm, a shrill "*tseep*." Song, a weak but pleasant chirruping twitter, less varied than Swallow's.
Habitat: Like Swallow, but more often near human habitation; also in open country. Builds enclosed mud nest, with entrance hole at top, cupped under eaves of houses and barns, locally on cliffs. Map below.

PIPITS AND WAGTAILS:
Motacillidae

Terrestrial birds, running and walking briskly. **Pipits** are brown and streaked, with white or whitish outer tail-feathers; less slender than wagtails. Sexes similar. Ground nesting. **Wagtails** are very slender, strongly patterned, with long tails, slender bills and slender legs. Ground, cranny or rock nesting.

← RED-RUMPED
    SWALLOW
Summer visitor.
Vagrant central
Medit., Brit. Isles,
Heligoland, Baltic,
Norway, Finland

HOUSE MARTIN →
    Summer visitor.
    Vagrant Iceland,
    Faeroes

302   303

GOLDCRESTS, DIPPER, WREN, CREEPERS, AND NUTHATCHES

● **GOLDCREST**   page 249
   Tiny; orange or yellow crown.
   No stripe through eye.

● **FIRECREST**   250
   From Goldcrest by sharp black and white eye-stripes;
   bronze "shoulders."

● **DIPPER**   224
   Portly; dark, with white "bib"; short cocked tail.

◉ **WREN**   225
   Tiny, rotund, brown; tail usually cocked.

● **TREE CREEPER**   281
   Slender, with curved bill; streaked brown with rusty
   rump; silvery white under-parts.

SHORT-TOED TREE CREEPER   281
   Nearly identical with Tree Creeper, but flanks more
   brownish. Safely separated only by voice and distribution (see text and maps).

△ **WALL CREEPER**   280
   Large crimson wing-patches; very rounded wings.

● **NUTHATCH**   279
   Stumpy; short tail; sharp bill; blue-grey back.
   Scandinavian form is whiter below.

CORSICAN NUTHATCH   279
   Small; white stripe over eye; black cap (male).
   Corsica.

ROCK NUTHATCH   280
   Paler than Nuthatch; larger bill; no spots on tail.
   Balkans, Greece.

GOLDCREST

♀ ♂

FIRECREST

♀ ♂

WREN

DIPPER

Winter

below

TREE
CREEPER

SHORT-TOED
TREE CREEPER

Summer

WALL CREEPER

Scandinavian
form

CORSICAN
NUTHATCH

NUTHATCH

ROCK NUTHATCH

GREAT   COAL   BLUE

Northern form

MARSH   WILLOW   AZURE

SOMBRE   SIBERIAN   CRESTED

♂   ♀

Northern form

BEARDED REEDLING   LONG-TAILED   **PENDULINE**

Plate 52 213

TITS

SMALL birds with stubby bills; extremely active, often hanging upside down in their busy search for food. Most true tits (*Parus*, first three rows) have black bibs, white cheeks and black or dark caps. In true tits the sexes are alike.

● **GREAT TIT**   page 278
Black stripe on belly.

● **COAL TIT**   274
White spot on nape.

● **BLUE TIT**   275
Blue cap; yellowish under-parts.

● **MARSH TIT**   272
Glossy black cap; small "bib"; no light edging on wing.

● **WILLOW TIT**   273
Dull black cap; light area on wing formed by feather edgings; distinctive voice (see text). Scandinavian form is much paler, with whiter cheeks.

  AZURE TIT   275
White cap; white under-parts; much white on wing.

  SOMBRE TIT   273
Large (size of Great Tit); drab, with large bill.

  SIBERIAN TIT   274
Brown cap; "dusty" appearance.

● **CRESTED TIT**   274
Crest; "bridled" face pattern.

● **LONG-TAILED TIT**   272
White crown-stripe, or white head; very long tail.

  PENDULINE TIT   278
Black mask through eyes; rusty back.

● **BEARDED REEDLING**   271
Male: Black "moustaches"; very long tail.
Female: No "moustaches"; brown; very long tail.

RICHARD'S PIPIT *Anthus novaeseelandiae*   page 245
    Du – Grote pieper   Fr – Pipit de Richard
    Ge – Spornpieper   Sw – Stor piplärka

Identification: 7″. A *large, long-tailed, long-legged* pipit. Upper-parts brown, broadly streaked blackish; breast buffish, *sparsely but boldly streaked.* Pale buff stripes above eye and below cheek. Narrow dark moustachial streak and black line below eye. Legs and hind claws very long. Slightly larger, more erect than Tawny, with shorter, stouter bill; also distinguished in spring by boldly marked back, longer legs and more streaked upper-breast and throat; in early autumn, not safely separated from immature (streaked) Tawny, except by voice and bill.
Voice: Harsher, louder and more grating than Tawny's.
Habitat and Range: Wet grass-lands, marshy steppes and rice fields. Almost annually on passage, or in winter, Heligoland and British Isles; also occurs Scandinavia, France, Portugal and E. Central Europe.

TAWNY PIPIT *Anthus campestris*   page 245
    Du – Duinpieper   Fr – Pipit rousseline
    Ge – Brachpieper   Sw – Fältpiplärka

Identification: 6½″. More slim and wagtail-like than other pipits. Pale, *almost uniform* sandy above, apart from line of dark spots on coverts near bend of wing, and with paler, usually *unstreaked* under-parts. *Conspicuous creamy supercilium.* Indistinct brown moustachial stripe. Legs long and yellowish, though shorter than Richard's. Further distinguished from Richard's by *paler,* less boldly marked plumage and slightly smaller size. In early autumn young birds with streaked breasts resemble young Richard's (see above).
Voice: More variable call-notes than other pipits, usually a drawn-out "*tsweep*", a brief "*chup*", or a sparrow-like "*chirrup*". Song, a repeated, metallic "*chivee, chivee, chivee,*" usually in high song flight.
Habitat: Waste-lands, with sand and scrub, in winter also frequents cultivated land. Nests in depression, sheltered by vegetation. Map below.

← TAWNY PIPIT
Summer visitor. Has bred Switzerland. Vagrant n. to Scotland, Ireland, Iceland, Finland

TREE PIPIT →
Summer visitor. Annual Ireland. Vagrant Iceland

TREE PIPIT *Anthus trivialis* page 245

Du – Boompieper Fr – Pipit des arbres
Ge – Baumpieper Sw – Trädpiplärka

Identification: 6″. Best distinguished from very similar Meadow Pipit by *voice*, slightly plumper form, stouter bill, *yellowish breast and pinkish legs*, with short hind claws. Upper-parts brown, streaked blackish. Creamy-buff below, with blackish moustachial stripe and boldly streaked breast and flanks. Yellowish supercilium. White outer tail-feathers. Perches readily on trees. Rock Pipit is larger and *darker*. See also Red-throated.

Voice: A rather hoarse "*teeze*"; alarm, a persistently repeated "*sip*." Song, loud and musical, with long trills, ending in characteristic "*seea-seea-seea*," or with very slow "*chew, chew, chew*"; sings during "parachute" descent to perch from short upward flight (Wood Lark plunges to ground).

Habitat: Heaths, clearings in woods, hillsides, fields with scattered trees and bushes. Nests under bracken, in long grass, etc. Map p. 214.

PETCHORA PIPIT *Anthus gustavi* page 284

Du – Petchora-pieper Fr – Pipit de la Petchora
Ge – Petschorapieper Sw – Tundrapiplärka

Identification: 5¾″. Resembles Tree Pipit; best distinguished by *call-note* and *two pale streaks down back*. Rump boldly streaked like Red-throated. Under-parts boldly streaked; outer tail-feathers buffish (not white). Rather skulking.

Voice: A stony, hard "*pwit*," usually repeated; unlike call of any other British pipit, lower and less sweet than call of Meadow Pipit. Song is in two parts, a trill followed by a low warble.

Habitat and Range: Except when nesting, inclined to stay close to cover, seldom perching on posts like Tree Pipit, but on breeding ground perches freely on trees. Vagrant from N.E. Europe, Asia to Britain (Fair Isle), Holland.

MEADOW PIPIT *Anthus pratensis* page 245

Du – Graspieper Fr – Pipit farlouse
Ge – Wiesenpieper Sw – Ängspiplärka

Identification: 5¾″. Very like Tree Pipit, but distinguished by *voice*, more olive upper-parts and usually *whiter, less yellow breast*, with smaller, more numerous streaks. White outer tail-feathers. Legs brownish, with long hind claws. Perches less frequently on trees than Tree Pipit. Rock Pipit is larger and darker. See also Red-throated.

Voice: A faint "*tseep*," rapidly repeated when alarmed; also a louder "*tissip*." Song, a thin piping, in gradually increasing tempo, ending in a musical trill, in short song-flight and during "parachute" descent.

Habitat: Moors, dunes, rough pastures; in winter prefers marshes, cultivated land, sea-coasts. Nests on ground. Map p. 216.

RED-THROATED PIPIT *Anthus cervinus* page 245
 Du – Roodkeelpieper Fr – Pipit à gorge rousse
 Ge – Rotkehlpieper Sw – Rödstrupig piplärka
Identification; 5¾". Distinguished from Meadow Pipit by darker upper-parts, *boldly streaked rump* and distinctive voice. In breeding season throat tinged *rusty-red* sometimes extending to upper breast. Distinguished in winter by heavy dark streaking on under-parts.
Voice: A hoarse "*tzeeez*," and a soft "*teu*." Song less musical and higher pitched than Meadow Pipit's.
Habitat: Swampy tundra, marshes and moist cultivated land, usually with dwarf vegetation, often near coast. Nests on ground. Map below.

ROCK PIPIT and **WATER PIPIT** *Anthus spinoletta* page 245
 Rock Pipit: Du – Oeverpieper Fr – Pipit maritime
   Ge – Strandpieper Sw – Skärpiplärka
 Water Pipit: Du – Waterpieper Fr – Pipit spioncelle
   Ge – Wasserpieper Sw – Vattenpiplärka
Identification: 6½". Slightly larger and longer than Meadow and Tree Pipits, with rather longer bill. Legs *much darker* than in other pipits. Typical mountain race (Water Pipit, *A. s. spinoletta*) has *white outer tail-feathers*, whitish supercilium, greyish upper-parts and whitish under-parts, which in autumn and winter are streaked, but are un-streaked and flushed pinkish in breeding season. Coastal races (Rock Pipit, *A. s. petrosus*, etc.) have darker, more olive appearance, with closely streaked olive-buff under-parts and *greyish* (not white) outer tail-feathers. Distinguished from Meadow Pipit in winter by browner upper-parts, *dark legs*; from Tawny Pipit by streaked under-parts, darker upper-parts, *dark legs*.
Voice: A thin "*tsip*," "*jeep*," or "*tseep-eep*." Song less tuneful than Tree and Meadow Pipit's, usually in "flapping" song-flight.
Habitat: Breeds in mountainous areas (Water Pipit), or near sea-shore (Rock Pipit). Winters in marshy lowlands, inland waterways, mud-flats and sea coasts. Nests in crevices in rocks, etc. Map p. 217.

← Meadow Pipit
Partial migrant

Red-throated
Pipit →
*Summer visitor.
Passage Europe w.
to Italy. Vagrant
to Britain, Ireland,
Portugal*

YELLOW WAGTAIL (and other races). *Motacilla flava*

pages 245, 252

Yellow Wagtail:
Du – Engelse gele kwikstaart   Fr – Bergeronnette flavéole
Ge – Englische Schafstelze   Sw – Engelsk gulärla

Blue-Headed Wagtail:
Du – Gele kwikstaart   Fr – Bergeronnette printaniére
Ge – Schafstelze   Sw – Gulärla

Identification: 6½″. A slender, long-tailed, long-legged bird with yellow under-parts. Several races occur in Europe and can, with practice, be separated in the field. Male of the yellowest race (*M. f. flavissima*), breeding in British Isles and on adjacent shores of Continent, has bright yellow supercilium, throat and under-parts; yellowish green upper-parts and cheeks. Females in summer and both sexes in winter are duller and browner above, paler below; juvenile has buff chin and brown bib. Male of central European race (Blue-headed Wagtail, *M. f. flava*), has bluish crown, slightly darker ear-coverts with a few white marks, white supercilium and white chin. Female much duller, with white chin. For further distinctions between races, see plate 59, page 252. Note: there is a tendency for populations to produce mutants and occasional individuals virtually identical with those of other subspecies. Most observers will be satisfied to call them all "Yellow Wagtails." See also Grey Wagtail.

Voice: A loud, musical "*tsweep*," or a more grating "*tsirr*." Song, a simple "*tsip-tsip-tsipsi*."

Habitat: Usually near water, marshes, stream-banks, meadows. Nests in depression under grass, crops, etc. Map below.

GREY WAGTAIL *Motacilla cinerea*   pages 245, 252
Du – Grote gele kwikstaart   Fr – Bergeronnette des ruisseaux
Ge – Gebirgstelze   Sw – Forsärla

Identification: 7″. Distinguished at any season from all other yellow-breasted wagtails by *very long* black tail with conspicuous white outer feathers *and blue-grey upper-parts*. Breast brilliant yellow in summer,

← ROCK PIPIT
Partial migrant.
Vagrant Iceland

YELLOW
WAGTAIL →
Summer visitor.
Has bred Ireland.
Vagrant Faeroes
and Iceland

310   311

buffish in winter. Rump greenish-yellow. Male has white supercilium and conspicuous white stripe from bill below dark grey cheek. Chin and throat of male *black* in summer, whitish in winter. Female is tinged greenish above, with whitish throat, summer and winter. Juvenile grey-brown above, buffish below; distinguished from Pied by *yellow* under tail-coverts. Not gregarious, except for roosting. See also Yellow Wagtail.

Voice: Call-notes more metallic than in Pied and song more varied and musical. Alarm, a shrill "*see-eet*," or "*siz-eet*."

Habitat: Shallow streams in hill country, but also lowlands, sewage farms and cultivated land, particularly in winter. Nests in holes in walls, bridges, banks, etc. Map below.

PIED WAGTAIL and WHITE WAGTAIL *Motacilla alba*
pages 245, 252

Pied Wagtail:
    Du – Rouwkwikstaart   Fr – Bergeronnette d'Yarrell
    Ge – Trauerbachstelze   Sw – Engelsk sädesärla
White Wagtail:
    Du – Witte kwikstaart   Fr – Bergeronnette grise
    Ge – Bachstelze   Sw – Sädesärla

Identification: 7". A well patterned black and white bird with slender legs, long tail. Summer male of British subspecies (Pied Wagtail, *M. a. yarrellii*) has *black back*, crown, throat and breast; blackish wings with double white bar; black tail with white outer feathers; white forehead, sides of head and belly. Female greyer above, less black on head and breast. In winter both sexes have *black* on crown, and white throat, with crescent-shaped black bib and grey back. Continental subspecies (White Wagtail, *M. a. alba*) is similar, but in breeding season has *light grey* back and *rump*. More easily confused in autumn.

Voice: A lively "*tchizzik*"; alarm, an abrupt "*tchik*"; song, a twitter, embodying variants of call-notes.

Habitat: Gardens, farms, open country and towns. Often, but not always, near water. Nests in holes in buildings, rocks, etc. Map below.

← GREY WAGTAIL
*Partial migrant.
Has bred Norway.
Vagrant Faeroes,
Iceland, Finland*

PIED WAGTAIL →
Partial migrant

SHRIKES: Laniidae

Strikingly patterned, with hook-tipped bills and hawk-like behaviour. Usually perch watchfully upright on conspicuous vantage points, fanning their rather long tails. Prey often impaled on thorn-bush "larders." Call-notes are harsh, but songs surprisingly musical. Sexes nearly similar, except Red-backed. Bush or tree nesting.

RED-BACKED SHRIKE *Lanius collurio*   page 253
      Du – Grauwe klauwier   Fr – Pie-grièche écorcheur
      Ge – Neuntöter   Sw – Törnskata
Identification: 6¾". Male distinguished by *chestnut back*, separating *pale blue-grey crown and rump*, and broad black face-marking through eyes to ear-coverts. Under-parts pinkish-white. Tail black with white sides, often swung side to side. Female normally lacks black face-marks and is dull rufous-brown above, buffish below, barred with brown crescent markings. Immature separable from young Woodchat by more rufous plumage, and lack of pale rump, shoulder-patch and wing-bar. Flight usually direct. Glides and hovers when hunting along hedges, but usually pounces on prey from elevated perch. Impales small birds and insects in thorn-bush "larders" more often than other shrikes.
Voice: A harsh, grating "*shack*," or "*chee-uk*." Song, a quiet musical and often prolonged warbling, interspersed with call-notes and a wide range of mimicry.
Habitat: Bushy commons, uncut hedges, thickets, old quarries. Nests in bushes, small trees, bramble patches. Map p. 222.

MASKED SHRIKE *Lanius nubicus*   page 253
      Du – Maskerklauwier   Fr – Pie-grièche masquée
      Ge – Maskenwürger   Sw – Masktörnskata
Identification: 6¾". Uniform black above, from crown to tail. Length of Woodchat but slighter; distinguished by *black rump*, *black crown* with bold white forehead and white supercilium; also by *reddish flanks* (otherwise white under-parts) and more conspicuous white sides to large tail. Wing-markings like Woodchat's. Behaviour like Red-backed, but with more graceful flight; seldom adopts prominent perch.
Voice: A harsh, but plaintive, repeated "*keer.*" Song, a subdued monotonous succession of scratchy notes.
Habitat and Range: Olive groves, gardens and lightly wooded country. Nests fairly high in trees. Summer visitor to Turkey, Greece, and S. Yugoslavia. Vagrant France, Spain.

THRUSHES

● **BLACKBIRD**　　　　　　　　　　　　　　　　　page 269
　　Male: All black; yellow bill.
　　Female: Dark brown.

● **RING OUZEL**　　　　　　　　　　　　　　　　　268
　　Black, with white breast-crescent; pale wing edges.

● **FIELDFARE**　　　　　　　　　　　　　　　　　267
　　Grey head and rump; rusty back.

● **SONG THRUSH**　　　　　　　　　　　　　　　　270
　　Brown, with spotted breast; buff wing-linings.

● **MISTLE THRUSH**　　　　　　　　　　　　　　　270
　　Larger, greyer; rounder spots; white wing-linings.

● **REDWING**　　　　　　　　　　　　　　　　　269
　　Reddish flanks and wing-linings; supercilium.

O **WHITE'S THRUSH**　　　　　　　　　　　　　　271
　　Bold "scaly" pattern above and below.

△ **DUSKY THRUSH**　　　　　　　　　　　　　　267
　　Double breast-band; supercilium.　Dusky and
　　Naumann's intergrade; probably conspecific.

△ **BLACK-THROATED THRUSH**　　　　　　　　　266
　　Hood and bib contrast with white below.　Black-
　　throated and Red-throated are races of same species.

△ **SIBERIAN THRUSH**　　　　　　　　　　　　　265
　　Male: Blackish, with striking white supercilium.
　　Female: Brown, see text.

△ **AMERICAN ROBIN**　　　　　　　　　　　　　268
　　Brick-red below; blackish head; broken eye-ring.

　NAUMANN'S THRUSH　　　　　　　　　　　267
　　Rusty breast; rusty wings.

　RED-THROATED THRUSH　　　　　　　　　266
　　Rufous supercilium, throat and breast.

△ **EYE-BROWED THRUSH**　　　　　　　　　　266
　　Grey upper breast; rusty sides; supercilium.

BLACKBIRD

♀

♂

RING OUZEL

SONG THRUSH

FIELDFARE

MISTLE
THRUSH

REDWING

SOME RARE THRUSHES

DUSKY

BLACK-
THROATED

SIBERIAN

♂

♀

HITE'S

AMERICAN
ROBIN

NAUMANN'S

RED-THROATED

EYE-BROWED

Winter

Black-throated form

White-throated form

WHEATEAR

BLACK-EARED WHEATEAR

PIED WHEATE...

Summer ♂

♂

♂

♂

♀

♂

REDSTART

BLACK REDSTART

S...
sin...

BLAC...
WHEATE...

♂

♀

♀

Juvenile

A...

RO...

STONECHAT

WHINCHAT

NIGHTINGALE

♂

♂

♀

Red-spotted form

♀

THRUSH-
NIGHTINGAL...

BLUETHROAT

White-spotted form

♂

♂

♀

♂

ROCK THRUSH

BLUE ROCK THRUSH

Plate 54 221

WHEATEARS, CHATS, ETC.

● **WHEATEAR** page 256
    Summer ♂: Grey back; white rump; black mask.
    Autumn: Brown above, buffish below; white rump.

△ **BLACK-EARED WHEATEAR** 257
    Black-throated form: Buff back; black throat.
    White-throated form: Buff back; black mask.

△ **PIED WHEATEAR** 257
    Blackish back; black throat.

△ **BLACK WHEATEAR** 258
    Black, with white rump.

● **REDSTART** 263
    Male: Rusty tail; orange under-parts; black bib.
    Female: Rusty tail; brownish breast.

● **BLACK REDSTART** 262
    Male: Black; rusty tail. *Female:* Slaty; rusty tail.

● **STONECHAT** 255
    Male: Black head; rusty breast; white neck-patch.
    Female: Brownish, with suggestion of male's pattern.

● **WHINCHAT** 255
    White stripes outline dark cheeks; white in tail.

● **ROBIN** 263
    Orange face and breast. Juvenile spotted and barred.

● **BLUETHROAT** 265
    Male: Blue throat; orange tail-patches.
    Female: U-shaped necklace; orange tail-patches.

● **NIGHTINGALE** 264
    Brown back; plain breast; broad chestnut tail.

△ **THRUSH NIGHTINGALE** 264
    Greyer; less chestnut in tail; mottled breast.

△ **ROCK THRUSH** 259
    Male: Blue head; white lower back; orange breast
    and tail. *Female:* Barred; orange tail.

  BLUE ROCK THRUSH 262
    Male: Slaty blue. *Female:* Barred and spotted.

WOODCHAT SHRIKE *Lanius senator*　　　　　page 253
　　Du – Roodkopklauwier　　　Fr – Pie-grièche à tête rousse
　　Ge – Rotkopfwürger　　　　　Sw – Rödhuvad törnskata
Identification: 6¾″. Distinguished from Great and Lesser Grey Shrikes
by *rich chestnut crown and nape.* Has broad black face-marking continuing across forehead, pure white throat and under-parts, blackish
wings and mantle with *conspicuous white shoulder patches* and short
wing-bar, black tail with white sides, *white rump conspicuous in flight.*
Female rather duller. Immature resembles young Red-backed, but
with larger, more angular head; is paler and less rufous, with pale
rump and shoulder-patch recalling adult pattern; shows traces of
whitish wing-bar. Corsican race *L. s. badius* lacks the white wing-bar.
See also Masked Shrike.
Voice: Like Lesser Grey, but more varied, with frequent House
Sparrow-like chatter. Song, a sustained musical warble, interspersed
with harsh notes and mimicry.
Habitat: Dry open country, olive groves, orchards, bushy commons,
occasionally large woods. Nests in trees of all sizes. Map below.

LESSER GREY SHRIKE *Lanius minor*　　　　　page 253
　　Du – Kleine klauwier　　　　Fr – Pie-grièche à poitrine rose
　　Ge – Schwarzstirnwürger　　Sw – Svartpannad törnskata
Identification: 8″. Resembles Great Grey, but is smaller, with *proportionately longer wings and shorter tail*; broad black face-markings
continuing across forehead (less evident in female); no white supercilium; *pale pinkish under-parts*; *shorter and much deeper bill*; very
prominent white wing-bar and white outer tail-feathers. Juvenile looks
yellowish at a distance, with relatively unbarred breast, finely barred
dark brown on head and flanks, with brownish-black wings and tail.
Behaviour like Great Grey but *perches more upright*. Flight usually
direct (not low and undulating as in Great Grey); hovers frequently.
Voice: Much as Great Grey; also a clear "*kviell.*"
Habitat: Fairly open cultivated country with scattered trees and bushes,

← Red-backed
Shrike
*Summer visitor.
Vagrant to Faeroes,
Ireland*

Woodchat
Shrike →
*Summer visitor.
Vagrant to Britain,
Ireland, Denmark,
Sweden, Finland*

roadsides, commons, etc. Nests fairly high in trees (even up to 60 ft.); often in loosely scattered colonies. Map below.

GREAT GREY SHRIKE *Lanius excubitor*   page 253
     Du – Klapekster   Fr – Pie-grièche grise
     Ge – Raubwürger   Sw – Varfågel
            N.Am – Northern Shrike

Identification: 9½". Largest of the shrikes. Identified by contrasting *black, white and grey plumage*. Distinguished from Lesser by larger size, grey (not black) forehead, *narrow white supercilium* between black eye-patch and grey crown; *longer, more slender bill*; much more white on scapulars; proportionately shorter wings *meeting at base of tail*; longer, more graduated tail; narrower white area on open wing (closed wing often gives effect of double white bar). Female usually has faint brown wavy bars on breast. Juvenile grey-brown, with brown wavy bars on under-parts. Perches on tree-tops or telegraph pole, from which it attacks small birds, mice, lizards, insects. Tail frequently waved or fanned. Flight low and usually undulating, with steep upward glide to perch; hovers frequently. South European race *L. e. meridionalis* is darker above and pinkish below.

Voice: Characteristic "*shek-shek*" note sometimes prolonged into Magpie-like rattle. Anxiety note, a grating "*jaaeg.*" Song, a subdued prolonged mixture of harsh and musical notes.

Habitat: Outskirts of woods, orchards, heaths, hedges, etc. Less fond of open country for breeding than other shrikes. Nest site varied, occasionally in high trees, usually in thorn bushes. Map below.

WAXWINGS: Bombycillidae

WAXWING *Bombycilla garrulus*   page 253
     Du – Pestvogel   Fr – Jaseur boréal
     Ge – Seidenschwanz   Sw – Sidensvans
         N.Am – Bohemian Waxwing

← LESSER GREY SHRIKE
Summer visitor. Vagrant to Finland, Sweden, Britain, Ireland

GREAT GREY SHRIKE →
Partial migrant. Vagrant to Faeroes, Ireland, Malta

317   318

Identification: 7″. Identified by unmistakable *pinkish-chestnut crest,* and short, *yellow-tipped tail.* Has black eye-stripe and throat patch. Upper-parts chestnut, with grey rump; under-parts pinkish-brown, with chestnut under tail-coverts; dark wings *boldly marked white and yellow,* with scarlet waxy tips to secondaries (less evident on female). Juvenile lacks black throat-patch and has soft streaks below. Flight strong and starling-like. Often very tame. Acrobatic feeding habits recall Crossbill. Gregarious.

Voice: Call-note a weak, high trill, "*zhreee.*"

Habitat: Breeds in open glades of northern coniferous and birch woods. Winters in more open country, seeking berried fruit in hedges and gardens. Map below.

DIPPERS: Cinclidae

DIPPER *Cinclus cinclus*   page 212
    Du – Waterspreeuw   Fr – Cincle plongeur
    Ge – Wasseramsel   Sw – Strömstare

Identification: 7″. A stout bird, Wren-like in shape but much larger, with rather large sturdy legs; short tail often cocked. *Blackish with white breast,* bordered below by dark chestnut merging into black in British race *C. c. gularis,* but some northern populations lack chestnut. Sexes alike. Juvenile slate-grey above, mottled grey and white below. "Bobs" spasmodically, perched on rock in stream. Plunges or walks into water, remaining submerged to feed on bottom; swims on or under water. Flight usually low, rapid and direct, following streams. Solitary, on same strip of water all the year.

Voice: A short "*zit,*" or, in flight, a metallic "*clink.*" Song, a succession of short, high, grating and explosive notes interspersed with liquid warbling. Sings nearly all year.

← Waxwing
*Partial migrant.
Extends most win-
ters beyond limit
shown. Vag. to Ice-
land, Faeroes, Ire-
land, Spain, Malta*

Dipper →
*Mainly resident.
Has bred Denmark
In winter extends
to Finland Estonia,
Sweden, Denmark*

Habitat: Swift hill streams; occasionally visits coasts in winter. Builds large globular nest in crevices under waterfalls, bridges, banks; invariably very near running water. Map p. 224.

WRENS: Troglodytidae

WREN *Troglodytes troglodytes*   page 212
   Du – Winterkoning   Fr – Troglodyte
   Ge – Zaunkönig   Sw – Gärdsmyg
         N.Am – Winter Wren

Identification: 3¾". A tiny, plump, closely barred brown bird with a *short cocked tail.* Extremely active; forages among litter on ground like a mouse, catches insects among vegetation like a warbler. Flight whirring and direct.

Voice: A loud, hard "*tit-tit-tit*," becoming a harsh churring when alarmed. Song, a prolonged, breathless jingle of strident but not unmusical notes and high trills. Sings almost all the year.

Habitat: Low cover, in gardens, thickets, woods, rocks, etc. Builds globular nest in hedges, hay-ricks, holes in trees, banks, or buildings. Map below.

ACCENTORS: Prunellidae

Rather drab and sparrow-like in appearance, but with slender bills. They have a distinctive shuffling gait, unobtrusive habits and brief, high-pitched jingling songs. Sexes similar. Bush or rock nesting.

ALPINE ACCENTOR *Prunella collaris*   page 276
   Du – Alpenheggemus   Fr – Accenteur alpin
   Ge – Alpenbraunelle   Sw – Alpjärnsparv
Identification: 7". Larger, plumper and more brightly coloured than

← WREN
Partial migrant

ALPINE
ACCENTOR →
*Part. mig. Spreads
to lower levels in
winter. Vagrant
Britain, Belgium,
Heligoland,
Sweden, Malta*

related Dunnock, though attitudes and unobtrusive habits are similar. Distinguished by *black-spotted whitish chin and throat*, greyish breast, *chestnut-streaked flanks*, irregular double white wing-bar and pale buffish tips to tail-feathers. Upper-parts streaked grey-brown. Legs coral red. Juvenile has unspotted grey throat.

Voice: A trilling, lark-like *"tchir-rip*," and a throaty *"churrg."* Song, a pleasant, sustained warbling, from ground or in brief display-flight.
Habitat: Rocky mountain slopes, up to snow-line. Winters lower. Nests in holes among rocks or vegetation. Map p. 225.

DUNNOCK   *Prunella modularis*   page 276
    Du – Heggemus   Fr – Accenteur mouchet
    Ge – Heckenbraunelle   Sw – Järnsparv

Identification: 5¾". Inconspicuous and rather featureless; combination of *rich brown and dark grey* is the best guide. Upper-parts dark brown streaked with black; head and neck slate-grey, with brownish crown and ear-coverts, *under-parts slate-grey* with darkly streaked flanks. Dark, thin bill. Feeds on ground, seldom far from cover, moving with slow, shuffling gait, with wings frequently twitched. Usually solitary.
Voice: A high, piping *"tseep"* and a high trilling note. Song, a hurried, weak but pleasant jingle, much shorter and weaker than Wren's, but somewhat similar in character. Sings almost all the year.
Habitat: Hedges, bushes, coppices. Nests in bushes, evergreens, wood-piles. Map p. 227.

WARBLERS, FLYCATCHERS, THRUSHES, etc.: Muscicapidae

Warblers are small, active, insectivorous birds, with slender bills. Many confusingly devoid of distinctive markings; plumages wear rapidly, adding to difficulty in identification. Call-notes often rather similar. Voices and behaviour diagnostically important. Usually nest in low vegetation on or near ground, or (in *Acrocephalus*) in reeds. Sexes similar, except in *Sylvia*. For convenience can be divided into four groups: swamp warblers, tree warblers, scrub warblers and leaf warblers.
Goldcrests are minute, olive-green arboreal birds, somewhat akin in behaviour to small tits and leaf warblers. Adults have brilliant streak of colour on crown. Sexes nearly similar. Tree nesting.
Flycatchers are usually seen perched *upright* on vantage points, from which they make short, erratic flights after passing insects. Bills broad at the base. Sexes similar in Spotted. Hole or tree nesting.
Chats and **Thrushes** are mostly colourful, rather upstanding song birds. Bills slender or fairly slender. Tails usually square-ended. Sexes usually similar in thrushes. Chats are hole-nesters; thrushes build substantial cup-nests in bushes, trees, rocks, ground.

CETTI'S WARBLER *Cettia cetti* page 228
    Du – Cetti's zanger   Fr – Bouscarle de Cetti
    Ge – Seidensänger   Sw – Cettisångare
Identification: 5½″ Skulking habits make sight identification difficult,
but *song is unmistakable*. Upper-parts *dark rufous brown*, short supercilium, under-parts greyish white with browner flanks and barred
under tail-coverts. Tail full and strongly rounded. Rather rufous
appearance may cause confusion with Nightingale, but latter is larger,
with longer tail more rufous than upper-parts. Tail often cocked.
Voice: A loud "*chee*," a short "*twic*," a soft "*huit*," and a churring
alarm. Song, a very loud, abrupt burst, chiefly a repetition of "*settee*"
or "*cheweeoo*" with varying emphasis. Sings from dense vegetation.
Habitat: Low, tangled vegetation, usually near water, ditches, swamps,
reed-beds. Nest well hidden in low vegetation. Map below.

SAVI'S WARBLER *Locustella luscinioides* page 228
    Du – Snor   Fr – Locustelle luscinioïde
    Ge – Rohrschwirl   Sw – Vassångare
Identification: 5½″. Superficially resembles large Reed Warbler, but
identified by Grasshopper Warbler-like song. Tail broad and well
graduated, often faintly barred. Upper-parts *unstreaked* dark reddish-
brown; under-parts brownish-white with slightly rufous-brown flanks.
Short indistinct buffish supercilium. Distinguished from Grasshopper
Warbler by *uniform* plumage; from River Warbler by *unstreaked*
breast; from both by distinctive song and larger size. Much less
skulking than Grasshopper Warbler.
Voice: A quiet, persistent "*tswik*" and a scolding chatter. Song very
like Grasshopper Warbler's reeling trill, but slower, often briefer and
can be confused with noise made by Marsh Cricket. Often preceded
by low ticking notes which accelerate until they merge into the typical
reeling. Sings from reed-top.

← DUNNOCK
*Partial migrant.
Vagrant Faeroes*

CETTI'S
WARBLER →
*Mainly resident.
Vagrant England,
Germany*

SWAMP WARBLERS

Field Marks and Habitat   *Song*

NO STREAKS ON BACK

● **REED WARBLER**   page 234
    Brown above; clear buffish-   Tendency to repeat phrases
    white below; pale eye-ring.   2-3 times: *"chirruc-chirruc,*
    Reeds, marshes.   *jag-jag-jag,"* etc.

○ **GREAT REED WARBLER**   235
    Large size; eye-stripe; large   Strident *"karra-karra, krik-*
    bill. *Reed-beds.*   *krik, gurk-gurk,"* etc.

● **MARSH WARBLER**   233
    More olive than Reed W.;   More musical and varied
    legs flesh-pink, not dark.   than Reed W., with canary-
    Wet thickets, ditches, crops.   like trills, mimicry, etc.

△ **CETTI'S WARBLER**   227
    Dark rufous; cocked tail.   A loud abrupt burst, chiefly
    Dense thickets, bushy ditches.   repetition of *"cheweeoo."*

● **SAVI'S WARBLER**   227
    Like large Reed, voice like   Like reeling trill of Grass-
    Grasshopper W. *Marshes.*   hopper W., but lower, briefer.

△ **RIVER WARBLER**   230
    Soft streaks on breast.   Rapid, but quiet *"chuffing"*
    Thickets, dense herbage.   notes, clearly separated.

WITH STREAKS ON BACK

● **SEDGE WARBLER**   233
    Streaks; creamy eye-stripe.   More varied than Reed W.;
    Widespread; reeds, wet scrub.   trills, mimicry, chattering.

△ **MOUSTACHED WARBLER**   232
    From Sedge by darker cap,   Recalls Reed; sweeter, in-
    whiter eye-stripe, rustier   cludes phrase suggesting
    back. *Reed-beds, swamps.*   Wood Lark's *"lu-lu-lu-lu."*

● **GRASSHOPPER WARBLER**   231
    Mottled upper-parts.   Long reeling trill or buzzing
    Marshy undergrowth, scrub.   on one high note.

○ **AQUATIC WARBLER**   232
    Buff stripe through crown.   Very like Sedge Warbler.
    Open marshes, sedge, etc.

  FAN-TAILED WARBLER   250
    Heavily streaked; short tail.   Sings in air; lisping *"zip ...*
    Marshes, crops.   *zip ... zip,"* etc. (or *"dzeep"*)

NO STREAKS ON BACK

GREAT REED

REED

MARSH

CETTI'S

SAVI'S

RIVER

STREAKS ON BACK

SEDGE

MOUSTACHED

GRASSHOPPER

ZIP···ZIP···ZIP···ZIP···ZIP···ZIP···

AQUATIC

FAN-TAILED

♀ ♂
BLACKCAP **ORPHEAN** **SARDINIAN**

**LESSER
WHITETHROAT**

♀ ♂
WHITETHROAT

♀ ♂
RUPPELL'S

SPECTACLED **SUBALPINE** **MARMORA'S**

DARTFORD

Brown-backed form

Adult

Rufous form

BARRED

**RUFOUS
BUSH CHAT**

Immature

SCRUB WARBLERS

Mostly *Sylvia*. With distinctive marks and "capped" appearance.

Field Marks and Habitat	*Song*	
BLACKCAP		page 239
Black cap to eye, ♂; brown in ♀. *Undergrowth, trees.*	Rich warbling notes, more varied than Garden W.	
ORPHEAN WARBLER		238
Black cap below white eye. *Woodlands, orchards, groves.*	Mellow thrush-like warble, phrases repeated 4-5 times.	
SARDINIAN WARBLER		241
Black cap below eye; flanks grey. *Dry thickets, scrub.*	Recalls Whitethroat's; longer with staccato *cha-cha-cha-cha.*	
WHITETHROAT		240
White throat, rusty on wing. *Bushes, bramble patches.*	A short, scratchy, urgent chatter, often in display flight.	
LESSER WHITETHROAT		240
Dark mask; not rusty on wing. *Hedgerows, shrubbery.*	Unmusical rattling on one note.	
RÜPPELL'S WARBLER		241
Black throat; white moustache. *Aegean. Rocky scrub.*	Like loud Sardinian: notes interspersed with loud rattle.	
SPECTACLED WARBLER		242
Like small Whitethroat; pinker breast; darker cheek. *Mediterr.; Salicornia, scrub.*	Short and Whitethroat-like; quieter, without grating notes.	
SUBALPINE WARBLER		241
Orange breast; moustache. *Bushes, wood-edges.*	Recalls Sardinian; slower, lacks hard scolding notes.	
DARTFORD WARBLER		242
Dark vinous breast; cocked tail. *Gorse, low scrub, etc.*	Musical chatter with liquid notes; recalls Whitethroat.	
MARMORA'S WARBLER		243
Dark slaty breast. *W. Med. Low scrub.*	Resembles Dartford's, but is less harsh.	
BARRED WARBLER		238
Barred breast; wing-bars. *Thorny thickets, bushes.*	Resembles poor Blackcap; more rapid, briefer phrases.	
RUFOUS BUSH CHAT		259
Rufous; large fan tail. *Mediterr. Gardens, groves.*	Musical, disjointed, some phrases recalling Sky Lark.	

Habitat: Swamps, reed-beds with scattered bushes. Nest well concealed among thick tangle of dead reeds and sedges. Map below.

RIVER WARBLER   *Locustella fluviatilis*   page 228

Du – Krekelzanger   Fr – Locustelle fluviatile
Ge – Schlagschwirl   Sw – Flodsångare

Identification: 5″. Distinguished from Grasshopper Warbler by *unstreaked*, dark earth-brown upper-parts; whitish under-parts with faint blurred brown streaking on upper breast; tail shorter, full and rounded, with slightly rufous coverts. Legs pinkish. Juvenile has only faint streaks on throat, more rufous upper-parts and buffish-white under-parts. Very secretive behaviour and reluctant flight as in Grasshopper Warbler, but differs in song and habitat.

Voice: Has low, harsh call-note. Song recalls Grasshopper Warbler's, but notes are softer and *slower*, with rhythmic "chuffing" quality, like distant steam-engine running at high speed; ends with 4-5 quiet "*zwee*" notes. Often sings from exposed bush-tops under trees.

Habitat: Moist localities, also often in woodland thickets, or tangled herbage and bramble patches in open ground, or in forest glades, including pine. Nests on or close to ground, in moist undergrowth. Map below.

PALLAS'S GRASSHOPPER WARBLER   *Locustella certhiola*
                                                              page 284

Du – Siberische snor   Fr – Locustelle de Pallas
Ge – Streifenschwirl   Sw – Starrsångare

Identification: 5¼″. Has very skulking character of Grasshopper, but plumage recalls Sedge. *Rump and upper tail-coverts rufous* (with some streaks) *contrasting with greyish-brown tail.* Tail has indistinct bars and blackish feather-centres broadening into dark terminal band; in unworn plumage *narrow greyish-white tips to all but central feathers form indistinct pale rim; under tail-coverts tawny buff.* Mantle streaked and generally browner than Grasshopper. Under-parts variable greyish-

← SAVI'S WARBLER
Summer visitor.
Breeds England.
Vagrant Scotland,
Sweden, Denmark

RIVER WARBLER →
     Summer visitor.
Vagrant to Nor-
way, Finland (has
bred), Switzerland,
Holland, Scotland

white; immature often has yellowish breast and flanks with indistinct spots forming breast-band. Bill blackish, legs pink.
Voice: Winter note described as *"chir-chirr."*
Habitat and Range: Damp meadows with long grass and in rank undergrowth. Winters in rice-fields, reeds, swamps. Vagrant from C. Asia, Siberia to Britain, Ireland, Heligoland.

GRASSHOPPER WARBLER *Locustella naevia* page 228
Du – Sprinkhaanrietzanger   Fr – Locustelle tachetée
Ge – Feldschwirl   Sw – Gräshoppsångare
Identification: 5". Very skulking. Usually identified by *distinctive song*. Upper-parts olive-brown (can be yellowish) *strongly streaked*; less streaked on rump; lightly streaked buffish-white under-parts; well-rounded, faintly barred tail; legs pinkish, variable. Creeps and runs with great agility among undergrowth, but reluctant to fly.
Voice: A short *"twhit,"* or *"pitt,"* merging into a chatter when alarmed. Far-carrying song is a "mechanical" churring on one high note, like winding an angler's reel, often for more than two minutes; ventriloquial effect obtained by turning head. Sings day or night. See also Savi's and Lanceolated.
Habitat: Undergrowth in marshes, water-meadows, dry heaths, hedge-rows, etc. Nest well concealed on or near ground in long grass, rushes, undergrowth. Map below.

LANCEOLATED WARBLER *Locustella lanceolata* page 284
Du – Temminck's rietzanger   Fr – Locustelle lancéolée
Ge – Strichelschwirl   Sw – Träsksångare
Identification: 4½". Resembles small Grasshopper Warbler, but is more heavily streaked above, particularly on the brown mantle. Best field-mark is the *well-defined gorget of close, parallel streaking on the upper-breast, below the whitish chin and throat*. Indistinct buffish-white streak through eye. Bill dark brown above, pale flesh below; legs pinkish. Behaviour very skulking.

← GRASSHOPPER WARBLER
Summer visitor. Vagrant Norway

MOUSTACHED WARBLER →
Partial migrant. Vagrant England (has bred), Germany, Switzerland. May breed N. Greece

Voice: Winter note described as *"chir-chirr,"* resembling Pallas's Grasshopper Warbler.
Habitat and Range: Rank vegetation and reeds bordering water, wet meadows and overgrown marshes. Vagrant from N.E. Russia, Asia to Britain, Holland, Denmark, Sweden, Germany, Yugoslavia.

MOUSTACHED WARBLER *Lusciniola melanopogon* page 228
　　　Du – Zwartkoprietzanger　　　Fr – Lusciniole à moustaches
　　　Ge – Tamariskensänger　　　Sw – Tamarisksångare
Identification: 5″. Distinguished with difficulty from Sedge Warbler by *almost black crown*, contrasting with *whiter supercilium* ending squarely at nape, *dark brown cheeks, very white throat*. Nape and mantle *rustier* than Sedge. Can be distinguished from Sedge and Aquatic by *perky habit of cocking its rather short, rounded tail*. Behaviour rather skulking.
Voice: A soft but penetrating *"t-trrt"* and a harsher *"tchuck,"* which runs into a scolding rattle of alarm. Song recalls Sedge Warbler's, but is sweeter and quieter, phrases repeated 4-6 times.
Habitat: Reed-beds and swamps. Nests in reeds or low bushes above shallow water. Map p. 231.

AQUATIC WARBLER *Acrocephalus paludicola* page 228
　　　Du – Waterrietzanger　　　Fr – Phragmite aquatique
　　　Ge – Seggenrohrsänger　　　Sw – Vattensångare
Identification: 5″. Looks like sandy Sedge Warbler, but distinguished by *boldly striped head*. Has *long* buff (instead of whitish) supercilium extending to nape and *conspicuous buff stripe down centre of crown*; prominent black streaks on back, extending less strongly *to rump*; in summer has thin, sparse streaks on breast and flanks. Distinguished from all other *Acrocephalus* and from Moustached Warbler by crown-stripe and streaked rusty rump. More skulking than Sedge Warbler. Often feeds on ground. Beware similarity to young Sedge.
Voice: Very like Sedge Warbler's.

← AQUATIC
WARBLER
*Summer visitor.
Has bred Latvia,
France. Passage
west to Spain &
Portugal. Vagrant
British Is., Sweden*

SEDGE
WARBLER →
*Summer visitor.
Vagrant Faeroes*

Habitat: As Sedge Warbler, but prefers open marshes with low vegetation, sedge, etc. Nests near ground. Map p. 232.

SEDGE WARBLER   *Acrocephalus schoenobaenus*   page 228
Du – Rietzanger   Fr – Phragmite des joncs
Ge – Schilfrohrsänger   Sw – Sävsångare

Identification: 5″. Distinguished from Reed Warbler by *conspicuous whitish supercilium, boldly streaked upper-parts* except for *unstreaked* tawny rump. Under-parts creamy, with rufous flanks. Adult crown can be very dark, causing confusion with Moustached. Tail rather pointed. Juvenile yellower, especially on rump, with faint spots on throat and upper-breast, and a streaked creamy stripe on crown; these features can cause confusion with Aquatic Warbler. Flight and behaviour like Reed Warbler. See also Aquatic and Moustached. Other *Acrocephalus* (Reed Warbler, etc.) have unstreaked upper-parts.
Voice: An explosive *"tuc,"* becoming a stuttering rattle when excited; also a harsh churring. Song *more varied* than Reed Warbler's, a loud, rapid sequence of repeated musical and harsh chattering notes, mingled with long trills and mimicry. Sings from perch and in short, vertical display flight.
Habitat: Reed-beds and lush vegetation near water, swampy thickets, crops. Builds untidy nest in low, dense vegetation. Map p. 232.

BLYTH'S REED WARBLER   *Acrocephalus dumetorum*
Du – Blyth's kleine karekiet   Fr – Rousserolle des buissons
Ge – Buschrohrsänger   Sw – Busksångare

Identification: 5″. Indistinguishable in the field from Marsh Warbler, but upper-parts usually greyer brown. Doubtfully distinguishable from Reed Warbler by slightly darker and usually less rusty-brown upper-parts. Identified with certainty only in the hand, by wing formula (see line drawing). Song, usually from tree, recalls Marsh Warbler's, but is less harsh and exceptionally long, loud, varied and musical. Summer visitor, breeding S. Finland and E. Estonia. Has bred Latvia. Accidental Britain.

MARSH WARBLER   *Acrocephalus palustris*   page 228
Du – Bosrietzanger   Fr – Rousserolle verderolle
Ge – Sumpfrohrsänger   Sw – Kärrsångare

Identification: 5″. Difficult to distinguish from Reed Warbler except by *remarkably musical song*; but upper-parts generally less rufous and more olive, chin and throat whiter; legs flesh-pink; short, faint supercilium. Behaviour less skulking; silhouette plumper. Juvenile resembles young Reed. See also Blyth's Reed Warbler.
Voice: A loud, repeated *"tchuc,"* a quiet *"tuc,"* a stuttering *"tic-tirric,"* *"tweek,"* etc. Song exceptionally musical and varied, with canary-like trills and a wide range of mimicry, interspersed with Reed Warbler-like chirrups and a distinctive nasal note.
Habitat: Dense, low vegetation in ditches, thickets, stream-banks,

osier-beds, crops, often near water. Builds untidy nest, supported by "handles" woven around low vegetation. Map below.

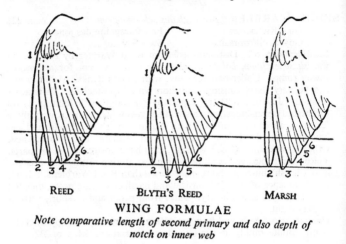

REED   BLYTH'S REED   MARSH

WING FORMULAE
Note comparative length of second primary and also depth of notch on inner web

REED WARBLER *Acrocephalus scirpaceus*   page 228
Du – Kleine karekiet   Fr – Rousserolle effarvatte
Ge – Teichrohrsänger   Sw – Rörsångare

Identification: 5″. Uniform brown above, slightly rufous on rump. Whitish below, with buffish flanks. Leg colour variable. Distinguished from Sedge Warbler by *unstreaked* head and back and very *indistinct* supercilium. Great Reed Warbler is much larger. Almost indistinguishable in the field from Marsh Warbler (except by voice), but is generally rustier-brown; in autumn juveniles look identical. Rounded tail is spread and depressed during brief flights over water. See also Blyth's Reed Warbler, and Paddyfield Warbler (Accidentals p. 321).

← MARSH
  WARBLER
Summer visitor.
Has bred Spain,
Vagrant Scotland,
Finland, Norway

REED WARBLER →
Summer visitor.
Vagrant Scotland,
Ireland (has bred)

Voice: A low "*churr*," a harsh "*skurr*" of alarm (very like Sedge's), and a weak ticking note. Prolonged song resembles Sedge's, but distinguished by tendency to repeat phrases 2-3 times: "*chirruc-chirruc*," "*jag-jag-jag*," etc., interspersed with liquid notes and mimicry. Sings day and night.

Habitat: Reed-beds and water-side vegetation; in parts of Europe also found in cultivated land away from water. Breeds colonially, suspending nest in reeds or bushes. Map p. 234.

GREAT REED WARBLER *Acrocephalus arundinaceus* page 228

<table>
<tr><td>Du – Grote karekiet</td><td>Fr – Rousserolle turdoïde</td></tr>
<tr><td>Ge – Drosselrohrsänger</td><td>Sw – Trastsångare</td></tr>
</table>

Identification: 7½". Easily distinguished from Reed Warbler by *much larger size, angular head, longer, much stouter bill,* usually bold *supercilium* and *strident voice*. Coloration like Reed Warbler. Behaviour less skulking: perches freely on trees or telegraph wires. Flight low, with characteristically spread tail, plunging heavily into reeds.

Voice: Strident and loud. Song harsh and prolonged, audible great distance. Wide range of grating notes, each repeated 2-3 times: "*karra-karra*," "*krik-krik*," "*gurk-gurk-gurk*," etc.

Habitat: Breeds colonially, building suspended nest like Reed Warbler, in reeds bordering open water, on river banks, clay-pits. Map below.

ICTERINE WARBLER *Hippolais icterina* page 244

<table>
<tr><td>Du – Spotvogel</td><td>Fr – Hypolaïs ictérine</td></tr>
<tr><td>Ge – Gelbspötter</td><td>Sw – Gulsångare</td></tr>
</table>

Identification: 5¼". A stout, perky, green and yellow warbler. Distinguished with difficulty from Melodious by usually brighter greenish-olive upper-parts (often with yellowish wash), *peaked* rather than rounded crown, *longer, more pointed wings projecting well beyond base of tail*. Except in worn autumn plumage, edges of inner secondaries form *distinct pale patch on folded wing* (whitish in immature, yellowish in adult). Some adults lack yellow below and are often greyer above. Immature greyer and more "washed-out" than immature Melodious.

← GREAT REED WARBLER
Summer visitor. Vagrant England, Ireland, Norway

ICTERINE WARBLER →
Summer visitor. Annual Britain & Ireland

Legs vary from blue-grey to bluish-black. Bill rather broad and large with dark upper and pinkish lower mandibles. *Voice and range* differ from Melodious.

Voice: A Blackcap-like *"tec,"* a characteristic, musical *"deederoid,"* a Chiffchaff-like *"hooeet,"* and a low churring alarm. Song recalls Marsh Warbler's, a loud, remarkably long sustained and varied jumble of melodious *and discordant* notes, each *repeated* several times, interspersed with jarring notes.

Habitat: Gardens, parks and cultivated land, but also found in woods, thickets and hedges. Builds snug nest in shrubs, hedges, etc. Map p. 235.

MELODIOUS WARBLER   *Hippolais polyglotta*   page 244
      Du – Orpheusspotvogel   Fr – Hypolaïs polyglotte
      Ge – Orpheusspötter   Sw – Polyglottgulsångare

Identification: 5″. Difficult to distinguish in the field from Icterine except by *voice*. Is slightly smaller, with browner or duller upper-parts, notably on rump. Has distinctly *rounded* crown and *shorter, more rounded wings which do not project beyond base of tail*. In breeding season many adults have yellow wing-patch, but less prominent than Icterine's; browner immature birds lack this. Legs vary from brownish-flesh to blue-grey, but are *usually browner* than Icterine's. Bill colour as in Icterine. Under-parts variable, but usually deeper yellow than Icterine's; some adults and immatures lack yellow and are browner above.

Voice: A House Sparrow-like chatter, a Chiffchaff-like *"hooeet"* and an abrupt *"tit, tit."* Song, often beginning slowly, is a *prolonged*, musical and very varied babbling, more hurried and less harsh than song of Icterine; often introduces sparrow-like chirping notes and mimicry, but with little repetition.

Habitat: Similar to Icterine, but more often in lush vegetation near water. Builds snug nest in bushes, rarely in trees. Map below.

← MELODIOUS
    WARBLER
*Summer visitor.
Annual Britain,
Ireland. Vagrant
Belgium, Ger-
many, Czecho-
Switzerland*

OLIVE-TREE
    WARBLER →
*Summer visitor.
Vagrant Italy*

OLIVE-TREE WARBLER *Hippolais olivetorum*   page 244
  Du – Griekse spotvogel   Fr – Hypolaïs des oliviers
  Ge – Olivenspötter   Sw – Olivgulsångare
Identification: 6″. A large *greyish* warbler with strikingly big, *dagger-like bill*, yellowish at base. *Bold whitish edges to secondaries* give streaky effect to closed wing. Primaries and tail darker grey-brown. Legs bluish-grey. Crown has peaked appearance at rear. Pale supercilium extends behind eye. Big bill, wing markings and larger size and longer wings easily distinguish it from Olivaceous.
Voice: Call-note *"tuc."* Distinctive song is louder, slower, more contralto and less "scratchy" than other *Hippolais* warblers.
Habitat: Frequents thorn scrub, olive and oak woods, keeping well out of sight. Nests in fork of branch. Map p. 236.

OLIVACEOUS WARBLER *Hippolais pallida*   page 244
  Du – Vale spotvogel   Fr – Hypolaïs pâle
  Ge – Blassspötter   Sw – Blek gulsångare
Identification: 5¼″. Form and behaviour recall Melodious, but normally lacks greenish and yellowish coloration. Distinguished by *longer bill*, with *yellowish* lower mandible, *flatter crown*, greyish or brownish-olive upper-parts and (apart from faint pale edges to inner secondaries) *unmarked, darker wings* reaching only to base of tail. Last-mentioned feature useful distinction from greyish first-winter Icterine. Under-parts dull white with pale buffish wash on flanks and under tail-coverts and sometimes across breast; throat often whiter. In spring under-parts often have yellowish wash. Pale grey eye-ring. Leg colours variable, overlapping those of both Melodious and Icterine. Has longer bill, more prominent supercilium and flatter crown than Garden Warbler.
Voice: Call-note similar to Icterine's *"tec, tec."* Alarm, a quiet ticking. Vigorous song recalls Sedge Warbler, though less varied and less harsh.

← OLIVACEOUS
  WARBLER
Summer visitor.
Vagrant Brit. Is.,
Heligoland, Italy

BARRED
  WARBLER →
Summer visitor.
Has bred Switz.
Rare passage E.
Britain. Vagrant
Ireland, Faeroes,
Norway

Habitat: Cultivated areas and gardens, with trees and bushes. Nests in bushes, hedges, etc., but sometimes in palm trees. Map p. 237.

BARRED WARBLER *Sylvia nisoria*　　　　　　　page 229
　　　Du – Gestreepte grasmus　　　Fr – Fauvette épervière
　　　Ge – Sperbergrasmücke　　　　Sw – Höksångare

Identification: 6″. Distinguished by whitish under-parts *barred with dark, crescent-shaped markings*, much less distinct in female. Male is ashy grey-brown above, female browner. Dark brown wings have *two whitish bars*. Rather long tail shows some white in outer feathers. Adults have *bright yellow eyes*. Juvenile has slightly buffish under-parts with little or no bars; distinguished from Whitethroat and Garden Warbler by greyer appearance, wing-bars and larger size. Appearance is heavy, with stout legs and bill. Behaviour skulking, tail often flicked.

Voice: A hard "*tchack*," a low churring and a distinctive, grating "*tcharr, tcharr*," which also occurs in song. Song resembles Blackcap's in richness and purity, but more rapid and *briefer phrases* recall Whitethroat.

Habitat: Thorny thickets, bushy commons and hedges, clearings in woods, etc. Usually nests in thorn bushes. Map p. 237.

ORPHEAN WARBLER *Sylvia hortensis*　　　　　　page 229
　　　Du – Orpheusgrasmus　　　　Fr – Fauvette orphée
　　　Ge – Orpheusgrasmücke　　　Sw – Mästersångare

Identification: 6″. Resembles large male Blackcap, but easily separated by *white in outer tail-feathers*; dull, blackish cap *extending clearly below the eye* and merging into grey mantle instead of being clean-cut; also by *white*, instead of grey, throat. Female slightly browner. Eyes are *distinctive pale straw*. Distinguished from Sardinian by much larger size, pale eyes, dull instead of clean-cut glossy black cap, and different habitat. Immature can be confused with young Barred, but tail is shorter and upper tail-coverts lack light tips.

← ORPHEAN
　WARBLER
Summer visitor.
Has bred Germany.
Vagrant England,
Belgium, Austria,
Czecho.

GARDEN
WARBLER →
Summer visitor.
Vagrant Faeroes,
Iceland

Voice: A Blackcap-like "*tac, tac,*" or "*tyut, tyut,*" and a loud, rattling alarm. Song, a loud, mellow, *thrush-like* musical warble, each phrase usually repeated 4-5 times, without discordant notes.
Habitat: Chiefly arboreal. Wooded districts, orchards, scrub, citrus and olive groves. Nests in bushes, low branches. Map p. 238.

GARDEN WARBLER *Sylvia borin*   page 244
    Du – Tuinfluiter   Fr – Fauvette des jardins
    Ge – Gartengrasmücke   Sw – Trädgårdssångare
Identification: 5½″. A plump, uniform, brownish warbler with pale under-parts and a characteristic *round head* and *stubby bill.* No distinctive plumage features, but may be identified by *sustained and beautiful song.* Distinguished from female and juvenile Blackcap by uniform brownish crown and upper-parts. Legs have bluish tinge.
Voice: Call-note "*check, check,*" like Blackcap's, but less hard; a low, harsh "*tchur-r-r*" and a faint "*whit.*" Song has same mellow quality as Blackcap's, but is quieter and much longer sustained. Sings from undergrowth.
Habitat: Woods with abundant undergrowth, thickets, bushy commons with bramble patches, overgrown hedges, fruit bushes. Nests in low bushes and brambles. Map p. 238.

BLACKCAP *Sylvia atricapilla*   page 229
    Du – Zwartkop   Fr – Fauvette à tête noire
    Ge – Mönchsgrasmücke   Sw – Svarthätta
Identification: 5½″. Male distinguished by *glossy black crown, down to eye-level*; upper-parts greyish brown, *sides of head* and under-parts ashy grey. Female has *red-brown crown* and browner under-parts. Juveniles are rustier above, yellow below; young males have blackish-brown crowns. Distinguished from Orphean and Sardinian by *sharply defined cap terminating at eye-level, and absence of white in tail.* See also Garden Warbler.
Voice: An emphatic "*tac, tac,*" rapidly repeated when alarmed, and a harsh churring. Song, a remarkably rich warbling, *more varied but*

← BLACKCAP
*Partial migrant.
Passage Faeroes,
Iceland*

WHITETHROAT →
*Summer visitor.
Vagrant Iceland*

less sustained than Garden Warbler's, often louder towards end.
Habitat: Woodland glades with undergrowth, overgrown hedges,
fruit bushes. Nests in brambles, honeysuckle, evergreens, etc. Map
p. 239.

WHITETHROAT   *Sylvia communis*   page 229

     Du – Grasmus   Fr – Fauvette grisette
     Ge – Dorngrasmücke   Sw – Törnsångare

Identification: 5¼″. A perky little bird with *conspicuously rusty wings*
and rather long tail with white outer feathers. Male has *pale grey cap*
extending to nape and below eye (brownish-grey in autumn), *pure
white throat*. Under-parts very pale pinkish-buff. Female duller, with
brownish head and only faint pink on breast. Restless, darting in and
out of undergrowth with raised crest and cocked tail. See also Lesser
Whitethroat.
Voice: A repeated "*check*," a hoarse, scolding "*tcharr*," and a quiet
"*wheet, wheet, whit-whit-whit*" ending hurriedly. Song, a vigorous,
urgent chatter, usually from bush, or in brief dancing song-flight.
Habitat: Fairly open country with bushes, brambles, gorse, nettle-
beds. Nests near ground in low vegetation. Map p. 239.

LESSER WHITETHROAT   *Sylvia curruca*   page 229

     Du – Braamsluiper   Fr – Fauvette babillarde
     Ge – Klappergrasmücke   Sw – Ärtsångare

Identification: 5¼″. Distinguished from Whitethroat by *shorter tail,
much greyer upper-parts, dark ear-coverts* (giving masked appearance),
lack of chestnut on wings and distinctive song. More skulking than
Whitethroat. See also Rüppell's and Sardinian Warblers.
Voice: Call-notes like Whitethroat's. Song begins with subdued
warble, followed by outburst of unmusical rattling *on one note*. Sings
in thick cover, and lacks Whitethroat's vertical song-flight.
Habitat: As Whitethroat, though usually in taller, denser vegetation,
with more trees. Map below.

← Lesser
    Whitethroat
*Summer visitor.
Vagrant Ireland,
Faeroes, Iceland,
Spain*

Sardinian
    Warbler →
*Mainly resident.
Vagrant Switzer-
land, England,
Heligoland*

RÜPPELL'S WARBLER *Sylvia rüppelli* page 229
Du – Rüppell's grasmus   Fr – Fauvette masquée
Ge – Maskengrasmücke   Sw – Svarthakad sångare
Identification: 5½″. Male has *black crown, face and throat, with conspicuous white moustachial stripe*, grey upper-parts, whitish under-parts, black tail with *bold white outer feathers*. Female duller, with pale or dusky throat, but white moustachial stripe still fairly visible. Eyes and legs brilliant red-brown. Male distinguished from Sardinian by *black throat*, and *white "moustache."*
Voice: Easily confused with loud Sardinian. Usual note like winding wooden rattle rapidly. Song resembles Whitethroat's, but interspersed with characteristic rattle.
Habitat and Range: Breeds in bushes among low scrub with rocky outcrops. Summer visitor, breeding Aegean region. Vagrant to Italy, Sicily.

SARDINIAN WARBLER *Sylvia melanocephala* page 229
Du – Kleine zwartkop   Fr – Fauvette mélanocéphale
Ge – Samtkopfgrasmücke   Sw – Sammetshätta
Identification: 5¼″. Male distinguished by *black cap extending well below eye*, pure white throat, grey upper-parts, whitish under-parts *with grey sides*. *Bright reddish eye-ring* is conspicuous. Frequently-spread, blackish, graduated tail, has bold white outer feathers. Female much browner, with grey-brown cap scarcely darker than back. Bobbing flight and restless behaviour recall Whitethroat. See also Orphean, Blackcap and Rüppell's.
Voice: Has loud, staccato alarm-note, *"cha-cha-cha-cha,"* like rapidly wound wooden rattle. Song faintly recalls Whitethroat's, but is longer, more musical, and interspersed with staccato alarm note. Sings from exposed or hidden perches and in brief, dancing display-flight.
Habitat: Dry, fairly open bushy scrub, thickets, pine and evergreen oak woods, etc. Nests in low bushes and undergrowth. Map p. 240.

SUBALPINE WARBLER *Sylvia cantillans* page 229
Du – Baardgrasmus   Fr – Fauvette passerinette
Ge – Weissbartgrasmücke   Sw – Rödstrupig sångare
Identification: 4¾″. Distinguished from Dartford, which has similar form and with which it often occurs, by much paler ash-blue upper-parts, unspotted throat, and conspicuous white outer feathers of dark, rounded tail. Male has *very narrow white moustachial stripe* contrasting with pinkish-chestnut throat and breast. Female and juvenile duller and paler, buffish-pink below, with much fainter moustachial stripes. Eyes appear red at close quarters. Behaviour like Dartford's, raising and spreading tail when excited, but tail is shorter. See also Spectacled.
Voice: A hard but quiet *"tec, tec,"* and a quick, chattering alarm. Song recalls Sardinian and Whitethroat, but is more pleasing, slower

and lacking hard scolding notes. Sings from bushes and during brief, dancing song-flight.

Habitat: Low bushes and thickets, often with scattered trees; also in open woodland glades and along stream banks. Nests in thick bushes. Map below.

SPECTACLED WARBLER *Sylvia conspicillata* page 229

> Du – Brilgrasmus Fr – Fauvette à lunettes
> Ge – Brillengrasmücke Sw – Glasögonsångare

Identification: 5″. Resembles small Whitethroat and also has bright rusty wings, but *white throat contrasts more strongly with dark head and pinkish-brown breast.* Narrow white eye-rim not very good field mark. Strikingly pale *straw-coloured legs.* Crown slate-grey, lores and ear-coverts darker; upper-parts brown. Juvenile is browner, without grey on head and with more buffish-white under-parts. Actions recall Whitethroat.

Voice: Song is short and Whitethroat-like, but quieter, without grating notes; sings from exposed perch, or in dancing song-flight. Alarm, a subdued, very characteristic, Wren-like rattle.

Habitat: Chiefly in *Salicornia* on coastal flats and (often with Dartford Warbler) in low scrub. Nests in low bush. Map below.

DARTFORD WARBLER *Sylvia undata* page 229

> Du – Provence-grasmus Fr – Fauvette pitchou
> Ge – Provencegrasmücke Sw – Provencesångare

Identification: 5″. Identified by *very dark plumage and long constantly cocked or fanned tail.* Male has slate-grey head (with characteristically raised crown-feathers), shading to *dark-brown* upper-parts; underparts *dark purplish-brown*; chin and throat spotted with white in autumn; tail graduated, dark brown with white border. Eye-ring ruby-red. Behaviour skulking. Flight weak, with characteristic "bobbing" action of tail and rapidly whirring wings. See also Subalpine and Marmora's.

Voice: A scolding metallic "*tchir-r*," a short "*tuc*," "*tchir-r-tuc-tuc*,"

← SUBALPINE
  WARBLER
*Summer visitor.
Vagrant Britain,
Ireland, Holland,
Switzerland*

SPECTACLED
  WARBLER →
*Summer visitor.
Resident Malta*

also a rattling alarm. Song, a short musical chatter, often in dancing flight, interspersed with liquid notes, recalling Whitethroat, but more pleasing.

Habitat: Open commons with heather and gorse, dwarf oak, cistus-covered hillsides, etc. Nests in scrub near ground. Map below.

MARMORA'S WARBLER *Sylvia sarda*　　　page 229

Du – Sardijnse grasmus　　　Fr – Fauvette sarde
Ge – Sardengrasmücke　　　Sw – Sardinisk sångare

Identification: 4¾″. Looks almost black at a distance. Size and shape of Dartford Warbler, but distinguished by *slate-grey* instead of purplish-brown throat and under-parts. Upper-parts dark slate-grey, with *almost black head, wings and tail*; belly brownish-white; tail slightly shorter than Dartford's; eye-ring red. Female slightly browner. Juvenile is paler and greyer above and much whiter below than young Dartford. Behaviour and habitat as Dartford, but is even more skulking.

Voice: A single sharp "*tzig*." Song like Dartford's, but less harsh.

Range: Resident E. coast of Spain, W. Mediterranean islands, perhaps Sicily.

WILLOW WARBLER *Phylloscopus trochilis*　　　page 244

Du – Fitis　　　Fr – Pouillot fitis
Ge – Fitis　　　Sw – Lövsångare

Identification: 4¼″. The most abundant summer visitor to northern half of Europe. Easily confused with Chiffchaff except for *distinctive song*. Plumage usually slightly yellower, but difference not reliable in late summer. *Legs usually light brown*, not blackish as in Chiffchaff but colour not reliable for identification. Behaviour and flight as Chiffchaff, but slightly less restless. See latter for comparison of wing formulae.

Voice: Note very like Chiffchaff's, but nearer to two syllables: "*hooeet*," or "*sooee*." Song, a liquid, musical cadence, beginning quietly and becoming clearer and more deliberate, *descending* to a distinctive flourish "*sooeet-sooeetoo*."

← DARTFORD
WARBLER
*Mainly resident.
Vagrant Ireland,
Holland, Switzerland, Malta*

WILLOW
WARBLER →
*Mainly summer
visitor. On passage
reaches Iceland*

LEAF WARBLERS

Field Marks and Habitat	*Song*	
● **WILLOW WARBLER**		page 243
"Cleaner" than Chiffchaff and (usually) pale legs. *Bushes, small trees.*	A liquid musical cascade; downscale, ending in flourish.	
● **CHIFFCHAFF**		246
"Dirtier" than Willow; dark legs. *Trees, thickets.*	Deliberately repeated "*chiff-chaff-chiff-chiff-chaff*," etc.	
○ **ARCTIC WARBLER**		248
Wing-bar; pale legs; large bill. *Arctic forests.*	A short, high trill "*ziz-ziz-ziz.*" Call, a husky "*tsssp.*"	
○ **GREENISH WARBLER**		249
Wing-bar; dark legs; weak bifl. *Forests, coppices.*	Loud, high-pitched jingle, merging into trill or gabble.	
● **YELLOW-BROWED WARBLER**		247
Two wing-bars; eye-stripe. *Mixed and conifer woods.*	Call-note "*weest.*" For song see text.	
○ **BONELLI'S WARBLER**		247
Pale head; yellow rump. *Pine forest, cork groves, etc.*	Loose trill on same note, flatter than Wood's.	
● **WOOD WARBLER**		247
Yellow throat; white belly. *Woodlands.*	Repeated notes on one pitch accelerating into dry trill.	

TREE WARBLERS

● **ICTERINE WARBLER**		235
Long wings; bluish legs. *N., E. and Cent. Eur.; bushes.*	Jumble of notes, each repeated, some discordant.	
● **MELODIOUS WARBLER**		236
Short wings; brownish legs. *S.W. Europe; bushes.*	Prolonged warbling babble, more musical than Icterine.	
OLIVE-TREE WARBLER		237
Big bill; pale wing-edging. *Olive groves, oaks.*	Louder, slower, deeper than other *Hippolais*.	
△ **OLIVACEOUS WARBLER**		237
"Mousey"; short wings. *Cultivation, scrub.*	Vigorous jumble, at times recalling Sedge Warbler.	
● **GARDEN WARBLER**		239
Unmarked, brownish. See text. *Woods, hedges, thickets.*	Mellow, suggests Blackcap, but much longer, less varied.	

WILLOW

CHIFFCHAFF

ARCTIC

GREENISH

YELLOW-BROWED

BONELLI'S

WOOD

ICTERINE

MELODIOUS

OLIVE-TREE

OLIVACEOUS

GARDEN

MEADOW PIPIT

TREE PIPIT

Winter

Summer

ROCK PIPIT

WATER PIPIT

RICHARD'S
PIPIT

TAWNY PIPIT

Summer
♂

Summer

Summer
♂

Winter

Summer

BLUE-HEADED WAGTAIL
YELLOW WAGTAIL

RED-THROATED PIPIT

♀

♂
Summer

WHITE WAGTAIL   PIED WAGTAIL

GREY WAGTAIL

♂
Summer

♂
Summer

Plate 58   245

PIPITS AND WAGTAILS

PIPITS are streaked brown ground birds with white, or whitish, outer tail feathers and long hind claws. They resemble larks (Plate 48) but are more slender.

WAGTAILS are boldly patterned ground birds, more slender and much longer tailed than pipits. Some pipits and all wagtails wag their tails. See further analysis of wagtails on Plate 59.

● **MEADOW PIPIT**   page 215
> Small; streaked above and below; white outer tail-feathers.

● **TREE PIPIT**   215
> From Meadow Pipit by buffer, less olivaceous colour, pinker legs.

● **ROCK/WATER PIPIT**   216
> The only pipits with *dark legs*.
> ROCK PIPIT. Dark; greyish outer tail. Coasts.
> WATER PIPIT. *Summer:* (mountains) pinkish un-streaked breast; greyish upper-parts; white outer tail-feathers. *Winter:* (wide-ranging) streaked whitish breast; white eye-brow; white outer tail-feathers.

○ **TAWNY PIPIT**   214
> Slim; unstreaked breast; long legs and tail.

○ **RICHARD'S PIPIT**   214
> Bulky; dark; very long stout legs; streaked breast.

○ **RED-THROATED PIPIT**   216
> *Summer:* Variable brick-red throat. *Winter:* From Meadow by blacker, heavier streaks; streaked rump.

● **YELLOW/BLUE-HEADED WAGTAIL**   217
> Yellow under-parts; olive-green back.
> YELLOW: Yellow and olive head.
> BLUE-HEADED: Blue-grey cap and cheeks.

◗ **WHITE/PIED WAGTAIL**   218
> No yellow in any plumage.
> WHITE: Grey back; black cap and bib separated.
> PIED: Black back; black cap and bib joined.

● **GREY WAGTAIL**   217
> Yellow under-parts, grey back. Longest tail of all wagtails. Male in summer has black throat.

Habitat: Less arboreal than Chiffchaff, more fond of low vegetation. Nests on ground in open bushy localities. Map p. 243.

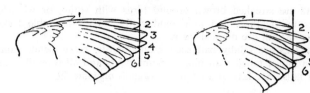

WILLOW WARBLER   CHIFFCHAFF

WING FORMULAE

Note Chiffchaff's shorter second primary and emargination on sixth primary

CHIFFCHAFF   *Phylloscopus collybita*   page 244
     Du – Tjiftjaf   Fr – Pouillot véloce
     Ge – Zilpzalp   Sw – Gransångare

Identification: 4¼″. Very similar to Willow Warbler, but plumage is a little dingier, shape a little dumpier and supercilium slightly less pronounced. Best identified by *distinctive song*. Legs usually *dark*, not light brown as in most Willow Warblers, but colour not always reliable. Upper-parts olive-brown, under-parts buffish-white faintly washed with lemon-yellow. (A useful check when trapped for ringing: 2nd primary is shorter than 6th, whereas Willow Warbler's is longer, see diagram.) Behaviour restless, wings and tail frequently flicked.

Voice: A soft "*hweet*," a louder "*twit*" and a subdued "*tsiff-tsiff-tsiff.*" Song, two notes deliberately repeated in irregular order, "*chiff, chiff, chaff, chiff, chaff,*" etc.

Habitat: More arboreal than Willow Warbler. Usually nests just above ground in brambles, evergreens, etc., in light woods and bushy commons. Winters in fairly open vegetation. Map below.

← CHIFFCHAFF
Partial migrant. May breed O. Hebrides. On passage Iceland

BONELLI'S
WARBLER →
Summer visitor. Vagrant British Isles, Sweden

BONELLI'S WARBLER *Phylloscopus bonelli*   page 244
   Du – Bergfluiter   Fr – Pouillot de Bonelli
   Ge – Berglaubsänger   Sw – Bergsångare
Identification: 4½". A very grey warbler, with pale grey-brown upper-parts, *paler grey head and whitish under-parts.* Touch of bright yellow at carpal joint and yellowish wing-patch stand out in contrast. Yellowish rump-patch can be conspicuous but is often difficult to see.
Voice: A soft *"hou-eet,"* more clearly disyllabic than familiar note of Willow Warbler. Song, a loose trill *on the same note*, slower, more musical and more clearly separated than faintly similar trill of Wood Warbler; can be confused with distant Cirl Bunting, or rattle of Lesser Whitethroat.
Habitat: Dense foliage of trees. Locally in dry pine or deciduous forests, open Cork Oak groves, or even scattered vegetation up to tree limit in mountains. Nests on ground under trees. Map p. 246.

WOOD WARBLER *Phylloscopus sibilatrix*   page 244
   Du – Fluiter   Fr – Pouillot siffleur
   Ge – Waldlaubsänger   Sw – Grönsångare
Identification: 5". Larger than Chiffchaff, with much longer wings. Distinguished by brightly contrasted yellowish-green upper-parts, *sulphur-yellow* throat and breast, and *white belly.* Broad yellow stripe above eye. Wings long, olive-brown, with yellow edges to feathers. Behaviour like Chiffchaff, but does not flick wings, though it often hangs them loosely.
Voice: A liquid *"piu"* and a soft *"whit, whit, whit."* Has two songs: a piping *"piu"* repeated 5-20 times, and a slowly repeated *"stip"* accelerating to a "shivering" grasshopper-like trill *"stip, stip, stip, stip-stip-stip-stip-shreeeee."* Sings while moving among tree foliage and in flight.
Habitat: Deciduous woods with light ground cover; also found in coniferous forests in central Europe. Nests on ground among light undergrowth, usually in beech or oak woods. Map p. 249.

YELLOW-BROWED WARBLER *Phylloscopus inornatus*
                                                page 244
   Du – Bladkoninkje   Fr – Pouillot à grands sourcils
   Ge – Gelbbrauenlaubsänger   Sw – Vitbrynad sångare
Identification: 4". Distinguished by very small size, whitish *double wing-bars,* the lower one being long, broad and *dark-edged;* broad whitish edges to secondaries, and *very long creamy supercilium.* Upper-parts greenish, becoming paler and yellower on rump. Under-parts whitish. Tail rather short. Sometimes has indistinct pale line down centre of crown. Often chases flies like flycatcher. Distinguished from juvenile Goldcrest by larger size and long, striking supercilium. See also Pallas's Leaf Warbler.
Voice: A loud *"weest,"* or *"wees-weest."* Song said to be a repetition of the call-note, or a rapid twitter on one note, usually from tree-top.

Habitat and Range: Mixed and coniferous woodlands, often in willows; scrub and undergrowth in winter. On autumn passage fairly regularly in Britain and Heligoland. Vagrant from Asia to Faeroes, Norway, Denmark, Ireland, France, Switzerland.

PALLAS'S LEAF WARBLER *Phylloscopus proregulus* page 284

Du – Pallas' boszanger   Fr – Pouillot de Pallas
Ge – Goldhähnchenlaubsänger   Sw – Kungsfågelsångare

Identification: 3½". Small size, plumage and behaviour, including hovering, recall Firecrest. Distinguished from Yellow-browed Warbler by brighter green upper-parts, *broad yellow stripe on dark-sided crown*; yellow forehead and supercilium; double *yellow* wing-bars; *primrose-yellow rump-patch* prominent when hovering.

Voice: A soft but shrill, rising "*weesp*," more prolonged than similar call of Yellow-browed; sometimes regarded as two notes "*wee-eesp*," the second higher than the first.

Habitat and Range: Mainly in tree-tops, nesting in birch, conifer and mixed forest. Vagrant from Asia to Britain, Belgium, Heligoland, Sweden, Finland, Yugoslavia.

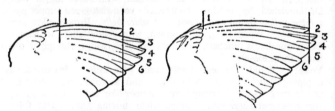

GREENISH WARBLER   ARCTIC WARBLER

WING FORMULAE
Greenish has longer first primary, shorter second primary than Arctic

ARCTIC WARBLER *Phylloscopus borealis* page 244

Du – Noordse boszanger   Fr – Pouillot boréal
Ge – Nordischer Laubsänger   Sw – Nordsångare

Identification: 4¾". Near size of Wood Warbler, but has whitish throat and conspicuous yellowish-white supercilium contrasting with long dark stripe through eye reaching almost to nape. Plumage variable: greyish-green to greenish-brown upper-parts (darker in 1st winter); greyish-white under-parts, sometimes with traces of yellow; usually a *narrow whitish wing-bar*, sometimes faint trace of second bar, but both may be lost in worn plumage. Legs *pale* yellowish-brown. Extremely active. See also Greenish Warbler.

Voice: A husky "*tssp*"; a hard "*zik*"; sometimes a chatter recalling Lesser Whitethroat. Song a distinctive trill of about 15 notes faintly recalling Bonelli's Warbler, followed by a short "*tseers*."

Habitat: Usually in lush undergrowth near water, but also in birch and coniferous woods. Nests on ground. Map below.

GREENISH WARBLER *Phylloscopus trochiloides* page 244
Du – Grauwe fitis   Fr – Pouillot verdâtre
Ge – Grüner Laubsänger   Sw – l undsångare

Identification: 4¼″. Very like Chiffchaff, but distinguished by voice, short whitish wing-bar (sometimes indistinct), less yellow under-parts and more pronounced supercilium. Size between Arctic and Yellow-browed, but is *greyer*, less green than these, and supercilium is less prominent. Legs *dark* grey-brown. In autumn difficult to separate from Arctic except by slightly shorter, finer bill and leg colour. (See wing formulae, p. 248.)

Voice: Usual note a thin "*chee-e.*" Song short and loud, beginning with rapidly repeated call-note, merging into a gabbled Wren-like trill.

Habitat: Very varied: occurs up to 11,000 ft.; deciduous or coniferous woodlands, coppices, orchards, etc. Nests on or near ground, not necessarily with undergrowth, occasionally in low stone walls. Map p. 250.

GOLDCREST *Regulus regulus* page 212
Du – Goudhaantje   Fr – Roitelet huppé
Ge – Wintergoldhähnchen   Sw – Kungsfågel

Identification: 3½″. Distinguished from tits and warblers by *very small size, plump form and bright yellow crown with black border*; crest (sometimes concealed) has orange centre in male, is paler yellow in female, absent in juvenile. Upper-parts olive green; under-parts dull whitish-buff, with greenish flanks. Wings have *two white bars and a broad black band*. Behaviour warbler-like. Roams with tits outside breeding season. Best distinguished from Firecrest by *lack of black eye-stripe.*

Voice: A frequent, shrill, high "*zee-zee-zee.*" Song, a high, thin, double note, repeated about six times, terminating with a short twitter. In autumn has longer, musical sub-song of high, soft twittering.

← WOOD
WARBLER
Summer visitor.
Has bred Ireland.
Vagrant Iceland

ARCTIC
WARBLER →
Summer visitor,
migrating east.
Vagrant to Brit.
Is., Holland and
Italy

Habitat: Coniferous or mixed woods; in winter also in hedges and undergrowth. Builds suspended nest, usually under tip of branch of conifer (but rarely in pine). Map below.

FIRECREST *Regulus ignicapillus* page 212

Du – Vuurgoudhaantje Fr – Roitelet triple-bandeau
Ge – Sommergoldhähnchen Sw – Brandkronad kunsfågel

Identification: 3½". Distinguished from Goldcrest by *bold white super-cilium and black stripe through eye*; upper-parts greener, under-parts whiter; golden tinge on sides of neck visible under good con-ditions. Juvenile has rudimentary black and white stripes on head, but lacks crest. Behaviour like Goldcrest.

Voice: Call-notes similar to Goldcrest's, but less persistent, lower-pitched and quieter, including a characteristic "*zit.*"

Habitat: As Goldcrest, but less partial to coniferous woods and more often in low undergrowth, bushy swamps, bracken, etc. Builds sus-pended nest in coniferous or deciduous trees, bushes, creepers, etc. Map p. 251.

FAN-TAILED WARBLER *Cisticola juncidis* page 228

Du – Waaierstaartrietzanger Fr – Cisticole des joncs
Ge – Cistensänger Sw – Grässångare

Identification: 4". During breeding season is most easily seen in display-flight, when *distinctive voice* is unmistakable; otherwise skulking. Suggests small, bright Sedge Warbler. Distinguished by *lack of pale eye-stripe* and much smaller size (the smallest European warbler) and *stubby tail*. Upper-parts dark brown, with broad reddish-buff margins and rufous rump, giving heavily streaked buffish impression; throat and under-parts unstreaked whitish, tinged with rufous-buff on breast and flanks; tail short and well rounded, with black and white tips to outer feathers.

Voice: Song a sharp, high, rasping "*dzeep . . . dzeep . . . dzeep . . .*"

← GREENISH WARBLER
Summer visitor; migrates east. Has bred Sweden. Vag-rant Brit. Is., Den-mark, Switzerland

GOLDCREST →
Partial migrant. Fairly regular passage Faeroes. Vagrant Iceland

corresponding with each rise in weak, undulating flight, well up in the air. Call-note "*tew*."

Habitat: Wet and dry localities, grain fields, rough grassy plains, marshes. Builds deep purse-shaped nest suspended in rushes, long grass, growing corn, or dense undergrowth. Map below.

PIED FLYCATCHER *Ficedula hypoleuca* page 253
  Du – Bonte vliegenvanger   Fr – Gobe-mouche noir
  Ge – Trauerschnäpper   Sw – Svartvít flugsnappare

Identification: 5″. Male in spring has head and upper-parts *black*; forehead, under-parts, *wing-patch and sides of tail white*; autumn plumage like female, but forehead remains whitish. Female is olive-brown above, buffish-white below, with smaller wing-patches. Juvenile distinguished from young Spotted by white on wings and tail. Fly-catching behaviour like Spotted, but seldom returns to same perch and often feeds on ground; tail constantly flirted. Wing-patches prevent confusion with other flycatchers, except Collared. See also Brown Flycatcher (Accidentals page 322).

Voice: A metallic "*whit*," an anxious "*phweet*," a persistent "*tic*" or "*wheetic*" and an explosive "*tschist*." Song chiefly on two up-and-down notes, a high "*zee-it, zee-it, zee-it*," interspersed with an occasional Redstart-like trill.

Habitat: In British Isles, usually deciduous woods and gardens, often near water. On Continent, also in coniferous forests. Nests in holes in trees, walls, nest-boxes. Map p. 254.

COLLARED FLYCATCHER *Ficedula albicollis* page 253
  Du – Withalsvliegenvanger   Fr – Gobe-mouche à collier
  Ge – Halsbandschnäpper   Sw – Halsbandsflugsnappare

Identification: 5″. Resembles Pied, but male distinguished by *bold white collar, whitish rump*, bolder white markings on wings and forehead and less white on sides of tail. In autumn black markings replaced by dark brown, collar almost disappears and white markings are reduced. Females doubtfully separable, but Collared is usually greyer above,

← FIRECREST
Partial migrant. Passage S. England (has bred). Vagrant Ireland, Faeroes, Sweden

FAN-TAILED
WARBLER →
Resident. Has bred W. coast France

HEADS OF WAGTAILS

WHITE WAGTAIL GROUP   *Motacilla alba.*   page 21
    Distinguished by lack of yellow or olive in plumage.

  ● **PIED WAGTAIL**
      M. a. yarrellii.   Back black (male) or very dark (female).
      Black cap and black bib joined in adults. Breeds British Isles
      and adjacent shores of Continent.

  ● **WHITE WAGTAIL**
      M. a. alba.   Clean grey back.   Black cap and black bib
      separated. Breeds on Continent.

GREY WAGTAIL   *Motacilla cinerea.*   21
    Distinguished by grey back, yellow under-parts.

  ● **GREY WAGTAIL**
      Male in summer: Black throat; yellow under-parts.
      Female in summer and both species in winter: Whitish throat;
      grey back; yellow under-parts.

YELLOW WAGTAIL GROUP   *Motacilla flava.*   2?
    Distinguished by olive-green back; yellow under-parts.

  ● **YELLOW WAGTAIL**
      M. f. flavissima. Yellow and olive head. Breeds in British
      Isles, a few on adjacent shores of Continent.

  ● **BLUE-HEADED WAGTAIL**
      M. f. flava. Male in summer: Eye-stripe starting at nostril.
      Central Europe (area not occupied by the other races).

  SPANISH WAGTAIL
      M. f. iberiae. Male in summer: White stripe starting from
      eye. Breeds Spain and Portugal, races merging in S. France.

  △ **ASHY-HEADED WAGTAIL**
      M. f. cinereocapilla. Male in summer: Grey crown, cheek;
      no eye-stripe. Italy, Corsica, Sardinia, Sicily, Albania.

  ○ **GREY-HEADED WAGTAIL**
      M. f. thunbergi. Male in summer: Grey crown, blackish
      cheek; no eye-stripe. Cent. and N. Sweden, Nor., Finland.

  △ **BLACK-HEADED WAGTAIL**
      M. f. feldegg. Male in summer: Black cap and cheek; no
      eye-stripe. Balkans.

NOTE: Systematics of the Yellow Wagtail group are complex. Som
authors classify various forms as distinct species. But inter-gradatic
occurs where ranges overlap. Mutants resembling other races breed wi
birds of normal appearance. Thus birds identical with Sykes's Wagta
M. f. beema of Russia breed with normal Yellow Wagtails *M. f. flavissir*
in England. In field work it is better to call them all "Yellow Wagtails

ummer   Summer   PIED   Winter

enile   ♂ Summer   WHITE   Winter

♂ mmer   ♀ Summer   GREY   Winter

enile   Summer   ♂   YELLOW   Winter

♂ ummer   SPANISH   Summer   ♂   BLUE-HEADED   Winter

mmer   ASHY-HEADED   ♂ Summer   GREY-HEADED   ♂ Summer   BLACK-HEADED

Sexes similar

SPOTTED FLYCATCHER

PIED FLYCATCHER

♀

Summer

♂ Summer

COLLARED FLYCATCHER

♀

♂

RED-BREASTED FLYCATCHER

WAXWING

Sexes similar

GREAT GREY SHRIKE

LESSER GREY SHR

Sex simi

Juvenile

♀

Sex sim

WOODCHAT

♂

RED-BACKED SHRIKE

MASKED SHRIKE

Plate 60   253

FLYCATCHERS, WAXWING AND SHRIKES

FLYCATCHERS are small birds which sit upright while waiting for passing insects. They frequently flick up their tails.

● **SPOTTED FLYCATCHER**   page 254
   No wing-patch; grey-brown back; streaked breast.

● **PIED FLYCATCHER**   251
   Male: Black and white, large white wing-patch. As
   female in winter.
   Female: Brown back; white wing-patch.

△ **COLLARED FLYCATCHER**   251
   Male in summer: White collar and rump; large wing-
   patch extends along wing.

● **RED-BREASTED FLYCATCHER**   254
   Male: Orange throat; grey cheek; white tail-patches.
   Female: Buffish breast; white tail patches (see
   Whinchat).

WAXWINGS are sleek, crested, Starling-like brown birds.

● **WAXWING**   223
   Long crest; yellow tip on tail.

SHRIKES are hook-billed song birds with the habits of little hawks, catching insects, mice and small birds.

● **GREAT GREY SHRIKE**   223
   Light grey forehead; white supercilium; slender bill;
   long tail; short wings; white on scapulars.

○ **LESSER GREY SHRIKE**   222
   Black forehead; stubbier bill; more upright pose;
   longer wings.

● **RED-BACKED SHRIKE**   219
   Male: Chestnut back; grey crown.
   Female: Rusty back; barred breast.

○ **WOODCHAT SHRIKE**   222
   Adults: Large white scapular patches; chestnut
   crown; white rump.
   Juvenile: Thickly barred; trace of wing-patch.

   MASKED SHRIKE   219
   From Woodchat by black crown and rump; white
   forehead; reddish flanks.

with longer wing markings and some indication of whitish collar and rump. Behaviour and habitat like Pied. Eastern race *F. a. semitorquata* lacks white collar and has more white on forehead and tail; more easily confused with Pied.

Voice: Call-notes resemble Pied's. Song is shorter and simpler: "*tsit-tsit-tsit-tsit-siu-si*," the penultimate note dropping. Map below.

RED-BREASTED FLYCATCHER   *Ficedula parva*   page 253
     Du – Kleine vliegenvanger   Fr – Gobe-mouche nain
     Ge – Zwergschnäpper   Sw – Liten flugsnappare

Identification: 4½″. Smallest European flycatcher. Male only has *bright orange throat*, summer and winter, and greyish head. Insignificant grey-brown above, pale buffish below, but quickly distinguished by *bold white patches* either side of blackish tail, which is often flicked when perched, with drooped wings. Breeding behaviour retiring; occasionally makes sallies in air or to ground after insects, when black and white tail-pattern is conspicuous, but more often feeds warbler-fashion among tree-tops. Male suggests tiny Robin, except for white on tail and different colour of face.

Voice: A brisk "*chic*" and a quiet, Wren-like chatter. Song varied, beginning rather like opening of Wood Warbler's and ending with a quicker trill recalling Redstart.

Habitat: Usually deciduous forests; on passage also in open cultivation. Nesting habits like Pied, but also builds open nest against tree trunk. Map p. 255.

SPOTTED FLYCATCHER   *Muscicapa striata*   page 253
     Du – Grauwe vliegenvanger   Fr – Gobe-mouche gris
     Ge – Grauschnäpper   Sw – Grå flugsnappare

Identification: 5½″. Apart from characteristic upright, watchful pose, is identified by ashy-brown plumage, spotted crown and *lightly streaked whitish breast*. Wings and tail often flicked. Sallies from low perch after passing insects with rapid, agile flight. Rather solitary.

← PIED
  FLYCATCHER
Summer visitor.
Passage Ireland.
Vagrant to Iceland,
Faeroes

COLLARED
FLYCATCHER →
Summer visitor.
Vagrant to Baltic
States, England,
Portugal

Voice: A very thin, grating "*tzee*" and a rapid "*tzee-tuc-tuc.*" Song, a few thin hasty notes: "*sip-sip-see-sitti-see-see.*"
Habitat: Gardens, parks, edges of woods. Nests on or in buildings against tree trunks, behind creeper, etc. Map below.

WHINCHAT *Saxicola rubetra*   page 221

    Du – Paapje   Fr – Traquet tarier
    Ge – Braunkehlchen   Sw – Busskvätta

Identification: 5″. Stocky, short-tailed appearance resembles female Stonechat, but distinguished at all seasons by *prominent eye-stripe, white patches at base of tail* and less upright pose. Male has strongly streaked brown cheeks, crown and upper-parts; *broad white stripes over eye and down side of throat*; white patch across blackish wings; warm buff throat and breast. Female paler, with buff instead of white eye-stripe, smaller white wing-patches. Juvenile lacks wing-patches. Behaviour like Stonechat.
Voice: A short "*tic-tic,*" "*tu-tic-tic,*" also several clicking and churring notes. Song, a very brief, rather metallic, but pleasing warble, recalling Redstart or Stonechat. Sings from bush-top, occasionally in flight.
Habitat: Commons, marshes, railway cuttings, open country, with a few bushes, bracken, gorse, etc. On passage in cultivated fields and bushy country. Nests in coarse grass, often at foot of small bush, or large plant. Map p. 256.

STONECHAT *Saxicola torquata*   page 221

    Du – Roodborsttapuit   Fr – Traquet pâtre
    Ge – Schwarzkehlchen   Sw – Svarthakad busskvätta

Identification: 5″. Plumper and more upright than Whinchat. Male has distinctive *black head and throat, with broad white half-collar* and narrow white wing-stripe; upper-parts dark with whitish patch on rump; under-parts rich chestnut, shading to buff; autumn plumage browner and duller. Female and juvenile upper-parts brown with black streaks, no white on rump, but some black markings on throat; distinguished from Whinchat by lack of eye-stripe, reddish

← RED-BREASTED
FLYCATCHER
*Summer vis. Bred
Denmark. Rare
passage Britain,
France, Italy. Vag.
Faeroes, Ireland*

SPOTTED
FLYCATCHER →
*Summer visitor.
Vagrant Faeroes*

instead of buff breast and lack of white on sides of tail. Perches with constantly jerked wings and tail, on tops of bushes or telegraph wires. Flight low and jerky.

Voice: A persistent scolding "*wheet, tsack-tsack*," like hitting two stones together, also a clicking note similar to Whinchat's. Song consists of irregular, rapidly repeated double notes, not unlike Dunnock's. Sings from elevated perch or in "dancing" song-flight.

Habitat: As Whinchat, but usually more fond of gorse-clad commons and of coastal areas. Map below.

WHEATEAR IN FLIGHT

WHEATEAR *Oeñanthe oenanthe* page 221
  Du – Tapuit   Fr – Traquet motteux
  Ge – Steinschmätzer   Sw – Stenskvätta

Identification: 5¾". Both sexes have conspicuous *white rump* and side of tail, contrasting with black centre and tip of tail (like broad inverted "T"). Breeding male has blue-grey back, *broad white supercilium*; black ear-coverts and wings (brownish in autumn); buffish underparts. Male in autumn is buffer, with brownish back. Female like autumn male. Behaviour restless, flitting across open ground, "bobbing" and waving fanned tail. Greenland race *O. o. leucorrhoa* (which

← WHINCHAT
Summer visitor.
Vagrant Faeroes

STONECHAT →
Partial migrant.
Vagrant Scandi-
navia, Baltic
Provinces, Faeroes,
Iceland

passes through western Europe) is larger, tends to be richer coloured, but many individuals are not safely identifiable. See also Black-eared Wheatear.

Voice: A hard "*chack*," "*chack-weet*," "*weet-chack*," etc. Song, a brief, lark-like warbling, combining musical and wheezy notes.

Habitat: Downs, moors, hilly pastures, cliffs, dunes. Nests in holes in walls, rabbit warrens, stone heaps, etc. Map below.

PIED WHEATEAR *Oenanthe pleschanka*   page 221
    Du – Bonte tapuit   Fr – Traquet pie
    Ge – Nonnensteinschmätzer   Sw – Nunnestenskvätta

Identification: 5¾″. Male distinguished from other European wheatears by *black back and breast* and whitish under-parts. Crown and nape whitish in summer, earthy brown in winter. White on outer tail-feathers sometimes extends nearly to tip, but centre pair is black from near base right to tip. Wings and coverts black in summer, edged pale buffish in winter. Female indistinguishable from female Black-eared, though back and wings usually more earthy brown. Often feeds shrike-fashion from perch on bush or tree.

Voice: A harsh "*zack*." Song resembles Black-eared, but more variable.

Habitat and Range: "Soft" coastal cliffs in Europe, elsewhere stony barrens, rocky hill-sides with a few bushes. Nests in holes. Summer visitor, breeding coastal Roumania and Bulgaria. Vagrant to Britain, Heligoland, Hungary.

BLACK-EARED WHEATEAR *Oenanthe hispanica*   page 221
    Du – Blonde tapuit   Fr – Traquet oreillard
    Ge – Mittelmeersteinschmätzer   Sw – Rödstenskvätta

Identification: 5¾″. Males are dimorphic, occurring either with a *black patch through eye and cheek and a whitish throat* or with the *black face extending to the whole throat*. Body very pale sandy-buff, with whiter crown and rump, buff breast and whitish under-parts; some birds can look black and white. Wings and scapulars conspicuously black.

← WHEATEAR
*Summer visitor.
May breed Sardinia*

BLACK-EARED
WHEATEAR →
*Summer visitor.
Vagrant Brit. Is.,
Heligoland, Holl.,
Switz., Austria*

Tail white with black centre feathers and tip. Autumn plumage buffer. Female resembles Wheatear, but distinguished by darker cheek-patch, *blacker* wings and more white on tail; indistinguishable from female Pied, though usually paler above. Perches readily on trees.
Voice: A rasping note followed by a plaintive whistle. Song rapid and high-pitched, "*schwer, schwee, schwee-oo*" in circling display flight and from perch.
Habitat: Open or lightly wooded arid country and stony mountain slopes. Usually breeds in holes among rocks, walls, etc. Map p. 275.

DESERT WHEATEAR *Oenanthe deserti*   page 284
    Du – Woestijntapuit   Fr – Traquet du désert
    Ge – Wüstensteinschmätzer   Sw – Ökenstenskvätta
Identification: 5¾″. Both sexes distinguished from other wheatears by *black tail almost to base* and noticeable white edges to wing-coverts. Rump and upper tail-coverts white, tinged buffish, particularly in female, which has whitish throat and browner wings than male. Male's *black throat* allows confusion with black-throated phases of Black-eared, but distinguished from latter by buffish instead of black scapulars and lack of conspicuous white on tail. Autumn males have white fringes to throat feathers.
Voice: Call-note a rather plaintive, soft whistle.
Habitat and Range: Barren and rocky or sandy wastes; in winter also in cultivated areas near barren ground. Vagrant from Africa, Asia to Britain, Heligoland, Finland, Sweden, Italy, Greece.

ISABELLINE WHEATEAR *Oenanthe isabellina*   page 284
    Du – Isabeltapuit   Fr – Traquet isabelle
    Ge – Isabellsteinschmätzer   Sw – Isabellastenskvätta
Identification: 6½″. Sexes similar. Distinguished by *large size and almost uniform pale greyish-sandy appearance*. At first glance resembles very pale female or young male Greenland Wheatear, but lacks their darker ear-coverts and *head and bill are noticeably larger*. Tail markings are dull, not jet black. Has distinctive running gait.
Voice: Call-note a loud "*cheep*," or a whistling "*wheet-whit*."
Habitat and Range: Usually in steppe, barren plain, or lower slopes of bare hills; shows preference for sandy locations in winter. Breeds N.E. Greece and European Turkey. Vagrant to Britain, Roumania.

BLACK WHEATEAR *Oenanthe leucura*   page 221
    Du – Zwarte tapuit   Fr – Traquet rieur
    Ge – Trauersteinschmätzer   Sw – Sorgstenskvätta
Identification: 7″. Easily identified by *large size* and striking, slightly glossy, *black plumage*, with white rump, under tail-coverts and side of tail. Female like male but usually duller, brownish-black. See also White-crowned Black Wheatear (Accidentals p. 322).
Voice: Song, a brief, but rich warble, comparable with Rock Thrush. Anxiety-note "*pee-pee-pee.*"

Habitat: Rocky deserts, sea-cliffs and mountainous regions. Nests in holes among rocks, frequently screening entrance with a little wall of pebbles. Map below.

RUFOUS BUSH CHAT (Rufous Warbler) *Cercotrichas galactotes*
page 229

Du – Rosse waaierstaart Fr – Agrobate roux
Ge – Heckensänger Sw – Rödsångare

Identification: 6". Slim, long-legged and rather thrush-like in some attitudes. Quickly recognised by *long, chestnut fan-tail, strikingly tipped with bold black and white.* Western race *C. g. galactotes* has all upper-parts foxy red-brown; eastern race *C. g. syriacus* (so-called Brown-backed Warbler) has chestnut confined to rump and tail, remainder of upper-parts grey-brown; both have bold creamy supercilium and sandy under-parts. Behaviour much bolder than warblers; perches conspicuously on bushes and ground, with wings drooped, long tail fanned and jerked vertically.

Voice: Call-note, a hard "*teck*." Song very musical but disjointed and varying in volume, recalling Sky Lark in some short phrases. Sings from prominent perch, telegraph wires, etc., and in slow, descending display flight.

Habitat: Gardens, vineyards, palm and olive groves. Nests in pricklypear hedges and palm bushes. Map below.

ROCK THRUSH *Monticola saxatilis*
page 221

Du – Rode rotslijster Fr – Merle de roche
Ge – Steinrötel Sw – Stentrast

Identification: 7½". In all plumages has *short chestnut tail,* with brown centre. Male in summer has *pale slate-blue head, neck and mantle, white lower back,* blackish wings and *chestnut-orange under-parts;* in winter, colours largely obscured by buffish fringes, giving dull mottled effect. Female has strongly mottled brown upper-parts, sometimes with trace of white on back, and mottled buffish under-parts. Behaviour

← BLACK
WHEATEAR
Resident. Vagrant Britain, Albania, Bulgaria

RUFOUS
BUSH CHAT →
Summer visitor. Irreg. S. France (?bred). Vagrant Italy, Heligoland, England, Ireland

FINCHES

FINCHES (and buntings) have stout bills, adapted for seed cracking. Three types of bills exist within the group: that of the Hawfinch, Bullfinch and grosbeaks, exceedingly thick and rounded in outline; the more ordinary canary-like bill of most of the finches; and that of the crossbills, the mandibles of which are crossed at the tips.

● **BULLFINCH**   page 299
     Black cap; white rump; stubby bill.
     Male: Rose-red breast.
     Female: Warm pinkish-brown breast.

● **LINNET**   295
     Male: Red forehead and breast; no black on chin.
     Female: Streaked, grey head; browner back.

● **REDPOLL**   295
     Red forehead; black chin; buff wing-bars.
     Male has pink breast.

○ **ARCTIC REDPOLL**   296
     From Redpoll by frostier appearance, unstreaked white rump; white wing-bars.

● **TWITE**   294
     Rich buff with black streaks; yellow bill in winter.
     Male has faintly pinkish rump, like Redpoll.

○ **SCARLET ROSEFINCH**   297
     Male: Rosy-carmine breast, crown and rump; no white wing-bars.
     Female: Yellowish-brown, streaked; round head; bold dark eye; pale wing-bars.

△ **PINE GROSBEAK**   297
     Male: Large, long-tailed, rosy; white wing-bars.
     Female: Golden-brown with brighter crown and rump; wing-bars.

● **CROSSBILL**   298
     Male: Dull red; dark wings and tail; crossed bill.
     Female: Yellowish-grey; dark wings and tail.

○ **PARROT CROSSBILL**   297
     Very stout bill. See text.

○ **TWO-BARRED CROSSBILL**   299
     Male: Carmine; white wing-bars; crossed bill.
     Female: Yellowish-olive; white wing-bars; streaks.

BULLFINCH

LINNET

REDPOLL

ARCTIC REDPOLL

TWITE

SCARLET ROSEFINCH

PINE GROSBEAK

PARROT CROSSBILL

CROSSBILL

TWO-BARRED CROSSBILL

HAWFINCH

♂

♀

CHAFFINCH

♂

♂ Summer

♀

♂ Winter

BRAMBLING

Sexes similar

GOLDFINCH

♀

♂

GREENFINCH

Sexes similar

CITRIL FIN

♀

♂

SISKIN

♀

♂

SERIN

Plate 62 261

FINCHES

● **HAWFINCH** page 300
 Massive bill and head; white wing-bands; short tail.

● **CHAFFINCH** 291
 Double white wing-bars; white sides of tail.
 Male with blue-grey crown, pinkish cheeks.

● **BRAMBLING** 291
 White rump; rusty chest and "shoulders."
 Male in summer has black head and back.

● **GOLDFINCH** 294
 Red and white face; broad yellow wing-band.

● **GREENFINCH** 293
 Male: Green; large yellow wing- and tail-patches.
 Female: Duller; dull yellow wing-patches.

△ **CITRIL FINCH** 292
 Unstreaked; greyish nape; dull green wing-bars.

● **SISKIN** 293
 Male: Black crown and chin; yellow on tail.
 Female: Streaked breast; yellow on tail.

○ **SERIN** 292
 Stumpy form; stubby bill; streaks; yellow breast;
 yellow rump.

Most finches have a strongly undulating flight.

shy and solitary; perches upright, like Wheatear, with loosely swinging tail, before diving out of sight behind rocks. Easily distinguished from Blue Rock Thrush by chestnut tail.

Voice: A moderate "*chack, chack.*" Song, a clear, fluty warble, from rock or post and in brief vertical display-flight.

Habitat: Breeds in open rocky regions and among trees from 3-8,000 ft., in eastern Europe down to sea level. Map below.

BLUE ROCK THRUSH *Monticola solitarius* page 221

Du – Blauwe rotslijster Fr – Merle bleu
Ge – Blaumerle Sw – Blåtrast

Identification: 8″. Slightly larger than Rock Thrush. Male easily distinguished by *deep blue-grey plumage*; in winter looks blackish. Female bluish-brown above, paler below, finely barred with grey-brown. Perches on rocks, with drooped wings and flaunted, relatively short tail, diving out of sight when approached. Solitary. See also Rock Thrush.

Voice: A hard "*tchuck,*" or a plaintive "*tseec.*" Song is deliberate, loud and fluty, recalling Blackbird's, but is limited in scope; sings from rock, or in vertical display-flight.

Habitat: Rocky desert regions and bare mountain-sides down to sea level. Nests in crevices in rocks, cliffs and buildings. Map below.

BLACK REDSTART *Phoenicurus ochruros* page 221

Du – Zwarte roodstaart Fr – Rougequeue noir
Ge – Hausrotschwanz Sw – Svart rödstjärt

Identification: 5½″. Both sexes at all ages have *constantly flickering rusty tail and rusty rump* (like Redstart), but are much darker, with *blackish* (not chestnut) under-parts and beneath wings. Male is sooty black with whitish wing-patch (some young breeding males lack this); plumage is paler in autumn, with partly obscured wing-patch. Female and juvenile resemble dark Redstarts, but have dark greyish instead of buff under-parts. Actions like Redstart, but prefers to perch on buildings or rocks.

← ROCK THRUSH
Summer visitor. Formerly S. Germany. Vagrant Britain, E. Prussia

BLUE ROCK
THRUSH →
Mainly resident. Leaves N.E. Greece in winter

Voice: A brief *"tsip"* and a stuttering *"tititic,"* more incisive than similar call of Redstart. Short, very rapid song is simpler and less musical than Redstart's, introducing curious spluttering, hissing notes. Sings from roof-top or other prominent perch.

Habitat: Cliffs, buildings, rocky slopes, occasionally vineyards, etc. Breeds in holes in walls, rocks, buildings. Map below.

REDSTART *Phoenicurus phoenicurus* page 221
    Du – Gekraagde roodstaart   Fr – Rougequeue à front blanc
    Ge – Gartenrotschwanz   Sw – Rödstjärt

Identification: 5½″. Both sexes distinguished at all ages (from all species except Black Redstart) by *constantly flickering rusty tail and rusty rump*. Male has *black face and throat*, white forehead, slate-grey upper-parts, *chestnut* breast and flanks; black throat partly obscured by white fringes in autumn. Female is greyish-brown above, buffish below; juvenile is mottled like young Robin, but with rusty rump and tail; both much paler and browner than female and juvenile Black Redstart. Behaviour much like Robin.

Voice: A rather tremulous *"whee-tic-tic,"* a liquid *"wheet"* very like note of Willow Warbler and a clear *"tooick."* Song, a short, pleasing jingle of hurried, Robin-like, but squeaky notes, ending in a feeble twitter.

Habitat: Woodlands, parks, heaths with bushes and old trees, occasionally ruins. Nests in holes in trees, stone walls, sheds, etc. Map below.

ROBIN *Erithacus rubecula* page 221
    Du – Roodborst   Fr – Rougegorge
    Ge – Rotkehlchen   Sw – Rödhake

Identification: 5½″. A plump, "neck-less" little bird. Adults have *rich orange* breast and forehead and uniform olive-brown upper-parts. Juvenile lacks orange and is strongly mottled with dark brown and buff; distinguished from young Redstart by *dark brown* instead of chestnut tail; from young Nightingale by smaller size, buffer under-

← BLACK
REDSTART
*Partial migrant.
Has bred Norway.
Vagrant n. to Iceland, Finland*

REDSTART →
*Mainly summer
visitor. Has bred
Ireland. Vagrant
Faeroes*

379   380

264 MUSCICAPIDAE

parts and *dark brown* tail. Confiding behaviour towards man and characteristically jaunty attitudes are well known in Britain, but Continental birds are usually shy.

Voice: A persistent and often rapidly repeated *"tic,"* a weak *"tsip,"* or *"tsissip,"* and a thin, plaintive *"tseee."* Song, heard all year, is a varied, deliberate series of short, high warbling phrases.

Habitat: Gardens, hedges, coppices, woods with undergrowth, etc. Nests in holes or crannies in walls, banks, trees, hedge-bottoms, ivy, tin cans, etc. Map below.

NIGHTINGALE *Luscinia megarhynchos*   page 221
　　　　Du – Nachtegaal　　　　　Fr – Rossignol philomèle
　　　　Ge – Nachtigall　　　　　Sw – Sydnäktergal

Identification: 6½″. Rather featureless, except for *brownish-chestnut tail and remarkable song*. Upper-parts uniform warm brown, under-parts whitish brown. Juvenile spotted and mottled like young Robin, but easily distinguished by larger size, chestnut tail and whiter under-parts; distinguished from young Redstart by larger size and much less bright chestnut tail. Behaviour skulking and solitary. Flight and attitudes while feeding on ground, like Robin. See also Thrush Nightingale.

Voice: A liquid *"wheet,"* a loud *"tac,"* a soft, very short *"tuc"* and a harsh *"kerr"* of alarm. Song is rich, loud and musical, each note rapidly repeated several times; most characteristic notes, a deep, bubbling *"chook-chook-chook"* and a slow *"piu, piu, piu,"* rising to a brilliant crescendo. Sings day and night, from deep cover, or from low exposed perch.

Habitat: Deciduous lowland woods, moist thickets, tangled hedges. Nest well hidden near ground in brambles, nettles, etc. Map below.

THRUSH NIGHTINGALE *Luscinia luscinia*   page 221
　　　　Du – Noordse nachtegaal　Fr – Rossignol progné
　　　　Ge – Sprosser　　　　　Sw – Näktergal

Identification: 6½″. Very like Nightingale, but distinguished by darker,

← ROBIN
Partial migrant.
Annual Iceland

NIGHTINGALE →
Summer visitor.
Vagrant Scotland,
Ireland

more olive-brown appearance *including tail*, and, at close quarters, by *brownish mottled breast*. Behaviour like Nightingale.

Voice: Call-notes like Nightingale's; song equally musical, with typical deep *"chook-chook-chook"* opening; distinguished by absence of rising crescendo phrases.

Habitat: Dense and damp thickets, particularly alder and birch, and in swampy undergrowth. Nesting habits like Nightingale's. Map below.

BLUETHROAT *Cyanosylvia svecica*   page 221
    Du – Blauwborst   Fr – Gorgebleue
    Ge – Blaukehlchen   Sw – Blåhake

Identification: 5½″. Redstart-like in form; tail spread and flirted frequently, showing *conspicuous chestnut panels at base*. Male in spring has *bright blue throat-patch*, separated from lower breast by black and chestnut bands. Scandinavian form (Red-spotted Bluethroat, *C. s. svecica*) has *chestnut spot* in centre of throat-patch; central and southern European form (White-spotted Bluethroat, *C. s. cyanecula*) has *white spot*. In autumn, throat is usually whitish with some blue and a black border and dark breast-band. Female has whitish throat-patch with black streaks at side, merging into an irregular dark necklace or breast-band, often with traces of blue and chestnut. Juvenile like streaky dark young Robin, but distinguished by chestnut at base of tail. Females and immatures of Red-spotted and White-spotted forms inseparable in the field; males doubtfully separable in autumn.

Voice: A sharp *"tac,"* a soft *"wheet"* and a guttural *"turrc."* Song, very musical and varied, in parts faintly resembling Nightingale and Wood Lark, but much higher pitched, weaker and less rich; introduces sharp, high note like striking tiny metal triangle, also a cricket-like note. Sings from perch and in zig-zag flight.

Habitat: Swampy thickets and heaths, tangled hedges, etc. Breeds close to ground among birch, willow and juniper scrub, in damp heaths; usually in high mountains, but in W. Central Europe also in lowlands. Map below.

← Thrush
  Nightingale
*Summer visitor.
Vagrant west to
Britain, Italy*

Bluethroat →
*Summer visitor.
Rare on passage
Britain, vagrant
Ireland, Faeroes*

RED-FLANKED BLUETAIL *Tarsiger cyanurus* page 284
  Du – Blauwstaart   Fr – Rossignol à flancs roux
  Ge – Blauschwanz   Sw – Blåstjärt
Identification: 5½″. Size and shape of Redstart. Male has *blue upper-parts* (bright cobalt on shoulders, rump and tail, darkest on cheeks and sides of neck); creamy under-parts, with *bright orange flanks*; white stripe across forehead and above eyes. Female is olive-brown above, paler below, with bluish rump and tail and orange flanks. Immature resembles young spotted Robin. Extremely shy.
Voice: Call-note a Robin-like "*tick-tick*." Song is distinctive, beginning and ending very quietly, with a loud, descending, thrush-like phrase "*tree-leee, tree-leee*" in the middle. Sings day or night, usually from high tree-top.
Habitat and Range: Dense virgin pine or spruce forests and damp thickets. Nests on ground. Now probably established as summer visitor to eastern Finland. Vagrant from central Russia to Britain, Germany, Italy.

OLIVE-BACKED THRUSH *Catharus ustulatus* page 284
  Du – Dwerglijster   Fr – Grive petite
  Ge – Zwergdrossel   Sw – Gråbrun dvärgtrast
Identification: 7″. Resembles very small Song Thrush with *buff eye-ring and buffish cheeks and throat*. These features distinguish it from very similar Grey-cheeked Thrush (Accidentals p. 323). Upper breast buffish, spotted with black; faint spots also on upper flanks; under-parts white; mantle and rump olive-brown. Bill blackish, legs pale brownish. Shy and retiring in undergrowth, but seen occasionally in tree-tops. Feeds chiefly on ground, but sometimes by fly-catching.
Voice: A high-pitched, weak "*whit*." Song musical and fluty, each phrase rising.
Habitat and Range: On passage frequents open woodland glades, gardens, damp woods. Breeds in damp parts of spruce and fir forests. Vagrant from N. America to Ireland, France, Belgium, Germany, Austria, Italy.

EYE-BROWED THRUSH *Turdus obscurus* page 220
  Du – Vale lijster   Fr – Grive obscure
  Ge – Weissbrauendrossel   Sw – Vitbrynad trast
Identification: 7½″. Look for combination of *grey* upper breast and *orange-buff* sides of breast and flanks. Olive-brown upper-parts with greyish crown, a *conspicuous white stripe above eye* and a wide white patch below eye to chin. Female is duller. Vagrant from Siberia to central Europe and W. to Britain, Belgium, France, Italy.

BLACK-THROATED THRUSH *Turdus ruficollis* page 220
  Du – Zwartkeellijster   Fr – Grive à gorge noire
  Ge – Schwarzkehldrossel   Sw – Svarthalsad trast
Identification: 9¼″. Male has striking *black face, throat and breast*

(partly obscured by pale fringes in winter), contrasting with whitish under-parts; upper-parts grey-brown. Female browner above, with whitish throat and breast closely spotted or streaked with black. In flight shows rusty-buff beneath wings. Behaviour and shape like Fieldfare. Eastern form, Red-throated Thrush *T. r. ruficollis*, has black throat of *T. r. atrogularis* replaced by brick-red.

Voice: Usual note said to resemble chuckling Blackbird alarm.

Habitat and Range: Winters in open country and sheltered areas near cultivation. Vagrant from Asia and Russia westwards across Europe to Norway, Britain, France, Italy.

DUSKY THRUSH   *Turdus eunomus*   page 220
    Du – Bruine lijster   Fr – Grive à ailes rousses
    Ge – Rostflügeldrossel   Sw – Sibirisk rödvingetrast

Identification: 9″. Distinguished from commoner European thrushes by *two blackish breast-bands* (the lower incomplete). Flanks have black crescentic markings in winter. Heavy bill. *Conspicuous whitish supercilium.* Broad chestnut areas on *upper and lower* surfaces of wings and rump. Distinguished from Redwing by larger size, blackish breast and flanks and chestnut on upper surfaces of wings; from Naumann's (with which it may be conspecific) by blackish instead of chestnut on breast and flanks and blackish instead of chestnut tail. Vagrant from Asia westwards across Europe to Norway, Britain, France, Italy.

NAUMANN'S THRUSH   *Turdus naumanni*   page 220
    Du – Naumann's lijster   Fr – Grive de Naumann
    Ge – Naumannsdrossel   Sw – Naumanns trast

Identification: 9″. Naumann's and Dusky Thrushes probably inter-breed, therefore may be conspecific. Naumann's is distinguished by *chestnut* instead of blackish, on breast, flanks and tail. Male has grey-brown upper-parts with *chestnut on wings*. Female is browner above, much paler below, with blackish spots on breast and flanks. Vagrant from Asia to central Europe, W. to Norway, Britain, France, Italy.

FIELDFARE   *Turdus pilaris*   page 220
    Du – Kramsvogel   Fr – Grive litorne
    Ge – Wacholderdrossel   Sw – Björktrast

Identification: 10″. Slightly smaller than Mistle Thrush, much larger than Song Thrush and Redwing. Distinguished by *pale grey head and rump, chestnut back* and almost black tail. Throat and breast rusty yellow, streaked with black, flanks heavily mottled with black. In flight, blue-grey rump, flashing white beneath wings and flight-call are distinctive. Flight less undulating than Mistle Thrush's. Has alert, upright attitude on ground. Gregarious.

Voice: A harsh, chattering "*tchak-tchak-tchak*" and a quiet "*see*." Song, a rapid mixture of feeble squeaking notes, frequently in flight.

Habitat: Winters in open country, seeking food in fields and along hedges. Breeds usually colonially near clearings or margins of woods, particularly in birch, occasionally on buildings and haystacks; on ground above tree limit. Map below.

RING OUZEL *Turdus torquatus*   page 220
    Du – Beflijster   Fr – Merle à plastron
    Ge – Ringdrossel   Sw – Ringtrast

Identification: 9½″. Unmistakable. Male has uniform dull black plumage, with a *broad white crescent* across breast; winter plumage has light feather edges, giving "scaly" appearance. Female is browner, with narrower, duller crescent. Juvenile has no crescent and looks like very spotty young Blackbird. Flight rapid, dodging behind rocks when approached. Distinguished from occasional pied Blackbird by *grey patch on closed wing-feathers.*

Voice: A clear, piping *"pee-u,"* and a scolding Blackbird-like *"tac-tac-tac."* Song, a few double or treble notes, *"tcheru," "tchivi," "ti-cho-o,"* etc., repeated 3-4 times, between pauses, interspersed with chuckling notes.

Habitat: Hilly moorlands and mountains, usually above 1,000 ft. Breeds among heather, juniper, rocks, often by track or stream; also within tree limit on Continent. Map below.

AMERICAN ROBIN *Turdus migratorius*   page 220
    Du – Roodborstlijster   Fr – Merle migrateur
    Ge – Wanderdrossel   Sw – Vandringstrast

Identification: 10″. Has character of Blackbird, with *uniform brick-red breast*, dark grey head and back, *bold white markings around eye* and white tips to outer tail-feathers. Chin white, streaked with black. Bill yellow. Sexes similar, but male has blacker head. See also Naumann's, Red-throated and Eye-browed Thrushes.

Voice: Harsh, scolding call-notes are typically thrush-like.

Habitat and Range: Woodlands and thickets, often seeking human habitation. Vagrant to Britain, Ireland, Germany, Belgium, Austria, Czechoslovakia, Yugoslavia.

← FIELDFARE
Partial migrant, at times to Malta, Sardinia. Has bred Iceland, Denmark, Holland, Hungary

RING OUZEL →
Partial migrant. Has bred Denmark. At times winters Italy. Vagrant Faeroes

BLACKBIRD *Turdus merula* page 220

Du – Merel Fr – Merle noir
Ge – Amsel Sw – Koltrast

Identification: 10″. Male, a sturdy *all-black* bird, with *bright orange-yellow bill and eye-rim*. Female is uniform dark brown above, paler brown below, with speckled whitish chin and brown bill. Juvenile more rufous and more mottled. Immature male brownish black with blackish bill. Occasional part-albino males distinguished from Ring Ouzel by lack of pale wing-patch and by difference in voice. Feeds on ground. Tail is raised and fanned and wings drooped on alighting.

Voice: A screeching chatter, when flushed; a persistent mobbing note "*tchink, tchink, tchink*"; an anxious "*tchook*"; a thin "*tsee*," etc. Song, a deliberate, loud and melodious warbling, easily distinguished from Song Thrush's by purer, fluty notes, *lack of repetitive habit* and characteristic "collapse" into weak, unmusical ending.

Habitat: Woodlands, hedges, gardens, bushy commons, etc. Nests in hedges, wood-piles, sheds, etc. Map below.

SIBERIAN THRUSH *Turdus sibiricus* page 220

Du – Siberische lijster Fr – Merle sibérien
Ge – Sibirische Drossel Sw – Sibirisk trast

Identification: 9″. Male identified by *slaty-black* plumage, *conspicuous white supercilium*, white centre to belly and in flight by white tips to tail. Female has olive-brown upper-parts, buffish eye-stripe, buffish-white under-parts closely spotted with brown. In flight both sexes show *conspicuous white bands across under-sides of wings*, providing easy distinction from Dusky and Black-throated Thrushes. Vagrant from Asia westwards across Europe to Norway, France, Italy, Scotland.

REDWING *Turdus iliacus* page 220

Du – Koperwiek Fr – Grive mauvis
Ge – Rotdrossel Sw – Rödvingetrast

Identification: 8¼″. Smallest common thrush. Resembles Song Thrush, but distinguished by *conspicuous creamy supercilium*, rich *chestnut*

← Blackbird
Partial migrant

Redwing →
Partial migrant. Has bred France, Belgium, Germany, Austria, Czecho. (where few winter)

flanks, *streaked* (not spotted) breast and flanks and, in flight, by *chestnut* (not buff) beneath wings. Gregarious, roaming countryside with Fieldfares in winter. See also rare Dusky Thrush.

Voice: Distinctive note (often during night migration) a thin *"see-ip"*; also a harsh *"chittuc."* Song varies greatly locally; a repeated phrase of 4–6 fluty notes, rising and falling, typically *"trui-trui-trui-troo-tri,"* followed by a weak, warbling sub-song.

Habitat: Winters in open country and light woods. Nests on tree stumps, wood-stacks, in trees or bushes, on ground, etc., in light woods, marshy localities, often on edges of Fieldfare colonies. Map p. 269.

SONG THRUSH   *Turdus philomelos*   page 220
     Du – Zanglijster   Fr – Grive musicienne
     Ge – Singdrossel   Sw – Taltrast

Identification: 9″. A brown-backed bird, with a spotted breast. Distinguished from Mistle Thrush and Fieldfare by much smaller size, uniform *brown* upper-parts and yellowish-buff breast and flanks with *small spots;* from Redwing by lack of chestnut on flanks and beneath wings and lack of prominent supercilium. Shows *buff* beneath wings. Often feeds on open ground, running spasmodically.

Voice: A loud *"tchuck,"* or *"tchick,"* repeated rapidly as alarm; flight-call a soft *"sip"* (shorter than Redwing's call). Song loud and musical, the short, varied phrases *repeated* 2–4 *times*, between brief pauses.

Habitat: Around human habitation, parks, woods and hedges. Nests in bushes, hedges, ivy, etc., occasionally in buildings. Map below.

MISTLE THRUSH   *Turdus viscivorus*   page 220
     Du – Grote lijster   Fr – Grive draine
     Ge – Misteldrossel   Sw – Dubbeltrast

Identification: 10½″. Distinguished from much smaller Song Thrush and Redwing by *greyish-brown upper-parts, closely spotted under-parts* and more upright stance, with raised head. Shows white beneath

← Song Thrush
Partial migr. Often winters S. Sweden. Vagrant Faeroes

Mistle Thrush →
Partial migrant. Vagrant Iceland

wings in flight, like Fieldfare, but readily distinguished from it by *greyish* instead of chestnut back, brownish-grey instead of blue-grey rump, *buffish-white* instead of rusty breast and longer, *paler tail* with whitish tips to outer feathers. Behaviour shy. Strong flight like Fieldfare's, but with longer, more regular wing closures. Juvenile strongly spotted above and can be confused with rare White's Thrush.

Voice: A dry, rasping chatter, a hard "*tuc-tuc-tuc*" and a thin Redwing-like "*see-ip*." Song is loud, somewhat Blackbird-like, but lacks mellowness and variety, repeating short, rather similar phrases. Sings in all weathers, from tree-tops.

Habitat: Large gardens, orchards, woods. Nests in bare fork in tree. Small flocks roam open country and fields in autumn. Map p. 270.

WHITE'S THRUSH *Zoothera dauma*   page 220

| Du – Goudlijster | Fr – Grive dorée |
| Ge – Erddrossel | Sw – Guldtrast |

Identification: 10¾″. Larger than Mistle Thrush. Distinguished by rich, *golden-brown* plumage patterned with black *crescent-shaped* tips to feathers of head and body. In flight, *bold black and white bands beneath wings* are distinctive. Flight deeply undulating. Distinguished from young "spotty" Mistle Thrush by black and white markings beneath wings and by golden appearance (instead of greyish).

Voice: Song, a penetrating Bullfinch-like whistle, interspersed with very quiet warbling.

Habitat and Range: Normally in deep forest with heavy undergrowth. Vagrant from Asia westwards across Europe to Norway, British Isles Iceland, France, Sardinia, Spain.

BEARDED REEDLING (TIT) *Panurus biarmicus*   page 213

| Du – Baardmees | Fr – Mésange à moustaches |
| Ge – Bartmeise | Sw – Skäggmes |

Identification: 6½″. A tit-like little bird with *tawny upper-parts*, *long tawny tail* and pinkish-grey under-parts. Male has ash-grey head with striking *black* "*moustaches*" and conspicuous *black under tail-coverts*. Female is paler, with tawny head, no "moustaches," and no black. Juvenile has dark back, wing-coverts and sides of tail. Flight "whirring," with loose tail. Acrobatic in reed-beds.

Voice: A distinctive, twanging "*tching*," a scolding "*p'whut*," a squeaky "*cheeu*," etc.

Habitat: Extensive and secluded reed-beds. Nests low down near edge of wet reed-bed. Map p. 272.

TITS: Paridae

Small, plump, short-billed birds, very acrobatic when feeding. Most tits roam in mixed bands in winter. Sexes generally similar. Most nest in holes, some in trees or bushes.

LONG-TAILED TIT *Aegithalos caudatus* page 213
    Du – Staartmees   Fr – Mésange à longue queue
    Ge – Schwanzmeise   Sw – Stjärtmes

Identification: 5½″ (incl. 3″ tail). Unmistakable *blackish, whitish and pinkish plumage, long graduated tail* and distinctive note. British race *A. c. rosaceus* and the W. and S. European races have head white, with bold blackish stripe over eye; mixed pink and black upper-parts; whitish below, with pinkish flanks and belly; black wings and tail with pure white outer tail-feathers. Juvenile has dark cheeks and no pink. Northern race *A. c. caudatus* has pure white head, neck and under-parts. Behaviour restless and acrobatic.

Voice: A distinctive, low *"tupp,"* a repeated trilling *"tsirrrup"* and a weak *"tzee-tzee-tzee."* Infrequent song, a mixture of call-notes and rapid *"see-see-siu."*

Habitat: Thickets, bushy heaths, coppices, hedgerows; also woods in winter. Builds ovoid mossy nest, usually in gorse, thorn or bramble bushes, occasionally well up in trees. Map below.

MARSH TIT *Parus palustris* page 213
    Du – Glanskopmees   Fr – Mésange nonnette
    Ge – Sumpfmeise   Sw – Kärrmes

Identification: 4½″. Has black cap and chin. Distinguished from Coal Tit by having *no white patch on nape*, no wing-bars and browner upper-parts; from very similar Willow Tit by *glossy* black crown (instead of dull sooty), smaller black bib, *absence of light patch on closed wing*, and distinctive call-note. Cheeks and under-parts dull greyish-white. Juvenile greyer above, with dull sooty crown, not distinguishable from young Willow Tit. Seldom more than two together in mixed winter flocks of tits.

Voice: Most distinctive. A loud *"pitchew,"* or *"piti-chewee"*; other notes are a deep, nasal *"tchair,"* and a scolding *"chick-adeedeedee."* Song varies from a repeated single musical note, to four- or five-note phrases such as *"pitchaweeoo."*

Habitat: Deciduous woods, hedges, thickets, etc., less often gardens.

← BEARDED
REEDLING
Wanders in winter.
Vagrant Denmark,
Belgium, Switzer-
land, Finland

LONG-TAILED
TIT →
Partial migrant

No particular fondness for marshes. Nests in existing holes in trees, usually willows or alders. Map below.

WILLOW TIT *Parus montanus*   page 213

      Du – Matkopmees   Fr – Mésange boréale
      Ge – Weidenmeise   Sw – Talltita
          N.Am – Black-capped Chickadee

Identification: 4½″. Very like Marsh Tit, but distinguished by *dull, sooty* black crown, *pale patch* formed by light edges to secondary wing feathers (less visible in summer) and *distinctive call-note*. Flanks darker buff than Marsh, and black bib usually rather larger; juveniles are indistinguishable. Northern race *P. m. borealis* is paler and greyer, with pure white cheeks.

Voice: Usual notes, a nasal buzzing "*eez-eez-eez*," and a very high thin "*zi-zi-zi*" and a loud "*chay*." Song, a warbling Nightingale-like "*chu, chu, chu*" and a Wood Warbler-like "*piu, piu, piu*."

Habitat: More fond of swampy thickets than Marsh Tit, where it can find rotting stumps. Excavates nest cavities in rotted alder, birch, willow, etc. Map below.

SOMBRE TIT *Parus lugubris*   page 213

      Du – Rouwmees   Fr – Mésange lugubre
      Ge – Trauermeise   Sw – Sorgmes

Identification: 5½″. Patterned like Willow Tit, but much larger, sides darker and bill very heavy for a tit, giving impression of Great Tit. *Crown and nape sooty brownish-black* (female's more chocolate brown), upper-parts grey-brown, *face and sides of neck whitish*, under-parts dull whitish with greyish-brown flanks and large black throat-patch. Behaviour as in Great Tit, but seldom joins mixed flocks in winter.

Voice: A distinctive "*sirrah*," a rather contralto chattering "*chur-r-r-r*" and Great Tit-like notes.

Habitat: Lowland plains and mountain slopes with mixed woods and

← Marsh Tit
Mainly resident

Willow Tit →
Mainly resident

401   402

rocky outcrops. Nests in holes in trees, occasionally among rocks. Map below.

SIBERIAN TIT   *Parus cinctus*   page 213

Du – Bruinkopmees   Fr – Mésange lapone
Ge – Lapplandmeise   Sw – Lappmes

Identification: 5¼″. Has distinctly *"dusty" and fluffy appearance*, unlike neatness of most tits. Crown and nape *dusky brown*, upper-parts paler, slightly rufous; face and under-parts dingy white, with slightly rufous flanks and sooty-black throat-patch merging indistinctly into breast. Juvenile plumage looks "cleaner" and neater. Easily distinguished from smaller Marsh and Willow Tits by obviously brown cap.

Voice: Resembles Willow Tit, but a longer *"eeez,"* repeated 4-5 times.

Habitat: Almost exclusively in birch and coniferous forests. Nests in old woodpecker holes, or excavates holes in soft dead trees. Map below.

CRESTED TIT   *Parus cristatus*   page 213

Du – Kuifmees   Fr – Mésange huppée
Ge – Haubenmeise   Sw – Tofsmes

Identification: 4½″. Easily distinguished by *prominent, speckled black and whitish crest and distinctive voice*. Face whitish with curved black mark from eye behind cheek, narrow black collar and bib. Upper-parts warm greyish-brown, under-parts whitish with buff flanks. Sometimes seeks food on tree trunks, like Tree Creeper. Less sociable than most other tits.

Voice: A short, low-pitched, purring *"choo-r-r,"* reminiscent of Long-tailed Tit, but deeper-toned. Also a repeated, high thin *"tzee-tzee-tzee."*

Habitat: Usually pine woods, but also mixed woods and thickets. Nests in holes in decayed trees, fence posts, etc. Map p. 275.

COAL TIT   *Parus ater*   page 213

Du – Zwarte mees   Fr – Mésange noire
Ge – Tannenmeise   Sw – Svartmes

← SOMBRE TIT
Resident. Vagrant Italy

SIBERIAN TIT →
Mainly resident

403

404

Identification: 4½″. Slightly smaller than Blue Tit. The only black-crowned tit with *bold white patch on nape*. Cheeks dingy white; chin to upper breast black; upper-parts olive-grey, with narrow double white wing-bar; under-parts whitish, with buff flanks. Juvenile has yellowish cheeks, under-parts and spot on nape. Less obtrusive than Great Tit.

Voice: A clear, thin "*tsui*" or "*tsee*" with a short twitter, also a scolding "*chi-chi-chich*," and a thin "*sissi-sissi-sissi*." Some notes very like Goldcrest's. Song, a repeated clear "*seetoo,*" or "*seetoooee*," more rapid and less strident than similar notes of Great Tit.

Habitat: Shows some preference for conifers. Nests in holes in banks and tree stumps, usually near ground. Map below.

BLUE TIT *Parus caeruleus*   page 213
  Du – Pimpelmees   Fr – Mésange bleue
  Ge – Blaumeise   Sw – Blåmes

Identification: 4½″. The only tit with *bright cobalt-blue crown, wings and tail*. Yellow under-parts; white cheeks with black line through eye and around nape and cheek to blue-black chin; white edging to crown, white spot on nape; greenish back. Juvenile has greenish-brown upper-parts, yellow cheeks. Behaviour like Great Tit.

Voice: Varied call-notes, "*tsee-tsee-tsee-tsit*," etc., and a harsh, scolding "*chur-r-r*." Song, a high "*tsee-tsee*," followed by a long trill.

Habitat: As Great Tit. Map p. 278.

AZURE TIT *Parus cyanus*   page 213
  Du – Azuurmees   Fr – Mésange azurée
  Ge – Lasurmeise   Sw – Azurmes

Identification: 5¼″. Resembles a whitish Blue Tit with a rather long tail. Distinguished by *snow-white head*, with narrow dark blue stripe through eye to back of crown, grey-blue upper-parts, *white* under-parts, with small blue streak or patch on breast, *broad white inverted "V" on dark wing* and conspicuous white on outer tail-feathers. Juvenile has grey crown and is greyer above.

← Crested Tit
Mainly resident

Coal Tit →
Partial migrant in northern part of range

SPARROWS, ACCENTORS AND BUNTINGS

● **HOUSE SPARROW** page 300
  Male: Black bib; grey crown.
  Female: Plain dingy breast; dull eye-stripe.

ITALIAN SPARROW (subspecies of House Sparrow) 300
  Male: Chestnut crown; no stripes on sides.
  Female: Similar to House Sparrow.

SPANISH SPARROW 301
  Male: Chestnut crown; heavy black streaks.
  Female: Similar to House Sparrow, but with faint flank-streaks.

● **TREE SPARROW** 301
  Black cheek-spot; chestnut crown. Sexes alike.

ROCK SPARROW 302
  Pale; striped crown; white tail-spots; indistinct yellow spot on breast.

● **DUNNOCK** 226
  Streaked brown; grey face and breast; thin bill.

△ **ALPINE ACCENTOR** 225
  Chestnut sides; spotted white throat; wing-bars.

○ **RUSTIC BUNTING** 288
  Summer: Black and white head; rusty breast-band.
  Winter: Brown; trace of head and breast patterns.

● **SNOW BUNTING** 290
  Large white wing-patches; head washed with buff. In summer, male has white head, black back.

SNOW FINCH 302
  From Snow Bunting by grey head, black chin.

● **LAPLAND BUNTING** 289
  Male in spring: Black face and chest; rusty nape.
  Female and winter male: Rusty nape; short tail.
  Immature: Light stripe through crown; see text.

● **REED BUNTING** 289
  Male: Black head and bib; white moustachial stripe and collar. *Female:* Streaked; blackish and creamy moustachial stripes.

HOUSE SPARROW

♂
♀

TREE SPARROW

Sexes
similar

♂ ♂

ROCK SPARROW

Sexes
similar

ALIAN SPARROW   SPANISH SPARROW

DUNNOCK

Sexes similar

Sexes similar

♂
Winter

ALPINE
ACCENTOR

♀

RUSTIC BUNTING   SNOW BUNTING

Winter ♂

SNOW FINCH

Sexes
similar

♂
mmer

Immature

♀

♂
Summer

LAPLAND BUNTING

♂
Summer

REED BUNTING

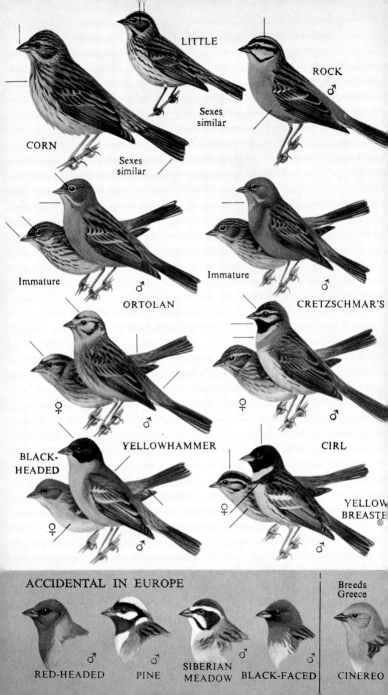

LITTLE

ROCK ♂

Sexes similar

CORN

Sexes similar

Immature ♂ ORTOLAN

Immature ♂ CRETZSCHMAR'S

♀ YELLOWHAMMER ♂

♀ CIRL ♂

BLACK-HEADED

♀ ♂

♀ ♂ YELLOW BREASTE

ACCIDENTAL IN EUROPE

Breeds Greece

RED-HEADED ♂   PINE ♂   SIBERIAN MEADOW ♂   BLACK-FACED ♂   CINEREO

Plate 64 277

BUNTINGS

● **CORN BUNTING**
    Large; streaked; stubby bill; no white on tail.

○ **LITTLE BUNTING**
    Rufous crown and cheeks; boldly striped with black.

△ **ROCK BUNTING**
    Black stripes on grey head; buffish-orange belly and
    rump.

● **ORTOLAN BUNTING**
    Olive head and breast; yellow throat and eye-ring.
    Immature: Streaked; pink bill; pale eye-ring.

CRETZSCHMAR'S BUNTING
    From Ortolan by rusty throat, blue-grey head.
    Immature: Resembles immature Ortolan.

● **YELLOWHAMMER**
    Yellowish, with rufous rump.

● **CIRL BUNTING**
    Male: Black throat; black and yellow face-pattern.
    Female: From Yellowhammer by olive-brown rump.

△ **BLACK-HEADED BUNTING**
    Male: Black hood; yellow below; rufous back.
    Female: Unstreaked below; bright yellow under
    tail-coverts; deep bill.

○ **YELLOW-BREASTED BUNTING**
    Male: Black face; chestnut band on yellow under-
    parts; bold white wing-bars.
    Female: Strongly striped head; flank streaks only.

△ **RED-HEADED BUNTING**
    Male: Red head and breast; yellow under-parts.

△ **PINE BUNTING**
    Male: White crown; chestnut throat-patch.

SIBERIAN MEADOW BUNTING
    Male: Chestnut crown and cheeks; white eye-brow;
    black "moustache."

BLACK-FACED BUNTING
    Male: Dark grey head; dull yellow under-parts.

CINEREOUS BUNTING
    Male: Dull yellow head; greyish body and nape.

Voice: Call-note recalls Long-tailed Tit's low *"tsirr"*; alarm a loud *"tcherpink."*

Habitat and Range: Trees (notably willow) and bushes along stream and river banks and around ponds. Vagrant from U.S.S.R. to central Europe and W. to Holland, France.

GREAT TIT *Parus major*   page 213

     Du – Koolmees   Fr – Mésange charbonnière
     Ge – Kohlmeise   Sw – Talgoxe

Identification: 5½″. Largest common tit. Glossy blue-black head and neck, with white cheeks; *yellow under-parts, with black band down centre* (the best field mark). Greenish blue-grey upper-parts. Juvenile has brownish crown and yellowish cheeks. Arboreal and acrobatic.

Voice: Most varied of the tits: a Chaffinch-like *"tsink, tsink,"* a nasal, Marsh Tit-like *"tchair, tchair,"* a scolding Blue Tit-like *"chi-chi -chi,"* etc. Song consists of two- or three-syllable variations on familiar, ringing *"teechew-teechew-teechew,"* and occasional mimicry.

Habitat: Mixed woods, hedges, gardens. Nests in holes in trees, walls, drain-pipes, nest-boxes, etc. Map below.

PENDULINE TIT *Remiz pendulinus*   page 213

     Du – Buidelmees   Fr – Mésange rémiz
     Ge – Beutelmeise   Sw – Pungmes

Identification: 4¼″. Easily distinguished by striking greyish-white head and throat, with *broad black patch across face*. Back *chestnut*; belly buffish-white. Juvenile mainly pale ash-brown, without black or chestnut markings.

Voice: Usual note a soft, plaintive *"seeou,"* recalling Robin, and a conversational *"tsi-tsi-tsi."*

Habitat: Marshy localities, thickets, along dykes, etc., but locally also in dry regions. Builds ovoid nest with funnel-shaped entrance, suspended in outer twigs of bush or tree and in reeds. Map p. 279.

← BLUE TIT
Partial migrant in northern part of range

GREAT TIT →
Partial migrant in northern part of range

NUTHATCHES AND WALL CREEPERS: Sittidae

Nuthatches recall tiny woodpeckers, having strong bills and large feet, but climb trees (or rocks) upwards or downwards, without using tail as prop. Wall Creeper has large wings, fine curved bill. Sexes similar. Hole nesting.

NUTHATCH *Sitta europaea* page 212

Du – Boomklever Fr – Sittelle torchepot
Ge – Kleiber Sw – Nötväcka

Identification: 5½″. A stubby, active, tree-climbing bird, with a powerful pointed bill. Distinguished by *blue-grey crown and upper-parts, buff under-parts with chestnut flanks*, white cheeks and throat, bold black streak through eye. Juvenile lacks chestnut. Climbs trees in short jerks, in any direction including *downwards*. Tail is *not* used as support. Hammers nuts wedged in bark. Under-parts are whiter in Scandinavian race *S. e. europaea*. See also Rock Nuthatch.

Voice: A ringing, metallic "*chwit, chwit, chwit*," a repeated "*tsit*," a shrill, trilling "*tsirr*," etc. Song, a repeated, loud "*tui*," a long, trilling "*chi-chi-chi-chi*," "*qui-qui, qui-qui*," etc.

Habitat: Old deciduous trees in woods, parks, gardens. Nests in holes in trees, occasionally in walls, bird-boxes, etc., plastering entrance hole and crevices with mud. Map below.

CORSICAN NUTHATCH *Sitta whiteheadi* page 212

Du – Zwartkopboomklever Fr – Sittelle corse
Ge – Korsikanischer Kleiber Sw – Korsikansk nötväcka

Identification: 4¾″. Much smaller than Nuthatch. Distinguished by *black* crown and broad stripe through eye, and *broad, sharply*

← PENDULINE TIT
*Has bred Switzer-
land; Wanders in
winter; apparently
absent from parts
of cen. and S.E.
Europe*

NUTHATCH →
*Resident. Vagrant
Finland*

defined white stripe above eye. Under-parts dingy *whitish.* Female is duller, with slate-grey crown.

Voice: More nasal and quieter than Nuthatch; most typical call a short nasal note recalling distant Jay; also a weak "*pupupupu*"; a louder, ascending "*pooi*"; a weak trilling " *tsi-tsi-tsi* ".

Habitat and Range: Confined to mountain forests and groves (particularly of Chestnut) in Corsica. Excavates nest holes in rotting trees.

ROCK NUTHATCH *Sitta neumayer* page 212

Du – Rotsklever Fr – Sittelle des rochers
Ge – Felsenkleiber Sw – Klippnötväcka

Identification: 5½″. Very different in habitat from other nuthatches frequenting bare rocks, but perches occasionally in trees. Resembles *very faded* Nuthatch, with *whitish* under-parts, *brownish-buff* (not chestnut) flanks and under tail-coverts and grey tail *without white markings.* Actions as Nuthatch.

Voice: Shrill, high-pitched and very varied, but lacking rich quality of Nuthatch. Song, a rapid trilling "*see-a, see-a, see-a*" on a descending scale.

Habitat: Rocky gorges, mountain-sides, cliffs. Breeds in caves and crannies in rocks, plastering entrance with mud, to form short funnel. Map below.

WALL CREEPER *Tichodroma muraria* page 212

Du – Rotskruiper Fr – Tichodrome échelette
Ge – Mauerläufer Sw – Murkrypare

Identification: 6½″. Distinguished by *brilliant crimson* on blackish, rounded wings. Has grey upper-parts, short tail and long, slender curved bill. *Large white spots* on edges of wings and tail. Throat and breast black in summer, whitish in winter. Has spasmodic, butterfly-flight; very broad wings constantly flicked while seeking food on rock-faces or old buildings. Juvenile like adults in winter, but brownish, with a straighter bill.

413

← ROCK NUTHATCH
Resident

WALL CREEPER →
Partial migrant. Vagrant to England, N. Germany, Corsica, Malta

414

Voice: A clear, piping *"zee-zee-titi-zwee,"* in rising cadence; usually sings while climbing.

Habitat: Rocky ravines, earth cliffs, ruins. Breeds in deep crevices, on inland cliff-face, in rocks, occasionally in buildings, usually from about 6,000 ft. to snow-line, wintering in rocky valleys and foothills. Map p. 280.

TREE CREEPERS: Certhiidae

Restless little birds with long, slender, curved bills. Usually seen creeping up tree trunks. Sexes similar. Nest in crevices.

TREE CREEPER *Certhia familiaris*   page 212

Du – Kortsnavelboomkruiper   Fr – Grimpereau des bois
Ge – Waldbaumläufer   Sw – Trädkrypare

Identification: 5″. A small, *brown*, tree-climbing bird. Easily distinguished from woodpeckers and nuthatches by small size, *thin curved bill* and distinctive behaviour. Brown upper-parts, streaked with buff; silvery white under-parts. Climbs up trees spirally in short spurts, with stiff tail pressed against bark. Travels with tits in winter.

Voice: A thin, high-pitched *"tsee"* or *"tsit."* Song weak, high-pitched, starting slowly and accelerating: *"tsee-tsee-tsee-tsizzi-tsee."*

Habitat: Woodlands, parks, gardens with large trees. Nests behind loose bark, in split trees, behind ivy, etc. In central and S. Europe prefers mountain woodlands and avoids lowlands. Map below.

SHORT-TOED TREE CREEPER *Certhia brachydactyla*

page 212

Du – Boomkruiper   Fr – Grimpereau des jardins
Ge – Gartenbaumläufer   Sw – Kortload trädkrypare

Identification: Not always safely distinguishable in the field from Tree Creeper, except by *voice* and *distribution*, but is less rusty on rump

← TREE CREEPER
Mainly resident

SHORT-TOED
TREE CREEPER →
Mainly resident

and has *brownish flanks* (a fairly good field mark), supercilium is less distinct. Bill usually slightly longer and more curved and claws shorter than Tree Creeper's.

Voice: Distinguished from Tree Creeper's by richer quality, often recalling Coal Tit. Song lacks Tree Creeper's thin, high-pitched notes: a rhythmic "*teet, teet, teeteroititt.*" Call-note a high, shrill "*srrieh.*"

Habitat: Gardens, parks, coppices, avoiding heavy woodlands. In central and S. Europe Tree Creeper usually restricted to mountains and regions above 3,000 ft., whereas Short-toed occurs from 5,000 ft. to sea level. Map p. 281.

BUNTINGS: Emberizidae

Seed-eating birds with short, thick-based bills. Males of most species brightly coloured, or patterned. Nest in trees, bushes, on ground, or in crevices.

CORN BUNTING *Emberiza calandra* page 277

    Du – Grauwe gors   Fr – Bruant proyer
    Ge – Grauammer   Sw – Kornsparv

Identification: 7″. Largest bunting. Heavily built. Brownish, streaked above and below. No white on wings or tail. Distinguished from larks and pipits by larger size, large round head and stubby bill. Sexes similar. Bill and legs yellowish. Flight heavy, often with dangling legs. Perches on posts and telegraph wires. Gregarious. Usually polygynous.

Voice: A short, rasping "*chip,*" a harsh, longer "*zeep*"; in autumn "*tip-a-tip.*" Flight-call a loud twitter. Song, a distinctive, rapid, dry jingle, like rattling bunch of keys.

Habitat: Open farm-lands, road-sides, waste-lands, hedges. Nests in long grass, among thistles, in hedge-bottoms, etc. Map below.

← CORN BUNTING
Partial migrant.
Has bred Norway.
Vag. to Finland

YELLOW-
HAMMER →
Partial migrant.
Vagrant Iceland,
Faeroes, Sicily

YELLOWHAMMER *Emberiza citrinella* page 277

    Du – Geelgors   Fr – Bruant jaune
    Ge – Goldammer   Sw – Gulsparv

Identification: 6½″. Male distinguished by *lemon yellow head and under-parts and chestnut rump*; streaked chestnut back and streaked flanks. White on outer tail-feathers conspicuous in flight. Female and juvenile much less yellow, with more dark markings, particularly on head; distinguished from Cirl by chestnut rump.

Voice: A metallic "*chip*" and "*twitic.*" Song, a rapid, "*chi-chi-chi-chi-chi . . . chweee*," usually written "little-bit-of-bread-and-no-cheese."

Habitat: Farm-lands, road-sides, commons, open country. Breeds on or near ground at foot of hedge, on ditch-side, etc. Map p. 282.

ROCK BUNTING *Emberiza cia* page 277

    Du – Grijze gors   Fr – Bruant fou
    Ge – Zippammer   Sw – Klippsparv

Identification: 6¼″. Distinguished by *ash-grey throat and head, with thin black stripes* on crown and through and below the eye. Frequently flicks tail open, to show conspicuous white when feeding on ground. Upper-parts chestnut, streaked black; rump *unstreaked* chestnut; under-parts *buffish-chestnut*. Female is duller, browner, with breast and flanks slightly streaked. Adult easily distinguished from all other European buntings by *pale ash-grey throat*. Immature distinguished from young Ortolan and Cretzschmar's by reddish-buff under-parts and chestnut rump.

Voice: Call-note a thin "*seea.*" Song recalls Reed Bunting's; a brief "*zi-zi-zi-zirr*," last note rising.

Habitat: Usually rocky mountain-sides, often on trees, occasionally at sea level. Breeds on or near ground. Map below.

← ROCK BUNTING
*Mainly resident.
Extends within
dotted lines winter.
Vagrant to Britain*

ORTOLAN
BUNTING →
*Summer visitor.
Prob. breeds Sar-
dinia. Passage E.
Britain. Vagrant to
Iceland, Ireland*

419   421

MISCELLANEOUS RARITIES

PALM DOVE

ISABELLINE
WHEATEAR

DESERT WHEATEAR

PETCHORA PIPIT

RED-FLANKED BLUETAIL

TRUMPETER
BULLFINCH

OLIVE-BACKED
THRUSH

LANCEOLATED WARBLER

Immature

PALLAS'S GRASSHOPPER
WARBLER

PALLAS'S
LEAF WARBLER

GREATER
SAND
PLOVER

SOCIABLE
PLOVER

SPUR-
WINGED
PLOVER

KILLDEER

Breeding

Non-breeding

WILSON'S PHALAROPE

GREATER
YELLOWLEG

Immature

BONAPARTE'S
GULL

Adult (winter)
ROSS'S GULL

Adult
(breeding

BAIKAL TEAL

AMERICAN WIGEON

BLUE-WINGED TEAL

Plate 66 285

MISCELLANEOUS RARITIES

GREATER SAND PLOVER   page 120
  Male: Heavy bill; rusty chest; black face marks.

△ **SOCIABLE PLOVER**   123
  Black crown; white supercilia join in "V" at nape.

SPUR-WINGED PLOVER   126
  Strikingly black and white except for brown back

○ **KILLDEER**   123
  Two breast-bands; rufous on rump and long tail.

△ **WILSON'S PHALAROPE**   147
  From other phalaropes by white rump, lack of wing-
  bar and longer bill. Compare with Lesser Yellowlegs.

△ **GREATER YELLOWLEGS**   137
  Larger than Lesser; bigger, slightly upturned bill.

△ **ROSS'S GULL**   163
  Graduated tail; delicate black bill; wing-marking.

△ **BONAPARTE'S GULL**   155
  Breeding: Like small Black-headed, but thinner *black*
  bill. *Immature:* Dark trailing edges to wings. *At all
  ages:* White beneath primaries.

△ **BAIKAL TEAL**   46
  Male: Creamy cheek with vertical black mark.
  Female: White spot near bill; broken supercilium.

△ **AMERICAN WIGEON**   50
  Looks pinkish-brown; broad creamy-white crown.

△ **BLUE-WINGED TEAL**   46
  Male: White crescent on head; black and white rear.
  Female: Like dark female Garganey, with longer bill.

CINEREOUS BUNTING *Emberiza cineracea* page 277

Du – Smyrna gors   Fr – Bruant cendré
Ge – Kleinasiatische Ammer   Sw – Gulgrä sparv

Identification: 6½″. A *greyish* bunting with a *dull yellow head*. Throat clear yellow. Nape and upper breast ash-grey tinged with yellow; under-parts mainly white. Upper-parts brownish-grey, darkly striped, with coverts and secondaries edged buffish. Bill bluish horn. Legs flesh-brown. Female duller, with browner, striped head and streaky yellow throat. Immature is darker, with streaked ash-brown under-parts, but throat shows pale sulphur wash; inner secondaries broadly edged buffish-rufous.

Voice: Call-note a short "*kip*." Brief song has typical bunting character, said to resemble "*dir, dir, dir, dli-di*."

Habitat and Range: Dry rocky or stony slopes with scanty vegetation up to tree limit. Breeds Greece.

ORTOLAN BUNTING *Emberiza hortulana* page 277

Du – Ortolaan   Fr – Bruant ortolan
Ge – Ortolan   Sw – Ortolansparv

Identification: 6¼″. Distinguished from other buntings by combination of *pinkish-buff under-parts and yellow throat*. Has pale *olive-green head and chest* and *pale yellow throat* with olive moustachial streak. At close quarters narrow yellow eye-ring and pink bill are visible. Upper-parts brown, streaked black. Female is paler, less green, with small dark streaks on chest. Immature browner, streaked on under-parts, but has characteristic *yellow eye-ring and pink bill*. See also Cretzschmar's and Rock Buntings.

Voice: A soft "*tsee-ip*" and "*tsip*" and a piping "*tseu*." Song slow and variable, usually 6-7 similar clear notes, with final note lower or higher.

Habitat: Open hilly country, often also in lowlands, gardens, scrub. Breeds on or near ground in growing crops or weeds. Map p. 283.

CRETZSCHMAR'S BUNTING *Emberiza caesia* page 277

Du – Bruinkeelortolaan   Fr – Bruant cendrillard
Ge – Grauer Ortolan   Sw – Rostsparv

Identification: 6¼″. Male suggests male Ortolan, but head and breast-band are unmistakable *bright blue-grey* (not olive), throat *rusty* (not yellow). Female distinguished from female Ortolan by *absence of yellow on throat*. Immature doubtfully distinguishable from young Ortolan by buffer appearance; from immature Rock Bunting by pink bill. In autumn both sexes have bright colours partly obscured.

Voice: An insistent "*styip*," less soft than Ortolan's call. Song resembles Ortolan's but is shorter.

Habitat and Range: Bare rocky hill-sides and semi-desert regions with scattered and stunted vegetation. Nests on ground. Summer visitor, breeding commonly in Greece and N. to Dalmatia. Vagrant elsewhere in Mediterranean Europe, W. to Spain, also Germany.

CIRL BUNTING *Emberiza cirlus* page 277

Du – Cirlgors Fr – Bruant zizi
Ge – Zaunammer Sw – Häcksparv

Identification: 6½″. Male has *yellow under-parts with greenish breast-band, black throat* (latter obscured in winter) and streaked flanks; olive-green head with dark crown, *yellow stripes above and below eye*, black stripe through eye; back and sides of breast chestnut; distinguished from Yellowhammer by characteristic head and breast markings. Female and juvenile duller, distinguished from Yellowhammer by *olive-brown rump*. See also Yellow-breasted and Ortolan.

Voice: A weak "*sip*," flight-call "*sissi-sissi-sip*." Song a monotonous, hurried jingle on one note, recalling Lesser Whitethroat's.

Habitat: Tall hedgerows and trees bordering cultivated land or downs; on Continent often on bushy and rocky hillsides. Winters in farmlands in mixed flocks. Nests low down in hedge, trees, sometimes on bank-sides. Map below.

LITTLE BUNTING *Emberiza pusilla* page 277

Du – Dwerggors Fr – Bruant nain
Ge – Zwergammer Sw – Dvärgsparv

Identification: 5¼″. Size of Linnet, but rather nondescript except in breeding season when crown and cheeks are *chestnut, boldly outlined with black*. Upper-parts brown, streaked black; under-parts whitish *with fine black streaks*, particularly on upper breast and flanks. Female duller. Distinguished from female Rustic and Reed Buntings by smaller size and dull chestnut cheeks. In flight looks small and compact, with less prominent tail than Reed Bunting.

Voice: A repeated, Robin-like "*tip*." Song, a short, melodious jingle.

Habitat and Range: Near water in tundra, valleys with undergrowth and marshes. Breeds on ground among willows or dwarf willow scrub. Rare summer visitor, breeding in N. Finland (and eastwards); has bred N. Norway and Sweden. Occasional on passage in most W. European countries S. to Mediterranean (in Britain especially on Fair Isle).

← CIRL BUNTING
*Mainly resident.
Vagrant Ireland,
Denmark*

RUSTIC
BUNTING →
*Summer visitor.
Vagrant W. Europe
s. to Italy, w. to
British Isles*

423

425

RUSTIC BUNTING *Emberiza rustica* page 276

Du – Bosgors   Fr – Bruant rustique
Ge – Waldammer   Sw – Videsparv

Identification: 5¾″. Distinguished from other buntings by pure white throat and under-parts, with large, irregular, *cinnamon breast-band* and a few similar streaks on flanks. Upper-parts chestnut, streaked black. Male has *blackish crown and cheeks* (brownish in winter) with *conspicuous broad white stripe behind eye.* Female has dark brown in place of black on head; faintly suggests big Whinchat. Has nervous habit of raising crest-feathers.

Voice: A repeated, high-pitched *"tsip, tsip, tsip."* Song rather Dunnock-like, but shorter.

Habitat: Thickets near water and mixed woods with rank undergrowth. Breeds in grass or low bushes. Map p. 287.

YELLOW-BREASTED BUNTING *Emberiza aureola* page 277

Du – Wilgengors   Fr – Bruant auréole
Ge – Weidenammer   Sw – Brunhuvad sparv

Identification: 5½″. Male has bright yellow under-parts with *distinctive narrow chestnut breast-band*; Chaffinch-like wing-pattern, with broad white shoulder patch and narrow bar; *black face*, dark chestnut nape and upper-parts; in winter, black and chestnut markings partly obscured, but still distinguishable from other buntings by wing-bars and breast-band. Female also yellow or yellowish below, but lacks breast-band; distinctive head pattern recalls Aquatic Warbler (pale crown-stripe and supercilium separated by dark lines); further distinguished from Cirl and Yellowhammer by paler appearance, unstreaked centre of breast and faint double wing-bars. Both sexes have some white on tail.

Voice: A Robin-like *"tick"* and a soft *"trssit."* Far-carrying song is melodious, quicker and more liquid than slightly similar Ortolan's.

Habitat and Range: Open country. In summer, chiefly birch and willow scrub near water, but also on steppes. Nests on ground or in small bushes. Breeds in West Finland. Migrates eastwards, vagrant westwards to British Isles and southwards to Malta.

BLACK-HEADED BUNTING *Emberiza melanocephala* page 277

Du – Zwartkopgors   Fr – Bruant mélanocéphale
Ge – Kappenammer   Sw – Svarthuvad sparv

Identification: 6½″. Male has *unstreaked* yellow under-parts; *black head, with yellow collar*; chestnut back; *no white on tail.* Head brownish in autumn. Female is dull streaked olive-brown above; distinguished from other yellow-breasted buntings by *unstreaked* under-parts; yellow under tail-coverts. But see Red-headed Bunting (Accidental, p. 323).

Voice: A soft *"chup,"* a short, loud *"zitt"* and a lower-pitched, quieter *"zee."* Song unusually pleasing for a bunting; 2-5 similar slow introductory notes, followed by a brief, quick, rather subdued warble.

Habitat: Open country with scattered woods and undergrowth, olive groves, gardens. Breeds in low vegetation. Map below.

REED BUNTING *Emberiza schoeniclus* page 276

Du – Rietgors Fr – Bruant des roseaux
Ge – Rohrammer Sw – Sävsparv

Identification: 6″. Male has *black head and throat, with white collar* (this pattern is almost obscured by brown mottling in winter); dark brown upper-parts with black streaks and greyish rump; conspicuous white outer tail-feathers; greyish-white under-parts, flanks streaked black. Female has brown head with pale buff supercilium and *conspicuous black and whitish moustachial streaks*; brownish rump; buff throat and under-parts with black streaks on breast and flanks.

Voice: A loud "*tseek,*" a metallic "*chink*" and (alarm note) "*chit.*" Song begins slowly, ends hurriedly, "*tseek-tseek-tseek-tississisk,*" usually delivered from reed-stem or bush.

Habitat: Reed-beds, sewage-farms, swamps; roams farm-lands in winter. Breeds on or near ground in rank vegetation. Map below.

LAPLAND BUNTING *Calcarius lapponicus* page 276

Du – IJsgors Fr – Bruant lapon
Ge – Spornammer Sw – Lappsparv
N.Am – Lapland Longspur

Identification: 6″. Male in spring has *black head, throat, breast and flanks, conspicuous buffish band from behind eye to white below cheek,* and *bright chestnut nape.* Upper-parts streaked dark brown; belly whitish, with streaked flanks; white sides to tail. Female lacks black markings, has striped crown and whitish throat. In autumn and winter both sexes are more nondescript and spend most of time *running* on ground; streaked buffish-brown, with narrow double whitish wing-bars, chestnut on coverts, some dark streaking on flanks, and varying amount of reddish on nape (in males); often with smudge of streaks

← BLACK-HEADED
BUNTING
*Summer visitor.
Vagrant w. to British Isles, Spain, n.
to Baltic Provinces*

REED BUNTING →
*Partial migrant.
Vagrant Faeroes*

across upper breast. Distinguished from rather similar female Reed Bunting by stouter form, *shorter tail* showing less white, *pale stripe through crown*, dark angular mark behind ear-coverts.

Voice: A musical *"teeu,"* *"ticky-tick-teu,"* etc. Song (in flight) vigorous but musical, not unlike short extract from Sky Lark's.

Habitat: Winters in coastal stubble fields, saltings, coastal moors and along beaches. Breeds in treeless barrens, open tundra and moss-heaths. Map below.

SNOW BUNTING *Plectrophenax nivalis*   page 276

Du – Sneeuwgors   Fr – Bruant des neiges
Ge – Schneeammer   Sw – Snösparv

Identification: 6½". Easily identified by *broad white patches on wings and tail*. In spring, male has black back, primaries and centre tail-feathers, remainder of plumage *snow-white*. Female's head grey-brown, with buffish stripe from eye around ear-coverts, back grey-brown flecked with black. In winter, male's head is sandy, back browner, under-parts creamy-white with tawny smudges on sides of breast; female browner, but in flight white wing-patches still conspicuous; immature has *brown* wings, rufuous-buff head and breast-band, creamy-white under-parts. Flight "dancing" and usually high. Gregarious; large flocks in flight resemble drifting snowflakes. See also Snow Finch.

Voice: A loud *"tsweet,"* a plaintive *"teup,"* and *"teu"* (like Lapland Bunting). Song, a high, very rapid, but musical *"turi-turi-turi-tetitui,"* of almost lark-like quality; sings on downward glide from circling display flight and from perch.

Habitat: Winters along sea-shores and open coastal regions, occasionally inland downs and fields. Nests deep in crevices, in rocky or mountainous regions. Map below.

← LAPLAND
BUNTING
Migrant. Passage Baltic, British Is., Iceland. Vag. s. to Italy

SNOW BUNTING →
Partial migrant. Some years nests Faeroes. Vagrant most other European countries

429

430

FINCHES: Fringillidae

Seed-eating birds, often brightly coloured, with short, strong bills, usually thick at the base. Nest in trees, bushes, or on ground.

CHAFFINCH *Fringilla coelebs*   page 261
    Du – Vink   Fr – Pinson des arbres
    Ge – Buchfink   Sw – Bofink

Identification: 6″. Commonest finch. Distinguished by *bold double white wing-bars* and, in flight, by *white outer tail-feathers*. Male pinkish-brown below, with chestnut mantle, greenish rump, and *slate-blue* crown and nape. Female pale olive-brown above, lighter below. Flight undulating. Gregarious, with other finches, except in breeding season; sexes often in separate flocks. Immediately distinguished from Brambling by *greenish* (not white) rump.

Voice: A loud, repeated "*chwink,*" "*wheet*" and "*chwit*"; flight-call a subdued "*tsip.*" Song, a brief, vigorous cascade of about a dozen notes, terminating in a flourishing "*choo-ee-o*"; varies widely locally.

Habitat: Hedges, woods, commons, gardens, farm-lands. Nests usually fairly low, in bush or tree. Map below.

BRAMBLING *Fringilla montifringilla*   page 261
    Du – Keep   Fr – Pinson du nord
    Ge – Bergfink   Sw – Bergfink

Identification: 5¾″. Easily distinguished from Chaffinch by *conspicuous though narrow white rump* and less white on wings and tail. Male has *bold orange shoulder-patch* and orange breast; head and mantle in spring are brilliant *black*, in winter brownish. Female can be confused with female Chaffinch but has paler, buffer plumage, white rump and dark stripes on crown. Flight more erratic than Chaffinch. Gregarious

← CHAFFINCH
*Partial migrant.
Annual in Iceland*

BRAMBLING →
*Migrant, annual in
Iceland. Vagrant
to Malta. Has
bred Scotland,
Denmark*

with Chaffinches in winter. Bullfinch also has white though wider rump-patch, but is much heavier bird, with very stubby bill.

Voice: A metallic "*tsweep*" and "*tchuc*"; latter repeated rapidly as flight-call. Song, a grating, monotonously repeated Greenfinch-like "*dzweea*," interspersed with a few very weak chipping notes.

Habitat: Winters in beech woods, and farm-lands. Breeds chiefly in birch, but also in conifers, usually on outskirts of wood. Map p. 291.

CITRIL FINCH *Serinus citrinella* page 261

  Du – Citroensijs   Fr – Venturon montagnard
  Ge – Zitronenzeisig   Sw – Citronsiska

Identification: 4¾″. Yellowish-green *with greyish nape and sides of neck*; bright yellow under-parts, greenish-yellow rump; blackish wings with greenish-yellow bar. Female duller and faintly streaked. Juvenile greyish-brown with paler under-parts, streaked above and below. Flight dancing. Sociable. Greyish neck and unstreaked under-parts distinguish it from Siskin and Serin. Corsican race *S. c. corsicana* has streaked rusty mantle, paler yellow under-parts and nests down to sea level.

Voice: A plaintive "*tsi-i*"; also a metallic "*chwick*." Song, a Siskin-like mixture of creaking notes and musical twittering, often during circling flight.

Habitat: Mountains with scattered conifers and open rocky ground; above 5,000 ft. in summer, lower in winter. Nests in conifers. Map below.

SERIN *Serinus serinus* page 261

  Du – Europese kanarie   Fr – Serin cini
  Ge – Girlitz   Sw – Gulhämpling

Identification: 4½″. A tiny, streaked, yellowish finch. Distinguished by *stubby bill*, and *bright yellow rump*. Male has *bright yellow forehead*, supercilium, throat and breast. Female more streaked, greyer below, browner above; distinguished from female Siskin by *shorter, stubbier*

← CITRIL FINCH
Mainly res. but spreads in winter. Has bred Balearics. Vagrant Britain, Heligoland, Sicily.

SERIN →
Partial migrant. Has bred Sweden. Vagrant Britain, Ireland, Finland

bill, lack of yellow in tail, bolder supercilium and heavier streaking below. Juvenile strongly streaked with brown, lacks yellow on rump. Flight swift and undulating; in nuptial flight rises vertically and descends in circles. Sociable.

Voice: Twittering flight-call; a rapid "*si-twi-twi-twi*," and a hard, wren-like "*chit-chit-chit*"; anxiety note a liquid "*tsooeet*." Song, delivered from tree-top, telegraph wire, or in flight, a rapid, sibilant, almost hissing, jingle, with occasional canary-like trills.

Habitat: Parks, gardens, vineyards, etc. Nests in trees, vines, small bushes. Map p. 292.

GREENFINCH *Carduelis chloris* page 261

Du – Groenling   Fr – Verdier
Ge – Grünling   Sw – Grönfink

Identification: 5¾″. Male olive-green, with *yellow-green rump and conspicuous yellow on wings and tail*. Heavy, whitish bill. Pinkish legs. Female duller, greyer, much less yellow. Juvenile browner and streaked. Flight undulating.

Voice: A loud, rapid trill; also a repeated short "*chup*," or "*teu*." In breeding season a prolonged nasal "*tswe-e-e*." Song, from tree-tops, or in bat-like flight, a canary-like twittering, mixed with call-notes.

Habitat: Gardens, shrubberies, farm-lands. Nests in hedges, bushes and small trees, particularly evergreens. Map below.

SISKIN *Carduelis spinus* page 261

Du – Sijs   Fr – Tarin des aulnes
Ge – Zeisig   Sw – Grönsiska

Identification: 4¾″. Male *yellowish-green*, paler beneath, with *black crown and chin*; yellow rump, wing-bar, sides of tail and stripe behind eye; brown-streaked back and flanks. Female greyer, with less yellow, no black on head, more strongly streaked whitish under-parts. Flight finch-like but very buoyant. Gregarious with redpolls in winter. See also Serin, Citril Finch and Redpoll.

← GREENFINCH
Partial migrant.
Vagrant Faeroes,
Iceland

SISKIN →
Partial migrant.
Has bred Holland.
Vagrant Faeroes,
Iceland

Voice: Almost constant twitter. Call-notes, a high squeaky "*tsy-zi*" and a wheezy "*tsooeet*." Song, a long, rapid musical twitter, often terminating with a long Greenfinch-like wheezing note.

Habitat: Coniferous woods, birch and alder thickets and uncut hedges. Nests high in conifers, usually at extremity of branch. Map p. 293.

GOLDFINCH Carduelis carduelis page 261

Du – Putter Fr – Chardonneret
Ge – Stieglitz Sw – Steglits

Identification: 4¾″. Sexes similar. *Boldly marked black and yellow wings*; black and white tail; *scarlet face, black and white head*; tawny-brown back merging into whitish rump. Juvenile head and upper-parts greyish-buff, streaked and spotted brown. Flight undulating and dancing. Sociable.

Voice: Unmistakable, liquid, "*swit-witt-witt-witt*" frequently re-peated; anxiety note a soft "*ah-i*"; song, a canary-like, liquid twitter, incorporating variations on the call-notes.

Habitat: Gardens, orchards, cultivated land. Forages for thistle-seed in waste-lands and road-sides during autumn and winter. Nests in trees, usually near tip of branch; occasionally in hedges. Map below.

TWITE Acanthis flavirostris page 260

Du – Frater Fr – Linotte à bec jaune
Ge – Berghänfling Sw – Gulnäbbad hämpling

Identification: 5¼″. Rather Linnet-like in appearance and actions. Dull buff above, streaked black and brown, lighter below. *Throat warm buff*. Male has *dark pinkish rump*, which in female is buff streaked with black. Bill greyish-yellow in summer, light yellow in winter. Distinguished from female and juvenile Linnets by less white in wings and tail, darker upper-parts, almost orange-buff throat and slightly longer tail, and, in winter, also by *yellow* bill; from Redpoll by buffer plumage, lack of black chin, lack of red cap and longer tail.

Voice: A nasal "*chweet*." Almost constant twitter in flight. Song, Linnet-like, but slower.

← GOLDFINCH
Partial migrant

TWITE →
Partial migrant.
Vagrant to Spain,
Italy

Habitat: Breeds sociably on moors and high waste-lands. In winter roams in flocks over coastal regions, fields, marshes, etc. Map p. 294.

LINNET *Acanthis cannabina*   page 260

 Du – Kneu   Fr – Linotte mélodieuse
 Ge – Hänfling   Sw – Hämpling

Identification: 5¼″. Male has chestnut-brown mantle; dark brown wings and forked tail are *edged with white*; head *greyish*; underparts buff, streaked brownish-black; breast *pinkish*; in breeding season also has *crimson crown and breast*, whitish throat with brown streaks. Female lacks crimson, is more streaked. Flight undulating. Gregarious. In winter distinguished from Twite and Redpoll by streaked chin and throat, prominent white on sides of tail (faint in Twite), and dark bill.

Voice: Usual call "*tsooeet*"; flight-note a rapid twitter; song, a varied, musical twitter, interspersed with pure and nasal notes, delivered from top of bush, sometimes in chorus.

Habitat: Open country with hedges; in winter roams in large flocks over waste-ground, farm-lands, marshes. Breeds sociably, in gorse, thickets and hedges, occasionally in marram grass and heather. Map below.

REDPOLL *Acanthis flammea*   page 260

 Du – Barmsijs   Fr – Sizerin flammé
 Ge – Birkenzeisig   Sw – Gråsiska

Identification: 5″. A little, streaked, grey-brown finch with a *bright crimson forehead* and a *black chin*. Male also has *pink* flush on breast. Flanks streaked. Flight undulating and buoyant. Sociable. British and Alpine race (Lesser Redpoll, *A. f. cabaret*) is smaller and browner, with more streaked upper-parts and less noticeable wingbars. Continental race (Mealy Redpoll, *A. f. flammea*) is somewhat larger, with whiter wing-bar and rump and, in winter, paler and greyer plumage. Greenland race (Greater Redpoll, *A. f. rostrata*) is even larger (5½-6″) and darker, with larger bill and darker flank-stripes, but

← LINNET
*Partial migrant.
Vagrant Faeroes*

REDPOLL →
*Partial migrant,
south to Mediterranean at times.
Has bred Holland*

usually not safely distinguishable unless in company with smaller redpolls. See also Arctic Redpoll.

Voice: High-pitched, metallic flight-calls: a very rapid, sustained twittering "*chuch-uch-uch*," "*tiu-tiu-tiu*," etc. Anxiety note, a plaintive "*tsooeet*." Song, a sustained series of brief trills interspersed with flight-calls.

Habitat: Copses, shrubberies, preferably of alder and willow; in northern forests chiefly deciduous; also rocky outcrops above tree line in mountainous areas and on tundra. Breeds, often sociably, in birch, alder, willow or juniper. Map p. 295.

ARCTIC REDPOLL *Acanthis hornemanni*   page 260
    Du – Witstuitbarmsijs   Fr – Sizerin blanchâtre
    Ge – Polarbirkenzeisig   Sw – Snösiska
                    N.Am – Hoary Redpoll

Identification: 5″. Breeding plumage looks "*hoar-frosted*," particularly on head and nape. Rump *unstreaked white* (as in some Mealy Redpolls); this and pale head contrast with grey back to give "*saddle*" *effect*. Wing-bars conspicuous. Under-parts *whiter and less streaked* than other races; male's breast is also much paler pink. Female lacks pink. Both sexes have crimson crown. Habits similar to other redpolls.

Voice: As other redpolls, but notes of flight-twitter slower, more clearly separated.

Habitat: Overlaps with other races, but usually in more open or marshy tundra, nesting in dwarf birch and tussocks of upper latitudes. Map below.

TRUMPETER BULLFINCH *Rhodopechys githaginea*   page 284
    Du – Woestijnvink   Fr – Bouvreuil githagine
    Ge – Wüstengimpel   Sw – Ökentrumpetare

Identification: 5½″. A sparrow-size ground-feeding bird with a stumpy bill. Male is greyish-brown *tinged with rosy-pink* on rump, wings,

← Arctic
    Redpoll
*Mainly migratory.
Vagrant Iceland,
Britain, central
Europe*

Scarlet
    Rosefinch →
*Summer visitor.
Vagrant Norway,
Iceland, Brit. Is.,
Spain, Italy. Has
wintered Czecho.*

under-parts and face; in spring bill is bright coral-red. Female and winter male duller, with yellowish bills. *Voice very distinctive.* Difficult to observe in typical habitat, crouching close to ground. Has rapid, finch-like flight.

Voice: A remarkable nasal, buzzing note and a harsh *"chizz."*

Habitat and Range: Deserts and barren hill country, but often near water sources. Nests in rocky crevices or stone walls. Vagrant from N. Africa to Malta, Greece and northern shores of Mediterranean.

SCARLET ROSEFINCH *Carpodacus erythrinus*   page 260
          Du – Roodmus   Fr – Roselin cramoisi
          Ge – Karmingimpel   Sw – Rosenfink

Identification: 5¾″. Male has brilliant *rosy-carmine head, breast and rump*, heavy bill, dark brown wings with two indistinct bars, white belly. Female, first-year male and juvenile rather nondescript: yellowish-brown above, brighter on rump, greyer on head; buff below with fine brown streaks; best distinguished by dumpy shape, bold black eye in large round head, pale double wing-bar and forked tail. Flight undulating. Distinguished from Pine Grosbeak by much smaller size, and indistinct wing-bars; from crossbills by longer tail and uncrossed mandibles.

Voice: A quiet, piping, *"tiu-eek"*; song, a clear, far-carrying and distinctive *"tiu-tiu-ti-tiu."*

Habitat: In summer, thickets, copses, undergrowth near water. Nests low down, usually in swampy vegetation, locally in dry oak woods. Map p. 296.

PINE GROSBEAK *Pinicola enucleator*   page 260
          Du – Haakbek   Fr – Dur-bec des sapins
          Ge – Hakengimpel   Sw – Tallbit

Identification: 8″. A large, heavy finch with a *longish tail*. Male has *deep rosy-pink head, neck, breast, and rump*; dark wings with *double white bars*; grey belly. In female the pink parts are a striking *greenish golden-brown*. Crown rather flat, bill heavy and Bullfinch-like. Flight very undulating. Usually very tame. Sociable in winter. Two-barred Crossbill and Scarlet Rosefinch are also rosy, with wing-bars, but are much smaller (sparrow-size).

Voice: A high, piping *"tee-tee-tew."* Alarm, a musical *"cheevli-cheevli."* Song consists of loud, whistling notes, interspersed with a twanging note.

Habitat: Northern mixed and coniferous woods. Usually nests in conifer. Map p. 298.

PARROT CROSSBILL *Loxia pytyopsittacus*   page 260
          Du – Grote kruisbek   Fr – Bec-croisé perroquet
          Ge – Kiefernkreuzschnabel Sw – Större korsnabb

Identification: 6¾″. Slightly larger than Crossbill, but *heavier, more* *rounded bill* gives more "top-heavy" appearance. Colouring and parrot-like actions similar, but seldom seen in such large numbers and usually keeps apart from other crossbills. Voice and habitat as Crossbill, but with greater preference for pines.

Voice: Deeper and stronger than Crossbill's, a rounder *"chup-chup-chup."*

Range: Breeds in S. Finland and Scandinavia from 67°, southwards sporadically to E. Germany; in winter occurs Denmark, Germany, Austria, occasionally Britain, France, Belgium, Italy, Yugoslavia.

CROSSBILL *Loxia curvirostra*   page 260

Du – Kruisbek	Fr – Bec-croisé des sapins
Ge – Fichtenkreuzschnabel	Sw – Mindre korsnäbb

N.Am – Red Crossbill

Identification: 6½″. A bird of the conifers. Distinguished by *crossed mandibles, parrot-like actions in feeding and short, forked tail.* Male plumage *brick-red,* brighter on rump, with dark wings and tail. Young male orange-brown. Female olive with yellowish rump and under-parts. Juvenile greenish-grey, strongly streaked below. Gregarious and tame. Heavy head and short tail distinctive in rapid, undulating flight. "Irrupts" in large numbers in late summer every few years and some continental birds wander to Britain to breed. Distinguished from Two-barred Crossbill by absence of white on wings. The Scottish race (*L. c. scotica*) has a much heavier bill and is sometimes regarded as race of *L. pytyopsittacus.* See also Parrot Crossbill, Pine Grosbeak and Scarlet Rosefinch.

Voice: A loud, emphatic *"chip-chip-chip."* Song faintly resembles Greenfinch's, but is a more regularly spaced mixture of short trills, creaking, warbling and chipping notes, notably *"ti-chee, ti-chee."*

Habitat: Coniferous woods, chiefly spruce, but also pine and larch. Dropped, opened cones on ground indicate presence. Breeds in conifers. Map below.

← PINE GROSBEAK *Vag. s. to England, France, Italy, Yugoslavia*

CROSSBILL → *Resid. After irreg. "irruptions" may nest outside normal range in Brit. Is., W. Europe. Vagr. to Iceland, Malta*

TWO-BARRED CROSSBILL *Loxia leucoptera*   page 260
    Du – Witbandkruisbek   Fr – Bec-croisé bifascié
    Ge – Bindenkreuzschnabel   Sw – Bändelkorsnäbb
           N.Am – White-winged Crossbill

Identification: 5¾″. Smaller than Crossbill. Distinguished even in flight by *bold, double white wing-bars,* which may give Chaffinch-like appearance in poor light. Male plumage more brilliant carmine than Crossbill; female lighter yellow and more streaked. Juvenile has less pronounced wing-bars than adults, otherwise like juvenile Crossbill. See also Pine Grosbeak.

Voice: A liquid *"peet"* and a dry *"chiff-chiff"* (latter corresponding to Crossbill's hard *"chip-chip"*). Song, a succession of loud trills on different pitches.

Habitat: As Crossbill, but prefers larch forests. Breeds rarely N. Finland, N. Sweden. Winters Baltic Provinces, sometimes reaching central, N.W. and W. Europe and British Isles.

BULLFINCH *Pyrrhula pyrrhula*   page 260
    Du – Goudvink   Fr – Bouvreuil pivoine
    Ge – Gimpel   Sw – Domherre

Identification: 5¾″. Male, a striking bird with *bright rose-red under-parts, conspicuous white rump,* blue-grey upper-parts, *black cap and chin* and *very stubby black bill.* Has black wings and tail, white wing-patch. Female has similar black cap and pattern but is pinkish-brown below, grey-brown above. Flight undulating. Secretive, seldom far from cover. N. European race *P. p. pyrrhula* is distinctly larger and brighter than British *P. p. nesa.* See Brambling, which has narrower white rump.

Voice: A soft, piping *"wheeb."* Song, a very subdued mixture of warbling and creaking notes, including *"teek, teek, tioo."*

Habitat: Plantations, thickets, hedgerows, gardens, orchards. Nests in evergreens, garden trees, hedges. Map below.

← BULLFINCH
*Mainly resident.
Vagrant Iceland*

HAWFINCH →
*Partial migrant.
Balearics in winter.
Has bred Finland,
Norway. Vagrant
Ireland, Malta,
Faeroes*

HAWFINCH *Coccothraustes coccothraustes* page 261
  Du – Appelvink   Fr – Gros-bec
  Ge – Kernbeisser   Sw – Stenknäck

Identification: 7″. *Huge bill*, bull-neck, *short* white-tipped tail, *bold white patches* high on blue-black wings. Tawny head, rich brown back, pale pinkish-brown under-parts, black throat and lores. Bill gunmetal blue in spring, pale horn in winter. Female paler, less rufous on crown. Juvenile is barred with brown and has yellow throat-patch. Flight rapid and usually high, but "bounding" over short distances. Flight silhouette (large head, short tail) is unmistakable; overhead, shows *transparent band across primaries..* Walks with upright, waddling gait, and hops powerfully. Often in flocks in winter, feeding on ground in woods. Extremely wary.

Voice: A loud, explosive "*ptik*," or "*ptik . . . ptik-it*," a thin "*tzeeip*," etc. Song, seldom heard, a halting "*teek, teek, tur-whee-whee*," with variations. Usually sings on tree-tops.

Habitat: Chiefly arboreal: mixed woodlands (particularly with beech and hornbeam), parks, orchards. Nests in tree-top, or on low horizontal branch, or against trunk, often in scattered groups. Map p. 299.

SPARROWS: Ploceidae

Thick-billed, sturdy little birds, mainly without bright colours. Sexes sometimes similar. Nest in holes, trees or rocks.

HOUSE SPARROW *Passer domesticus* page 276
  Du – Huismus   Fr – Moineau domestique
  Ge – Haussperling   Sw – Gråsparv

Identification: 5¾″. Perhaps the most familiar bird. Male distinguished by *dark grey crown, chestnut nape, black throat* and whitish cheeks. Female and juvenile lack the black throat and are dull brown above and dingy white below, without distinctive marks.   Male Italian

← House
  Sparrow
Mainly resident. Black line surrounds range of Italian Sparrow

Spanish
Sparrow →
Mainly resident. Vagrant S. France, Corsica

Sparrow *P. d. italiae* (now regarded as conspecific) has brighter coloration in breeding plumage, with *rich chestnut* crown, *whiter* cheeks and
under-parts. See map. See also Tree and Spanish Sparrows.
Voice: Garrulous and varied. A loud "*cheep*," "*chissis*" and various
grating, twittering and chirping notes.
Habitat: Built-up areas and cultivated land, seldom far from human
habitation. Nests in holes or crevices in buildings, ivy, ricks, etc.
Map p. 300.

SPANISH SPARROW *Passer hispaniolensis* page 276

Du – Spaanse mus   Fr – Moineau espagnol
Ge – Weidensperling   Sw – Spansk sparv

Identification: Male has rich, *chestnut-red* crown, as in Italian race of
House Sparrow *P.d. italiae* but is distinguished by *much more extensive
black throat and upper-breast, black-streaked flanks, and much more
heavily marked back.* Female and juvenile resemble House Sparrows,
but have faint pattern of male's flank-streaks, white cheeks and darker
upper-parts. Behaviour and flight much as in House Sparrow, but
often seen in dense flocks far from houses.
Voice: A full, rich "*chup*" and other notes resembling House Sparrow's,
but all are richer in tone.
Habitat: Not restricted to houses, preferring bushy woods, roadside
trees and forests. Breeds colonially and singly, in foundations of
occupied or unoccupied nests of storks, eagles, etc., and in old martins'
nests and in branches of wayside or forest trees. Map p. 300.

TREE SPARROW *Passer montanus* page 276

Du – Ringmus   Fr – Moineau friquet
Ge – Feldsperling   Sw – Pilfink

Identification: 5½". Sexes alike. Distinguished from male House
Sparrow by rich *chocolate-brown crown, and black spot on purer white
ear-coverts* which almost form white collar. Smaller and more slender
than House Sparrow and more retiring. See also Spanish Sparrow.
Voice: Higher pitched than House Sparrow's. A short, metallic

← TREE SPARROW
*Partial migrant.
Breeds irregularly
Orkney, Shetland.
Has bred Faeroes*

ROCK SPARROW →
*Resident. Has bred
Czecho., formerly
S. Germany. Vag-
rant Switzerland,
Belgium, Poland*

"*chik*" or "*chop*," a repeated "*chit-tchup*" and a rapid, chuckling twitter. Unmistakable flight call "*tek, tek*."
Habitat: In western Europe more rural than House Sparrow. In south and eastern countries occurs around houses and in the north in tundra. Nests in holes in trees (particularly pollard willows), nest-boxes, haystacks, etc., but in houses in S. and E. Europe. Map p. 301.

ROCK SPARROW *Petronia petronia* page 276
        Du – Rotsmus   Fr – Moineau soulcie
        Ge – Steinsperling   Sw – Stenfink
Identification: 5½". Pale and plump, with short tail. Centre of crown is grey-brown, sides of crown and cheeks dark brown, with *long, broad supercilium to nape*. White spots on tips of tail-feathers conspicuous, *particularly in flight*. Under-parts faintly mottled with pale brown lines. Inconspicuous pale yellow spot on throat visible only when head is raised and seen at close quarters. Juvenile paler, without yellow throat-patch. Very active, often *running* briskly among rocks.
Voice: A characteristic, squeaky "*pey-i*," recalling Goldfinch. Varied chipping notes recall House Sparrow.
Habitat: High rocky mountain slopes, stony ground, ruins, etc., also in dry river-beds and farm-lands; seldom among houses though sometimes among trees. Nests in crevices in rocks and trees. Map p. 301.

SNOW FINCH *Montifringilla nivalis* page 276
        Du – Sneeuwvink   Fr – Niverolle
        Ge – Schneefink   Sw – Snöfink
Identification: 7". A mountain species. Distinguished from Snow Bunting by *grey head and black throat*, but unlikely to be seen in same localities. Warm chocolate-brown above, creamy-white below. Wings mainly white, with black primaries. Tail mainly white, with black centre, more conspicuous in flight than when perched. Female and juvenile duller, with less white on wings and tail. Bill blackish in spring, yellow in winter and juvenile. Perches upright, with nervous jerking of tail.
Voice: A harsh "*tsweek*." Song, in nuptial flight and when perched, a repeated "*sitticher-sitticher*."
Habitat: Bare mountain-tops above 6,000 ft., lower in winter. Visits mountain huts and camps. Nests in rock crevices, walls, under eaves, etc. Map p. 303.

STARLINGS: Sturnidae

Stocky birds, with short tails, long pointed bills. Jaunty, garrulous and very active. Feed on open ground. Sexes similar. Hole nesting.

ROSE-COLOURED STARLING *Sturnus roseus* page 197

Du – Rose spreeuw Fr – Martin roselin
Ge – Rosenstar Sw – Rosenstare

Identification: 8½″. Similar to Starling in form and movements, though flight subtly different. Plumage unmistakable *rose-pink, with glossy black head, neck, wings and tail, and a distinctive crest.* Bill orange-yellow, legs pink; in winter bill is brown. Juvenile is sandy brown, with darker wings and tail and no crest; *paler* than young Starling, even in flight, and further distinguished by *yellowish bill.* (But beware occasional rather similar biscuit-coloured young Starlings.) Gregarious, even when nesting. Often associates with Starlings, particularly when feeding among cattle.

Voice: Flight-notes like Starling; feeding flocks maintain rapid, high-pitched chatter, louder and more musical than Starlings'.

Habitat and Range: Open country, agricultural land, cliffs, steppes. Breeds in holes among stones on open ground, and in walls or wood-stacks. Passage in Greece, breeding irregularly in S.E. Europe, W. to Hungary and Italy and occurring in summer and autumn increasingly erratically westward over rest of Europe to British Isles, Iceland.

STARLING *Sturnus vulgaris* page 197

Du – Spreeuw Fr – Etourneau sansonnet
Ge – Star Sw – Stare

Identification: 8½″. Blackish, glossed bronze-green and purple. *Short tail; pointed wings; long sharp bill.* Plumage closely speckled in winter, particularly female. Juvenile mouse-brown, with whitish throat. Bill of adult dark in winter, lemon-yellow in spring. Jaunty, quarrelsome and garrulous. Flight direct and rapid, gliding occasionally. Feeds and roosts gregariously. Occurs in huge flocks in autumn and winter, congregating in dense, noisy throngs on city buildings, woods or reed-beds at dusk.

Voice: A harsh descending "*tcheeer*." Also a medley of clear whistles, clicks, rattles and chuckles, woven into a long, rambling song, delivered from chimney-pot or tree-top. A good mimic.

← SNOW FINCH
Resident, rarely to lower levels in winter. Vagrant Heligoland, central Europe, Balearics

STARLING →
Partial migrant. Has bred Spain

Habitat: Equally at home in town or country. Breeds in holes in trees, buildings, thatches, nest-boxes, etc., or holes in ground in barren areas. Map p. 303.

SPOTLESS STARLING *Sturnus unicolor* page 197

Du – Zwarte spreeuw Fr – Etourneau unicolore
Ge – Einfarbstar Sw – Svart stare

Identification: 8½″. Indistinguishable at a distance from Starling, but at short range male in breeding plumage is obviously *blacker*, glossed with purple and *without spots*; bill yellow. Female is duller. In winter both adults are greyish-black, speckled with small, arrow-shaped white spots. Juvenile like dark young Starling. Behaviour and flight like Starling.

Voice: Louder and shriller than Starling's; notably a whistling "*seeooo*."

Habitat and Range: Usually in small colonies on cliffs and in towns and villages, locally in wooded regions and around isolated farms. Nests in holes in trees, cliffs, ruins, under eaves, etc. Resident in Spain, Portugal, Corsica, Sardinia, Sicily.

ORIOLES: Oriolidae

GOLDEN ORIOLE *Oriolus oriolus* page 197

Du – Wielewaal Fr – Loriot
Ge – Pirol Sw – Sommargylling

Identification: 9½″. Male unmistakable *brilliant yellow, with black wings and tail*, latter boldly marked with yellow. Female and juvenile yellowish-green with darker wings and tails and lightly streaked greyish under-parts, difficult to see in foliage. May be confused with Green Woodpecker, which has yellow rump but is much heavier, with red on head. Flight rapid, in long undulations with characteristic upward sweep to regain tree-cover. Normally stays well hidden in tree-tops.

Voice: A loud, fluty whistle "*weela-weeo*," or "*chuck-chuck-weeo*," from hidden perch. Alarm a harsh "*chr-r-r*." Also several harsh, rather Jay-like notes.

Habitat: Essentially arboreal; well timbered parks, old orchards, river banks, woods, seldom in open. Nest usually slung between horizontally forked branches. Map p. 305.

CROWS: Corvidae

The largest of the perching birds, with black or boldly patterned plumage. Longish, powerful bills. Sexes similar. Tree, cliff or hole nesting.

SIBERIAN JAY *Perisoreus infaustus*   page 197
    Du – Taiga gaai   Fr – Mésangeai imitateur
    Ge – Unglückshäher   Sw – Lavskrika

Identification: 12″. *Fox-red wing feathers, rump and especially outer feathers of well-graduated tail* are conspicuous in flight. Crown and nape dull sooty brown; wings, back, centre tail-feathers and underparts mouse-grey, with rufous flanks and under tail-coverts. Retiring and usually silent in breeding season, otherwise perky and confident. Agile in clinging to tips of pine branches to reach cones.

Voice: A cheerful *"kook, kook,"* and a raucous *"chair"*; also *"whisk-ee."*

Habitat: Thick northern coniferous and birch woods, resorting to outskirts of camps and villages in winter. Usually nests in pine, on branch close to trunk. Map below.

JAY *Garrulus glandarius*   page 197
    Du – Vlaamse gaai   Fr – Geai des chênes
    Ge – Eichelhäher   Sw – Nötskrika

Identification: 13½″. Pinkish-brown body, *white rump contrasting with black tail,* bold white patch on wings, *blue and black barred wing-coverts,* streaked black and white erectile crown feathers. Eyes pale blue. Flight heavy. Often in small noisy parties.

Voice: A penetrating, raucous *"skraaak,"* sometimes in chorus. Various harsh notes and subdued chuckling, clicking and mewing.

Habitat: Rarely far from trees. Usually nests in well secluded coniferous and deciduous woods. Map p. 306.

AZURE-WINGED MAGPIE *Cyanopica cyanus*   page 197
    Du – Blauwe ekster   Fr – Pie-bleue
    Ge – Blauelster   Sw – Blåskata

Identification: 13½″. Easily recognised by *rich black cap* extending to nape and below eyes, *blue wings* with black inner edges to primaries, and long, graduated *blue tail,* or by *distinctive voice.* Upper-parts brownish-grey, under-parts pale, with white throat. Behaviour con-

← GOLDEN ORIOLE
*Summer visitor.
Annual S.E. England (sometimes nests). Vagrant Ireland, Scotland, Iceland, Faeroes, Norway*

SIBERIAN JAY →
Mainly resident. Vagrant s. to Czechoslovakia

458
459

fident and perky, roaming the country in noisy bands; more secretive in breeding season. Actions resemble Magpie's.

Voice: A querulous "*zhreee*," with rising inflection.

Habitat and Range: Gardens, orchards, olive and eucalyptus groves and woods, particularly where ilex and pine are abundant. Builds open nest, usually in fork of pine, ilex, poplar or oak. Breeds in scattered groups. Resident in central and S. Spain, Portugal.

MAGPIE *Pica pica* page 197

Du – Ekster   Fr – Pie bavarde
Ge – Elster   Sw – Skata

Identification: 18″. Unmistakably *contrasting black and white plumage and long tail*. Scapulars, flanks and belly white; remainder black, glossed blue, green and purple. Often in small parties; large gatherings occur in winter.

Voice: A loud, rapid "*chak-chak-chak-chak*." Various not unmusical chattering and piping notes in breeding season.

Habitat: Farm-lands and open country with hedges and some trees. Builds domed nest in tall trees, thorn bushes, hedgerows, wood-edges, even bramble-patches. Map below.

NUTCRACKER *Nucifraga caryocatactes* page 197

Du – Notenkraker   Fr – Casse-noix moucheté
Ge – Tannenhäher   Sw – Nötkråka

Identification: 12½″. Dark chocolate brown, *boldly speckled with white*. Long, heavy, blackish bill. Very conspicuous *white under tail-coverts*, with broad white border to under-side of shortish black tail (upper side shows only narrow white tip). Wings blackish and very broad in flight. Flight Jay-like. Often in small parties, except in breeding season. Likes perching on tree-tops.

Voice: A harsh "*kror*" and a loud, rasping "*krair*," often repeated fairly quickly 4-6 times, also a Jay-like "*skraaak*." In breeding season various croaks, clicks and mewing notes.

← JAY
Partial migrant in northern part of range

MAGPIE →
Resident

Habitat: Mainly coniferous forests in mountainous regions, also deciduous woods in winter. Breeds in conifers. Map below.

CHOUGH *Pyrrhocorax pyrrhocorax* page 197

Du – Alpenkraai   Fr – Crave à bec rouge
Ge – Alpenkrähe   Sw – Alpkråka

Identification: 15½″. Glossy, blue-black plumage, *long, curved red bill and red legs.* Flight strong, buoyant and frequently acrobatic, with widely separated, up-curved primaries when soaring. Sociable. Easily distinguished from Jackdaw by total absence of grey plumage and from yellow-billed Alpine Chough by *longer, red bill.*
Voice: A long, high-pitched "*kyaw*," not unlike Jackdaw, but more musical. Also several gull-like calls "*kwuk-uk-uk*," etc.
Habitat: Mountains and locally cliffs and rocky outcrops near the sea. Nests in cleft rocks, cliff ledges, caves. Map below.

ALPINE CHOUGH *Pyrrhocorax graculus* page 197

Du – Alpenkauw   Fr – Chocard à bec jaune
Ge – Alpendohle   Sw – Alpkaja

Identification: 15″. Distinguished from Chough by much *shorter and straighter yellow bill.* Legs are red. At short range plumage looks blacker, less shot with blue. Behaviour similar. Juvenile is duller, with blackish legs.
Voice: Less vocal than Chough; a rippling "*chirrish*" and a shrill, explosive "*tchiupp*."
Habitat: Mountains. Does not normally descend to lowlands, nor occur on sea-coasts. Nests in cleft rocks and in ruins. Map 308.

JACKDAW *Corvus monedula* page 309

Du – Kauw   Fr – Choucas des tours
Ge – Dohle   Sw – Kaja

Identification: 13″. Black, with *grey nape* and ear-coverts. Underparts dark grey. Eye distinctively pale grey. *Smaller size,* quicker wing-beat, jaunty actions, *shorter bill* and characteristic voice easily

← NUTCRACKER
Mainly resident, but at times Siberian race invades Europe as far as Britain, France, Spain, Portugal

CHOUGH →
Resident

463   464

distinguish it from Rook and crows. Gregarious, often with Rooks and Starlings. Scandinavian form *C. m. monedula* generally has paler collar and under-parts and a barely discernible white patch either side of neck.

Voice: Unmistakable *"chak"* and, when excited, a chattering *"chaka-chaka-chack"*; also *"kya"* and widely varying breeding calls.

Habitat: Parks, cliffs, old buildings, farm-lands. Nests sociably in holes in trees, buildings, cliffs, occasionally in burrows and in branches of trees. Map below.

ROOK *Corvus frugilegus*   page 309

    Du – Roek   Fr – Corbeau freux
    Ge – Saatkrähe   Sw – Råka

Identification: 18″. Black, with iridescent gloss. Distinguished from crows by *bare, whitish face and more slender, more pointed greyish-black bill*; thighs appear noticeably shaggy when walking. Juvenile is duller, with fully feathered black face; more easily confused with Carrion Crow, but bill is always more slender. Flight direct and regular, with faster wing-beats than Carrion Crow's. Gregarious.

Voice: Has wide vocabulary. Usual notes, *"kaw"* or *"kaaa."* Voice much less harsh than Carrion Crow's.

Habitat: Prefers agricultural areas with some trees. Nests and roosts *in colonies* in tree-tops. Map p. 310.

CARRION CROW *Corvus corone*   page 309

    Du – Zwarte kraai   Fr – Corneille noire
    Ge – Rabenkrähe   Sw – Svart kråka

Identification: 18½″. All black; glossy in good light. Heavy black bill. Flight direct, slow and regular; soars rarely. Usually solitary or in pairs, except when roosting. Distinguished from immature Rook by heavier, more rounded bill; from Hooded Crow (a subspecies) by uniform black plumage; from Raven by much smaller size, less massive bill, squarer tail, but most readily recognised *by voice*.

← ALPINE CHOUGH
Resident. Vagrant Czechoslovakia

JACKDAW →
Partial migrant. Vagrant to Iceland, Corsica

CROWS

Grey back and belly

HOODED CROW

All black; heavy bill

CARRION CROW

Grey nape

Bare face patch

JACKDAW

Shaggy "trousers"

ROOK

Shaggy throat; massive bill

RAVEN

Wedge-shaped tail

THE CROW FAMILY

Voice: A harsh, croaking "*kraa*" repeated 3-4 times. Also querulous, repeated "*keerk*" and a muffled metallic "*konk*."

Habitat: Moors, cultivated country with some trees, sea-shores, even town parks. Usually nests in trees, occasionally on cliffs. Map below.

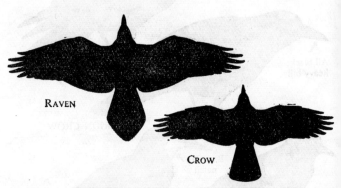

RAVEN

CROW

FLIGHT SILHOUETTES OF RAVEN AND CROW
(Carrion Crow and Hooded Crow have same silhouette)

HOODED CROW *Corvus corone cornix*   page 309

Du – Bonte kraai   Fr – Corneille mantelée
Ge – Nebelkrähe   Sw – Grå kråka

Identification: 18½″. Easily distinguished from Carrion Crow (of which it is a subspecies) and Rook by *grey back and under-parts*. Remainder black. Voice, habits and habitat as Carrion Crow, with which it interbreeds where ranges overlap. Northern race is *C. c. cornix*; southern is *C. c. sardonius*. Map 211.

← ROOK
Partial migrant.
Has bred Switz.
Vagrant Iceland,
N. Scandinavia

CARRION CROW →
Mainly resident.
Vagrant Ireland,
Hungary, Poland,
Scandinavia

RAVEN *Corvus corax* page 309

Du – Raaf Fr – Grand corbeau
Ge – Kolkrabe Sw – Korp

Identification: 25″. Large size, *massive black bill*, shaggy throat-feathers, *wedge-shaped* end of tail and *deep*, distinctive voice, easily distinguish it from smaller crows. Plumage black, iridescent in good light. Powerful, direct flight; often soars and glides; acrobatic flight especially during courtship.

Voice: A repeated, deep "*prruk*"; also a high metallic "*tok*"; many other croaking and clucking notes.

Habitat: Frequents and breeds on cliffs, mountains, also in trees Map below.

← Hooded Crow
*Partial migrant.
Vagrant Iceland,
Spain, Balearics*

Raven →
*Mainly resident.
Winters through-
out Sweden*

Accidentals

"Accidentals" are defined as species which have been recorded fewer than twenty times within the geographical area embraced by this book. The following notes give the salient field marks of 114 species. The geographical origin of each species is indicated in brackets, followed by the European countries in which it has been recorded at least once. In the case of species most likely to be seen in Europe in immature or winter plumages, these are briefly described.

WANDERING ALBATROSS *Diomedea exulans*. Largest ocean bird (11 ft. wing-span). Mainly white, with black wing-tips and a little dark mottling on wing-coverts and tip of tail. Bill pale flesh. Female has darkish patch on crown. Immature mainly brown, with white face and throat; wings blackish above, white below, except for black tips. (Southern oceans.) Accidental France, Belgium.

BLACK-BROWED ALBATROSS *Diomedea melanophris*. 6-7 ft. wing-span. Easily confused with Yellow-nosed and Grey-headed. All have white or greyish head and neck and white rump and under-parts, contrasting with dark grey or sooty back, tail and upper-surfaces of wings. All have dark mark near eye, but in Black-browed this usually extends as streak *through and behind*. Adult has *pinkish-yellow bill*; white under-surfaces of wings *broadly* margined blackish on leading edges, *narrowly* on trailing edges. Immature has greyish head and nec (like many adult Yellow-nosed and most Grey-headed) and dark or light horn-coloured bill, but under-wings have *very broad dark margins*, with *narrow white* centres. (Southern oceans.) Accidental northwards to British Isles, Norway, Faeroes.

YELLOW-NOSED ALBATROSS *Diomedea chlororhynchos*. 6-7 ft. wing-span. Adult distinguished from Black-browed by *black* bill, with *golden-yellow along the top*; under-wings white, with *narrow blackish border front and rear*. Immature has *black* bill; head and neck white, with no grey tinge; under-wing pattern as adult. (Southern oceans.) Accidental Iceland.

GREY-HEADED ALBATROSS *Diomedea chrysostoma*. Resembles Yellow-nosed, but adult has *yellow streak along base as well as top of bill*. Under-wing pattern like Black-browed. Immature has dark bill and greyish head and is difficult to distinguish from young Black-browed, but under-wing is dusky with pale centre, rather than distinctly margined; usually has only indistinct triangular spot in front of eye. (Southern oceans.) Accidental Norway.

LIGHT-MANTLED SOOTY ALBATROSS *Phoebetria palpebrata.* 6 ft. wing-span. Distinguished by *pale ash-grey* back and underparts, *sooty face* (darkest around eye), and conspicuous broken white eye-ring. (Southern oceans.) Accidental France (?).

CAPE PIGEON (PINTADO PETREL) *Daption capensis.* Near size of Manx Shearwater. *Boldly chequered* upper-parts, *two large round white patches* on upper surface of each wing, dark head, white underparts. (Southern oceans.) Accidental Holland.

BULWER'S PETREL *Bulweria bulwerii.* Noticeably larger than Storm Petrel, a little larger than Leach's. *Entirely sooty-black*, except for grey on chin. Tail wedge-shaped and longer than in most petrels. Feet *pinkish.* (Atlantic islands.) Accidental Britain, Italy.

CAPPED PETREL (DIABLOTIN) *Pterodroma hasitata.* Size of large Manx Shearwater. Resembles Great Shearwater, but distinguished by *whitish nape and forehead* (contrasting with black cap) and more extensive white or greyish on rump. Bill is shorter and thicker than Great Shearwater's. Very rare. (Caribbean.) Accidental England.

KERMADEC PETREL *Pterodroma neglecta.* About size of Manx Shearwater. Upper-parts uniform dark brown. Head and under-parts may be either brown or white, or intermediate, but always with some white on throat. Best distinguished by *white bases to primaries*, and white patches near tips of *under-surfaces* of wings. (S. Pacific.) Accidental Britain.

COLLARED PETREL *Pterodroma leucoptera.* Smaller than Manx Shearwater. Blackish above, with grey middle of back, tail-coverts and wing-coverts. Tail blackish with *pale grey outer feathers.* Face and under-parts white, with complete or partial *grey breast-band* (sometimes under-parts are all-grey except for throat). Under-surfaces of wings white, with black edges. Feet yellowish. (S. and W. Pacific.) Accidental Wales.

LITTLE SHEARWATER *Puffinus assimilis.* Resembles miniature Manx, but feet are very dark (not pink) and *black crown does not extend below eye.* Two races occur accidentally in Europe—the Madeiran, *P. b. baroli*, is the most frequent, and the Cape Verde, *P. b. boydi*; latter has *black* under tail-coverts and is probably indistinguishable in the field from Audubon's Shearwater. (Atlantic islands.) Accidental British Isles, France, Spain, Italy, Denmark.

FRIGATE PETREL *Pelagodroma marina.* Distinguished from all other small petrels by *entirely white under-surfaces of wings and body.* Upper-parts dark, rump pale grey. White forehead and *stripe over eye*; *dark crown* and *stripe below eye.* (Atlantic islands.) Accidental Britain.

MADEIRAN PETREL *Oceanodroma castro.* Not usually distinguishable from Leach's, but has *pure white* (not grey-centred) rump-band and less deeply forked tail. (Atlantic islands.) Accidental British Isles, Spain.

MAGNIFICENT FRIGATE-BIRD *Fregata magnificens.* Large (7 ft. wing-span), black, piratical sea-bird, with very long, *deeply-forked* tail (usually carried in a long point), red throat-patch and a long, slender, hook-tipped bill. Female has white breast. Immature has completely white head and most of under-parts. (S. Atlantic.) Accidental France, Scotland.

BALD IBIS *Geronticus eremita.* Black plumage, with green, bronze and purple gloss. Head mainly bare and red, with decurved red bill. Legs dark red. (Africa, W. Asia.) Accidental S. Spain.

BAR-HEADED GOOSE *Anser indicus.* A pale "grey goose" with a *white head and two bold dark bars* around the back of the crown and nape; long white stripe down side of dark neck. (Asia.) Accidental Hungary, Finland, Sweden, Denmark, Germany.

BLACK DUCK *Anas rubripes.* Size and flight silhouette of Mallard. Dark brown (looks black at distance), with pale cheeks and sides of neck, yellowish bill, purple speculum without white border. In flight *dark body and white wing-linings* are conspicuous. (N. America.) Accidental Ireland.

FALCATED TEAL *Anas falcata.* Male has iridescent bronze-green head, with *thick shaggy nape overlying mantle*, white throat with narrow dark collar and long drooping scapulars. Female larger than Teal, brown with mottled (not streaked) flanks. (N.E. Asia.) Accidental Sweden, Czechoslovakia, Austria (France?).

RING-NECKED DUCK *Aythya collaris.* Superficially resembles Tufted, or a *black*-backed Scaup, but *pale grey flanks come to bold white peak* in front of wing. High-crowned head lacks crest. Chestnut collar visible at close range. *Two white bands across bill.* Female recalls female Pochard, but with white around eyes and base of bill. Broad grey rear-edge to wings in flight. (N. America.) Accidental British Isles, Holland.

SPECTACLED (FISCHER'S) EIDER *Somateria fischeri.* Easily distinguished from other eiders by *large, circular, pale eye-patch.* Male has back of head *and forehead* pale green; upper-parts yellowish-white; under-parts blackish. Female closely barred brown and black, with greyish-buff head and neck. (Siberia.) Occasional in Arctic Ocean, W. to Norway.

BUFFLEHEAD *Bucephala albeola.* A tiny duck. Male at rest looks chiefly white with black back; high-crowned black head, *broadly marked with white from eye around back of crown*. Female brown above, with dusky flanks, a white cheek-spot and white wing-patch. (N. America.) Accidental Britain, Iceland, Czechoslovakia.

HOODED MERGANSER *Mergus cucullatus*. Slightly longer than Smew, with typical spike-like saw-bill and slim flight silhouette, but has generally dark appearance. Male is black and white, with *fan-shaped, white, erectile crest*, outlined with black; breast white, with two black bars in front of wing, brownish flanks. Female much smaller and darker than female Goosander and Red-breasted Merganser, with dark head and neck and *prominent, bushy, buff crest*. (N. America.) Accidental Britain, Ireland.

PALLAS'S SEA EAGLE *Haliaetus leucoryphus*. Dark brown, with whitish throat and sides of head, buffish crown and nape and *a broad white band* on dark tail. Immature all-dark, with pale streaks on head. (Russia, Asia.) Accidental Norway.

AMERICAN KESTREL *Falco sparverius*. Resembles Kestrel, but tail of male is *rufous* (not grey), wings blue-grey, head much more strikingly patterned. Female resembles female Kestrel, except for strong black and white pattern on side of head. (N. America.) Accidental Denmark.

ASIATIC WHITE CRANE *Grus leucogeranus*. Snow-white plumage with elongated scapulars and black primaries. Bare fore-part of head and base of bill red. Legs reddish. (Asia.) Accidental Sweden.

SORA RAIL *Porzana carolina*. Very similar to Spotted Crake, but adult has *black patch* on face and throat. Lacks red at base of yellow bill, and the white spots on neck and upper-breast. (N. America.) Accidental British Isles.

AMERICAN PURPLE GALLINULE *Porphyrula martinica*. Size and shape of Moorhen but with *much longer, yellow legs*. Brilliant bronze above, purple head and under-parts; *all-white* under tail-coverts; red bill tipped yellow, with pale blue frontal shield. Immature like young Moorhen, but with pure white under tail-coverts and no white flank-stripe. (N. America.) Accidental Britain.

GREEN-BACKED GALLINULE *Porphyrio madagascariensis*. Very similar to Purple Gallinule (perhaps conspecific,) but smaller, with dark *blue-green* upper-parts, instead of purplish-blue. (Africa.) Accidental Sardinia, Sicily, Italy.

ALLEN'S GALLINULE *Porphyrio alleni*. Smaller than Moorhen. Plumage black, glossed bronze-green on upper-parts, reddish-blue on neck and under-parts. Bill and legs *dark red*; frontal shield *green.* (Africa.) Accidental France, Spain, Italy, Sicily, Denmark, Germany.

CASPIAN PLOVER *Charadrius asiaticus.* Slightly larger than Ringed Plover. Hair-brown above, white below. Has *broad rusty breast-band* narrowly bordered with black below. Face and eye-stripe white. Female has only faint breast-band. Male in winter resembles female. (Asia.) Accidental Britain, Heligoland, Italy, Bulgaria.

WHITE-TAILED PLOVER *Vanellus leucurus.* Lapwing size. Has *short white tail, long, bright yellow* legs; conspicuously marked, rounded black and white wings, white throat and *pale pinkish-brown* under-parts. (Asia.) Accidental France, Malta.

WESTERN SANDPIPER *Calidris mauri.* Difficult to distinguish in autumn plumage from Semi-palmated, but often has some *rusty colour on nape and scapulars* and is more coarsely marked. Bill thicker at base, *longer, often drooping slightly at tip* and carried pointing more downwards. Legs black. Less wing-stripe than Dunlin. Call a distinctive "*cheet.*" (N. America.) Accidental Scotland, Ireland.

SEMI-PALMATED SANDPIPER *Calidris pusilla.* In summer much less rufous than Least or Western, with bill thicker than Least's and usually shorter than Western's. In winter closely resembles Little Stint, but carriage less "hunched," bill stouter and upper-parts paler ochre. Calls include a distinctive "*chrrup.*" (N. America.) Accidental Britain, France.

LEAST SANDPIPER *Calidris minutilla.* Smaller and darker brown than Little Stint (in adult and first winter) and with paler yellowish or greenish legs. Bill extremely fine, often with slight downward kink at tip. Call a distinctive "*kreet.*" (N. America.) Accidental Britain, Ireland, France, Finland.

BAIRD'S SANDPIPER *Calidris bairdii.* Smaller than Pectoral, larger than stints, with *long wings well overlapping tail when folded.* Adult in summer recalls Sanderling, but first-winter birds have dark, "scaly" upper-parts and white under-parts with buff breast-patches. Bill longish with decurved tip. Call "*chur-rut,*" recalling Curlew Sandpiper. (N. America.) Accidental Britain, Ireland, Sweden.

SHARP-TAILED SANDPIPER *Calidris acuminata.* Closely resembles Pectoral, but summer adults distinguished by even black scalloping on under-parts *not forming clean-cut breast-band*; distinctly *reddish crown* and buff wash across breast. Legs greenish-grey or black (not yellowish). Call a Swallow-like "*tree-treep.*" (N.E. Asia.) Accidental Britain.

STILT SANDPIPER *Micropalama himantopus.* In summer has *strongly barred under-parts,* rusty cheek-patch below white eye-stripe and *long, spindly,* greenish legs, which project well beyond tail in flight. Slender, slightly down-curved bill is longer than in other sandpipers of similar size. No wing-bar. Lower rump white. In winter is paler and greyer, without rusty marking and with little barring, recalling Lesser Yellowlegs (but feeds like Dowitcher). (N. America.) Accidental England.

SHORT-BILLED DOWITCHER *Limnodromus griseus.* Closely resembles Long-billed Dowitcher (see p. 134), but immature is buffer, with spotted under and lateral tail-coverts; wings just overlap tail and bill is usually shorter. Call a rapid, triple *"kut-kut-kut."* (N. America.) Accidental British Isles.

SOLITARY SANDPIPER *Tringa solitaria.* A dark-winged sandpiper with *conspicuous white sides to dark tail.* Blackish under-sides of wings and olive-green legs recall Green Sandpiper, but *dark rump* is quick distinction. (N. America.) Accidental Britain, France, Iceland.

SPOTTED SANDPIPER *Tringa macularia.* In winter only slightly greyer than Common Sandpiper, but in summer distinguished by *large round black spots* (not streaks) on breast and black-tipped *yellow* bill. (N. America.) Accidental Britain, Ireland, Belgium, Germany.

ESKIMO CURLEW *Numenius borealis.* Resembles small Whimbrel, with shorter, straighter bill and *no white on rump.* Distinguished from rather similar but larger Hudsonian Whimbrel (American race of Whimbrel, which lacks white rump) by *paler,* more buffish under-parts, *cinnamon-buff* under surfaces of wings. Legs dark greenish. (N. America.) Has occurred British Isles. Now nearly extinct.

GREAT BLACK-HEADED GULL *Larus ichthyaetus.* Size of Great Black-backed. The only *big* gull with a black head in breeding season (with white marks above and below eye). Distinguished at all seasons by *massive yellow bill, with black band.* Legs yellowish-green. In winter, head is white, with dusky marks on crown and near eye. Immature has white tail with bold black band. (European Russia, Asia.) Accidental Britain, Belgium, Denmark, Sweden, Greece, Roumania. Sardinia, Malta.

LESSER CRESTED TERN *Sterna bengalensis.* About size of Sandwich, but with *rich orange-yellow* bill, and more deeply forked tail. Feet black. Crown of adult slightly crested, all-black in summer, streaked with white in winter. (Africa, Asia.) Accidental Sicily, Switzerland, S. France, Spain.

ROYAL TERN *Sterna maxima.* Resembles rather small Caspian, with *less heavy orange bill*; tail longer and more deeply forked; tips of primaries show a little less black; forehead is *white* except at beginning of breeding season; call-note *higher* and less raucous. (N. America and W. Africa.) Accidental Ireland, Spain (?).

FORSTER'S TERN *Sterna forsteri.* Adult in summer distinguished in flight from Common Tern by *silvery* primaries (paler than rest of wing), less white tail, more orange bill. In autumn has heavy spot *like an ear-cap* on side of head; bill blackish, feet sometimes yellowish. Immature lacks Common's dusky patch on forewing. (N. America.) Accidental Iceland.

BRIDLED TERN *Sterna anaethetus.* Resembles Sooty, but is smaller, with greyer back, a wide whitish collar, and the narrower white forehead-patch extending in a point *behind the eye.* (Caribbean, Africa.) Accidental British Isles.

NODDY *Anous stolidus.* The only *dark brown* tern (except immature Sooty) and the only tern with a full, *rounded* tail (Sooty has forked tail). The *whitish crown* on a dark bird gives a reverse, or "negative" effect, by contrast with other terns having dark caps and pale bodies. (Tropical and sub-tropical seas.) Accidental Germany.

CRESTED AUKLET *Aethia cristatella.* Larger than Little Auk. *Entirely dark, above and below.* Easily distinguished by *short black crest, curving forward,* and tufts of white feathers drooping from behind eye in summer (as in Parakeet Auklet). Bill orange-red with whitish tip. (N. Pacific.) Accidental Iceland.

PARAKEET AUKLET *Cyclorrhynchus psittacula.* Much larger than Little Auk. Distinguished by proportionately larger *orange-red bill and tufts of elongated white feathers* drooping from behind eye in summer. (N. Pacific.) Accidental Sweden. See also Crested Auklet.

SPOTTED SANDGROUSE *Pterocles senegallus.* Male almost uniform sandy above and below, with *orange-yellow crown, throat and cheeks* and a pale blue-grey band bordering the crown. Female is *heavily spotted* with black and has paler yellow throat and cheeks. Both sexes have long "pin-tails," white wing-linings and a *black ventral streak.* (Africa, Asia.) Accidental Sicily.

CHESTNUT-BELLIED SANDGROUSE *Pterocles exustus.* Very long "pin-tails" and *dark chestnut belly and thighs*; blackish axillaries. (Spotted has white). Male sandy-buff above, with fine dark markings, yellowish face, pinkish-buff breast, below which a *narrow black band.* Female more closely marked above; breast spotted. (Africa, Asia.) Accidental Hungary.

RUFOUS TURTLE DOVE *Streptopelia orientalis.* Slightly larger, *darker* and more rufous than Turtle Dove and *without white on tail.* Upper-parts rich dark chestnut, more closely speckled than Turtle Dove. Tips of black feathers of neck-patches and of tail-feathers are *grey* (not white). Under tail-coverts also grey. (Asia.) Accidental Britain, Scandinavia, Denmark, Italy.

BLACK-BILLED CUCKOO *Coccyzus erythrophthalmus.* Closely resembles Yellow-billed (see p. 183), but *lacks rufous on wings,* has *small* white spots on tail, entirely *black* bill and narrow red eye-ring. (N. America.) Accidental British Isles, Germany, France, Italy.

AFRICAN MARSH OWL *Asio capensis.* Not unlike dark Short-eared, but under-parts are spotted and vermiculated, not streaked, and wings have *large pale patch on distal half;* eyes are black. Toes almost bare, feet blackish. Short ear-tufts. (N.W. Africa.) Accidental Spain, Portugal.

AMERICAN NIGHTHAWK *Chordeiles minor.* Smaller, darker and greyer than European nightjars and less crepuscular. Has slightly forked tail and *bold white bands* across very long, pointed wings. Flight recalls Kestrel rather than Nightjar. (N. America.) Accidental England, Iceland.

NEEDLE-TAILED SWIFT *Hirundapus caudacutus.* A large swift with a very short, squared tail. Blackish, with metallic green gloss on wings, crown and tail and *greyish patch high on back.* White forehead, throat and *conspicuous horse-shoe mark* on under tail-coverts. (E. Asia.) Accidental Britain, Ireland, Italy, Finland.

WHITE-RUMPED SWIFT *Apus affinis. Smaller and shorter-winged* than Swift, and has almost square tail and *broad white rump.* (Africa, Asia.) Acccidental Italy, Malta.

PIED KINGFISHER *Ceryle rudis.* A large, shaggily crested, *black and white* kingfisher (twice size of Kingfisher), with a broad and a narrow black band across white breast. Female has only one breast band. Occurs on fresh and salt water. (Africa, Asia.) Accidental Greece, Poland.

BELTED KINGFISHER *Ceryle alcyon.* Larger than Pied (size of Jackdaw). *Blue-grey* above, white below, with a prominent, ragged crest and a broad grey breast-band; female also has a chestnut band below the grey. (N. America.) Accidental Holland, Iceland.

BLUE-CHEEKED BEE-EATER *Merops superciliosus.* Immediately distinguished from *M. apiaster* by almost uniform green plumage without any brown on upper parts, *warm orange* throat-patch and *flashing copper under-surfaces of wings.* (Africa, Asia.) Accidental Britain, Italy, Greece, Malta, S. France, Scilly Isles.

YELLOW-BELLIED SAPSUCKER *Sphyrapicus varius.* Size of Great Spotted Woodpecker. Male has brilliantly patterned red, black and white head, with red on forehead *and throat,* above black breast-patch. Female's throat is white. Long white wing-patch much narrower than Great Spotted's. Back finely barred black and white; rump white; under-parts pale yellowish. Immature barred brownish above and below. (N. America.) Accidental Iceland.

DESERT LARK *Ammomanes deserti.* Dumpy, with rather flat crown and *longish, yellowish, pointed* bill. Pale grey-brown above, faintly streaked on head; buffish-white below, faintly mottled on throat. In flight rump and primaries show warm buff. (N. Africa, Middle East.) Accidental Spain.

BAR-TAILED DESERT LARK *Ammomanes cincturus.* Recalls small Desert Lark, but neater, with *round head and small, stubby bill* giving bunting-like appearance; often more rufous, with primaries and tail feathers variably tipped with black. (N. Africa, Middle East.) Accidental Malta.

HOOPOE LARK *Alaemon alaudipes.* A swift-running, long-tailed desert species, suggesting small Hoopoe in flight. Pale sandy-grey above, with whitish eye-stripe and dark mark through eye. Long, slightly down-curved bill. Long creamy legs. *Two brilliant white bands almost full length of blackish wings.* Under-parts dirty white, strongly spotted on upper breast. (N. Africa, Asia.) Accidental Malta.

INDIAN SAND LARK *Calandrella raytal.* Slightly smaller than Short-toed Lark, with *very pale silvery grey upper-parts* and white throat and upper breast. (Asia.) Accidental Spain.

BIMACULATED LARK *Melanocorypha bimaculata.* Distinguished from Calandra by smaller size, *more rufous* plumage, *buff* (not white) outer tail-feathers and tips to secondaries. *Double* neck patches are less clear-cut. (Asia.) Accidental Britain, Finland, Italy.

INDIAN TREE PIPIT *Anthus hodgsoni.* Smaller than Tree Pipit; more olivaceous above, with softer streaking; more heavily streaked on breast. (Asia.) Accidental Norway, Heligoland.

CITRINE (YELLOW-HEADED) WAGTAIL *Motacilla citreola.* Under-parts, *head and neck* canary-yellow; upper-parts blue-grey, with black hind-collar. Female browner and duller, lacks hind-collar. In winter resembles typical winter *flava* from in front, *alba* from behind. Wags tail and bobs head less than *alba.* (Siberia.) Accidental Britain, Germany.

COMMON BULBUL *Pycnonotus barbatus.* Recalls long-tailed thrush, perky and voluble. Earth-brown above, with *rounded, noticeably dark head*. Throat, wings and tail also dark; under-parts paler, with *yellow or white under tail-coverts*. (Africa, Asia.) Accidental Spain.

ISABELLINE SHRIKE *Lanius isabellinus*. *Strikingly pale*, sandy to grey-brown above, whiter below, with pale rufous crown and rump. Lores and ear-coverts jet-black. Tail *reddish to pale red*, without white. Wings brown, with conspicuous white patch at base of primaries, forming bar in flight. May be conspecific with Red-backed Shrike. (Asia.) Accidental Britain, Ireland, Heligoland.

CATBIRD *Dumetella carolinensis*. A slender, long-tailed, dark *slate-grey* bird, with a *black cap* and *chestnut-red* under tail-coverts. About size of Starling, but tail is much longer. Has distinctive mewing call-note. (N. America.) Accidental Germany.

SIBERIAN ACCENTOR *Prunella montanella*. Male has *black crown and face*, with *broad ochreous stripe* over eye and around dark cheek. Upper-parts dark red-brown, rump and tail grey-brown. Under-parts warm buff, with streaked flanks. Female duller, with whiter under-parts. (N. Asia.) Accidental Czechoslovakia, Greece, Italy.

GRAY'S GRASSHOPPER WARBLER *Locustella fasciolata*. Resembles large Savi's Warbler, near size of Great Reed. *Unstreaked* olive-brown above, with greyish cheeks and breast contrasting with white throat. Rufous under tail-coverts. (Asia.) Accidental France, Denmark.

PADDYFIELD WARBLER *Acrocephalus agricola*. Difficult to distinguish from Reed, Blyth's Reed and Marsh Warblers, though supercilium slightly more evident. Usually paler and more rufous above than Reed and Blyth's Reed; more rufous and less olive than Marsh. (S. Russia, Asia.) Accidental Scotland, Heligoland, Sweden, Roumania.

THICK-BILLED WARBLER *Acrocephalus aedon*. Very similar in size, shape and coloration to Great Reed Warbler, but *bill is deeper and shorter*, tail longer in proportion, rump redder, legs blue and *lacks eye-stripe*. In the hand, rounded first primary is diagnostic. (S.E. Asia.) Accidental Scotland.

BOOTED WARBLER *Hippolais caligata*. Like small Olivaceous, but more *buffish* above, with *shorter, finer* bill and more rounded head. Rudimentary supercilium. In winter looks very pale, silvery-white below, with faint buff upper-breast and flanks. (Asia.) Accidental Scotland, Heligoland.

DESERT WARBLER *Sylvia nana*. Very pale, sandy-greyish above, slightly rufous on rump; whitish below, with slightly buffish flanks; tail well rounded, pale rufous-brown, with whitish outer feathers. Eyes and legs *pale yellowish.* Spectacled Warbler is much darker, larger, with dark cheeks and dark eyes. (N. Africa, European Russia, Asia.) Accidental Italy, Sweden, Greece.

DUSKY WARBLER *Phylloscopus fuscatus.* Darker and browner than other *Phylloscopus* occurring in Europe. Lacks green and yellow coloration. Unstreaked darkish brown above (no wing-bar), buffish flanks, whitish under-parts, *rusty-white* eye-stripe contrasting with darkly mottled rusty brown ear-coverts. Distinguished from rather similar Radde's Warbler by darker, more rufous appearance, rusty (not creamy) eye-stripe, browner legs, finer bill and harsh "*tchak-tchak*" call-note. Usually feeds *on ground* in damp localities. (Asia.) Accidental Britain, Heligoland (?).

RADDE'S WARBLER *Phylloscopus schwarzi.* Larger and longer-tailed than Chiffchaff, recalling Dusky Warbler. Has *very long, conspicuous creamy supercilium above blackish streak from bill through eye almost to nape.* Stout bill, yellowish legs, pale brownish-olive upper-parts, *creamy-white* under-parts. Arboreal. Call-note, a nervous "*chik-chik.*" (Asia.) Accidental Britain, France, Heligoland, Sweden.

BROWN FLYCATCHER *Muscicapa latirostris.* Resembles small female Pied Flycatcher; distinguished by *absence of white wing-patch* and, at close range, by *narrow white eye-ring.* Distinguished from Spotted Flycatcher by smaller size and *lack of streaking* on crown and breast. (E. Asia.) Accidental Britain, Norway, Denmark, Faeroes.

WHITE-CROWNED BLACK WHEATEAR *Oenanthe leucopyga.* Very like Black Wheatear, though both sexes are usually *blue*-black, usually (but not always) with some white on crown. Rump, under tail-coverts *and ventral region* are always white, as is tail, except for terminal half of centre feathers, which is black. (N. Africa, W. Asia.) Accidental Malta.

MOUSSIER'S REDSTART *Phoenicurus moussieri.* Short tail and bush-perching habit give impression of cross between Redstart and Stonechat. Male distinguished from other redstarts by *white half-collar and wing-patch.* Upper-parts and head are black; forehead and eye-stripe white; rump, tail and under-parts *orange.* Female is grey-brown above, brownish-orange below, usually lacking white wing-patch. (N. Africa.) Accidental Italy, Malta.

SIBERIAN RUBYTHROAT *Luscinia calliope.* At a distance resembles large Bluethroat. Male's throat is *bright scarlet*, eye-stripe and moustachial stripe white, breast grey, remainder of plumage olive-brown. Female has whitish throat, buffish eye-stripe. (E. European Russia, Asia.) Accidental France, Italy, Iceland.

HERMIT THRUSH *Catharus guttatus.* Considerably smaller than Song Thrush, which it superficially resembles. Distinguished by *bright rufous rump and tail*. Legs are flesh colour. Has distinctive habit of cocking its tail and dropping it slowly. (N. America.) Accidental Iceland, Germany.

GREY-CHEEKED THRUSH *Catharus minimus.* Very like Olive-backed Thrush, but with very pale buffish tinge on upper breast and less distinct buff eye-ring. Identified at close range by *greyish cheeks*. (N. America.) Accidental Germany, Britain, France.

TICKELL'S THRUSH *Turdus unicolor.* Size of Song Thrush. Uniform grey, or grey-brown, above; greyish or buffish across breast, usually (not always) with necklace of sparse streaking on upper breast. (Himalayas.) Accidental Heligoland.

PINE BUNTING *Emberiza leucocephala.* Male has *white* crown and cheeks, edged with black; chestnut throat, eye-stripe and rump; whitish under-parts, with indistinctly speckled breast-band and flanks. Female like Yellowhammer, with all latter's yellow parts white. (E. European Russia, Asia.) Accidental Europe, westwards to Britain, Iceland.

SIBERIAN MEADOW BUNTING *Emberiza cioides.* Male has bold white supercilium and throat, isolated black moustachial stripes and *dark chestnut crown and cheeks*. Usually has pale chestnut breast-band. Upper-parts like Rock Bunting. Female has similar, though fainter, pattern and streaked crown. (E. Asia.) Accidental Italy.

YELLOW-BROWED BUNTING *Emberiza chrysophrys.* Black head, with *narrow white crown-stripe and yellow eye-stripe*. Upper-parts brown, streaked blackish; under-parts white, with blackish streaks on breast and flanks. Female duller, more spotted below. (E. Asia.) Accidental Belgium, France.

CHESTNUT BUNTING *Emberiza rutila.* Male has *chestnut-red* head, upper-parts and breast; under-parts bright yellow, with chestnut flank-stripes. Female olive-brown above, streaked blackish; crown slightly rufous, rump uniform chestnut; under-parts dull yellow; throat white, bordered with chestnut. (E. Asia.) Accidental Holland, France.

RED-HEADED BUNTING *Emberiza bruniceps.* Male has chestnut head and throat, yellow nape and rump contrasting with greenish mantle. Female resembles Black-headed, with greener mantle, no yellow on under tail-coverts. Frequent cage-bird—beware "escapes." (Asia.) Accidental westward across Europe to Norway, Britain, Italy.

BLACK-FACED BUNTING *Emberiza spodocephala.* Male has dark *olive-grey head*, blacker around bill, and *yellow belly*; wings and tail blackish-brown. Female is browner, without black on face and with yellow throat and breast streaked with brown. (Siberia.) Accidental Heligoland.

PALLAS'S REED BUNTING *Emberiza pallasi.* Resembles Reed Bunting, but has *pale yellow* instead of white nape and noticeably paler upper-parts. Song quite distinct from Reed Bunting's, more like Ortolan's, but faster and higher-pitched. (Asia.) Accidental Denmark.

SONG SPARROW *Melospiza melodia.* Bunting-like. Boldly streaked brown above and below, with *black spot in centre of breast*; heavy streaking extends well down flanks. *Broad buff supercilium.* Slightly rufous on wings. Immature may lack breast-spot. Flits tail open during flight. (N. America.) Accidental Scotland.

FOX SPARROW *Passerella iliaca.* Much larger than House Sparrow, with *conspicuous chestnut tail* and bunting-like shape. Upper-parts boldly streaked rufous brown; under-parts creamy; breast and flanks heavily streaked with rufous brown. (N. America.) Accidental British Isles, Germany, Italy, Iceland.

WHITE-THROATED SPARROW *Zonotrichia albicollis.* Grey breasted, with clean-cut *white throat-patch*, boldly striped *black and white* crown, and broad supercilium (yellow before eye, white behind). Wings and under-parts resemble House Sparrow. Immature has brown and buff head-stripes. (N. America.) Accidental Britain.

SLATE-COLOURED JUNCO *Junco hyemalis.* Smaller than Chaffinch. Uniform dark *slate-grey*, with *conspicuous white lower breast, belly and outer tail-feathers*, and stubby whitish bill. (N. America.) Accidental Ireland, Iceland, Italy.

ROSE-BREASTED GROSBEAK *Pheucticus ludovicianus.* Size of thrush, with *Hawfinch-like bill.* Male striking black and white above, with *rosy patch on white breast*; in winter under-parts streaked. Female has conspicuous white stripes on head, dull brown above, with dark streaks on back and under-parts. Both sexes have double white wing-bars. (N. America.) Accidental Ireland.

INDIGO BUNTING *Passerina cyanea.* Smaller than House Sparrow. Male *rich, deep blue all over*; in winter resembles brown female though retaining some blue on wings and tail. Female featureless, plain brown, paler below with indistinct streaking. (N. America.) Accidental Iceland.

SUMMER TANAGER *Piranga rubra.* Size of Corn Bunting. Adult male unmistakable, *rose-red all over*, with rather large whitish bill. Female yellowish-olive above, deep yellow below. Immature male patched red and green. (N. America.) Accidental Wales.

BLACK-AND-WHITE WARBLER *Mniotilta varia.* Strongly striped *black and white* on head, body and wings. Female has whiter under-parts. Has habit of *tree-creeping.* (N. America.) Accidental Scotland.

TENNESSEE WARBLER *Vermivora peregrina.* Size and pattern of Arctic Warbler. In summer male has distinctive *blue-grey head* contrasting with greenish back; conspicuous white supercilium. Female has less grey head and yellow under-parts. In autumn plumage both sexes are closer to Arctic Warbler, though *greener* above with *yellower* under-parts and supercilium and *dark* legs. (N. America.) Accidental Iceland.

PARULA WARBLER *Parula americana.* Unmistakable *bluish* above, with *yellow* throat and breast and two conspicuous white wing-bars. Male has *dark rusty breast-band.* (N. America.) Accidental Iceland.

MYRTLE WARBLER *Dendroica coronata.* In all plumages has *bright yellow rump*, yellow on crown and in front of each wing. Male blue-grey above (brownish in winter and female), with bold inverted "U" on white breast and flanks (partly obscured into streaks in winter). White patches each side of spread tail. (N. America.) Accidental England.

BLACK-THROATED GREEN WARBLER *Dendroica virens.* Male has *bright yellow* face framed by black throat and olive-green crown and upper-parts; two conspicuous white wing-bars and white under-parts, with black-streaked flanks. Female and autumn birds have much less black on throat and flanks. (N. America.) Accidental Heligoland.

NORTHERN WATERTHRUSH *Seiurus noveboracensis.* Resembles plump, sparrow-size thrush with short tail, conspicuous *yellowish supercilium* and heavily streaked yellowish under-parts. Behaviour and habitat recall sandpiper, running along water's edge and "teetering" constantly. (N. America.) Accidental France, England.

YELLOWTHROAT *Geothlypis trichas.* Size of Wood Warbler. Male greenish-brown above, with *broad black "mask" from cheek across forehead* (partly obscured in winter) framed with pale ash-grey; *canary-yellow* throat, with pale buffish breast and flanks and *white belly.* Cocks tail. Female duller, lacks black "mask," but retains white belly. (N. America.) Accidental England.

AMERICAN REDSTART *Setophaga ruticilla.* Largely black with *bright orange patches on wings and tail*; belly white. Female olive-brown, white below, with *yellow* patches on wings and tail. Immature resembles female, but the yellow is tinged orange in young males. Tail constantly fanned. (N. America.) Accidental France.

RED-EYED VIREO *Vireo olivaceus.* Size and shape of Blackcap, but with shorter tail. Adult olive-green above, whitish below, with *blue-grey crown* and conspicuous *black-bordered white supercilium.* Red eyes. Immature has duller head-pattern. Call, a nasal *"chway."* (N. America.) Accidental British Isles, Iceland.

BOBOLINK *Dolichonyx oryzivorus.* Larger than Sky Lark. A stout meadow-bird, with *black face and under-parts*; conspicuous white band on "shoulders" and white rump; *back of head dull yellow*; back strongly striped. Female and immature yellowish-buff, heavily streaked on crown and upper-parts. (N. America). Accidental Britain.

YELLOW-HEADED BLACKBIRD *Xanthocephalus xanthocephalus.* Blackbird-size. Male black, with *brilliant golden-yellow head and breast*; shows white wing-patch in flight. Bill rather heavy. Female smaller and browner, with paler yellow face, throat and breast; lower breast streaked with white. Calls a low *"kruck,"* or *"kak."* (N. America.) Accidental Denmark, Sweden.

BALTIMORE ORIOLE *Icterus galbula.* Smaller than Golden Oriole. Male vivid *orange with black head, back, wings and tail.* Bold white wing-bar conspicuous in flight. Female olive above, yellow below, with two white wing-bars. (N. America.) Accidental Britain, Ireland, Iceland.

PALLAS'S ROSEFINCH *Carpodacus roseus.* Larger than Scarlet Rosefinch (of similar form). Male is crimson, browner on back, wings and tail; under-parts crimson, with small white speckles. Female streaked pale brown, slightly rosy on rump. (Asia.) Accidental Hungary.

DAURIAN JACKDAW *Corvus dauuricus.* Easily distinguished from Jackdaw by *whitish breast* and broad *whitish collar around throat.* Immature resembles young Jackdaw. (Asia.) Accidental Finland.

Selected Bibliography

Reference list of the leading ornithological handbooks and check-lists concerning the birds of Europe

A Field Guide to the Birds of Britain and Europe is now available in an American edition, also in French, German, Dutch, Swedish, Danish, Finnish, Icelandic, Spanish and Italian. Hungarian and other editions are in preparation. Each has been translated and edited by leading local ornithologists.

GENERAL
VAURIE, C. (1959-65), *The Birds of the Palearctic Fauna.* Vol. 1 (Passeri-formes). Vol. 2 (Non-passerines). The latest complete taxonomic work.

VOOUS, K. H. 1960, *Atlas of European Birds.* Illustrated. Shows total breeding ranges of all species occurring in Europe.

SCOTT, PETER (1949), *Key to the Wildfowl of the World.* Illustrated. Published in the Annual Report of the Wildfowl Trust.

BOSWALL, JEFFERY (1964). *A Discography of Palearctic Bird Sound Recordings.* Lists all published and many unpublished recordings of voices of European (and Palearctic) birds. Supplement to *British Birds.*

AFRICA (NORTH)
ETCHÉCOPAR, R. D. & HÜE, F. (1964), *Les Oiseaux du Nord de l'Afrique.* Illustrated.

AUSTRIA
BAUER, K., and ROKITANSKY, G. (1951), *Verzeichnis der Vögel Oster-reichs.* The latest Austrian check-list.

BELGIUM
VERHEYEN, R. (1934-51), *L'Institut Royal des Sciences Naturelles de Belgique* has published a comprehensive illustrated work on the birds of Belgium, each of the 8 volumes having a different title.

BULGARIA
PATEFF, P. (1950), *The Birds of Bulgaria.* Illustrated. English summary.
IORDANS, A. von (1940), *Beitrag zur Kenntnis der Vögel Bulgariens.*

DENMARK

SALOMONSEN, F. (1963), *Oversigt over Danmarks Fugle*. The latest Danish check-list, with English explanatory notes.

JESPERSEN, P. (1946). *The Breeding Birds of Denmark*. In English.

FRANCE

MAYAUD, N., HEIM DE BALSAC, H., and JOUARD, H. (1936), *Inventaire des Oiseaux de France*. Check-list, with details of distribution. Supplemented by *Liste des Oiseaux de France*, in *Alauda* (1953).

BARRUEL, P. (1949), *Les Oiseaux dans la Nature*. Illustrated guide to the birds of France. See also Géroudet, Switzerland.

FINLAND

MERIKALLIO, E. (1958), *Finnish Birds, their Distribution and Numbers*.

GERMANY

NIETHAMMER, G. (1937-42), *Handbuch der Deutschen Vogelkunde*. The standard handbook for Germany.

GREAT BRITAIN and IRELAND

WITHERBY, H. F., *et al.* (1938-41), *The Handbook of British Birds*, 5 vols, illustrated. A very detailed work.

HOLLOM, P. A. D. (1962), *The Popular Handbook of British Birds*. A revised and abridged edition of the above, in one volume. Illustrated.

HOLLOM, P. A. D. (1960), *The Popular Handbook of Rarer British Birds*. Describes all the rare vagrants up to 1960.

BANNERMAN, D. A. & LODGE, G. E. (1953-63), *The Birds of the British Isles*, 12 vols., illustrated.

SCOTT, PETER (1950-51), *The Swans, Geese and Ducks of the British Isles*. Published in the Annual Report of the Wildfowl Trust.

GREECE

LAMBERT, A. (1957), *A specific Check-List of the Birds of Greece*. *Ibis* 99: 43-68.

MAKATASCH, W. (1950), *Die Vogelwelt Macedoniens*. Illustrated. Embraces all Macedonia, but chiefly concerned with the southern area. In German.

HUNGARY

KEVE, A., *et al.* (1958), *Aves-Madarak*. The latest handbook on Hungarian birds.

KEVE, A. (1960), *Nomenclator Avium Hungariae*. The latest Hungarian check-list, with notes on distribution.

ICELAND

TIMMERMANN, G. (1938-49), *Die Vögel Islands*. A handbook in German.

ITALY

MOLTONI, E. (1945), *Elenco degli ucceilli italiani*. The latest check-list, with notes on distribution.

LUXEMBOURG

MORBACH, J. (1939-43), *Die Vögel der Heimat*. A handbook in German. See also Verheyen, Belgium.

NETHERLANDS

EYKMAN, C., *et al*. (1937-49), *De Nederlandsche Vogels*, 3 vols.
VAN IJZERDOORN, A. L. J. (1950), *The Breeding Birds of the Netherlands*. A systematic list, giving past and present breeding status. In English.

NORWAY

LOVENSKIOLD, H. L. (1947-50), *Håndbok over Norges Fugler*. Excellent handbook, in Norwegian. See also Curry-Lindahl, Sweden.

POLAND

SOKOLOWSKI, J. (1958), *Ptaki ziem Polskich* (The Birds of Poland), 2 vols., in Polish.

PORTUGAL

TAIT, W. (1924), *The Birds of Portugal*.

ROUMANIA

DOMBROWSKI, R. VON (1912), *Ornis Romaniae*.
LINTIA, D. (1946-55), *Pasarile din R.P.R.* (The Birds of Roumania), 3 vols., in Roumanian.

SPAIN

LLETGET, A. G. (1945), *Sinopsis de las Aves de España y Portugal*. Trab. Inst. Cienc. Nat., vol. 2. A check-list with keys.
BERNIS, F. (1954), *Prontuario de la Avifauna Española*. Check-list, giving distribution in Spain, Portugal, Balearics and Canaries.

SWEDEN

CURRY-LINDAHL, K. (1959-63), *Våra Fåglar i Norden*, 4 vols., 2nd ed. illustrated, embracing all species in Denmark, Finland, Norway and Sweden.
SWEDISH ORNITHOLOGICAL SOCIETY (1962), *Förtechning över Sveriges Fåglar*, 5th ed. Swedish check-list, with English equivalents.
ROSENBERG, E. (1961), *Fåglar i Sverige*, 4th ed., in Swedish, illustrated. Describes all species found in Sweden.

SWITZERLAND

GLUTZ VON BLOTZHEIM U. (1961), *Die Brutvögel der Schweiz.* Breeding birds of Switzerland, in German.

HALLER, W. (1951), *Unsere Vögel, Artenliste der schweizerischen Avifauna.* Swiss check-list, in German.

GEROUDET, P. (1940-51), *La Vie des Oiseaux.* An illustrated handbook of the birds of Switzerland, France and Belgium, in French. Six vols.

UNITED STATES OF AMERICA

PETERSON, ROGER (1947), *A Field Guide to the Birds.* Fully illustrated. Describes all N. American species likely to occur in Europe.

U.S.S.R.

DEMENTIEV, G. P., *et al.*, (1951-52), *Birds of the U.S.S.R* A complete illustrated handbook, in Russian, with distribution maps. Six vols.

IVANOV, A. I., *et al.* "*Ptitsy SSSR*" *Akademii Nauk. SSSR.* Part I (1951), Part II (1953) in Russian. Contains (non-Passeriformes).

PORTENKO, L.A. "*Ptitsy SSSR*" *Akademii Nauk SSSR.* Part III (1954), Part IV (1960) (contains Passeriformes).

YUGOSLAVIA

MATVEJEV, S. D. (1950), *Ornithogeographia Serbia (La Distribution et la vie des oiseaux en Serbie).* Monograph 161 of the Academie Serbe des Sciences. In Serbian, with French summary. See also Makatsch, Greece, and Stresemann's *Avifauna Macedonica* (1920).

Index

Vernacular English names are printed in bold type. Scientific names are in italics. The figures in bold type refer to the pages on which the illustrations appear. The other figures refer to the descriptive text pages. The scientific names are followed only by the text page numbers. Note that the title pages opposite the illustrations also indicate the page numbers of the corresponding text matter

331

FIELD NOTES

The Guide is intended for work in the field. When you see an unusual bird which you cannot readily identify, use these blank pages for notes made *on the spot*, so that you can analyze them at leisure later. Notes made at the time with the subject in view are far more valuable than what you may later remember about colours, markings, size, voice, habitat, etc.

FIELD NOTES

FIELD NOTES

FIELD NOTES